GENDER, CREATION MYTHS AND THEIR RECEPTION IN WESTERN CIVILIZATION

Bloomsbury Studies in Classical Reception

Bloomsbury Studies in Classical Reception presents scholarly monographs offering new and innovative research and debate to students and scholars in the reception of Classical Studies. Each volume will explore the appropriation, reconceptualization and recontextualization of various aspects of the Graeco-Roman world and its culture, looking at the impact of the ancient world on modernity. Research will also cover reception within antiquity, the theory and practice of translation, and reception theory.

Also available in the same series:

ALEXANDER THE GREAT IN THE EARLY CHRISTIAN TRADITION: CLASSICAL RECEPTION AND PATRISTIC LITERATURE
by Christian Thrue Djurslev

ANCIENT MAGIC AND THE SUPERNATURAL IN THE MODERN VISUAL AND PERFORMING ARTS
edited by Filippo Carlà and Irene Berti

ANCIENT GREEK MYTH IN WORLD FICTION SINCE 1989
edited by Justine McConnell and Edith Hall

ANNE CARSON/ANTIQUITY
edited by Laura Jansen

ANTIPODEAN ANTIQUITIES
edited by Marguerite Johnson

CLASSICS IN EXTREMIS
edited by Edmund Richardson

FAULKNER'S RECEPTION OF APULEIUS' THE GOLDEN ASS IN THE REIVERS
by Vernon L. Provencal

FRANKENSTEIN AND ITS CLASSICS
edited by Jesse Weiner, Benjamin Eldon Stevens and Brett M. Rogers

GREEK AND ROMAN CLASSICS IN THE BRITISH STRUGGLE FOR SOCIAL REFORM
edited by Henry Stead and Edith Hall

GREEKS AND ROMANS ON THE LATIN AMERICAN STAGE
edited by Rosa Andújar and Konstantinos P. Nikoloutsos

HOMER'S ILIAD AND THE TROJAN WAR: DIALOGUES ON TRADITION
by Jan Haywood and Naoíse Mac Sweeney

IMAGINING XERXES
by Emma Bridges

JULIUS CAESAR'S SELF-CREATED IMAGE AND ITS DRAMATIC AFTERLIFE
by Miryana Dimitrova

KINAESTHESIA AND CLASSICAL ANTIQUITY 1750–1820: MOVED BY STONE
by Helen Slaney

ONCE AND FUTURE ANTIQUITIES IN SCIENCE FICTION AND FANTASY
edited by Brett M. Rogers and Benjamin Eldon Stevens

OVID'S MYTH OF PYGMALION ON SCREEN
by Paula James

PERFORMING GODS IN CLASSICAL ANTIQUITY AND THE AGE OF SHAKESPEARE
by Dustin W. Dixon and John S. Garrison

READING POETRY, WRITING GENRE
edited by Silvio Bär and Emily Hauser

SEX, SYMBOLISTS AND THE GREEK BODY
by Richard Warren

THE CLASSICS IN MODERNIST TRANSLATION
edited by Miranda Hickman and Lynn Kozak

THE CLASSICS IN SOUTH AMERICA: FIVE CASE STUDIES
by Germán Campos Muñoz

THE CODEX FORI MUSSOLINI
by Han Lamers and Bettina Reitz-Joosse

THE GENTLE, JEALOUS GOD
by Simon Perris

THE THUCYDIDEAN TURN: (RE)INTERPRETING THUCYDIDES' POLITICAL THOUGHT BEFORE, DURING AND AFTER THE GREAT WAR
by Benjamin Earley

TRANSLATIONS OF GREEK TRAGEDY IN THE WORK OF EZRA POUND
by Peter Liebregts

VICTORIAN CLASSICAL BURLESQUES
by Laura Monrós-Gaspar

VICTORIAN EPIC BURLESQUES
by Rachel Bryant Davies

VIRGIL'S MAP: GEOGRAPHY, EMPIRE, AND THE GEORGICS
by Charlie Kerrigan

GENDER, CREATION MYTHS AND THEIR RECEPTION IN WESTERN CIVILIZATION: PROMETHEUS, PANDORA, ADAM AND EVE

Edited by Lisa Maurice and Tovi Bibring

BLOOMSBURY ACADEMIC
LONDON • NEW YORK • OXFORD • NEW DELHI • SYDNEY

BLOOMSBURY ACADEMIC
Bloomsbury Publishing Plc
50 Bedford Square, London, WC1B 3DP, UK
1385 Broadway, New York, NY 10018, USA
29 Earlsfort Terrace, Dublin 2, Ireland

BLOOMSBURY, BLOOMSBURY ACADEMIC and the Diana logo are trademarks of Bloomsbury Publishing Plc

First published in Great Britain 2022
Paperback edition published 2023

For legal purposes the Acknowledgements on p. xvi constitute an extension of this copyright page.

Cover design: Terry Woodley
Cover image © *Eve*, 1896, by Lucien Levy-Dhurmer (1865–96), pastel and gouache, 49 cm x 46 cm. (Photo by DeAgostini/Getty Images)

A catalogue record for this book is available from the British Library.

Library of Congress Cataloging-in-Publication Data
Names: Maurice, Lisa, 1968– editor. | Bibring, Tovi, 1973– editor.
Title: Gender, creation myths and their reception in western civilization : Prometheus, Pandora, Adam and Eve / Lisa Maurice, Tovi Bibring.
Description: 1. | New York : Bloomsbury Academic, 2022. | Series: Bloomsbury studies in classical reception | Includes bibliographical references and index.
Identifiers: LCCN 2021034472 (print) | LCCN 2021034473 (ebook) |
ISBN 9781350212824 (hardback) | ISBN 9781350212831 (ebook) | ISBN 9781350212848 (epub)
Subjects: LCSH: Creation–Mythology. | Prometheus (Greek deity) | Pandora (Greek mythological character) | Adam (Biblical figure) | Eve (Biblical figure) | Gender identity–Religious aspects.
Classification: LCC BL227 .G46 2022 (print) | LCC BL227 (ebook) | DDC 231.7/65—dc23
LC record available at https://lccn.loc.gov/2021034472
LC ebook record available at https://lccn.loc.gov/2021034473

ISBN: HB: 978-1-3502-1282-4
PB: 978-1-3502-1286-2
ePDF: 978-1-3502-1283-1
eBook: 978-1-3502-1284-8

Series: Bloomsbury Studies in Classical Reception

Typeset by RefineCatch Limited, Bungay, Suffolk

To my grandchildren

Kfir, Ayal, Manor and Ori

To my one and only Shani

In memory of Dr Lana Schwebel z'l

CONTENTS

FIGURES AND TABLES

Figures

Tables

CONTRIBUTORS

Thierry J. Alcoloumbre is an associate professor at Bar-Ilan Department of Comparative Literature (chair from 2010 to 2013). An alumnus from École Normale Supérieure de la rue d'Ulm (Paris), he received his PhD in Ancient Philosophy from the University of Paris 1 Sorbonne. His research embraces the interactions between Judaism and Ancient Greek legacy (philosophy, religion and literature). Alcoloumbre has been selected as co-editor of *Perspectives: Revue de l'Université Hébraïque de Jérusalem.*

Tovi Bibring is an associate professor at the Department of French Culture at Bar-Ilan University. Her research focuses on Old and Middle French and Medieval Hebrew literature and the possible interactions between them. Recent publications include *Marie de France's 'Lais', Literary Study and a Critical Translation from Anglo-Norman, Fully Annotated, with Introduction and Variants* (2014) (in Hebrew) and *Corps, Ame, Psyché, lectures de l'érotique dans les Lais de Marie de France* (2016). She is also the author of a number of articles about Berechiah ha-Naqdan's fables and of two forthcoming monographs: *The Patient, The Imposter, and The Seducer: Medieval Literature in Hebrew* and *The Tale of Old Bearded Achbor by Yaakov ben El'azar: A Close Reading of A Medieval Overwhelming Story.*

John Bradley was occupied in a thirty-year career in the construction industry before changing profession, thereupon gaining a first-class degree and Masters in Classics at Royal Holloway College, University of London, with dissertations on early Christian art and republican Roman religion. In 2017 he completed his PhD at the same college under the supervision of Dr Zena Kamash; his thesis was published the following year. An initial project on the broader aspects of the evolution of art in the catacombs of Rome ultimately focused on the Hypogeum of the Aurelii when existing theories and explanations appeared unsatisfactory, and he now continues his interest in ancient Roman art as an independent scholar.

Edmund Cueva is Professor of Classics and Humanities at the University of Houston-Downtown. His research interests include the ancient Graeco-Roman novel, comparative mythology, ancient literature and the occult, mythology and film, and patristics. He has published and lectured extensively on these topics.

Lily Glasner teaches Literature at the Department of Comparative Literature at Bar-Ilan University and at Kibbutzim College of Education. Her research and publications are mainly on children's literature and comics. In recent years one of her main projects has been the recovery and bringing to light of literary works for children written by Jewish immigrants from Islamic countries and by their descendants. Glasner has taken part in several collaborative research groups, amongst them the research group led by Lisa

Maurice that focused on the joint Graeco-Roman and Judaeo-Christian roots of Western civilization. She is currently participating in an innovative research group on digital pedagogy at Kibbutzim College of Education. She is also a member of the Literature Committee of the Israeli national programme, Sal Tarbut Artzi.

Hava Bracha Korzakova received her MA from the Leningrad State University and her PhD from Bar-Ilan University where she is a member of the Classics Department. She has published several articles on papyrology, epigraphy and Greek poetry, as well as several poetry books in Hebrew and Russian.

Isabelle Mathian is a former student of the École du Louvre and member of its research team. In 2016 she presented a thesis under the supervision of Jean-Pierre Caillet entitled 'Le nu tardo-antique et ses prolongements médiévaux: genèse et devenir des figures de Daniel et d'Adam et Ève'. Her research focuses on the iconography of late antiquity and the early Middle Ages as well as on the problematics of the historiography of late antiquity.

Lisa Maurice is an associate professor and chair of the Department of Classical Studies at Bar-Ilan University, and her research focuses on the reception of the classical world in modern popular culture. She is the author of *The Teacher in Ancient Rome* (2013) and *Screening Divinity* (2019), as well as many articles on the reception of the ancient world in popular culture. In addition, she has edited a volume on the use and reception of classical myth in formal education, *Our Mythical Education* (2020), as well as three volumes on the reception of the ancient world in popular culture: *The Reception of Ancient Greece and Rome in Children's Literature: Heroes and Eagles* (2015), *Rewriting the Ancient World: Greeks, Romans, Jews and Christians in Modern Popular Fiction* (2017) and *The Reception of Ancient Virtues and Vices in Modern Popular Culture* (2017). She also heads the Israeli branch of the international ERC-funded research project, *Our Mythical Childhood ... The Reception of Classical Antiquity in Children's and Young Adults' Culture in Response to Regional and Global Challenges* (ERC consolidator grant 681202).

Ayelet Peer is a member of the Department of Classical Studies at Bar-Ilan University. She is the author of the monograph *Julius Caesar's Bellum Civile and the Composition of a New Reality* (2015) and a number of articles on the works of Julius Caesar. She has also published within the field of classical reception and is a member of the international ERC-funded research project, *Our Mythical Childhood ... The Reception of Classical Antiquity in Children's and Young Adults' Culture in Response to Regional and Global Challenges* (ERC consolidator grant 681202).

Revital Refael-Vivante is an associate professor and chair of the Department of Literature of the Jewish People, Bar-Ilan University. Her research fields are medieval Hebrew literature, especially secular Hebrew poetry in medieval Spain; the Maqama and the rhymed prose in medieval Spain; Hebrew and general aphorisms in the Middle Ages; medieval fables (*Mishlé Shu'alim* by Berechiah ben Natronai ha-Nakdan); medieval Hebrew manuscripts; and Hebrew literature after the expulsion from Spain, mainly from the Balkans and Salonica. Refael-Vivante has published articles in these areas and most recently the monograph *A Treasury of Fables: Isaac ibn Sahula's Meshal Haqadmoni – Text and Subtext* (2017; 440 pp. in Hebrew).

Yael Shemesh is an associate professor in Hebrew Bible at Bar-Ilan University and the head of the Fanya Gottesfeld Heller Center for the Study of Women in Judaism. Her publications include *Mourning in the Bible: Coping with Loss in Biblical Literature* (2015; Hebrew); 'The Stories of Women in a Man's World: The Books of Ruth, Esther, and Judith', in *Feminist Interpretation of the Hebrew Bible in Retrospect*, vol. 1: Biblical Books, edited by Susanne Scholz (2013); and 'Directions in Jewish Feminist Bible Study', in *Currents in Biblical Research* 14 (2016).

Jared A. Simard is a Clinical Assistant Professor in Liberal Studies at New York University. His scholarly work focuses on ancient mythology in literature and art, classical reception studies and classical influences on New York City. His research has appeared in the *Journal of the Society of Architectural Historians*, Fordham University Press, Bloomsbury Academic Publishing and De Gruyter.

Benjamin Eldon Stevens works in two main areas: 'classical receptions', that is, how ancient materials are transmitted and transmuted in more recent sources, with focuses on underworlds and other afterlives, science fiction and fantasy, and film; and the ancient Mediterranean world, especially Latin literature and Roman history, with special attention to linguistics and sensory anthropology. He has published four co-edited volumes of essays on receptions in science fiction and fantasy, a monograph on silence in the Roman poet Catullus, and numerous articles; he is also a published translator of French and Spanish. A graduate of the University of Chicago (PhD 2005) and Reed College (BA 1998), he taught at Bard College, Hollins University, Bryn Mawr College and the University of Colorado at Boulder (his home town) before reaching Trinity University in San Antonio, Texas in 2015. Outside of academia, Ben enjoys learning new languages (currently Icelandic and Swedish), baking and a cappella music.

Vered Tohar is Senior Lecturer in the Department of the Literature of the Jewish People at Bar-Ilan University. Her research focuses on Jewish traditional narratives from a diachronic and comparative perspective. She is the author of *Abraham in the Furnace: A Rebel in a Pagan World* (2010; in Hebrew) and *The Book of Tales, Sermons and Legends (Ferrara 1554): An Anthology of Hebrew Stories from the Print Era* (2016; in Hebrew). Tohar is also a co-editor of *Tell Me About It: Aspects in Narrative Analysis* (2010), *Religious Stories in Transformation: Conflict, Revision and Reception* (2016) and *Jerusalem and Other Holy Places as Foci of Multireligious and Ideological Confrontation* (2020).

Roslyn Weiss is Clara H. Stewardson Professor of Philosophy at Lehigh University. She earned her PhD in Philosophy from Columbia University (1982) and an MA in Jewish Studies at the Baltimore Hebrew University (1992). She has published four books on Plato's dialogues and fifty articles on Greek philosophy, Jewish philosophy, ethics and the philosophy of religion. Weiss has also lectured widely on Greek philosophy and Jewish philosophy in the United States, Israel, Canada, South America, Europe and Asia. She has recently published the first complete English translation of *Or Hashem* (*Light of the Lord*), the magnum opus of the great medieval Jewish philosopher Ḥasdai Crescas.

Susan Weiss is an attorney and holds a PhD in anthropology and sociology. In 2004 she founded, and has since served as the director of, the Center for Women's Justice (CWJ). CWJ is an NGO located in Jerusalem whose mission is to shift the discriminatory status quo of religion and state in Israel regarding women, securing the way towards a more just and democratic society. Weiss is an editor of *The Law and Its Decisor*, a journal published by Bar-Ilan University Law School, and the co-author of *Marriage and Divorce in the Jewish State: Israel's Civil War* (2013).

ACKNOWLEDGEMENTS

This book would not have come about without the stimulus of a request from the then rector of Bar-Ilan University for proposals for collaborative research groups. As a result of this opportunity, a group was initiated by Lisa Maurice, whose title was 'The Roots of Western Civilisation and their Reception throughout History' and which aimed to examine the interplay between Graeco-Roman and Judaeo-Christian traditions in the formation of the cultures of Western civilization. After the successful submission of the proposal, resulting in generous funding, the initial product of the group was a conference entitled 'Prometheus, Pandora, Adam and Eve: Archetypes of the Masculine and Feminine and their Reception throughout the Ages', which took place from 20 to 22 March 2017 at Bar-Ilan University. This volume expands the work still further. For all these developments, we are indebted to Professor Miriam Faust, who, in her term as rector, made them possible, and also to our gracious keynote speakers, Simon Goldhill, Catherine Conybeare and Nick Lowe.

Thanks are also due to others without whose substantial support the conference could not have taken place: the Lechter Institute for Literary Research and the Lewis Family Foundation for International Conferences in the Humanities; Andrew Goldman of Tsemed, a big-hearted and open-handed friend; and most of all Lilly and Philip Schwebel z'l and Pam Swickley, who generously donated financial support matched only by gracious enthusiasm, in memory of their daughter and sister Lana Schwebel z'l, tragically taken from this world at far too young an age. This book is as much tribute to her, and to her parents, sadly no longer with us, as it is a work of scholarship.

On the more practical production side, I must thank the anonymous reviewers of the proposal for this volume, who did so much to improve it, and also the wonderful team at Bloomsbury, whose professionalism is outstanding and with whom it has been a pleasure to work throughout, even under the strains of Covid-19. I am also inordinately grateful to the wonderful contributors to this book, who worked to deadlines, responded to emails, and remained co-operative to the end, making the venture an unusually enjoyable one to co-ordinate. Particular thanks go to my co-editor, Tovi Bibring, whose care and attention to detail as well as unflagging enthusiasm make her both a delightful colleague and friend.

Finally, as always, my grateful thanks and love go to my happily increasing family who have continued to produce offspring at a gratifying (and somewhat speedier) rate over the course of the development of this book. My husband, sons, daughters, sons-in-law and daughters-in-law, and of course my grandchildren to whom this volume is dedicated, are the light of my life. Thank you for everything.

Lisa Maurice

INTRODUCTION

Lisa Maurice

The date was 15 October 2017. 'If you've been sexually harassed or assaulted write "me too" as a reply to this tweet,' tweeted actress Alyssa Milano, and with this the 'Me Too' movement was born.[1] The manner in which it captivated the popular imagination and gained momentum is indicative of the fact that gender issues remain central to popular discourse, even in the twenty-first century. The issue of whether such differences are rooted in nature or nurture is one that has been debated throughout history, and goes back to the very myths of creation found in Western civilization, the reception of which has been influenced by, and influenced in turn, various aspects of that civilization. Prometheus shines above the lower plaza at the Rockefeller Center in Manhattan, in New York City. To open a 'Pandora's box' is a phrase found in multiple languages. Similarly, Adam and Eve's story, narrated in Genesis 2–3, has taken on an independent afterlife producing what Theresa Sanders calls a 'cultural memory' of its own that is often dramatically different from the version in the Bible.[2]

This book has evolved from a conference held at Bar-Ilan University in Israel in 2017, which examined the joint classical and Judaeo-Christian foundations of Western civilization, and their reception. The terms 'classical' and 'Graeco-Roman' refer in this work to those texts, artefacts and traditions from the ancient Near Eastern societies of Greece and Rome, and in the context of the theme of this book, specifically the stories and representations of Prometheus and Pandora. Similarly, 'Judaeo-Christian', despite the complexity of the term in its unification of disparate traditions, is used for the tradition emanating from the Bible and the works of subsequent Jewish and Christian theologians.

Although the book stems from the conference, it is not a conference proceedings volume in its usual rendering, providing a narrower focus than the original forum and with the addition of new material as well. The impetus for the conference was an understanding that both the classical and Judaeo-Christian strands have contributed to Western societies in areas as diverse as art, philosophy, politics and architecture, and in many cases, the two intertwine and play off each other. Yet very little sustained research to date has examined the two elements in relation to each other by means of incorporating experts from a wide range of different fields. These include Jewish Studies, Christianity, Classical Studies, European literature, history and art, politics and philosophy. A belief that such collaboration would lead to greater understanding was the inspiration behind both the original conference and the present study, which is intended to provide enlightenment in a way that individual researchers, in their own closed specializations, cannot.

Within this broad understanding, this book focuses on the topic of gender in both traditions, as highlighted through the creation myths of each. In general, we refer to gender rather than sex, in recognition that the issues raised are generally more concerned with the way in which society addressed the differences between male and female, and the roles that have been allotted to each. The study takes as its starting point the idea that the way in which a culture regards humanity, and especially the roots of humanity, both male and female, is crucial to an understanding of that society. Different models for the creation and nature of human beings, and their changing receptions at different periods and places, reflect fundamental evolutions and developments in society, particularly with regard to gender. This volume thus investigates the Graeco-Roman and Judaeo-Christian stories of the creation of the primordial couples, and their reception in the Western world. It sheds light on attitudes towards male and female on a range of influential periods and places, utilizing both general overviews of the subject, and more specific readings and interpretations of individual works or collections.

The central conceptual orientation of the volume is the examination of a number of questions that go beyond merely categorizing the various figures found in the creation myths under discussion. These questions include:

- What do the respective depictions of male and female reveal about the roles and perceptions of the different genders both in their original sources and in their receptions in later societies?
- How do the Judaic, Christian, Greek and Roman myths stand out from each other and also cross-fertilize between each other at different times and cultures?
- How have the tales been recast at various periods and for what purposes?
- How far do these creation myths, and their adaptations, reflect concerns of the societies producing and manipulating them?
- In what ways have variations of the creation myths been adapted for children and for different religious groups?
- How have these stories been exploited in order to target issues of gender?
- How far do the myths still have relevance in the modern Western world?

In short, this book considers the use, adaptation and abuse of two ancient creation myths and the gendered figures upon which they are centred, figures that, while different in nature, have been interwoven and combined within Western tradition. This study aims not only to examine both but also to tease apart and explain points at which they intermingled or separated, thereby deepening our understanding of the two main threads that are assumed to have given shape to Western civilization.

With regard to this assumption, it is necessary to make one more point: while the phrase 'Western civilization' was an uncontroversial term at the outset of this project in the first half-decade of the 2010s, this outlook has altered considerably since then, and it has become increasingly controversial in recent years to talk of Western culture or tradition, a change that perhaps only reflects how timely was the founding of the research group in 2016. Recognition of the role of Western Europe (and consequently of those areas settled by those originally from the West) in the imposition of its own ideas and values on native, non-Western cultures has led to an unwillingness to think in such terms. Fears concerning the dominant influence of this culture, overlaid with connotations of colonialism, have led to attempts to replace a 'western template' with an appreciation of 'non-western' worldviews and a polarization has sprung up between West and non-West, Occidentalism and Orientalism.[3] This is understandable. As one recent article stressed:

> The cautions against western dominance and western templates [. . .] are anchored in a very understandable rejection of European empire building and the enduring global inequalities it produced. Understandable too, is the desire to reverse the negative identifications the west made of 'the rest' and thus to denounce a conviction that the west was best (more civilized, educated, democratic etc.) or that it arose from an untarnished enlightenment model of progress.[4]

Yet there is no reason to suppose, much less impose, a sense of cultural superiority in what is commonly regarded to be the Western tradition. While the roles it has played at various times in history are regrettable according to modern perception, that is no reason to deny or ignore the considerable impact that Western culture has had on the world as a whole; on the contrary, it is all the more important to recognize the myriad influences from this tradition, for better or for worse, and to analyse and dissect the various manipulations, agendas and practices that were employed at different times and places, and for a wide variety of purposes. Beyond this, it is important to bear in mind that the so called modern 'Western' civilization is actually a product of multiple traditions and ideologies, including elements as diverse as European capitalism, the Renaissance, the Enlightenment, revolutionary America and the Abrahamic faiths.[5] Teasing out the myriad strands and examining how they connect with each other makes us more aware of the depth of what has come to be regarded as a somewhat monolithic (and negative) concept, and to appreciate the different elements of 'Western civilization' in a more nuanced manner. Although we acknowledge the importance of current sensitivities regarding issues such as colonialism and the appropriation of the classical tradition to the West, nevertheless we feel that the term still has value as a shorthand for that long period of history in which, ignoring the rights and wrongs of the situation, European and North American cultures claimed both Graeco-Roman and Judeao-Christian traditions as their own.

Although this book focuses on the creation narratives, it differs from works such as Paul Morris and Deborah Sawyer's *A Walk in the Garden Biblical, Iconographical, and Literary Images of Eden* (1992) and, more recently, Bob Becking and Susanne Hennecke's *Out of Paradise: Eve and Adam and Their Interpreters* (2010), which examine only the Biblical narrative. By considering the reception of two different creation myths, this book has some overlap with studies of comparative mythology, such as Jean Puhvel's *Comparative Mythology* (1989), and comparative religion, such as Craig Martin's *A Critical Introduction to the Study of Religion* (2017), but has a much narrower focus than works such as these. It does not aim to look for similarities and differences between the two traditions or to decipher the roots of the myths; as such, it differs from works such as Bruce Louden's *Greek Myth and the Bible* (2018), which examines the relationship of Jewish and Christian scriptures to Greek mythology, and sees the latter as deriving from the former. Similarly, the stress here is different from that of Sarah Iles Johnston who, in her *The Story of Myth* (2018), compares Greek myths to those myths of other cultures as well as to other genres ranging from fairy tales to television series, in order to examine both the role played by myth in Greek society specifically, and more generally the part played by stories and storytelling in every culture. While these issues have relevance for the current volume, this book does not look for universal themes or usages, nor try to compare the creation myths with other narratives, standing as a work of reception rather than comparison.

With regards to methodology, the work falls into the field of Classical Reception that has developed over recent decades, largely replacing the now redundant term Classical Tradition. Where the Classical Tradition considered how the Graeco-Roman world was 'handed down' to subsequent (inferior) generations, Classical Reception focuses on the ongoing ways in which later centuries and cultures connected with and reinterpreted those earlier texts and societies; thus the point of contact is a vital element in the discussion and a fundamental aspect of the new product.

Within this general framework, various theoretical approaches have been developed in recent years by classical scholars. Charles Martindale's original methodology recognized later receptions of the ancient world as valid interpretations and legitimate works in their own right.[6] He went on to apply Kantian aesthetics to this idea, arguing that ideology is overly dominant in considerations of receptions, and that Kant's theory, as set out in the *Critique of Judgement*, can still provide powerful analytic tools for scholars. With this belief, Martindale clashes with other scholars such as Simon Goldhill, Lorna Hardwick and Edith Hall, who also take into account the social contexts of each work, seeing reception as a form of cultural history.[7] David Hopkins, trying to bridge the gap between these two schools of thought, argues that receptions are part of a trans-historical *conversation* with earlier times, and that the consideration of reception should take into account not only how the ancient texts have been transformed, but also how modern understanding of these receptions influences comprehension of the ancient world in a two-way process.[8] By employing the language of 'conversation', Hopkins avoids both the prejudicing of the ancient world over later periods, which is implicit in the term 'Classical Tradition', and the passivity inherent in the word 'reception'.[9]

Despite these diverse methodologies, one thing all the theories have in common is that they are concerned with *interaction*. Although research within this field explores how ancient Greece and Rome have connected both with each other and with aspects of societies in later periods, there is another element that is rarely considered within this context, namely how two different ancient traditions, the classical and the biblical, interact both with each other and with the receiving culture. This book is a step in this direction, examining how both the Judaeo-Christian and Graeco-Roman narratives of creation, and in particular of the questions of gender within these narratives, have evolved, both independently and through interaction with each other, at various times from the medieval period up to and including the modern day. Inspired by Hopkins' ideas, it seeks to understand the 'conversations', both between the biblical and Graeco-Roman creation stories as seen in their various receptions and between those myths and the wider societies adapting the traditions at each point.

The book is divided thematically into five sections. Part I focuses on visual symbolism, examining how the iconography of the creation myths of the classical and biblical traditions has been employed. Visual representations have great power and reflect (and help create) societal assumptions, particularly when concerning subjects connected with a belief system. This is certainly the case in a less literate society, but is no less so in the contemporary world, as the papers in this section reflect. The first two chapters provide cases studies from different historical and geographical points: third-century Rome and late antique Italy. John Bradley's chapter, the first of these, examines the use of Prometheus as an exemplar in the fresco decoration of a third-century tomb in Rome known as the hypogeum of the Aurelii. One of the frescoes in the upper chamber of the hypogeum has been interpreted as being either the earliest depiction of Adam and Eve together with an image of the Creator making the first human, or the proto-human couple moulded by Prometheus. Since the Aurelii were *liberti*, Bradley suggests that the 'Creator' image is not God or Prometheus but the *patronus* of the Aurelii in the guise of Prometheus, creating new human beings by granting liberty to slaves. By so doing, the *patronus* has carried out an act of fundamental metamorphosis from mercantile object to human in this example of the use of Prometheus in classical funerary decoration.

Isabelle Mathian considers a medieval reception of Prometheus in her examination of the basilica of San Paolo fuori le Mura at the time of its most recent restoration, towards the end of the thirteenth century. In this basilica, a half-bust Logos can be seen leaning out of a starry lunette directly above the Agnus Dei and a dove hovering over verdant hills; a man and a woman are arranged on either side, each in their own mandorla. These mandorlas, also called *clipei*, which express the divine nature of the man and woman inhabiting them, are, she argues, based on pagan iconography of the Promethean creation's '*septemplicis clipei*', and present an example of how the Italian ecclesial environment between the tenth and thirteenth century reappropriated pagan iconography in creating the Genesitic nude, through the definitive assumption of a didactic responsibility expressed in Christian typology.

Jared A. Simard closes the first section with a survey covering the issues from antiquity to the modern day, tracing the mutual influence of depictions of Promethean and biblical creation by means of an art historical survey. Beginning in antiquity, comparisons are made between sarcophagi depicting Promethean and biblical creation. Close attention is paid to iconography demonstrating that early Promethean sarcophagi influenced depictions of biblical creation. As the survey moves into late antiquity and the early modern period, this chapter argues for a reversal of the trend, with depictions of God creating Adam and Eve influencing early modern depictions of Prometheus creating man. The early modern period witnesses a shift in Promethean creation imagery. Artists have borrowed key elements from depictions of biblical creation. They have also moved towards a more secularized Prometheus by self-fashioning themselves as Promethean. Finally, the chapter argues that this shift culminates in perhaps the most well-known depiction of Prometheus, that of Paul Manship's *Prometheus* at the Rockefeller Center in New York City.

The second part of the book moves from visual symbolism to pinpoint specifics of the creation narratives, as it raises the issue of the depiction of the first men and women as ideals of marriage; since until very recently the male–female union was the central family unit upon which society was structured, consideration of the ideal nature of this relationship was of relevance to all.[10] Thierry Alcoloumbre's chapter examines both the Greek myth and the Genesis creation story as received in Jewish belief, considering how the two different narratives work from a common basic premise and yet arrive at opposite conclusions about human reality. This, he argues, stems from contrasting attitudes in the mindsets of Greece and Judaism, a conclusion that highlights dialogue possible between the two traditions.

Lisa Maurice's chapter also draws together both the biblical and classical narratives, as she examines the depiction of Pandora and Eve in children's picture books. She argues that although neither Eve nor Pandora have traditionally been depicted in a positive light, and the messages that are often read from the stories are ones reflecting negative attitudes towards the female gender, the two females are treated differently from each other in this form of literature. This difference stems from the religious connotations which, even in the twenty-first century, still impact strongly on the Eve narrative in a manner that does not affect the Pandora story.

Revital Refael-Vivante presents another presentation of the perfect woman in her examination of receptions of the love story of Pygmalion narrated in Ovid's *Metamorphoses*. Refael-Vivante discusses the complex avenues of this theme and the intercultural literary correspondence on this subject over the centuries, as she examines 'The Ring of the Dove' by a Spanish poet, Ibn Hazm of Andalusia (Cordova, eleventh century), demonstrating that while the Pygmalion effect generally has a positive connotation, Ibn Hazm's writings indicate that this is a negative, needless, disappointing and even dangerous phenomenon, apparently due to cultural and religious differences. She then traces the migration of this theme to the Hebrew literature that was written in Spain, and to Arabic *maqamas*.

From the ideals of marriage, the book then moves in the third section to examine more specifically the female, generally depicted as the source of evil in both Graeco-Roman and Judaeo-Christian traditions, and examines the concept of the ideal woman, opening with two complementary personal readings of the creation of woman in Genesis. Roslyn Weiss turns the spotlight on the biblical tale in Genesis 2, attempting to approach the text without an agenda and without prejudice, and deliberately without recourse to biblical commentaries, in an attempt to be open to the text and to hear anew what it is saying. In examining the text, she emphasizes that the relationship between male and female is asymmetrical and alters over the course of the narrative. While at first it is man who leaves his parents and cleaves to his woman, who is the more perfect of the two, after the sin of the eating of the forbidden fruit, God effects a radical upheaval in the course of nature, reversing the initial hierarchical order of the first human beings by placing man in a position of power over woman.

Yael Shemesh also scrutinizes Eve, seeing her as a female and, indeed, human archetype, whose choice to eat the forbidden fruit in Genesis 3 exemplifies the exercise of free will and independent thinking. This trait is demonstrated once again after Cain's murder of Abel, when she takes a positive attitude by producing and naming her son, Seth, in a proactive manner. Shemesh's chapter illuminates this aspect of Eve's personality, as a woman who makes conscious choices. She considers readers' own responsibility for how they interpret her decision to eat the forbidden fruit, an act that can be interpreted either negatively or positively, through the presentation of a range of views, from that of Ben Sira through to modern feminists.

Finally, Tovi Bibring focuses this debate on the Middle Ages, in a study that highlights works that resist misogynistic interpretations of Eve. Analysing two original meditations on Genesis composed by women, a fable by the twelfth-century Marie de France and a redaction composed in the thirteenth century by an anonymous woman, as well as the fourteenth-century *Livre de Leesce* by Jehan Le Fèvre, she shows that these works present a situation in which man and woman were initially created as equal, and that Adam and Eve share equal responsibility for the Fall. Through her analysis, Bibring presents some medieval voices that were rather more feminist in approach than might have been expected, and which oppose the prevailing traditional discourses that viewed Eve as physically and mentally inferior to Adam.

The utilization of the creation narratives to promote ideas about gender and relationships seen in parts II and III is brought into sharper focus in Part IV, where the exploitation of these tales for ideological purposes is the focus. Hava B. Korzakova looks at a society in which the Bible was alien, namely the Soviet Union, where the Bolsheviks established their own religion and tried to destroy any other religion in the areas where they came to power. Despite this opposition, a masterpiece of art was produced under this ideology. This was a puppet show called *The Divine Comedy*, based on the play by Isidor Shtok (1908–80), staged in 1961 and filmed for television in 1973. It was an extremely popular TV show, partly because it was almost the only way for Soviet children (and adults) to become familiar with the first story of the Bible. This work was also notable for the fact that Shtok was Jewish, as were a number of the actors, who added a, probably intentional, 'authentic' Jewish taste to the show. In this paper, Korzakova examines the reception of the biblical narrative in this creation within the Soviet, and specifically Soviet-Jewish, context.

While the Bible was the tradition rejected in the Soviet Union, in modern Israel it is the Graeco-Roman world that has been seen as alien, and the Judaeo-Christian root as the natural point of identification, as reflected by the two remaining chapters in this section, which examine Israeli receptions of the biblical tradition. The first, Vered Tohar's paper, explores the creation myth in two versions of one of the most popular Hebrew children stories from the twentieth century: the Israeli daffodil in the swamp. Composed in both versions (one a play and the other a picture book) by Levin Kipnis in the first half of the twentieth century and regarded as an Israeli classic, the story is an allegory of the hardships of the early Zionist immigrants. It tells of the generosity of a strange and ugly plant, who is the only one who agrees to live in the disgusting swamp, and for this receives a divine reward, becoming a beautiful flower with marvellous petals and a strong and pleasing scent; it becomes the king of the swamp. Tohar examines the multiple layers of meaning in this story, demonstrating how it is rooted both in classical myth and the biblical creation story and also fits into the pattern of creation narratives, as it adapts this to the evolution of the new, young Israeli pioneer.

Still concentrating on the biblical tale, Susan Weiss's 'Genesis 3.15 and 16 and the State of Israel' focuses on two verses in the third chapter of Genesis, which place limits on Eve, both of them imposed on her by God. First, she is 'severed' from the snake, a symbol of the fertility goddess and female sexuality exercised freely and autonomously. Second, she is to be ruled by her husband, thus establishing the 'law' of patriarchy. In this chapter, Weiss shows through examples of actual laws, regulations and cases in Israel how this twofold construction of gender is very much potent today in the state of Israel, where personal status law compounds and legitimates these two notions, as the state both polices the 'free' sexuality of women and completely subordinates women to their husband in matters of marriage and divorce.

The final section turns from traditional readings to some rather less conventional depictions, reflecting the ongoing fascination with these creation myths, with the presentation of some postmodern contemporary receptions from the world of popular culture, covering popular fiction, anime and film. Benjamin Eldon Stevens presents a study of how modern science fiction features versions of the ancient Graeco-Roman mythic figure of Pandora. Closely linked to Prometheus in myths, Pandora evokes similar themes about the human relationship with knowledge and technology. As an artificial or synthetic creation who is also an archetypal woman, Pandora literally embodies how 'technology' and 'art' are intertwined with 'human nature', suggesting that mortals themselves are somehow intrinsically technological or artificial. Pandora is traditionally understood as a negative exemplar, but some Pandora figures in science fiction suggest instead that curiosity, including interest in technology, has more positive potential. Stevens demonstrates these differing interpretations through investigation of several Pandora figures in science fiction, considering how such figures enable us to see more clearly how modern classical receptions are shaped in part by science fiction.

Remaining with science fiction, Edmund Cueva's chapter focuses on Ridley Scott's 2012 film, *Prometheus*, which, as Cueva shows, is carefully constructed upon the ancient myth on a multitude of levels. While there is no one person or creature that is solely recognizable as Prometheus in the film, other than the scientific spacecraft that bears this name, elements of Pandora and Eve manifest themselves in the Elizabeth Shaw character, in that she is an inquisitive female who seeks knowledge no matter the cost or the warnings given in the pursuit of this knowledge, and, at the same time, serves as the mother of a new race. Analysing these elements, Cueva contends that Ridley Scott, Jon Spaihts and Damon Lindelof have re-envisioned the roots of humanity in a way that appeals to a modern, movie-going audience.

Moving from Prometheus to Pandora, Lily Glasner examines a book aimed at female young adult female readers: *Cruel Beauty* by Rosamund Hodge (2014). Envisioned as a popular text, the book is a rather complex retelling of *Beauty and the Beast* (in itself a transformation of the classic myth of Cupid and Psyche). Within this general frame, the author plays with and weaves in several other sources, most notably the classic myth of Pandora and the box (or jar) of miseries. Glasner demonstrates that many of the central traits and issues of Hesiod's creation resonate in *Cruel Beauty*, as Hodge interprets the ancient myth and recreates it under a feminist agenda which seeks to empower women, through developing a new model of heroine.

Finally, moving from juvenile fiction to Japanese anime, Ayelet Peer scrutinizes the reception of the biblical creation of humans, which is combined with the Pandora narrative, in several examples of anime and manga. In this chapter, Peer demonstrates how the Japanese creators use these specific Judaeo-Christian and classical references to the creation of humans and reinterpret them in their works, arguing that such receptions of the source material are not randomly chosen and that the Japanese creators have deliberately used them to convey a message that is the result of a long and painful process of cultural integration that has taken place in Japanese society.

The papers in this collection cover a wide range of time periods, cultures, languages and media. Some use only the biblical narrative, others only the Graeco-Roman, while still others utilize elements of both. All of the receptions, however, use stories of the creation of humankind in ways that reflect and shape their own needs, and many are influenced not only by the original stories, but also by the later versions of them. Neither the Graeco-Roman nor the Judaeo-Christian tales of the creation of male and female have ever operated in isolation of each other, but rather have intersected and reacted against each other. This mixing was intensified through the merging of traditions as Christianity spread throughout the Roman Empire and became the dominant religion in the West, which was also the foremost propagator of the classical tradition, especially from the Renaissance onwards. In the concluding chapter, I attempt to elucidate some overall trends regarding how the different narratives have been adapted, where they overlap and where they differ, and what light these issues can shed on how the tales of creation of the two traditions have been utilized in Western tradition with regard to gender.

This introduction opened with reference to a contemporary debate concerning discourse regarding gender, in the form of the 'Me Too' movement. Yet the issues go much further than this, with ideas concerning issues of sexual orientation and gender identification having changed radically in the twenty-first century. Terms such as Lesbian, Gay, Bisexual, Transgender, Cisgender and Transsexual, some of which were unheard of a century ago, now pepper the newspapers on a regular basis and are the topic of ongoing research.[11] The right to choose the gender with which one identifies, now widely accepted by Western society – and this is, despite the issues surrounding the term, a phenomenon only found widely in the West[12] – is a radical new direction, made possible in the modern age by medical advances and changing ideologies regarding personal freedom.[13] Considering the ways in which gender has historically been considered in the civilization that now rejects much of these ideas is surely an exercise of paramount importance, and one to which we hope this volume contributes in some small way.

Notes

1. The phrase was actually coined more than ten years previously, by Tarana Burke, a survivor of sexual assault who wanted to do something to help women and girls of colour who had also survived sexual violence. It came to national and indeed global prominence with Milano's usage however.
2. Theresa Sanders, *Approaching Eden: Adam and Eve in Popular Culture* (Lanham, MD: Rowman and Littlefield, 2009), 2.
3. C. Shiel, 'Developing the global citizen', *Exchange* 5 (2006): 15–20 (Higher Education Academy, York, Higher Education Research & Development); B. Szkudlarek, 'Through western eyes: insights into the intercultural training field', *Organization Studies* 30, no. 9 (2009): 975–86.
4. Glynis Cousin, 'Rethinking the concept of "western"', *Higher Education Research & Development* 30, no. 5 (2011): 585 (585–94), DOI: 10.1080/07294360.2011.598449. This last point is made by S. Hall, 'The west and the rest: discourse and power', in S. Schesh and J. Haggis (eds), *Development: A Cultural Studies Reader* (Oxford: Blackwell, 2002), 56–64, and cited by Cousin.
5. It should also be noted that these faiths were also themselves influenced by other Middle Eastern cultures such as Sumerian, Assyrian, Babylonian, Hittite and Egyptian.
6. Charles Martindale played a central role in the development of the field, pushing classicists to theorize reception, first in his pioneering article 'Redeeming the Text: The Validity of Comparisons of Classical and Post-Classical Literature. A View from Britain', *Arion* (3rd series) 1, no. 3 (1992): 45–75, and then in a number of publications over the following fifteen years. These include *Redeeming the Text: Latin Poetry and the Hermeneutics of Reception* (Cambridge: Cambridge University Press 1993); 'Reception', in Simon Hornblower and Anthony Spawforth, *The Oxford Classical Dictionary*, 3rd edn (Oxford: Oxford University Press, 2003), 1294–5; 'Reception and the Classics of the Future', *Council of University Classics Departments Bulletin* 34 (2005), http://www.rhul.ac.uk/classics/cucd/martindale05.html; Charles Martindale and Richard F. Thomas, *Classics and the Uses of Reception* (Oxford: Blackwell Publishing, 2006); Charles Martindale, 'Reception – a new humanism? Receptivity, pedagogy, the transhistorical', *Classical Receptions Journal* 5, no. 2 (2013): 169.
7. Major works include Lorna Hardwick, *Translating Words, Translating Cultures* (London: Duckworth, 2000); Lorna Hardwick and Christopher Stray, *A Companion to Classical Receptions* (Oxford: Blackwell, 2008); Edith Hall, 'Putting the class into Classical reception', in Lorna Hardwick and Christopher Stray, *A Companion to Classical Receptions*, Blackwell Companions to the Ancient World (Oxford: Blackwell, 2008), 386–97; Edith Hall, *The Return of Ulysses: A Cultural History of Homer's Odyssey* (London and New York: IB Tauris, 2008); Edith Hall and Stephe Harrop (eds), *Theorising Performance: Greek Drama, Cultural History and Critical Practice* (London: Duckworth, 2010); Simon Goldhill, 'Cultural History and Aesthetics: Why Kant is No Place to Start Reception Studies', in Edith Hall and Stephe Harrop (London: Duckworth, 2010), 56–70.
8. David Hopkins, *Conversing With Antiquity: English Poets and the Classics, from Shakespeare to Pope*, Classical Presences (Oxford: Oxford University Press, 2010), 1–14.
9. For a more detailed description of the various theories of classical reception and the history of the debate between them, see, L. Maurice, *Rewriting the Ancient World: Greeks, Romans, Christians and Jews in Modern Popular Fiction*, Metaforms: Studies in the Reception of Classical Antiquity (Leiden: Brill, 2017), 5–8.

10. The impact upon society of recent changes with regard to gay marriage and LGBTQ+ rights in general is a matter of ongoing research; see below p. 9.

11. See, e.g., Kim Gelé, Susan McNamara, Sidney H. Phillips, R. Dennis Shelby, Gary Grossman, Susan C. Vaughan and Ralph Roughton, 'Emerging views on gender and sexuality: celebrating twenty years of new perspectives on lesbian, gay, bisexual, and trans people', *Journal of the American Psychoanalytic Association* 60, no. 5 (2012): 949–67, https://doi.org/10.1177/0003065112459956; Walter R Schumm, 'Changes over the decades in selected LGBTQ research findings', *JSM Sexual Medicine* 4, no. 2 (2020): 1029.

12. See, e.g., Q. F. Zhang, 'Transgender Representation by the *People's Daily* Since 1949', *Sexuality & Culture* 18, no. 1 (2014): 180–95, https://doi.org/10.1007/s12119-013-9184-3, on the situation in China.

13. For changing attitudes, see Mignon R. Moore and Michael Stambolis-Ruhstorfer, 'LGBT Sexuality and Families at the Start of the Twenty-First Century', *Annual Review of Sociology* 39 (July 2013): 491–507, https://doi.org/10.1146/annurev-soc-071312-145643; Peter Hart-Brinson, *The Gay Marriage Generation: How the LGBTQ Movement Transformed American Culture* (New York: New York University Press, 2018).

PART I

VISUAL SYMBOLISM: THE ICONOGRAPHY OF CREATION

CHAPTER 1
THE USE OF PROMETHEUS AS AN EXEMPLAR IN THIRD-CENTURY ROME

John Bradley

In 1919, whilst constructing an underground garage close to the Viale Manzoni in Rome, a group of workmen came upon a richly decorated funerary monument dated, stylistically and archaeologically, to the late Severan era.[1] Its three principal chambers, two wholly subterranean, contained a highly eclectic collection of images.[2] The name it is now known by, the Hypogeum of the Aurelii, is derived from a dedicatory mosaic floor inscription in one of the subterranean *cubicula* that names four individuals, all with the same *nomen*: Aurelius or Aurelia.[3]

Despite the efforts of restorers in recent years, today the frescoes are significantly degraded, especially in the blue/green end of the spectrum. The clear but faded frescoes were published by Fabrizio Bisconti in 2011 with, unfortunately, not always perfect results.[4] Fortunately, a series of aquatints were produced by Tabanelli for the monograph of Josef Wilpert in 1924.[5] These, together with Goffredo Bendinelli's comprehensive record of the tomb's excavation,[6] have ensured that the decoration was well documented before the effects of time erased much detail. One image has been interpreted as an early, if not the earliest, depiction of Adam and Eve; another has had a variety of interpretations: Prometheus, philosopher, or, the most common interpretation, the Christian God as Creator.[7] My conclusion is that none of these interpretations is strictly correct. The interpretation put forward here not only alters our perception of the monument as a whole, but also, in the context of this volume, may shed a light on the evolution of Graeco-Roman creation iconography during the period before and after the toleration of Christianity in the early fourth century.

This chapter concerns these two images; fragments of a single fresco in the upper *cubiculum*. The position of the fresco is of importance. The two images are either side of what was probably a stone or marble inscription (the removal of which, together with a later additional burial, caused most of the plaster loss) beneath an inhumation burial within an arched recess (*arcosolium*); the fresco is in the first burial chamber that one comes upon when entering the hypogeum. Furthermore, it is in the most significant position immediately opposite the entrance.

It is not the place here to elaborate on other areas of the hypogeum, but it is important to note that there is no self-evident religious imagery anywhere within the monument – Christian or pagan. Our sole evidence about the status of the occupants of the tomb, apart from the frescoes themselves, is the mosaic floor inscription in one of the subterranean *cubicula* which clearly states that some, if not all, of them were freedmen and women. Given the lack of religious imagery and the connection with *liberti* it is worth re-examining the frescoes without preconceptions. The first to be examined is that on the left side of the wall (see Figure 1.1). Upon its discovery, this image was almost immediately interpreted as Adam and Eve.[8] The reasonably well-preserved figure on the left is clearly a nude male. The right-hand figure, of which only the lower legs are extant, is also nude. Though its gender is unknown, it has been interpreted as female; an interpretation with which I would not argue. But are they Adam and Eve? At first sight, the presence of a snake and a tree would suggest they are, and following the discovery there were a series of Christian and Gnostic interpretations over the next half-century.[9] There are, however, difficulties and the Christian/Gnostic view was first challenged by the eminent art historian Nicolaus Himmelmann in 1975.[10]

Figure 1.1 'Adam and Eve', Wilpert, *Le pitture*, tav. I (detail).

One major problem raised by Himmlemann is that the left-hand, male figure does not appear to exhibit any shame in his nakedness. In nearly all depictions of Adam and Eve, both male and female display a modesty that appears absent here. An image from the house church at Dura-Europos,[11] dated to *c.* 253–256 and thus near-contemporary with the Hypogeum of the Aurelii frescoes, clearly has both female and male figures covering themselves up in accordance with the story as it is told in the Book of Genesis in the Christian Bible (Gen. 2.15–3.24). Although much Christian iconography had yet to evolve, at this time the image of Adam and Eve was established and continued in a consistent manner throughout the Roman period: that is, both male and female figures exhibit shame, while the Tree of Knowledge is positioned between the two individuals and a snake twists itself around the tree.

There are a few instances where the First Couple do not exhibit shame: one is evident on a sarcophagus cover, now in the museum at Velletri in the hills above Rome.[12] In this instance the tree is to one side; the male figure displays no shame and the couple, both nude, are shown in a pose of *dextrarum iunctio*. There is a very particular reason, however, for the lack of shame: the snake still has the apple in its mouth; that is, the apple is yet to be eaten and a state of innocence still exists. Another exception to the usual Adam and Eve iconography is seen on the 'Dogmatic' sarcophagus in the Vatican.[13] Here the tree and snake are moved to one side, allowing the image of Christ to be placed between the First Couple where He passes a wheatsheaf to Adam and a lamb to Eve. The iconography illustrates the consequences of the Fall from Grace: men produce food through hardship and women bear children in sorrow. The Velletri and 'Dogmatic' examples are, however, very much the exception rather than the rule and each exception demonstrates a specific exegetical point. The complete lack of Christian reference elsewhere in the Hypogeum of the Aurelii, combined with a representation that does not comply with the canonical image of Adam and Eve, suggests that an explanation independent of Christianity is the more likely. For this, we now have to turn to the other significant area of remaining plaster.

The image on the right-hand side of the rear wall, though damaged, is of a seated, barefoot man dressed in tunic and *pallium* who turns his gaze towards the viewer (see Figure 1.2). Immediately in front of him is a much smaller figure, apparently nude. Degradation of the fresco makes it unclear whether or not this smaller figure is seated on some form of pedestal, but it must be resting on something for the image to be coherent. Both figures are pictured beneath an overhanging tree: a similar tree overhangs the scene on the left side of the wall. Although now severely degraded, both are clearly visible in Tabanelli's aquatint.

A Christian interpretation has been posited on perceived similarities between this image and the scene of creation on the 'Dogmatic' sarcophagus adjacent to the Adam and Eve mentioned above. In the 'Dogmatic' scene of creation there are three figures involved. The senior, seated figure, who can only be God, is in the middle facing right towards another figure, generally considered to be the Holy Spirit, who places his right hand on a diminutive, upright and nude female while an inanimate male lies at the feet of both.[14] Behind God stands a third figure, who has the characteristics of St Paul.[15] There are,

Figure 1.2 'Creator' image, Wilpert, *Le pitture*, tav. I (detail).

therefore, marked differences with the Aurelii 'Creator' who is operating on his own, whereas the 'Dogmatic' Creator acts through the agency of others. The 'Dogmatic' sarcophagus, giving prominence to Father, Son and Holy Spirit, expresses the Trinity in a manner coherent with its post-Nicene date, the second quarter of the fourth century, that is, a century after the Aurelii fresco.

Another sarcophagus (of uncertain date, but with definite Christian imagery), now in a church in Campli, Abruzzo (see Figure 1.3), has an image closer still to the Aurelii figure, with a small human being created on a pedestal. In both the 'Dogmatic' and Campli examples, God the Creator is shown as a bearded figure whereas the Aurelii 'Creator' is clean-shaven with shorter hair. Individuals with short hair and clean-shaven or with very short beards are very much in line with male portraits of the mid-third century.[16] For this reason, Himmelmann, having highlighted the inconsistencies in the

Figure 1.3 Campli sarcophagus, Wilpert, *I sarcophagi*, tav. CVI (detail).

'Adam and Eve' picture, believed that the Aurelii figure was a contemporary individual, not a Prometheus (because of lack of comparanda), but in the guise of a philosopher, a form of commemoration that became progressively more popular during the third century.[17] Yet 'philosopher' imagery, found frequently on sarcophagi,[18] bears little or no relation to the Aurelii figure with its outward gaze, bare feet and accompanying small figure.[19] 'Philosophers' display their learning by holding papyrus scrolls (*rotuli*) and often have an audience of admirers or pupils. Figures represented on sarcophagi may have the attributes of, or be attended by, one or more of the Muses; they may be depicted with beards and/or *pallium* alone. There is a variety of poses, but there is no convincing parallel with a 'philosopher' represented in the manner of the Aurelii figure, that is, with short hair with little or no beard, barefoot and looking towards the viewer in the sole company of a small figure.

Helga Kaiser-Minn also noted, in 1981, that the Hypogeum of the Aurelii figure is similar in many respects to the pagan myth of the creation of mankind by Prometheus, yet blamed inconsistencies in the iconography on supposed idiosyncrasies in Severan art.[20] An objection Kaiser-Minn might have added was the absence of Athena to animate the humans.

God, philosopher or Titan? None are wholly satisfactory. I shall now propose a solution that is consistent with the imagery under discussion and with funerary practices prevalent in the years leading up to the construction of the Hypogeum of the Aurelii in the early third century. I noted in the introduction that the only secure fact that we possess about the Aurelii is that they were *liberti*. A popular theme employed in funerary commemoration by *liberti* was a celebration of themselves honouring, or in the company of, their patron. There are many examples of this: one, the second-century tomb O of the necropolis under St Peter's Basilica, has an inscription stating that it was erected by two freedmen,[21] Entimus and Zmaragdus, in honour of their *patronus* Titus Mattucius Pallas.[22] A second example, from Ravenna,[23] shows the *familia* of the patron, both freeborn and *liberti*, and exhibits an explicit pride in their occupation as shipwrights. In this latter example, the *patronus* Longidienus and his wife Stacte (herself a former slave of Longidienus) are shown above the *liberti* who paid for the stele. Whether or not the Hypogeum of the Aurelii *patronus* was in fact buried among his *liberti* in between the two scenes under discussion is unknowable due to the loss of any inscription that may have confirmed the point one way or the other. It is quite feasible, however, especially as the images we are discussing are in the first room in the monument and positioned immediately opposite the entrance, that is, in the most prominent position.

In addition to the tradition of celebrating the patron as described, the second century saw the rise of a phenomenon which has been described as 'private deification': the depiction of the deceased in a heroized or deified form.[24] A deceased male infant may be portrayed as the young Hercules, or the goddess Diana may represent a deceased female child. The most common example is that of a deceased wife being depicted as Venus, with an ordinary portrait head of the deceased melded to the idealized body. I suggest that these two trends, namely celebration of the patron and heroization of the deceased, combine to produce the image found here, in which the patron is represented as Prometheus.

Henrik Mouritsen has drawn attention to the psychological effect on the former slave of his or her manumission.[25] The effect would have been profound and is exemplified in Petronius' first-century satire *Satyricon* where, during Trimalchio's Feast, there is a heated exchange of words between one of Trimalchio's freedmen friends and the freeborn Asclytus (Petron. *Sat.* 57). The *libertus* rounds on Asclytus' insult saying, 'et nunc spero me sic vivere, ut nemini iocus sim. homo inter homines sum' ('And now I hope to live so that I'm a laughing-stock to no-one. I am a man amongst men'). The satire may have been written by the high-born Petronius but is no less indicative of the sensitivities of the ex-slave. The *libertus* was no longer an object to be used and abused at the whim of the owner, but a human being. In the Hypogeum of the Aurelii we have an amalgam of 'private deification' and gratitude towards a *patronus*. Where the memorial is set up by a family member, a bereaved widower might commemorate his deceased wife as Venus or *infelicissimi parentes* might represent a deceased child as the young Hercules or Diana. These representations are not to be taken literally, but as examples of what the deceased meant to the surviving widow or parent; they are expressions of the emotional attachment that remained beyond the grave. In the Hypogeum of the Aurelii we have a *patronus* depicted with realistic mid-third-century hairstyle combined with a pose emulating Prometheus in the act of creation: the scene articulates an emotional bond between *patronus* and *libertus* using the same conceptual framework. The goddess Athena is missing, because it is not through divine intervention that a one-time chattel has been transmuted into a socially and legally recognized citizen, but through the agency of the *patronus*.

In the light of this change from slave to freedman, does it come as any surprise that a *patronus* would be depicted as Prometheus, the creator of humanity, when by an act of manumission he has effectively converted an object into a human being? As previously mentioned, Himmelmann rejected the idea because that there was no comparandum: a premature conclusion I believe. Promethean depictions, though few, exist in a number of media, primarily in a funerary context (see Table 1.1 at the end of the chapter). What is unusual in the case of the Hypogeum of the Aurelii is the amalgamation of two concurrent traditions: the honouring of the patron and the heroization in funerary decoration.

A possibly analogous situation, however, may be found in a mid to late second-century tomb on the Isola Sacra, near Ostia, albeit with a different myth. It has the same relative position in this tomb as the Aurelii fresco, that is, the rear wall, facing the entrance. Unfortunately, the fresco is now lost, but it was recorded by Guido Calza in 1940.[26] In this instance the myth clearly depicted is of Pyramus and Thisbe: Pyramus lies prostrate on the ground with Thisbe kneeling next to him in the act of stabbing herself. In a similar manner to the Hypogeum of the Aurelii, the tableau is positioned immediately beneath a niche (*aedicula*) containing cinerary urns instead of an *arcosolium*. Unlike the Aurelii fresco, however, this tomb still has several extant, *in situ* dedicatory inscriptions one of which is inset into the centre of the fresco. This and other inscriptions record that the tomb was erected by the *liberti* P. Varius Ampelus and Varia Ennychis to their *patrona* Varia Servanda.[27] The fact that there is no *patronus* nor is Varia Servanda commemorated by a husband or father suggests that the choice of myth may reflect some incident in her life resulting in her being commemorated by her *liberti* rather than a blood relative or husband. In the Isola Sacra example, the unambiguity of the image and the presence of an inscription allows a conclusion to be drawn as to its meaning – yet the same cultural forces were at work on the decorators of the Hypogeum of the Aurelii.

How does the Promethean explanation affect the so-called 'Adam and Eve'? Kaiser-Minn did not concern herself with that part of the fresco and Himmelmann could not provide an alternative solution. One first has to explain the presence of the snake. There is no reason to link a snake to Christianity, as there are many instances of snakes used in pagan funerary contexts. On sarcophagus covers the deceased were sometimes portrayed with attendant snakes,[28] and, unlike their sinister reputation in Judaeo-Christian religion, were generally considered to be benign creatures: a guardian spirit or even the spirit of the departed (Virg. *Aen.* 5.85). Pliny the Elder also mentions snakes that act as guardians over the soul of the deceased (Pliny *NH* 16.234). This ability of snakes to go from the everyday world to the underworld is reflected in the entwined snakes on the *caduceus* of Mercury Psychopompus, who led the souls of the deceased to the realm of Dis.[29]

Snakes can be associated with Tellus as seen on a sarcophagus now in the Terme museum, Rome,[30] and as late as the fourth century they are shown in conjunction with humans in funerary contexts.[31] There is no reason to suppose that they were associated with any one religion, least of all Christianity. Which leaves the two naked individuals themselves and the tree; can these be connected with the myth of Prometheus? Although plaster loss has made the decorative detail fragmentary, giving the impression of being two separate images, there is no indication of anything other than a unified schema on this wall. There are no red-green line divisions evident on what plaster remains: rather the space between the two extant images seems to have been filled, in addition to the probable stone inscription mentioned above, with a field of fruit-bearing foliage.[32] Consequently, the two images are linked and this too accords with some of the surviving Promethean images. The first is the so-called Albani relief in the Louvre, which shows Prometheus in the company of Athena creating a human of much smaller size than goddess or Titan and various, presumably recently made, male and female human beings.[33] There are similarities here with the Hypogeum of the Aurelii scene: the male figures display no element of shame and the position of a tree whose branches are spread over the scene. In this instance the human figures are physically close to Prometheus, but that is not always the case. In another example, this time in the Capitoline Museum, Prometheus continues to create new human beings on the front of the sarcophagus (see Figure 1.4) while those already made are on a side panel, separated from their creator by a variety of mythological figures including Vulcan at work. Note the tree in the background and the female figure below and slightly in front of the male.

The so-called 'Adam and Eve' and 'Creator' images have been construed as Christian by comparing them to later, assuredly Christian, iconography. Yet, this is looking at the pictures through the wrong end of the art historical telescope. The position of the frescoes, in the principal *cubiculum*, opposite the entrance doorway, make it likely that the person commemorated here is the *patronus*. If so, the frescoes illustrate a concept, that of gratitude towards a *patronus*, well established within the canon of ancient funerary art. In this case the honouring of the *patronus* using the myth of Prometheus would have

Figure 1.4 Capitoline sarcophagus Palazzo Nuovo, 329, Robert, *Die Antiken Sarkophag-Reliefs*, 355.

Table 1.1: Prometheus and the creation myth, first to third centuries CE[36]

	Date.	*Prometheus seated.*	*Prometheus faces away from figure.*	*Prometheus wears tunic.*	*Prometheus has curly hair.*	*Prometheus has beard.*	*Position of Athena in respect of Prometheus.*	*Tree closely associated with scene.*	*Additional animated human figures.*
1) Lamp.[37]	1st C. CE	✓	✗	✓	✓	✓	In front	✗	✗
2) Medallion.[38]	140–3	✓	✗	✗	✓	✓	In front	✓	✗
3) Sarcophagus. Prado 140-E.	150	✓	✗	✗	✓	✓	In front	✗	✗
4) Tomb fresco, Ostia.[39]	*c.* 200	✓	✗	✗	✓	✓	In front	✗	✗
5) Sarcophagus. Louvre Ma 355.	220	✓	✗	✗	✓	✓	In front	✓	✗
6) Sarcophagus. Louvre Ma 339.	240–70	✓	✗	✗	✓	✓	Behind	✗	✓
7) Sarcophagus. Louvre Ma 445.	3rd C.	✓	✓	✗	✓	✓	Behind	✓	✓
8) Glass plate.[40]	3rd C.	✓	✗	✗	✓	✓	Absent	✗	✗
9) Sarcophagus. Cap. Mus. Pal. Nuovo 329.	250–300	✓	✗	✗	✓	✓	In front	✓	✗
10) Sarcophagus. Vat. Mus. Sala dei Busti 638.	3rd C.	✓	✗	✗	✓	✓	Absent	✗	✓
11) Painting found near S. Stephano Rotundo.[41]	?	✓	✗	✗	✓	✓	In front	✗	✗
Hypogeum of the Aurelii.	*c.* 240	✓	✓	✓	✗	✗	Absent	✓	✓

been particularly appropriate amongst *liberti*.[34] This in turn influenced the later Christian images of the creation of humanity, with God seated in direct contact with the proto-human or through the agency of Christ and/or the Holy Spirit as seen in the Campli and 'Dogmatic' sarcophagi. Pagan funerary iconography thus evolved to suit the *mores* and texts of the new religion.

The use of Prometheus in pagan funerary contexts sought and found a Christian equivalence in the Book of Genesis. Eventually, the image of God as creator recedes and the pictorial emphasis is on the Fall from Grace and Original Sin rather than the actual manufacture of humanity. This process was no doubt accelerated as first the pagan myth, including concomitant imagery of Prometheus as creator of proto-humanity, then the judicial process of manumission died out in late antiquity. Theodore Klauser,[35] in the 1960s, revealed how imagery such as the 'Good Shepherd' had its origins in the non-Christian world. The Hypogeum of the Aurelii's use of Prometheus as an exemplar for a *patronus* is a nascent example of a similar, albeit short-lived, process of iconographic migration from a pagan belief system to Christian imagery.

Notes

1. Goffredo Bendinelli, 'Il monumento sepulcrale degli Aureli al Viale Manzoni in Roma', *Monumenti Antichi di Accademia Nazionale dei Lincei* 28 (1922): 510, dated the structure to 200–20 based upon brick stamps found in the vicinity. Similarities between the Hypogeum of the Aurelii and the Villa Piccola beneath S. Sebastiano on the via Appia dated to *c.* 240 (F. Wirth, *Römische Wandmalerei von Untergang Pompeijs bis ans Ende des 3. Jahrhunderts* (Berlin: Darmstadt, 1934, reprinted 1968), 86) and the *cubiculum* of the Good Shepherd in the catacomb of Domitilla dated to the first quarter of the third century (V. Fiocchi Nicolai, F. Bisconti and D. Mazzoleni, *The Christian Catacombs of Rome: History, Decoration, Inscriptions*, 3rd edn, trans. C. Carlo Stella and Lori-Ann Touchette (Regensburg: Schnell and Steiner, 2009), 22–3) suggest to the author that a dating in the 230s or 240s to be more likely. See J. W. Bradley, *The Hypogeum of the Aurelii: A New Interpretation as the Collegiate Tomb of Professional* Scribae (Oxford: Archaeopress, 2018), 84.
2. A fourth, much smaller, chamber existed above ground level and had no figural decoration. This chamber was destroyed during consolidation work.
3. *ICUR n.s.* 6.15391 = EDR072917 = EDB9222. For an analysis of this inscription, see L. De Maria, 'L'inscrizione musiva dell'ipogeo degli Aureli in Viale Manzoni: restauri e nuove riflessioni', in *L'ipogeo degli Aureli in Viale Manzoni: restauri tutela, valorizzazione e aggiornamenti interpretativi*, ed. F. Bisconti (Vatican City: Pontificia Commissione di Archeologia Sacra, 2011), 125–34, and, for a less traditional interpretation, Bradley, *The Hypogeum of the Aurelii*, 18–27. The term 'hypogeum' is that used by most authors on the subject. Though strictly speaking such a term should be reserved for a wholly subterranean structure, I have continued to use the term given in the original excavation report by Bendinelli rather than the less frequently used terms *monumentum* or *sepulcrum*. The term 'Aurelii' is also one of convenience rather than accuracy, as, other than the presence of the extremely common *nomen* Aurelius, -a, there is no evidence that the hypogeum was used by a single family of that name.
4. F. Bisconti (ed.), *L'ipogeo degli Aureli in Viale Manzoni: restauri tutela, valorizzazione e aggiornamenti interpretativi* (Vatican City: Pontificia Commissione di Archeologia Sacra, 2011). The colour reproduction of the illustrations is of variable accuracy and the context of

individual images is not always made clear. Nevertheless, the restoration brought to light a number of features that were previously obscured by water damage. The archive of the Pontificia Commissione Archeologia Sacra has further detailed photographs that could not be included in the 2011 publication.

5. J. Wilpert, 'Le pitture dell'ipogeo di Aurelio Felicissimo presso il Viale Manzoni in Roma', *Atti della Pontificia Accademia Romana di Archeologia, Memorie* 1, no. 2 (1924): 5–43.

6. The photographs in the excavation report in Bendinelli, 'Il monumento sepulcrale', are of poor quality, but a handful of aquatints combined with accurate textual description of the monument read in conjunction with Wilpert's, and now Bisconti's, publication results in a comprehensive recording of the site's frescoes.

7. A summary of most interpretations of these images can be found in A. Pergola, 'Il Quadrante delle Interpretazioni', in *L'ipogeo degli Aureli in Viale Manzoni: restauri tutela, valorizzazione e aggiornamenti interpretativi*, ed. F. Bisconti (Vatican City: Pontificia Commissione di Archeologia Sacra, 2011), 82–3.

8. Bendinelli, 'Il monumento sepulcrale', 433.

9. Wilpert, 'Le pitture', 2. In addition to the 'Adam and Eve', Wilpert's misinterpretation of a fragmentary garland as a cross plus a misunderstanding of the number of large figures depicted in *cubiculum* A (there were only ever eleven, not twelve; see Bradley, *The Hypogeum of the Aurelii*, 108–9) led to a half-century of Christian interpretations of varying complexities.

10. N. Himmelmann, 'Das Hypogäum der Aurelier am Viale Manzoni', *Akademie der Wissenschaften und der Literatur* 7 (1975): 8–16.

11. C. H. Kraeling, 'The Christian Building', in *The Excavations at Dura-Europos: Final Report VIII, Part II*, ed. C. Bradford Wells (New Haven, CT: Dura-Europos Publications,1967), plate XXXII, 3.

12. J. Wilpert, *I sarcophagi cristiani antichi*, vol. 1 (Rome: Pontificio Istituto di Archeologia Cristiana, 1929), tav. IV, 3.

13. Vatican Museums Pio-Christiano inv. 31427 (ex. 104).

14. R. Bucolo, 'Himmelmann e l'ipogeo degli Aurelii', in *L'ipogeo degli Aureli in Viale Manzoni: restauri tutela, valorizzazione e aggiornamenti interpretativi*, ed. F. Bisconti (Vatican City: Pontificia Commissione di Archeologia Sacra, 2011), 125–34.

15. The high forehead suggests St Paul based upon iconography of the fourth century; since the sarcophagus was found beneath the *baldacchino* of S. Paolo fuori le mure this reading seems secure.

16. A survey of third-century portraiture is found in S. Wood, *Roman Portrait Sculpture 217–260 AD* (Leiden: Brill, 1986). Such male figures reflect the fashions of imperial portraiture.

17. Himmelmann, 'Das Hypogäum der Aurelier', 14.

18. The seminal work on this subject is B. C. Ewald, 'Der Philosoph als Leitbild. Ikonographische Untersuchungen an Römischen Sarkophagreliefs', *MDAI(R)* Ergänzungsheft 34 (Mainz am Rhein: von Zabern, 1999).

19. Excluding single figures in tondos, out of Ewald's 218 examples of the deceased as philosopher only two (C24 and E24) are shown barefoot and two (D3 and D4) shown looking at the viewer.

20. H. Kaiser-Minn, 'Die Erschaffung des Menschen auf den spätantiken Monumenten des 3. und 4. Jahrhunderts', *Jahrbuch für Antike und Christentum*, Ergänzungbund 6 (Munster: Aschendorff, 1981), 88.

21. EDR000668

22. J. M. C. Toynbee and J. B. Ward-Perkins, *The Shrine of St Peter and the Vatican Necropolis* (London: Longmans; New York: Green, 1956), 119, n. 2, xvii.

23. MN Ravenna, 7.

24. The seminal work on this topic is H. Wrede, 'Consecratio in formam deorum', in *Vergöttlichte Privatpersonen in der römischen Kaiserzeit* (Mainz am Rhein: von Zabern, 1981).

25. H. Mouritsen, *The Freedman in the Roman World* (Cambridge: Cambridge University Press, 2011), 279.

26. G. Calza, *La necropoli del Porto di Roma nell'Isola Sacra* (Rome: Istituto di Archeologia e Storia dell'Arte, 1940), 113–17.

27. Calza, *La necropoli*, nr 346 = EDR101461; Calza *La necropoli*, nr 346 (1) = EDR101462; Calza, La *necropoli*, nr 347 = EDR101627.

28. For example, the sarcophagus of a youth found at Tre Fontane dating to the Julio-Claudian period, MNR Terme, 61586; an adult male of the early second century, Vatican Museums Gregorio Profano, 10025; and, also from the late second century, an adult female Vatican Museums Cortile del Belvedere, 891.

29. J. H. Charlesworth, *The Good and Evil Serpent* (New Haven, CT: Yale University Press, 2010),140.

30. MNR Terme, 255953.

31. The mid-fourth century *cubiculum* E of the catacomb of Via Latina/Dino Campagni has an image, sometimes known as the 'Death of Cleopatra', of a half-draped female reclining among roses with a snake twisting around her left arm. A. Ferrua, *The Unknown Catacomb: A Unique Discovery of Early Christian Art* (New Lanark: Geddes and Grosset, 1991), 102–3, Figure 79. On the date of the *cubiculum*, see W. Tronzo, *The Via Latina Catacomb: Imitation and Discontinuity in Fourth-Century Roman Painting* (Philadelphia: Pennsylvania State University Press, 1986), 15.

32. It is worth noting that each of the two side walls which have suffered much less damage each have a single unified decorative scheme.

33. Louvre, Ma 445. Bucolo, 'Himmelman', 128, figure 4.

34. It is also plausible, of course, that those sarcophagi which also portray the myth might have been similarly inspired, but that would require an investigation into context etc., outside the scope of this chapter.

35. T. Klauser, 'Studien zur Entstehungsgeschichte der christlichen Kunst III', *Jahrbuch für Antike und Christentum* 3 (1960): 112–33.

36. A sarcophagus from Puteoli, now in the Naples museum (MAN Naples, 6705) and listed in *Lexicon Iconographicum Mythologiae Classicae* as Promethean (*LIMC* vol. VII, 2 s.v. 'Prometheus' nr 110, pl. 429), has enough discrepancies, e.g. lack of Athena, the presence of many other gods, only one inanimate body (and that the same size as 'Prometheus'), as to question its listing among Promethean sarcophagi. Two Eastern mosaics – one from Edessa, the other from Philippopolis – I have omitted as both being heavily influenced by Eastern artistic style and much later than the third century.

37. P. S. Bartoli, *Le antiche lucerne sepolcrali figurate* (Rome: Buagni, 1691), vol. 1, 1–2.

38. F. Gnecchi, *I medaglione Romani* (Milan: Hoepli, 1912), tav. 54, 1.

39. E. M. Moormann, *La pittura parietale romana* (Assen: van Gorkum, 1988), 81.

40. F. Fremersdorf, *Figürlich Geschliffene Gläser* (Berlin: de Gruyter, 1951), tav. 4–5.

41. Recorded by F. Bartoli. Vatican manuscript Capponi 285, 23r, https://digi.vatlib.it/mss/detail/Cappon.285.

CHAPTER 2
INNOCENT IN SENSE AND IN BODY: ADAM AND EVE IN THEIR MANDORLAS (FOURTH CENTURY–THIRTEENTH CENTURY)

Isabelle Mathian

The story of Adam and Eve might be considered one of Christian art's most immediate and imaginative themes. The apparent simplicity of the Genesis narration, its universality and its dissemination in the collective unconscious tend to inspire a literal visualization. For these reasons, its iconographical translation may also seem relatively static in time, requiring the observer to adopt a long historical view in order to divine changes, derivations and breaks which would otherwise remain hidden.

This chapter addresses the representation of *Human's creation on the sixth day of the Creation of the World* (Genesis 1.26–7) over a lengthy window of time, as a case of figurative transmission, an iconic itinerary, perhaps, drawing from late antiquity (fourth century) to the medieval era (thirteenth century).

In this regard, the very particular case of the medieval mandorlas of the Genesis executed by Jacopo Torriti in Assisi in approximately 1280 (see Figure 2.1) is a visual surprise. They are rare enough to oblige us today to take into account the traces of their transmission, which, according to consolidated historiography,[1] trace back to the supposed fifth-century walls of the Basilica of Saint Paul Outside the Walls (see Figure 2.2).

In other words, this case requires us to have multiple interactions with the visual history surrounding it. A first period of observation extending from the fourth to the eighth or ninth centuries shows a debt to Roman canons thought to have become obsolete, while the awareness of the provenance of the origins of the images of creation seems to indicate fidelity to more ancient conceptualizations. The second period can be traced between the beginning of the eleventh century to the end of the thirteenth century, when the awareness of the origins dissolves and the ancient canons find favour anew in *Latin consciousness*.

Two premises are necessary for this viewpoint of interaction. The first is that addressing the theme of the creation implies high political and epistemological stakes. According to Paul the Apostle, prefiguring the form of man, that is to say the Image itself (*imago*), relies on Adam's topos as he has been redeemed in Christ.[2] Therefore, addressing Adam and Eve's figurative debts from late antiquity to the Middle Ages means nothing less than addressing the very idea of the human figure and, of course, of its *incipit*. To this end, one can read in the dedication that Constantina (*c.* 321–*c.* 354), the daughter of

Figure 2.1 Jacopo Torriti, Upper Basilica of Assisi, right side of the corbel arch of the transept, *c.* 1280, detail. Photo Marcello Fedeli, Spoleto 2014. © Archivio Fotografico del Sacro Convento di San Francesco in Assisi.

Figure 2.2 First panel of the Nave of Basilica of Saint Paul Outside the Walls, Vatican City, seventeenth century. Apostolic Library, ms. Barb. lat. 4406, fol. 23, the Vatican Library, https://digi.vatlib.it/view/MSS_Barb.lat.4406.

Constantine, addressing Christ in the first apse of Saint Agnes's basilica on Via Nomentana, formulates the affirmation of a parousiac typological synthesis:

> [. . .] nomen enim Christi celebratur sedibus istis,
> tartaream solus potuit qui vincere mortem,
> invectus caelo solusq(ue) ieferre triumphum,
> nomen Adae referens [. . .].[3]
>
> [. . .] for the name of Christ is celebrated in these places,
> the only one who could overcome the death of Tartarus
> entered heaven and the only one to bring back the triumph,
> the name of Adam [. . .].[4]

Secondly, as far as art history is concerned, scholars usually hold that the Genesitic image is a very common one,[5] but they do not consider its actual rarity in early Christian art. In fact, the theme does not appear predominant during the period of the third to the seventh centuries, nor are the representations of Genesis narrative cycles particularly abundant. All the thematic variations of the first three chapters of Genesis[6] amount to a total of twenty-five paintings set in catacombs[7] and approximately sixty-four sarcophagi or fragments of sarcophagi.[8] This is a small number if one considers, for instance, the roughly 350 representations of the Jonah theme extant from that period.[9]

A Roman debt

The imagining of Genesis was from the beginning associated with the illustration of the creation of man. For that matter, and as suggested in the careful studies by Helga Kaiser Minn,[10] the *eidolon*/Adam/Eve adopted as the simulacrum of the 'first fashioning' in the hands of the Creator/Logos on the Sarcophagus of Cyriaca comes very close to the representation of man's creation in earlier depictions of the Promethean myth.[11] Such a representation can undoubtedly be linked to the centuries-old myth of the dead person's revivification, relying upon the dualistic anthropology[12] which melds the two concepts of enlivenment and shaping. Indeed, the last late antique Gallic sarcophagus from Loudun,[13] possibly datable to the very end of the fifth century, borrowed none other than the Promethean creation's iconic schema for the creation of Adam (Gen. 1.26–7 and Gen. 2.7–8).

Quite rightly, this object's position in the chronology has been emphasized, and this by virtue of its conceptual proximity to a Trinitarian composition of the Creator/Logos, hesitantly made explicit in folio 1v of the *Ashburnham Pentateuch* (Paris, BNF ms. nouv. acq. lat. 2334), itself datable to the very end of the sixth century/beginning of the seventh century.[14] Nevertheless, the perpetuation of the Promethean scheme must be considered not entirely certain since, at some point, its use ceased. It should be noted, indeed, that the last 'Promethean' pagan type of sarcophagus must be dated to around the year 300 CE.[15] On the other hand, the chronology of the so-called Christian 'creation' sarcophagi, of which there are no more than six,[16] cannot be dated earlier than the end of the first quarter of the fourth century, that is, 325 CE. This window of time must be recognized as the moment when the iconography of creation was forged, parallel to the rise of the Christian religion under the reign of Constantine, a very ambivalent period. One may mention the case of the fine front of a Promethean sarcophagus of the end of the third century being reused, inside out, to close a Christian sepulchre in the catacombs of Domitilla (leaving its imprint in the muddy earth that accumulated inside the grave).[17] I understand this to signify that the gravediggers who overturned the stone did not consider the Prometheus myth entirely pertinent to Christian beliefs.

Another aspect that deserves examination concerns the lexicon of the Genesitic image interpretation. This point is critical as it can assist in interpreting what early Christians could understand of this particular representation. No text dating to the late antique period has ever clearly commented on it.

From a lexical perspective, the Latin expression *faciamus hominem* ('let us make man') attests to how firmly the narrative is embedded in the image. If the distinctive elements in the biblical text can support an iconic system, they nevertheless assume a canon of the created human body that is difficult to grasp. The biblical syntax evokes a creation that is carried out in two distinct moments (Gen. 1.26–7 and Gen. 2.7–25) and is both sexless and yet produces two sexes. The text's proleptic nature, noted by many,[18] would imply, at an iconographical level, just what seems to have actually happened; that is to say, the chronological anticipation of events that were not close to each other. Contrary to every causal logic, the first mention of shame in Genesis 2.25 precedes the transgression narrated in Genesis 3.2–6; the creation in Genesis 1.26–7 precedes the clay creation in Genesis 2.7–8, 21–3.

As is known, at the beginning of the fifth century, Augustine (354–430) suggested the most intelligible solution by distinguishing the double passage of the speculative *informatio* (i.e., the information about the act of creating man contained in Genesis 1.26–7) from the *formatio* (the forming of Adam's body in Genesis 2.7–25). In any case, as Ernst Dassman[19] has noted, Augustine's thinking, which many people, unfortunately, tend to misapply to far earlier figurative works, means that the representational problem was not at all solved by the beginning of the fifth century. Augustine, nevertheless, recognized the need to prevent the pitfalls of a purely allegorical vision (that is to say, an image bearing no resemblance), creating the risk that the drawing both of the human body and of creation might be excluded. For him, the act of the creation becomes a 'trans-historic' act on which the whole of creation depends.[20]

It is very likely that Augustine and his contemporaries' concerns persisted even in the following two centuries when the Genesitic creation seemed to disappear almost entirely from the visual arts. This fact suggests the evidence of a consistent twofold concern: first, how to qualify the Creator/Logos, and second, how to qualify man. One can discount as insignificant in this regard the famous *Carrand Diptych* (fifth century) in the Bargello, some examples of sixth-century mosaic church floors in the East,[21] and the back of the ninth-century right ivory leaf of the Areobindus diptych kept today in the Louvre.[22] The lack of interest in and minimal awareness of creation's ideal human body paralleled a frenzied outpouring of renderings of the divine celestial majesty. Early on, when a considerable number of theological disputes still had to be resolved, the *Maiestas Domini* image was to be accorded its own separate and prevalent identity in the Apse.[23]

Taking all this into consideration, can it be authoritatively said that Prometheus has definitively disappeared from the Christian horizon? The question is controversial with regard to Christian figurative sources, but it is particularly noteworthy that shortly after the Second Council of Nicaea in 787, and probably expressed through the pen of Bishop Theodulf, Charlemagne declared in his controversial *Opus Caroli regis* (also called *Libri Carolini*), addressed to Pope Hadrian I, that representations of the Promethean creation were incompatible with Holy Scripture. The subject is treated in Chapter 23 of Book III, in the context of a literary strategy tending to denounce a range of figurative themes.[24] If the full, polemical, ecclesio-political contribution of the *Opus Caroli regis* remained highly limited, and regardless of what was to be the positive aesthetic Carolingian inflexion,[25] we know that the pontiff was to respond to Charlemagne's offensive by informing him of his intention to proceed *cum patrimoniis nostris*,[26] that is, in the awareness that a pre-Christian imaging past had been transformed into a heritage.

In this context, the description of a possible painting furnished by the *Libri Carolini* constitutes a proportional and valuable iconographic testimony to the sacralization of art around the year 790:

> An non divinis Scripturis contrarium est, quod Prometheum homines ex luto finxisse inanimatos fingunt et eundem Prometheum a Minerva in caelum levatum inter horas septemplicis clypei et, dum omnia caelestia vidisset, fingunt eum ferulam Phoebiacis adplicasse rotis ignemque esse furatum et pectusculo hominis, quem finxerat, adplicato animatum reddidisse corpus?[27]
>
> Is it not, perhaps, in conflict with the Holy Scriptures that men are represented as having come, inanimate, out of Prometheus' clay mould and then from Minerva, raised skywards by the same Prometheus towards the seven-coated shields, and while he saw all things from on high, they received new life through the stick of fire applied to their puny breasts, after having stolen it from the wheels of Phoebus' chariot?

Theodulf is not evoking an allegory or a metaphorical figure here, but an exact scene. Does this mean that by challenging the value of this antiquity the author is denouncing a still very current perception, that is from our viewpoint an ancient perception,[28] of the theme?

Latin consciousness

We shall now consider the Roman pontifical basilicas' decorative programmes that lead to interventions in both late antiquity and during medieval times. The founding document of this consideration is the seventeenth-century watercolour recording the state of the Basilica of St Paul Outside the Walls on the occasion of its most recent restoration, at the end of the thirteenth century (see Figure 2.2). A much-consolidated historiography[29] considers it to be a wonderful synthesis of the creation in Genesis 1. We know of it thanks to the transcription in folio 23 of the Vatican Apostolic Library's manuscript Barb. Lat. 4406, dated to the end of the seventeenth century. The folio refers to the first fresco panel marking the beginning of the decoration of the left nave. A half-bust bearded Logos appears in a ringed celestial half-orb above the Lamb of God and a dove hovering over verdant hills; a man and a woman are arranged on either side, each in their own mandorla. These surprising navette-shaped mandorlas are painted in grisaille, tone upon tone, on a uniform blue background for the woman and on an iridescent ochre and gold background for the man. The woman is in three-quarters view and her hips are loosely wrapped by drapery. She is moving off in the opposite direction to the man, who seems to be floating, naked, with his right arm twisted up towards his head.

Apart from the evidence analysed so far, the use of these mandorlas is only documented from the beginning of the eleventh century,[30] on two frontispieces to the so-called Atlantic Bibles of Italian production (ms. Vat. Pal. 3 manuscript and ms. L 59 from Perugia). These details must reflect the divine nature of the occupants, to be so honoured, and they are usually designated as *clipei*.[31] As such, they express meanings that are difficult to discern. In this particular case the images are open to disparate interpretations as they might constitute, either alternatively or simultaneously, the personifications of the sun and moon (*sol/luna*), light and darkness (*lucem/tenebras*) and, in my opinion, Adam and Eve. However, here they are undoubtedly drawn from a cosmic vision of the universe's six days of creation. In the end, they could also suggest, through their visual mediation, an authoritative understanding of a more secular tradition.

A Carolingian italic transcription of the work *De universo* by Rhabanus Maurus (*c.* 780–856), dated to the year 1023, refers to the same subject. On page 231 of the Monte Cassino Codex 132, in the great cosmic zodiacal disk of the regions of the universe, the Logos-Son, as a Creator, is bending over His creature who floats there, naked[32] (see Figure 2.3). The naive, antiquarian draughtsmanship marks the intention to condense the entire chapter of Genesis 1, corresponding to a pure typological Paulinian interpretation of Genesis 1.26–7. The iconography on this page (which, elsewhere, also presents the full catalogue of idolatrous forms of paganism) is a *unicum*.[33] It is, to our knowledge, the only one that so clearly establishes the ideal human prototype of the sixth day of creation inside a full disc of *Æternitas*. There is no doubt that here the naked man in the *clipeus* is actually Adam and not a generical representation of a divine figure.

Like the other two Atlantic Bibles referred to earlier, the date of the Monte Cassino Codex leads back very accurately to the years 1020–40, years that are commonly classified as the premises for the Gregorian Reform undertaken by the Pope of the same name, Gregory VII. Definitively documented, at around the middle of the twelfth century, by the creation panels in the Churches in Ceri under the name of *dies* and *nox*, and in Ferentillo (see Figure 2.4), these mandorlas seem however to suggest that we could be viewing personifications of day and night.[34] Each includes the little masculine and feminine torch-bearer characters, which are quite similar, incidentally, to the Promethean stick of fire figures that Theodulf was deploring four centuries earlier.

Figure 2.3 Monte Cassino, Library of the Abbey, *De rerum naturis* (Hrabanus Maurus), ms. 132, p. 131 (ex fol. 234), *c.* 1023. © Archivio dell'Abbazia di Monte Cassino, cod. 132, p. 231.

Figure 2.4 Church of San Pietro in Valle, twelfth century, Ferentillo.

In the dozen other occurrences that, in total, can be reviewed (see Table 2.1), the standardization and dissemination of the creation image that was carried out, at the direct urging of the papacy,[35] between Umbria and Monte Cassino, can also be found, integrally transposed onto as spectacular a liturgical object as the Lateran's *Crux Magna* (tenth to twelfth century)[36] (see Figure 2.5).

The gold flat relief aims here to promote the visual perception of a unitary space in order to tell the story of human history very clearly. Its starting point is the figure of a young hairless Logos/Creator, in a half-celestial orb, who let a dove slip away (*Spiritus Dei*). The man and the woman, half-immersed in the aquatic element, illustrate the ultimate creative instance of the sixth day. The *Crux Magna* recapitulates the theorizations of Hrabanus Maurus and the liturgical custom, designed by Pope Leo III, of using the great cross to carry the ecclesial construction out of the building itself, so as then to, upon return, restore it to ornament the church's altar.[37] This sacramental iconic pilgrimage of the Old and New Testament liturgical ornamentation is demonstrated, with a not-dissimilar function, in some mandorlas of the Exultet scrolls[38] in southern Italy, in order to promote the same unitary visual perception of space.

The iconographic formula of the *Crux Magna*, due to its conjoinment with the Lateran, leads us to examine the intervention in the Lateran and Assisi sites of Jacopo

Table 2.1: Distribution of the emblems of creation of Genesis 1.26–7.

	Date.	*Creator/ Logos*	*Agnus Dei*	*Angels*	*Dove*	*Oceanus/ Abyssus*	*Sol/Luna*	*Lamellar cockle form mandorla*	*Radiant mandorla*
Ms. Barb.lat. 4406, f. 23 (Rome, St Paul o.t.w.)	5th C. CE–1280	✓	✓		✓		✓	✓	✓
Cod. Cass. 132	1023	✓		✓					
Ms. Pal.lat. 3	*c.* 1050	✓						✓	✓
Ms. Vat.lat. 3784	*c.* 1060–70	✓		✓				✓	
Ms. L59	*c.* 1100–50	✓		✓	✓				✓
Ceri	*c.* 1100	✓			✓		✓	✓	
Ferentillo	*c.* 1150–1170	✓		✓	✓		✓		✓
Rome, Porta Latina	*c.* 1150–80	✓			✓	✓	✓	✓	
Rome, Crux Magna, Lateran	*c.* 10th – 12th C.	✓			✓			✓	
Ms. Vat.lat. 9071	*c.* 1200 (1640)	✓			✓		✓	✓	
Castro dei Volsci	*c.* 1250	✓		✓	✓	✓	✓		✓
Assisi	*c.* 1260 – 80	✓			✓		✓	✓	✓

Torriti in the second half of the thirteenth century.[39] By virtue of this process, Torriti was able to formulate his 'neo-classical' Adam around 1280, thereby reactivating his conception of the creation of the world in late antiquity. This Adam, it must be noted, no longer has the stability and support of the earth, but has at least reacquired its projection and volume in space, and thence its conception as a complete and independent being.

At the dawn of the fourteenth century, it was no longer possible to exclude all the textual interpolations elucidating an image that was by then directly associated with the modus operandi of scholastic thought and the assumption, at last, of a didactic and fully typological responsibility for Christian images. Amidst the political support of Roman supremacy expressed by the whole of the Gothic building in Assisi, Iacopo Torriti's radiant Adam mandorla emits the same light from which the Eve in St Paul Outside the Walls had fled at least four centuries earlier.

Figure 2.5 The so-called *Crux Magna* or 'Cross of Constantin', detail, *c.* tenth–twelfth century, Archbasilica of St John Lateran, Museo del Tesoro, Rome.

Overcoming Prometheus

The Genesitic image that might have been thought to be non-existent or subordinate to others may have become, in reality, from the Constantinian era onwards, the exemplary motif for the architectural space in places of worship. In the part designed to receive ordinary people, that is, the nave, which, unlike the choir, is not an eschatological space, the narrative of humankind's history is condensed.

As far as the illuminated manuscripts are also concerned, further illustrations, like those in the *Cotton Genesis* (London, British Library, Cod. Cotton Otho B. VI) and the *Ashburnham Pentateuch* (Paris, BNF, ms. nouv. acq. lat. 2334), bear witness to variants in the development of the theme. But it must be first emphasized that none of these illustrates the sixth day of creation.[40] All of them seem to avoid, or, possibly, have lost,[41] the crucial moment in Genesis 1.26–7.[42]

The hypothetical reconstruction carried out by K. Weitzman and H. L. Kessler in 1986 in relation to the missing folio 5v (the one theoretically treating the creation of man) is far from being conclusive.[43] In fact, the reconstructed hypotheses of the two scientists seems resigned to a methodological inversion of the evidence, mostly due to the fact that the cycle of Genesis 1 in the famous creation cupola over the (thirteenth-century) narthex in San Marco, Venice, presents a much more articulated scrutiny of the days of creation than the *incipit* deriving from St Paul Outside the Walls.[44] Nonetheless, it is very likely that the *Cotton Genesis* inspired the Promethean figure of the Creator in the creation cupola in Venice.[45] Within the subtle distinctions to be drawn between two seals, namely, the considerable Constantinopolitan reference and the exceptional antique revival of the Promethean creation schema in Venice (Gen. 2.7–8), the particular case of Venice had remained almost unparalleled in the Byzantine programmes and reflected generic primary lines of development in the medieval Latin iconographic tradition.[46] From the extraordinary scansion and colorimetry of the Venetian cupola, it is difficult to perceive a line of thought that adheres to both Roman precepts and a more Oriental thought. In Venice, the mystical vision of Adam, or at least the theophanic vision, does not exist. Venice shows us the gap which increased in semantic mutations beginning actually in the fifth century.

* * *

We ought to expect a univocal semantic meaning common to all the iconography of the creation of the world – but this is not the case. If Eve's body remains prosaically traced along the lines of Adam's male body until the end of the medieval era, a genuine emancipation from the ancient iconographic heritage started shortly after the turn of the first millennium. Then we perceive a man and a woman escaping or floating in a movement that is suspended above the elements. We can distinctly see them actually running in a multicoloured cubist remodelling of the morphological volumes.

In a pictorial versification of Carmen 27, vv. 607–9, Paulinus of Nola (*c.* 354 –431) poetically reverses the visual inspiration of the 'first' Adam of Genesis 1.26–7 to that of Genesis 2.7–8:[47]

> de Genesi, precor, hunc orandi collige sensum, ne maneam terrenus
> Adam, sed uirgine terra nascar et exposito ueteri noua former imago
>
> Take this way of praying from Genesis, that I might not remain the terrestrial Adam but that I might be the one born from virgin soil, and that what is left of the old me may be raised up as a new image.[48]

The beautiful ekphrasis of Paulinus in reference to monumental art would invite us to understand the two slightly offset mandorlas welcoming the naked proto-parents' figures in St Paul as a compression of the theophany foreshadowing Adam that Paulinus, who is not a theologian, calls for in paintings of the basilica. Stephan Waetzolt,[49] for his part, suggests the same theophanic reading of the image of the man created by Agnellus of Ravenna in the ninth century. Indeed, Agnellus noted a *titulus* (title) for Adam, *insons hic corpore senso* ('innocent in sense and in body')[50] over the mosaic that Bishop Neon in the fifth century had inscribed above the figures of the triumphal arch delimiting the apsidal conch of the triclinium of the episcopal palace of Ravenna.

In his turn, the painter and mosaicist in Assisi was probably the last erudite witness of almost a millennium of typological reading of Genesis 1.26–7. From Augustine to Hrabanus Maurus onwards, Torriti understood the liberation of the antique brought about by that reading: a conscious acceptance of the analogy with paganism and the latter's rejection through its integration into the Genesis story. He transcended the literal word of the Bible, tracing a point of no return: the fully completed creation of the world and, above all, the visionary ontology of a man and a woman created innocent and free.

Notes

1. S. Romano, 'San Pietro, San Paolo, e la narrazione cristiana', in *Les stratégies de la narration dans la peinture médiévales. La représentation de l'Ancien Testament aux IVe–XIIe siècles*, ed. M. Angheben (Turnhout: Brepols, 2020), 127–41; C. Proverbio, *I cicli affrescati paleocristiani di San Pietro in Vaticano e San Paolo fuori le mura. Proposte di lettura* (Turnhout: Brepols, 2017); H. L. Kessler, *Old St Peter's and Church Decoration in Medieval Italy* (Spoleto: Centro italiano di studi sull'alto Medioevo, 2002).
2. M. Harl, 'La prise de conscience de la nudité d'Adam. Une interprétation de Génèse 3, 7 chez les Pères Grecs', *Studia Patristica* 7 (1966) : 486–95; P.-A. Deproost, 'Formatur . . . Limatur . . . Le corps d'Adam et Éve dans la poésie latine chrétienne', in *Le corps dans les cultures méditerranéennes – Actes du colloque des 30–31 mars et 1 avril 2006*, ed. P. Veyne et al. (Perpignan: Presses universitaires de Perpignan, 2007), 106.
3. P. Liverani, 'Epigrafia monumentale e immagine pubblica in epoca tardoantica', in *Using Image in Late Antiquity*, ed. S. Birk et al. (Oxford: Oxbow Books, 2014), 3–32, n. 25 = ICUR VIII, 20752.
4. All translations are my own unless otherwise stated.
5. T. Mathews, 'La nudità nell'arte paleocristiana', in *Aurea Roma: dalla città pagana alla città cristiana (mostra nel Palazzo delle Esposizioni, 22 dicembre 2000–20 aprile 2001)*, ed. S. Ensoli and E. La Rocca (Rome: 'L'Erma' di Bretschneider, 2000), 399–403.
6. H. Kaiser-Minn, 'Adam and Eve', in *The Eerdmans Encyclopedia of Early Christian Art and Archaeology*, vol. 1, ed. P. Corby Finney, 2nd edn (Grand Rapids, MI: William B. Eersdmans Publishing Compagny, 2017), 10–12.
7. A. Nestori, *Repertorio topografico delle pitture delle catacombe romane* (Vatican City: PIAC, 1993).
8. S. Salvadori, 'Sin and Redemption, Sexuality and Gender: Adam and Eve in the Funerary Art of Late Antique Rome', in *ΑΝΑΘΕΜΑΤΑ ΕΟΡΤΙΚΑ: Studies in Honor of Thomas F. Mathews*, ed. J. D. Alchermes with H. C. Evans and T. K. Thomas (Mainz am Rheim: Verlag Philpp von Zabern, 2008), 271–82.
9. N. Bonansea, *Simbolo e narrazione. Linee di sviluppo formali e ideologiche dell'iconografia di Giona tra III e VI secolo* (Spoleto: Fondazione Centro italiano di studi sull'alto medioevo, 2013).
10. H. Kaiser-Minn, 'Die Erschaffung des Menschen auf den spätantiken Monumenten des 3. und 4. Jahrhunderts', *Jahrbuch für Antike und Christentum*, Ergänzungbund 6 (Munster: Aschendorff, 1981), 32–52.
11. F. W. Deichmann et al. (eds), *Repertorium der christlich-antiken Sarkophage: Bd. Rom und Ostia*, vol. 1 (Wiesbaden: Reichert Verlag, 1967), n. 180 = CIL VI, 31967.
12. P. Prigent, *Le Judaïsme et l'image* (Tübingen: Mohr, 1990), 293–4.
13. F. W. Deichmann et al. (eds), *Repertorium der christlich-antiken Sarkophage: Frankreich, Algerien, Tunesien*, vol. 3 (Mainz am Rhein: Verlag Philipp von Zabern, 2003), n. 456.

14. Y. Christe, 'À propos de la création de l'homme du sarcophage de Crozant – Creuse – et des peintures de Saint-Eutrope des Salles-Lavauguyon (Haute-Vienne)', *Cahiers Archéologiques* 38 (1990): 7–16.
15. H. Sichtermann and G. Koch, *Griechische Mythen auf Römischen Sarkophagen* (Tübingen: Wasmuth, 1975), 162–3, n. 67.
16. Deichmann et al., *Repertorium der christlich-antiken Sarkophage*, vol. 1, nn. 43, 86, 164; vol. 2, nn. 101, 180; vol. 3, n. 456.
17. F. Bisconti and M. P. Del Moro, 'Via Latina 135: cronaca di un intervento di emergenza. Un'area cacatacomba recuperata al II miglio della via Latina', *Rivista di Archeologia Cristiana* 75 (2009): 11–94.
18. R. Giordani, 'Fenomeni di prolepsis disegnativa nei mosaici dell'arco di Santa Maria Maggiore', *Rendiconti della Pontificia Academia Romana di Archeologia* 47 (1974–5): 225–49.
19. E. Dassmann, *Sündenvergebung durch Taufe, busse and Martyrerfürbitte in den Zeugnissen frühchristlischer Frömmigkeit und Kunst* (Munster: Aschendorff, 1973), 232.
20. M. Dulaey, 'L'apprentissage de l'exégèse biblique par Augustin. Années 393–394', *RÉAug.* 51 (2005): 21–65. See also, J. Pépin, '"Ut scriptura pictura": un thème de l'esthétique médiévale et ses origines', in *From Augustine to Eriugena: Essays on Neoplatonism and Christianity in Honor of John O'Meara*, ed. F. X. Martin and J. A . Richmond (Washington, DC: Catholic University of America Press, 1991), 168–82.
21. P. Canivet, 'Lecture d'une image: une mosaïque d'Adam au Ve s.', in *Rencontres de l'École du Louvre. Image et signification* (Paris: Documentation française, 1983), 141–51.
22. D. Gaborit-Chopin, *Ivoires médiévaux: Ve–XVe siècle, Catalogue du Musée du Louvre. Département des objets d'art* (Paris: Éditions de la RMN, 2003), n. 41; A. Goldschmidt, *Die Elfenbeinskulpturen aus der Karolingischen und Sächsischen Kaiser*, vol. 1 (Oxford : n.p., 1969), 77, n. 158; D. Gaborit-Chopin, 'Les ivoires du Ve au VIIIe siècle', in *Byzance. L'art byzantin dans les collections publiques françaises. Musée du Louvre, 3 nov.–1er fév. 1993* (Paris: Éditions de la RMN, 1993), 42–5.
23. J.-M. Spieser, 'Le décor figuré des édifices ecclésiaux', *Antiquité Tardive* 19 (Turnhout: Brepols, 2011): 95–108.
24. MGH Conc. 2, 1: 577–82.
25. P. Meyvaert, 'Medieval Notions of Publication: The "Unpublished" "Opus Caroli regis contra synodum" and the Council of Frankfort (794)', in *The Art of Words: Bede and Theodulf*, Variorum Collected Studies (Aldershot: Ashgate Publishing, 2008), 78–89.
26. MGH Epist. V: 2, 57.
27. MGH Conc. 2, 1: 443–4.
28. For the 'lack of prejudice' from the Carolingian toward antiquity, see E. Panofsky, 'Renaissance and Renascences', *Kenyon Review* 6 (1944): 201–36. For the opposite, see N. Himmelmann, 'Nudità ideale', in *Memoria dell'Antico nell'arte italiana*, vol. 2, ed. S. Settis (Turin: Ed. Einaudi, 1985), 201–78, 252–3.
29. Proverbio, *I cicli affrescati paleocristiani*, chapter 2 and 178–80.
30. M. Maniaci and G. Orofino, *Le Bibbie atlantiche: il libro delle Scritture tra monumentalità e rappresentazione* (Milan and Rome: Centro Tibaldi, 2000), 120–6.
31. H. Brandenburg, 'Meerwesensarkophage und Clipeusmotiv. Beitrage Zur Interpretation Römischer Sarkophagreliefs', *Jahrbuch des Deutschen Archäologischen Instituts* 82 (1967): 195–245; O. Brendel, 'Origin and meaning of the Mandorla', *GazBA* 25, no. 6 (1944): 5–24;

A. Grabar, 'The Virgin in a Mandorla of Light', in *Late Classical and Medieval Studies in Honor of Albert Mathias Friend, Jr.* (Princeton, NJ: Princeton University Press, 1955), 305–11.

32. G. Orofino, 'Citazione e interpretazione. Il rapporto con l'antico nel ciclo illustrativo dell'enciclopedia di Rabano Mauro', in *Medioevo: il tempo degli antichi – Atti del Convegno internazionale di studi, Parma, 24–28 settembre 2003*, ed. A. C. Quintavalle (Parma: Electa, 2006), 197–206.

33. Orofino, 'Citazione e interpretazione', 197–206.

34. Kessler, *Old St Peter's and Church Decoration in Medieval Italy*, 159–78.

35. H. L. Kessler, *The Illustrated Bibles from Tours* (Princeton, NJ: Princeton University Press, 1977), 145–8.

36. M. Andaloro, 'Il tesoro della basilica di S. Giovanni in Laterano', in *San Giovanni in Laterano*, ed. C. Pietrangeli (Firenze: Nardini, 1997), 271–95; E. B. Garrison, *Studies in the History of Medieval Italian Painting*, vol. 4, 1 (Florence: 'L'impronta', 1960), 201–10.

37. J.-P. Caillet, 'L'arredo dell'altare', in *L'arte medievale nel contesto. 300–1300. Funzioni, iconografia, tecniche*, ed. P. Piva (Milan: Jaca Book, 2006), 181–203.

38. It is, in fact, the case of ms. Vat. lat. 3784. A description in B. Brenk, 'Città del Vaticano, Biblioteca Apostolica Vaticana, Vat. lat. 3784, Exultet', in *Exultet. Rotoli liturgici del Medioevo meridionale*, ed. G. Cavallo and G. Orofino (Rome: Istituto Poligrafico e Zecca dello Stato, 1994), 211–13.

39. A. Tomei, *Iacobus Torriti. Una vicenda figurativa del tardo Duecento romano* (Rome: Argos, 1990), 59–65.

40. K. Weitzmann and H. L. Kessler, *The Cotton Genesis: British Library, Codex Cotton Otho B. VI* (Princeton, NJ: Princeton University Press, 1986), 16–26.

41. H. L. Kessler, 'The Cotton Genesis and Creation in the San Marco Mosaics', *CArch* 53 (2009–10): 17–32.

42. This is also the case with the *Byzantine Octateuchs* (ninth century). K. Weitzmann, *Illustrations in Roll and Codex: A Study of the Origin and Method of Text Illustration* (Princeton, NJ: Princeton University Press, 1970), 193–4.

43. Weitzmann and Kessler, *The Cotton Genesis*, 52. Reassessed by H. L. Kessler, 'La Genèse Cotton est morte', in *Les stratégies de la narration dans la peinture médiévales. La représentation de l'Ancien Testament aux IVe–XIIe siècles*, ed. M. Angheben (Turnhout: Brepols, 2020), 373–402.

44. Garrison, *Studies in the History of Medieval Italian Painting*, 201–10.

45. Garrison, *Studies in the History of Medieval Italian Painting*, 201–10.

46. Garrison, *Studies in the History of Medieval Italian Painting*, 201–10.

47. G. Herbert de la Porbarré Viard, 'Choisir des décors pour une église. Culture classique et culture biblique chez un commanditaire privilégié au début du Ve siècle', in *Poïkiloï karpoï. Récoltes diverses. Études réunies en hommage à Gilles Dorival*, ed. M. Loubet and D. Pralon (Paris: n.p., 2015), 249–259.

48. My translation from PL, 61, cols. 648–63.

49. S. Waetzoldt, *Die Kopien des 17. Jahrhunderts nach Mosaiken und Wandmalereien in Rom, Römische Forschungen der Bibliotheca Hertziana* 18 (Vienna: Schroll-Verlag, 1964): 57.

50. I quote the translation of D. M. Deliyannis, *The Book of Pontiffs of the Church of Ravenna*, Medieval Texts in Translation (Washington, DC: Catholic University of America Press, 2004), 125.

CHAPTER 3
PROMETHEUS PLASTICATOR: RECEPTIONS OF THE CREATION MYTHEME IN ART

Jared A. Simard

In antiquity, Prometheus as the Hesiodic trickster and fire thief along with the punished rebel and philanthropist of *Prometheus Bound* dominate representations of the myth. Prometheus as the creator of humanity is a less dominant strain of the myth. This is partially explained by the challenge it presented to late antique Christian apologists, for whom Prometheus plasticator was a pagan rival to God in Genesis.[1] Furthermore, his clear benefactions to humanity and his willingness to sacrifice himself for their benefit position him as an earlier Christ-like figure.[2] Therefore, this chapter posits that a focus on the visual record offers a better explanation for the reception of the Prometheus creator mytheme. It is in the visual record that the fullest depictions of Prometheus plasticator emerge and provide new associations for Prometheus. It is also in the visual record that this particular mytheme influences early Christian depictions of creation in Genesis. Later, Prometheus plasticator emerges in the Renaissance more clearly associated with artistic creation, both literary and in the visual arts. The reception of Prometheus ultimately culminates in a modern syncretism of all three major mythemes in what has become one of the most iconic images of Prometheus: that of Paul Manship's gilded *Prometheus* at Rockefeller Center.

Prometheus plasticator

Some of the earliest depictions of Prometheus creating man appear in Etruscan and Hellenistic era gems.[3] They present a challenge in terms of their dating, but here it is beneficial to follow Gabriella Tassinari's comprehensive work.[4] Many of these gems feature the same set of depictions. Prometheus is sometimes seated and working on a statue-like creation, often placed standing atop a column. At times, he may hold a sculpting tool or a hammer. At other times the creation is only partially formed and Prometheus is seen measuring with a plumb line. Finally, some of these gems depict Prometheus' creation as a skeleton.[5] Taken together, these depictions of Prometheus at work on his creation represent an area that needs further research.[6] The important aspect for us in the present study is a tantalizing link between the Titan figure at work on humanity and artisans at work on their sculptures.[7] Here we recall that Prometheus is said to have made men out of clay, a mixing of mud and water. The plasticity and applicability of clay as a modelling material further enhances this association. Is Prometheus plasticator the father of sculpture? The Prometheus creation mytheme,

Figure 3.1 *La creation de l'homme par Prométhée*, Louvre, Paris, Inventory Number MA445, https://www.photo.rmn.fr/archive/05-509172-2C6NU076ER_M.html. L'Agence Photo RMN Grand Palais, https://www.photo.rmn.fr/archive/05-509172-2C6NU076ER_M.html.

while an important strand of the larger Prometheus myth on its own, additionally provides for the new association of Prometheus with artists and fruitful comparisons with other creators in myth: Hephaestus, Athena and Pygmalion.[8] His association with artists is important as a potential (pagan) secular reception in light of the myth's treatment and allegorization by early Christian writers.[9]

Another rich source of ancient depictions of Prometheus as creator appear in the third and fourth centuries CE in fragments and Roman sarcophagi. A particular marble relief fragment from the third century CE, now at the Louvre, provides an interesting set of motifs in the Prometheus creation myth (see Figure 3.1). Prometheus is seated on the right with a stool between his legs. He holds a sculpted man with his left hand while looking back over his right shoulder to Athena, who stands a few feet behind him. Athena is installing souls into Prometheus' creations. As is archetypal, the soul is characterized by a butterfly. This relief depicts a number of motifs in the Prometheus creation mytheme. The pairing with Athena is typical here. Prometheus' seated position with stool and statue-like creation harkens back to some of the gems discussed earlier,[10] but unlike those, Prometheus' creation is nearly complete but for its soul. Curiously, Prometheus uses two fingers, his index and middle digits of his right hand, to point to or bless the creation he is holding. The ring and pinky digits remain folded toward the palm of the hand. Noticeably absent from this depiction is the use by Prometheus of any tools to sculpt his creations. Nonetheless, the stool positioned between his legs is reminiscent of the position of a potter's wheel and one can easily imagine Prometheus forming his creation from a block of clay positioned in front of him, much like a sculptor might. That is to say, the literary sources have us conjure an image of Prometheus bent over the ground and forming his creation from the earth. This third-century CE fragment, like the previous Hellenistic gems, deliberately seeks to associate Prometheus with a sculptor.

In addition to fragments like the one at the Louvre, Roman sarcophagi provide another source of depictions of the Prometheus creation mytheme. A sarcophagus of a child now at the Capitoline Museum and dating to the third century CE is richly decorated, for example.[11] So is another example at the Louvre also dating to the third century CE.[12] Both of these sarcophagi depict a Prometheus seated, with a statue-like creation standing before him on a column and also on his lap in the case of the Capitoline example. Both, as in the third-century fragment, also feature Athena close at hand to infix the soul in Prometheus' creations. The Capitoline sarcophagus also clearly shows Prometheus holding a sculptor's stylus in his right hand, furthering his association with artisans as was shown with the gem representations. But it is the example of a fourth-century CE sarcophagus now at the Museo Archeologico Nazionale di Napoli which is of interest for our current study (see Figure 3.2).

Discovered in a mausoleum near ancient Puteoli, the sarcophagus furthers the remarkable trend in the third and fourth centuries CE where the deceased decorated their sarcophagi with the Promethean creation myth.[13] Olga Raggio has argued that this sarcophagus depicts the 'eternal journey of man from birth to death',[14] but this particular

Figure 3.2 Fourth-century CE sarcophagus, Museo Archeologico Nazionale di Napoli, https://commons.wikimedia.org/wiki/File:MANNapoli_6705_creation_of_the_man_sarcophagus.jpg.

instantiation of the myth is a departure from the previous visual record.[15] It is remarkable for what is missing as much as for what is depicted. Athena is absent, but her function is here likely replaced by the presence of Psyche, who appears by the left hand of the creation with her right hand raised. Prometheus is seated low to the ground with his creation unanimated, lying horizontal on the ground between his legs. A pantheon of gods surrounds them. While Prometheus does not seem to hold any sculpting tools, perhaps distancing this depiction from earlier ones where his association with sculptors was emphasized more, what is clear is that this creation was moulded out of the earth. The mud earth from which he was moulded is still visible beneath his right side: it is as if he emerged from the ground. His horizontal position further emphasizes his telluric origins. The presence of the gods also seems to indicate that this particular creation is important and worthy of their presence. The sarcophagus depicts Prometheus creating the *first* man.

Prometheus plasticator and Christianity

Prometheus plasticator is well and fine for Greco-Roman mythology, but less so for Christianity. Beginning in the fourth century CE and possibly earlier, the Prometheus creator mytheme both influenced early Christian iconography and was allegorized away so as to prevent it from remaining a problematic challenge to God and Christ. Here we focus on two somewhat well-trodden examples to demonstrate this influence: the so-called Dogmatic Sarcophagus and the Moutier-Grandval Bible.[16] The sarcophagus dates to the early part of the fourth century CE and is also known as the Trinitarian sarcophagus for its depiction of the divine Trinity in the upper-left register.[17] From our interest in Promethean depictions of creation several things are remarkable. The first is the depiction of Eve on the sarcophagus, whose statue-like stance recalls the Promethean tradition of him holding his still-lifeless creations atop a column.[18] The second is that the seated God blesses Eve with two fingers in a gesture that is nearly identical to the one Prometheus uses in our Figure 3.1. The gesture is replicated on the male figure in the central tondi on the sarcophagus and could be an early depiction of the benediction sign.[19] Finally, Adam is depicted lying flat and motionless on the ground. While this is not a depiction of Adam's creation, nevertheless his position on the ground recalls the position of the Promethean first man in our Figure 3.2.

The horizontal Adam in depictions of Christian creation is uncommon and in the view of Raggio originates with our Figure 3.2 in the pagan and Promethean visual tradition.[20] Another example of Adamic creation in the horizontal position is the well-known Moutier-Grandval Bible from Tours, dating to the ninth century CE.[21] In the folio depicting Genesis, God is shown creating Adam in the top-left panel. God is bent over Adam, who is lying flat and motionless on the ground. This directly echoes the position of Prometheus and his first man in our Figure 3.2.[22] What has failed to be noted about this comparison is a detail which furthers the comparison. In the hexameral Genesis, God is said to have commanded the earth to bring forth all the living creatures of every kind of the earth (cattle, creeping things, wild animals).[23] God next creates Adam, but nowhere does it mention he is created from the earth, unlike the other animals that inhabit the earth.[24] The Moutier-Grandval Bible depicts Adam lying on the ground next to mud and water. This detail recalls the Prometheus myth, where the Titan moulded the first man out of mixing mud and water, a form of clay, and a detail that is consistent in many of the ancient literary sources.[25] As was noted before, the depiction of Prometheus creating the first man in Figure 3.2 makes sure to indicate he is moulded out of the earth. Thus, not only does Christian iconography adopt the horizontal position for Adam, echoing earlier pagan iconography, but it also appears at least in the case of the Moutier-Grandval Bible to adopt the concept of the first man made out of mud and water.[26] In an example of earlier pagan iconography being fully adopted well into the ninth century, the two-finger blessing sign from our Figure 3.1 is also present as God animates Adam with his right hand.

The Christian reception of the myth of Prometheus, as we have seen thus far, largely focused on the mytheme of creation. This was the locus of potential conflict from a monotheistic point of view. The more well-known mythemes articulated long ago (even for early Christian times) by Hesiod and *Prometheus Bound* and, to some extent, Plato, were pushed aside and perhaps forgotten.[27] In addition to the brief examples above of Christian iconography, Christian writers forcefully sought to allegorize and otherwise bring the Prometheus plasticator mytheme into harmony with prevailing doctrine (for two creator gods cannot occupy the same space).[28] Lactantius and Augustine provide examples for us. Lactantius wrote in the fourth century CE and cast Prometheus as the father of idolatry and thus the founder of the art of sculpture.[29] Augustine likewise strips Prometheus of his divinity, shapeshifting him into a mere wise man learned in lore.[30] Lactantius is certainly the more hostile of the two in his regard for the myth. In Augustine, however, there is a discernable secularizing as much as it is Christian allegory. The continued association of Prometheus plasticator with artisans and sculptors also stands out among the early Christian apologists. This thread continued into the late Middle Ages and early Renaissance.

While Christian writers were busy turning Prometheus into an obscure mortal, manuscript illuminators also put forth interpretations of the Prometheus creation myth. The previously discussed Moutier-Grandval Bible is just one example of a biblical illuminator's reception of the myth. In our discussion of ancient literary sources for Prometheus, Ovid's version of the Prometheus creation mytheme stood out among the Greek and Latin literary sources because it forms part of a larger cosmogony and thus its creation tale was also in need of Christian allegorizing.[31] One of the most well-known and best examples of this is the early fourteenth-century CE *Ovide moralisé*. Combining both literary and visual interpretations and commentary on Ovid's *Metamorphoses*, the *Ovide moralisé* presents one of the most striking examples of Christian religious syncretism. Of particular interest to us are the depictions of creation from the Lyon and Paris manuscripts. Both present Prometheus animating what can be both the first man and Adam. In fact, the depictions do not seem to follow the Latin text at all.

In manuscript 742, f.1 of the Lyon *Ovide moralisé*, the illuminator chose to begin with a depiction of creation. Since both the Christian Bible and Ovid's *Metamorphoses* begin with creation, this choice is not unusual per se. Of all the scenes from the *Metamorphoses* with which to begin the first depiction, the choice of creation, however, does seem to indicate the motivations behind the manuscript. One could have just as easily chosen to begin with the ages of mankind. Instead, the illuminator begins with creation and thereby betrays a desire, as does the commentary of the *Ovide moralisé*, to allegorize and make the pagan myths of Ovid fit into a Christian worldview. Thus, it is not a surprise to see Prometheus present (he appears just right of centre), but it is a surprise to see the Christian God present. His presence makes clear the subordination of Prometheus to the biblical Genesis. Sébastien Douchet argues in one of the most in-depth studies of this sequence published to date that this Christian God is not necessarily the same one as the *in principio* God we see in the hexameral tradition of Genesis.[32] Considering that both the Bible and Ovid begin with creation and follow a natural progression culminating in the creation of man, what is unexpected in this depiction is not the presence of the Christian God taking the place of the unnamed Ovidian '*deus*' nor the presence of Prometheus creating the first man, but the fact that Prometheus animates him with fire.[33] The illuminator needed a way to indicate the figure as Prometheus and not the Christian God.[34] The illuminator's solution was to overlap the Hesiodic Prometheus with his iconic fire and the Ovidian creator Prometheus. In doing so, the illuminator maintains the readability of their manuscript while still subordinating pagan myth to Christian doctrine. That is to say, the depictions of creation in the *Ovide moralisé* might as well be that of Genesis, except for the presence of Prometheus animating what appears to be Adam or the first man (more on this below). Prometheus in the Lyon manuscript is not clearly marked as the creator; the Christian God is, however. Prometheus *is* marked as animating Adam or the first man with fire, which replaces the more typical Athena plus butterfly motif because the illuminator needed an easily recognizable icon for Prometheus.

The Paris BnF manuscript 871 f.1r depicts creation in much the same way as the Lyon manuscript, except that the Paris manuscript breaks up creation into four panels.[35] For our purposes, the fourth and final panel on this folio is the key to understanding the *Ovide moralisé* and its depiction of creation. While it may have been unclear in the Lyon manuscript whether the illuminator was depicting Genesis with Prometheus subordinated to the Christian God or depicting Ovid's creation with a Christian God superimposed over the narrative, the presence of the first woman, Eve, in the Paris manuscript makes it clear it is the former. That is to say, the illuminator is making Ovid fit into the Christian worldview, and while it might be easier to moralize the various myths in Ovid's *Metamorphoses*, the act of creation can only be that of Genesis. Thus, in Paris ms. 871 we find Prometheus in very nearly the same depiction as that of the Lyon manuscript. He is animating the first man, here clearly Adam, with fire. The fourth panel shows the Christian God pulling the first woman, in this case it must be Eve, from the rib of Adam. Thus, the depiction of creation in Paris ms. 871 and I would add Lyon ms. 742 is that of Genesis, with Prometheus animating Adam in both depictions.[36] This subordination of pagan narratives to Christian ones continues a long tradition of Christian allegorizing of the Prometheus creation mytheme, here even going so far as to strip him of his demiurge status and his status as man's benefactor. Instead, much like

Athena's function in the pagan sarcophagi, he acts as a clearly lesser figure akin to the Christian God's helper in his depiction of simply animating Adam with the spark of divine fire (the spark of life).

Renaissance reception

This transfer from one mytheme to the other is picked up later in Giovanni Boccaccio's take on the myth, which will set the stage for our final discussion in this chapter. Boccaccio in many ways represents a sort of final transformation for Prometheus and the Prometheus creator mytheme in particular. This transformation builds upon previous Christian allegorical interpretations of Prometheus and sets the stage in the Renaissance for the wide-open reception of all three strands of the Prometheus myth. In both the *De Genealogiia Deorum Gentilium* and in the *Decameron*,[37] Boccaccio puts forth a comprehensive view of the Prometheus myth, seeking to incorporate the three major mythemes (fire-bringer/philanthropist, punished rebel and creator) into one harmonious allegory.[38] In this, Boccaccio is far more ambitious than his earlier Christian counterparts who focused on the creator mytheme and the problems it presented for Genesis. Boccaccio's allegorical synthesis picks up various ancient strands of interpretation, including the idea that Prometheus was an Assyrian sage who withdrew to the Caucasus and taught man various skills.[39] Boccaccio also further develops the imagery depicted in the *Ovide moralisé* of Prometheus animating Adam with the divine spark, turning it into the moment where the previously dormant rational mind is awakened.[40] But the key transformation for Boccaccio is the merging of identities between Prometheus the poet and Prometheus the sage.[41] As Susanna Barsella concludes her argument, Boccaccio the famed Renaissance poet transforms Prometheus into an allegory for the self.[42] This recalls a long tradition going back to the Hellenistic gems where Prometheus was modelled as a sculptor, depicted creating statue-like first men. Just as the ancient sculptors saw themselves in Prometheus plasticator, so Boccaccio centuries later in the Renaissance sees himself in Prometheus plasticator-poet.

Boccaccio thus opens the door for *everyone* to see themselves in Prometheus. As much as he allegorizes the Prometheus myth according to Christian doctrine, this secular shift in the Prometheus mytheme also serves the purpose of opening up Prometheus for everyone: we are all Prometheus now. Boccaccio inadvertently restores Prometheus as our benefactor. If Boccaccio, a Renaissance mythographer, philosopher and poet, can see himself as, and in, Prometheus, why not a Renaissance painter? This is exactly the sense of Piero di Cosimo's dual panel depiction of the Prometheus myth.

Over a century after Boccaccio, Piero di Cosimo, an Italian Renaissance painter, produced two panels on the Prometheus myth in 1515. The first in the series is *Prometheus Fashioning the First Man*.[43] Prometheus' creation, centre, stands contrapposto, life-size and on a pedestal. Its right arm is raised and appears to be pointing to the sky. Prometheus wearing a white sash is off to the right speaking animatedly with Athena. There is much debate about the group of figures on the left.[44] What stands out for our study is the return of Prometheus at work on statue-like creations. The image of the first man on a pedestal recalls those from the Hellenistic gems and Roman sarcophagi (cf. Figure 3.1). Here the life-sized proportions and elevated height of the creation as well as its central position in the frame of the panel casts Prometheus' work as triumphant. Another detail which stands out is the mirror effect established between Prometheus and his creation. Where the creation has its right arm raised, Prometheus has his left arm raised, and where the creation has its weight on its left leg, Prometheus holds his on his right leg. This merging of identities between Prometheus and his creation, combined with the artisan tools at both of their feet, establishes an allegorical representation of Piero di Cosimo's self-reflection in this panel. Just as Boccaccio the poet saw himself as a new Prometheus, so Cosimo the painter, echoing previous ancient sculptors' identification with the Prometheus creation mytheme, sees and has fashioned himself as a new Prometheus plasticator.[45] This meta-allegory of self represents a shift away from Christian interpretations of the Prometheus creation mytheme toward a secular and generative interaction with the myth.

Cosimo's second Prometheus panel, *The Theft of Fire and the Punishment of Prometheus*, fleshes out the rest of the Prometheus myth.[46] Key scenes include, in the centre, the theft of fire from the chariot of the sun shown in the distance in the clouds; front left, Prometheus enlivening his creation with divine fire in the heart; and front right, Hermes chaining Prometheus as an eagle stands ready to begin its daily feast. A group of figures are shown in the mid-centre set back a little and could be a depiction of the creation of Pandora.[47] Two aspects of this panel stand out. The first is the attempt by Cosimo to synthesize all the strands of the Prometheus myth into a coherent narrative. The second is the continuation, as with Boccaccio and the illuminator of the *Ovide moralisé*, to have Prometheus use the divine fire/spark to enliven the first man. In the case of Cosimo, that creation is likely made out of clay, as the greyish colour in the first panel would indicate. Thus, Cosimo in his two panels on the Prometheus myth has synthesized all three major mythemes for Prometheus to centre on the action of his creation of the first man and his awakening of that man with the divine fire. This centrality of the creation mytheme also serves to further Cosimo's self-identification with Prometheus plasticator.

Post-Renaissance and modern receptions

In terms of visual receptions of the Prometheus creation mytheme, Pompeo Batoni's *Prometheus Fashioning Man from Clay* from *c.* 1742 continues the trend of artistic self-fashioning while returning to an old motif in the Prometheus creation mytheme.[48] Prometheus is seated centre, draped in lush pink. He holds a sculpting stylus in his right hand and looks back over his right shoulder to Athena who is looking at his creation and placing the soul, symbolized as a butterfly, to awaken it. Prometheus' creation stands before him, sculpted out of clay. The creation is diminutive compared to the gods and appears the size of a young man. His smooth clay skin and neat short curly hair emphasize his youth. As Edgar Bowron and Peter Kerber note, Batoni likely modelled the creation after the *Belvedere Antinuos*.[49] The left hand of Prometheus wrapping around the back of the creation and the creation's right hand form a sort of mirror of one another.[50] This gesture, combined with the clear depiction of Prometheus here as a sculptor, as Prometheus plasticator, follows in the artistic footsteps of Cosimo, Boccaccio and others who have continually thought of themselves as Promethean since the Renaissance. That the Titan is here shown in a dark cave secluded from the world also draws upon Boccaccio's telling of the myth and previous Christian allegory which placed Prometheus as a hermitic wise old man.[51]

Bowron and Kerber note that Batoni's previous sketch drawings of the fragment that is our Figure 3.1 indicates the set-up here is a condensed version of our ancient fragment which Batoni knew intimately.[52] The two fail to note, however, that in addition to the general composition, Batoni also clearly mimics the two-fingered blessing sign in Prometheus' right hand, here shown with the addition of the sculpting stylus delicately perched between the index and middle digits. Batoni's piece is important because it also demonstrates that the mode in which the creation is enlivened is not the essential part of a Promethean self-fashioning. Here it is with the Athena plus butterfly motif, while earlier Cosimo used divine fire to enliven his creation. Neither were key contributions to the self-fashioning. That was indicated by composition and mirroring in the case of the artists, and was purely a literary creation for Boccaccio, while ancient gems emphasized Prometheus' sculpting the first man out of clay as a sculptor might.

Before ending with Paul Manship's epic *Prometheus* at Rockefeller Center in New York City, Heinrich von Füger's *Prometheus Brings Fire to Mankind* of 1817 is a necessary addition to emphasize another aspect of the modern reception of the Prometheus creation mytheme.[53] Here, Füger distilled the mytheme even further than Batoni who had just three figures, including the creation. Füger has just Prometheus and the creation. The duality allows him to play with contrasts to full effect. Prometheus is bathed in light as he holds a torch in his right hand, his right arm uplifted above his head. His left forefinger grabs his chin as Prometheus looks upward, pondering his actions. Because of the billowing fabric behind him, Prometheus appears to have arrived in haste despite his inquisitive look. The creation lies beneath him, cast in shadow, made darker by the grey clay of its anatomy. The bright fire of Prometheus' torch barely casts a glow upon the creation. It is seated slumped over, head down. Füger has masterfully played the light and dark contrast to allegorize Prometheus (whose name means forethought) as a fountain of knowledge and his creation as yet still motionless in ignorance. Thus, Füger's Prometheus is very much the benevolent caretaker of mankind, as he was in *Prometheus Bound* where he lists off the many things his gift of fire taught mankind. Here too, as we saw in earlier pieces, Prometheus will quite literally awaken his creation with fire, an awakening not just of life but of knowledge too.

Therefore, we end this chapter with a final culmination. Just as Boccaccio synthesized all three Prometheus mythemes into one where creation took precedent, so Paul Manship's statue of *Prometheus* (see Figure 3.3), installed in January 1934 in Rockefeller Center, is the modern culmination of millennia of Promethean receptions.[54] Prometheus is here shown holding fire in his right hand as he descends from the heavens. Next to him

Figure 3.3 Paul Manship, *Prometheus*, Rockefeller Center, New York, https://digitalcollections.nypl.org/items/510d47e2-c3b0-a3d9-e040-e00a18064a99. The New York Public Library Digital Collection, https://digitalcollections.nypl.org/items/510d47e2-c3b0-a3d9-e040-e00a18064a99.

are *Man* and *Woman*, who are shown in Figure 3.3 in their original location.[55] Manship's *Prometheus* recalls Hesiod's fire-bringer and *Prometheus Bound*'s philanthropist. He also recalls Ovid's Prometheus the creator by virtue of the *Prometheus Bound* quotation inscribed on the wall just behind the statue (not shown in Figure 3.3), which reads 'Prometheus, teacher in every art, brought the fire that hath proved to mortals a means to mighty ends.' In this way, Prometheus here is symbolic of the creative ingenuity on display by the first tenants of Rockefeller Center: the RCA corporation and NBC – radio and television, the two new mass media technologies, the new media of their day.[56] Prometheus is bringing fire to humanity, and while he may not be awakening them, his fire does awaken in them the *techne*[57] and ingenuity that will lead to the technological achievements of modernity and the digital age. Further, as humanity's philanthropist, I have argued elsewhere that Manship's *Prometheus* is also a self-fashioned representative of his own times and of John D. Rockefeller Jr., the benefactor of Rockefeller Center and one of the founders of modern philanthropy.[58]

This wide-ranging survey of the reception histories of the Prometheus creator myth demonstrates a fluke of history. If not for Christianity's obsession with allegorizing pagan creation myths, the myth of Prometheus may have remained that of Hesiod and *Prometheus Bound*. From the very beginning of visual representations of Prometheus, a strand has existed that connected his creation of man with sculptors who saw themselves and their craft in him. This is why he is Prometheus *plasticator* and not anthroplast. He is fundamentally one who moulds and shapes and in this we too, like the ancient artists and Boccaccio and Cosimo and countless others, can see ourselves in Prometheus. We are all Prometheus.

Notes

1. For some of the Christian perspectives on Prometheus, see Philipp Theisohn, 'Prometheus', in *Brill's The Reception of Myth and Mythology*, ed. Maria Moog-Grünewald (Leiden: New Pauly), 552–68.
2. Gedaliahu G. Stroumsa, 'Myth into Metaphor: The Case of Prometheus', in *Gilgul: Essays on Transformation, Revolution and Permanence in the History of Religions*, ed. Shaul Shaked, David Shulman and Gedaliahu G. Stroumsa (Leiden: E.J. Brill), 311. See also, Caroline Corbeau-Parsons, *Prometheus in the Nineteenth Century: From Myth to Symbol* (London: Legenda, Modern Humanities Research Association and Maney Publishing, 2013), 19–22, and Raymond Trousson, *Le thème de Prométhée dans la littérature européenne* (Geneva: Librairie Droz, 2001), 91ff.
3. Please note throughout that when I use 'gem' I am referring to ancient engraved gemstones, rather than to great artistic works.
4. Gabriella Tassinari, 'La raffigurazione de Prometeo creatore nella glittica romana', *Xenia Antiqua* 1 (1992). For a discussion of Tassinari's work in relation to Prometheus and ancient automata, see Adrienne Mayor, *Gods and Robots: Myths, Machines, and Ancient Dreams of Technology* (Princeton, NJ: Princeton University Press, 2020), 114–23.
5. For a discussion of the skeleton frames and the wooden skeletal structures of ancient artists, see Mayor, *Gods and Robots*, 121–2.
6. I agree with Mayor that these gems are fascinating and more studies on them are welcome. See Mayor, *Gods and Robots*, 114.
7. Mayor, *Gods and Robots*, 114–23. See also Meredith Shedd, 'Prometheus the Primeval Sculptor: Archaeology and Anatomy in Emeric-David's "Recherches Sur L'art Statuaire"', *Zeitschrift Für Kunstgeschichte* 54, no. 1 (1991): 91–3.
8. The association of Prometheus with Athena and Hephaestus has deep roots. See Mayor, *Gods and Robots*, 124, n. 37. See also, Carol Dougherty, *Prometheus* (London: Routledge, 2006), 49–50, and Karl Kerényi and Magda Kerényi, *Die Mythologie der Griechen* (Stuttgart: Klett-Cotta, 1997), 156–7.
9. For an interesting discussion of Lucian's self-fashioning as Prometheus, see James Romm, 'Wax, Stone, and Promethean Clay: Lucian as Plastic Artist', *Classical Antiquity* 9, no. 1 (April 1990).
10. For examples of Prometheus with his creations atop a column, see Tassinari, 'La raffigurazione de Prometeo', 81–5.
11. Olga Raggio, 'The Myth of Prometheus: Its Survival and Metamorphoses up to the Eighteenth Century', *Journal of the Warburg and Courtland Institutes* 21, no. ½ (Jan.–Jun. 1958): 5a.
12. Raggio, 'Myth of Prometheus', 4f. For additional examples, see John W. Bradley, 'An Interpretation of the Frescoes of the Hypogeum of the Aurelii in Rome', PhD diss., Royal

Holloway and Bedford New College, University of London, London, 2017, 256–61 and especially 262, Table 4, for a comparison, as well as Chapter 1 in this volume.

13. Raggio, 'Myth of Prometheus', and Bradley, 'Frescoes of Hypogeum', provide examples. See above notes.
14. Raggio, 'Myth of Prometheus', 47. She also notes two other sarcophagi which showcase this same theme.
15. There are two gems in Tassinari's catalogue which depict the creation in a horizontal position. In those, Prometheus is holding the creation in his lap. Tassinari, 'La raffigurazione de Prometeo', 93.
16. Raggio, 'Myth of Prometheus', 5c and 6c.
17. Likely produced following the Council of Nicaea in 325 CE. Located in the Musei Vaticani, Cat. 31427.
18. See, for example, Raggio, 'Myth of Prometheus', 4e–f, 5a. Compare numerous gems in Tassinari, 'La raffigurazione de Prometeo', 1992.
19. Bennett Futterman, 'Analysis of the Papal Benediction Sign: The Ulnar Neuropathy of St. Peter', *Clinical Anatomy* 28, no. 6 (2015). Futterman argues for a medical source for the benediction sign. Rather than being of a medical origin, it originates with Promethean and pagan imagery as shown here, example Figure 3.1. On this, I agree with Raggio, who in a different comparison notes Christian adoption of this sign is likely from the Louvre fragment. See Raggio, 'Myth of Prometheus', 48.
20. Raggio, 'Myth of Prometheus', 48–9.
21. Raggio, 'Myth of Prometheus', 6c. The British Museum page has a robust bibliography on the manuscript, http://www.bl.uk/manuscripts/FullDisplay.aspx?ref=Add_MS_10546. The depiction of creation appears in f.5 of ms. 10546.
22. Raggio, 'Myth of Prometheus', 48–9, appears to be the first to make this connection directly between our Figure 3.2 and the creation depiction in the Moutier-Grandval Bible.
23. Genesis 1.24.
24. Genesis 1.26ff. Outside of the hexameral creation of Genesis 1, in Genesis 2.7 God again creates Adam, this time from the dust of the ground.
25. See my discussion below, especially Ovid, *Metamorphoses*, 1.80–8.
26. Even accounting for Genesis 2.7, the inclusion of water in the Moutier-Grandval creation scene and Adam's placement in the zone where earth and water mix recalls the language of Promethean creation.
27. Raggio, 'Myth of Prometheus', 50ff., and Theisohn, 'Prometheus', 555ff.
28. Theisohn, 'Prometheus', 555–8.
29. Theisohn, 'Prometheus', 556, and Raggio, 'Myth of Prometheus', 51–2.
30. Theisohn, 'Prometheus', 556. Raggio places this tradition with Servius' commentary. Raggio, 'Myth of Prometheus', 51.
31. On why it's important Ovid has Prometheus create man and not a philosophical god, see Richard McKim, 'Myth against Philosophy in Ovid's Account of Creation', *Classical Journal* 80, no. 2 (1984).
32. Sébastien Douchet, 'Création du monde et poétique de l'œuvre', *Cahiers de recherches médiévales et humanistes* 30 (2015): 65.
33. Douchet, 'Création du monde', 65, argues that the Lyon ms. in fact depicts the Ovidian *deus* rather than the Christian God. We disagree, as is outlined below.

34. Douchet seems to suggest the illuminator got the notion of fire from Ovid's text, but is more interested in the origin of the turban and the three stars. Douchet, 'Création du monde', 59–61. The horizontal position recalling our Figure 3.2 lends credence to the idea that the illuminator is drawing from ancient traditions.

35. For an image, see Douchet, 'Création du monde', Figure 11.

36. Raggio, 'Myth of Prometheus', 49, sees only the Paris manuscript as Adam.

37. Important treatments are Susanna Barsella, 'The Myth of Prometheus in Giovanni Boccaccio's "Decameron"', *Modern Language Notes* 119, no. 1 (2004); and Lucia Marino, 'Prometheus, or the Mythographer's Self-Image in Boccaccio's "Genealogie"', *Studi sul Boccaccio* 12 (1980) 263–73.

38. *De Genealogiia Deorum Gentilium* IV.44. Boccaccio's treatment of the Prometheus myth is one of his lengthiest. A new topic is not picked up until IV.54.

39. Marino, 'Prometheus', 267–8. It's unclear whether Boccaccio was drawing upon Servius' commentary or ciphered through some other Christian source.

40. Marino, 'Prometheus', 268.

41. Marino, 'Prometheus', 269–70. Marino argues this is done through Boccaccio's treatment of Fulgentius' theory of cognition, which Boccaccio himself cites in *Genealogiia* XI.2. Boccaccio's Prometheus fulfils part of the requirements while Boccaccio's own treatment of the myth fulfils the remaining parts.

42. Barsella, 'Myth of Prometheus', 138.

43. Dennis Geronimus, *Piero di Cosimo: Visions Beautiful and Strange* (New Haven, CT: Yale University Press, 2006), 116ff., has a good image and discussion. The painting is housed at the Alte Pinakothek in Munich, inventory number 8973.

44. For a brief discussion of the group, see Geronimus, 'Piero di Cosimo', 117.

45. Indeed, Raggio argues that Cosimo borrowed many of the details for his composition from Boccaccio. Raggio, 'Myth of Prometheus', 56.

46. For an image, see Geronimus, 'Piero di Cosimo', 117.

47. For a discussion of the puzzling group, see Geronimus, 'Piero di Cosimo', 118–19, and especially Patricia Simons, 'Piero di Cosimo's Creation of Pandora', *Source: Notes in the History of Art* 34, no. 2 (2015).

48. Jane Davidson Reid, *The Oxford Guide to Classical Mythology in the Arts 1300–1990s* (Oxford: Oxford University Press, 1993), 927. Reid locates the painting in the private collection of Conte Piero Minutoli-Tegrimi in Lucca. For an image, see Anthony M. Clark and Edgar Peters Bowron, *Pompeo Batoni: A Complete Catalogue of his Works with an Introductory Text* (Oxford: Phaidon, 1985), no. 69.

49. Edgar Peters Bowron and Peter Björn Kerber, *Pompeo Batoni: Prince of Painters in Eighteenth-Century Rome* (New Haven, CT: Yale University Press, 2008), 21.

50. Timothy Alves notes the oppositional nature of the hands. See Timothy Alves, 'Pompeo Batoni Exhibition, The National Gallery, London', *Birkbeck Early Modern Society Bulletin* 65 (Spring 2008): 27.

51. See above note 42.

52. Bowron and Kerber, *Pompeo Batoni*, 21. For an image of Batoni's sketch of the fragment, see Hugh Macandrew, 'A Group of Batoni Drawings at Eton College, and Some Eighteenth-Century Italian Copyists of Classical Sculpture', *Master Drawings* 16, no. 2 (Summer 1978): Plate 15.

53. Located in the Liechtenstein Museum Princely Collections, inventory number GE1362. In literature of the 1800s especially, the Prometheus myth has a robust reception and scholarship.

Of interest to our project here is McCallum-Barry's work on Napoleon and Victor Hugo's self-fashioning as Prometheus. See Carmel McCallum-Barry, 'Myth under Construction', *Classics Ireland* 7 (2000). For a good introduction to the reception of Prometheus during the Romantic period, see Corbeau-Parsons, *Prometheus in the Nineteenth Century*.

54. For other receptions of Prometheus in modern art, see Judith E. Bernstock, 'Classical Mythology in Twentieth-Century Art: An Overview of a Humanistic Approach', *Artibus et Historiae* 14, no. 27 (1993): 160–2.

55. They have since been moved multiple times and currently are located flanking the top of the stairs leading down to the sunken plaza. Jared A. Simard, 'The Titans of Rockefeller Center: Prometheus and Atlas', in *Classical New York: Discovering Greece and Rome in Gotham*, ed. Elizabeth Macaulay-Lewis and Matthew M. McGowan (New York: Fordham University Press), 150.

56. Simard, 'The Titans of Rockefeller Center', 151.

57. For a discussion of *techne* in Plato's discussion of Prometheus, see Alfredo Ferrarin, 'Homo Faber, Homo Sapiens, or Homo Politicus? Protagoras and the Myth of Prometheus', *Review of Metaphysics* 54, no. 2 (2000).

58. Simard, 'The Titans of Rockefeller Center' and Jared A. Simard, 'Classics and Rockefeller Center: John D. Rockefeller Jr. and the Use of Classicism in Public Space', PhD diss., Graduate Center, City University of New York, 2016.

PART II

CREATION NARRATIVES AS A MODEL FOR MARRIAGE

CHAPTER 4
EVE AND PANDORA: MYTHS IN DIALOGUE

Thierry J. Alcoloumbre

In this chapter, I propose to compare the Greek myth of Pandora with the myth[1] of Adam and Eve as it appears in Judaism. For this, I will base myself not only on the biblical text of Genesis, but also on the interpretation that the rabbis gave it in the Talmud and the Midrash.[2] Indeed, for Judaism, the biblical text is indissociable from the tradition that comments on it. This comparison has two goals: on the one hand to show how two civilizations, starting from an identical question, explored different directions as answers in order to each construct its representation of the world; on the other hand, to put these myths in dialogue, by reading each according to the other. We cannot know how exactly a Greek read Genesis or a Jew read Hesiod during the Hellenistic period. But we can, as readers of the twenty-first century, develop a critical reading of each story based on its counterpart. How are the values of the one represented in the other? What changes would have to take place to pass from the Greek myth to the Jewish one and vice versa? I hope therewith to clarify certain issues that have been hitherto ignored and to contribute to better understanding the heritages of Hellenism and Judaism.

In order to study the Greek myth, I will base myself on the two poems by Hesiod: *Theogony* and *Works and Days*. For a Jewish reading of Genesis, I will primarily use the Talmud and the most well-known compilation of the Midrash, that is to say the *Midrash Rabba* (fourth and fifth century).[3] My analysis is inspired by the philosophical commentaries developed by French anthropology and philology (Claude Lévi-Strauss, Jean-Pierre Vernant, Jean Bollack and the Philological School of Lille), the hermeneutics of Paul Ricoeur, and the Paris School of Jewish Thought.[4]

1. The myth of Prometheus and Pandora

In Hesiod,[5] the myth of Prometheus appears in different but complementary contexts. It is both part of the narrative of the emergence of the gods and their respective rights (*Theogony*, 506–616) and also a moral reprimand that evokes the misfortunes of humanity to call for respecting justice (*Works*, 27–105). In both cases the myth marks the limits that separate gods and men, while also explaining the origin of the human condition and its miseries.

1.1. The actors: Zeus, Prometheus and Man

We can distinguish three protagonists: Zeus (the Olympian god), Prometheus (the Titan) and man: a rivalry develops between Prometheus and Zeus, for whom man (favoured by

Prometheus) is the stake and finally the victim; a passive victim overall, since his initiative consists in accepting or not accepting the divine gifts. The conflict, which plays out in three parts, revolves around the sharing of the prerogatives between the gods and men. Everything starts, *Theogony* tells us, 'when the gods and men separated,[6] at Mecone' (vv. 535–6).

Prometheus tries to give to man the benefits that Zeus wanted to keep for the gods. In the first instance, during the establishment of sacrifices, the Titan managed to impart to man the best section of the animal offering, leaving to the gods nothing but the fat and the bones; the second time, when Zeus, as a retaliation, deprives man of fire by removing it from the earth, Prometheus steals the flame by hiding it in an hollow reed; on the third occasion, Zeus definitively re-establishes the balance in his favour: no longer by taking away the source of good, but by giving to men an irremediable evil, from which they will no longer be able to deliver themselves *because they desire it*. As Zeus says (*Works*, 57–58), 'I shall give them an evil [*kakon*] that they will all enjoy to their heart's content [*terpontai kata thumon*] as they embrace with love [*amphagapontes*] their own evil.'

This evil is the first woman created by the gods, whose gifts she capitalizes on (hence the name Pan-dora) but who hides beneath her blessed appearance a harmful nature; trapped by what seems to him to be a divine gift, Epimetheus (the brother of Prometheus, father of man) accepts this 'magnificent evil' (*Theogony*, 585) and this 'adorable misfortune' (*Works*, 82), which leads to the opening of the famous jar[7] from which all of the evils of the earth escape. Hope is the only power to remain prisoner in the jar once it is closed again, but it is unclear whether it represents a consolation or an additional curse, since the hope of tomorrow makes man persist in his misery. The evils that hit man are linked to the necessity of working and procreating, necessities from which man was exempt before the creation of woman.

In a parallel manner to the curse of man, Prometheus suffers the famous punishment of being tied to a cliff, his liver regularly devoured by an eagle. He will later be delivered by Heracles, with the permission of a reconciled Zeus.

1.2. The great themes of the Hesiodic story

(i) The ruse and the theft

The confrontation between Zeus and Prometheus takes place primarily through the use of ruse and dissimulation. Zeus and Prometheus compete here in the art of hiding, from the establishment of the sacrifice when the Titan conceals the bad part under a good layer of fat up until Pandora's curse, hidden under her divine appearance, passing by the confiscation of fire, hidden in a carved reed.[8] Prometheus, as his name indicates (*prometheus*) distinguishes himself by his foresight and his cunning. The lesson of the final myth, which consecrates the victory of the god over men, is precisely that 'one cannot deceive Zeus' (*Works*, 15) or 'steal the spirit of Zeus' (*Theogony*, 613).

(ii) Woman: good and evil

Created by Zeus, woman is an instrument of evil in the world. Though she has become indispensable to human continuity, she is not strictly speaking a human being. Pandora, the first woman, is a pure artefact and the women who are born from her are a race (*genos*) apart, a fatal race.[9] She has a divine and cosmic aspect since she brings together the gifts of all of the gods and since the crown of gold that she wears represents the animals of the earth and of the seas.[10] However, it is but a simulacrum destined to trick men. Hesiod recognizes certain virtues in her,[11] but nevertheless she brings together in herself all of the vices: lazy and thieving,[12] she is nothing but a stomach hungry for food and sex, in which man risks exhausting his strength.[13] The jar from which all of the evils leave is probably the symbol of the matrix.[14]

Nevertheless, a positive femininity does exist for Hesiod: that of the goddesses; in particular, Hecate. Pandora herself, by virtue of her origin and her beauty, tends sometimes to receive a quasi-divine importance: she inspires the admiration of the gods (*Theogony*, 588), and other versions of the myth preserved in the fragments of Hesiod show her married to Prometheus or even having sexual relations with Zeus himself![15] The last verse of *Theogony* announces a poem of the celebration of women.

It is therefore not femininity as such that poses a problem for Hesiod but femininity as *something human*. Pandora is a curse, because she resembles a divinity but *in reality* enslaves man to his economical and biological condition. She incarnates a mix of Good and Evil: she is a Good in appearance, but an Evil in reality; she brings Evil, as the counterpart of Good acquired unduly by man (fire).[16]

2. The Jewish myth (Bible and Midrash)[17]

Mentioned in the beginning of Genesis (1–3), the creation of Adam and his fall are part of the story of the origins of humanity. This story describes the emergence, among the 'families of the earth', of the line of Abraham finally chosen by God. This line is the origin of the people of Israel, whose birth will be described in the Book of Exodus. Genesis, in contrast, tells the story of Canaan's curse, legitimating in advance its future conquest by Israel.[18] To this geopolitical purpose is added an aetiological one, analogous to that of the Hesiodic story. Adam's sin explains the origin of evil present in the human condition.

2.1. The actors of the Jewish story

(i) Man, woman and their Creator

The biblical story attributes to the original man a more elevated condition than the Greek myth. In Hesiod, men appear like an anonymous collectivity, created by the gods[19] but characterized by their mortal and inferior condition[20] even before Pandora could open the jar of misfortunes. In Genesis, on the contrary, God decides to create a being in His image (*tzelem, demut*) which will rule over all of the living beings; unlike all the other animals produced from the earth or the water, he is fashioned by God himself, who blows a 'soul of life' (*nishmat ḥayyim*) into his nostrils. The creation of man crowns the work of all of creation (*tov meod*, 1.31). This man is already characterized by work and procreation, which are thus not considered to be a curse (1.28).[21] Further, man is immortal:[22] God places him in the Garden of Eden where he should rejoice from the material goodness (1.29, 2.8–16), and it is in order to help him, not to punish him, that woman is created (2.18).

It is precisely about woman that the fundamental difference between the two traditions appears. In the Bible (1.27 and 2.18–24), even if woman seems inferior to man (she is his helpmate), she has a very great dignity: her body is fashioned from that of Adam with whom she is supposed to form an organic unit (2.24). She receives the name of 'Eve' because she is 'the mother of all living creatures' (3.20),[23] a function that other cultures attribute to a goddess. Finally, the first story of the creation defines 'Adam' as both male and female,[24] which implies that the true human being is only achieved within the couple.[25]

The Midrash expands on these biblical themes. Man is the goal of creation, he is a quasi-divine being with cosmic proportions[26] and endowed with a universal knowledge.[27] He is superior to angels, who are at his service.[28] This dignity introduces the risk of a competition, whether with God[29] or with the angels who are jealous of Adam.[30] Adam's sin will deprive him of his divine dimension, without however nullifying his resemblance to the Creator (the *tzelem*). As to woman, she participates in Adam's divinity. One of the opinions of the Talmud sees in the original Adam 'male and female' – an androgynous being; woman was created by the taking of one of the 'sides' or faces of this androgynous being.[31]

(ii) The forbidden fruit

Like Hesiod, Judaism blames the transgression of an interdiction for the origins of evil. But if the benefits of fire, hidden by Zeus and stolen by Prometheus, were obvious, the Bible is not explicit about the advantages of 'the knowledge of good and evil'. This is a divine privilege, as the serpent affirms and as God himself confirms.[32] But the immediate result of his acquisition (the shame of being naked) is not clearly an advantage; and the consumption of the fruit leads to the immediate mortality of man, even before his judgement by God.[33]

The rabbis proposed identifying the forbidden tree with known plants: wheat, the grapevine or the fig tree.[34] The production of these three plants seem inseparable from the progress of human civilization. But why does the Creator, despite His concern about the fate of His creation, oppose this progress? How can the knowledge of 'good and evil' be interpreted here? One source for the answer can be found in the typology of the vine and of wine developed by the rabbis. Wine is the source of blessing, it 'gladdens the heart of man' (Psalm 104.15), but it is however the cause of all vices, and in particular of debauchery, as the example of Noah shows.[35] Wine makes good and evil known, in the sense that it gives the taste, the desire, to do good as much as evil. When it comes to God, the knowledge of good and evil is a power; when it comes to men, it is a desire and a pleasure. For the rabbis, the forbidden wheat, grapes and figs are thus emblematic of the ambivalence of human desire, its susceptibility to distance man from his Creator. By consuming these fruits, Adam would have let this ambivalence enter into him. This idea is sharpened when we study the discourse of the serpent.

(iii) The serpent and the sin

In contrast to Prometheus, a benevolent god who stole the fire in order to give it to man, the serpent clearly appears as a malevolent creation. He offers nothing to man, but rather seduces his wife in order to make her transgress the interdiction. He uses lies, since he denies that the consumption of the fruit leads to death (v. 4).

Like Prometheus, the serpent distinguishes himself by his cunning, but the narrative presents him like a created animal, which puts aside the supposition that it was an ancient god.[36] The Midrash presents him as very similar to man, with whom he shared intelligence, a bodily form (erect chest, arms and legs) and food.[37] It is thus a sort of natural man, who was only missing the soul emanating from God (*nishmat ḥayyim, tzelem*) in order to be a true human being. Originally, he was supposed to cross the earth in the service of man, trading and prospecting treasures.[38] But envy guides him: he wants to usurp Adam's place either to unite with Eve[39] or to inherit the earth. He plans therefore to provoke the sin of the first man in order to make him die.[40] According to later traditions,[41] the serpent would not have been able to desire or seduce Eve if he had not been 'ridden' by a superior force, that is the angel Samael, who was jealous of Adam's supremacy and decide to destroy it. Thus, the sin of Adam is part of a cosmic drama implying the involvement of celestial forces. Adam nevertheless retains the responsibility for this act.

The seduction by the serpent provoked the sin of the woman, then that of man. The three characters appear before God like before a judge (2.9–19). Their punishment leads to the deterioration of their condition of life: the serpent plummets to the bottom of the ladder of the living, whereas humans lose their divine superiority (immortality, cosmic size) and henceforth suffer (as in Hesiod) the difficulties of economy and procreation. The Bible further insists on the suffering of woman (submission to her husband, the pains of childbirth). The Greek myth hardly considered this aspect, since Pandora was seen primarily as a malevolent artefact.

2.2. The great themes of the Jewish narrative

(i) Adam as thief

As in the Hesiodic myth, man is condemned for having appropriated a forbidden object. The theme of the dissimulation can be found in the attempt of the human couple to hide after the sin, even though it was less a matter of escaping judgement than of covering up their nudity (Genesis 2.7). The Midrash, in turn, insists on Adam's hope of deceiving his Creator, in terms that are almost identical to the terms found in Hesiod ('stealing Zeus's spirit'): Adam is condemned for having tried to 'steal the spirit' of his Creator (*ganav da'at*), an expression which in Hebrew and Aramaic signified (as in Greek) deceiving someone, hiding oneself from him.

(ii) Adam's sin as a choice between civilizations

(a) Eden as Torah and 'mitzvot' In order to explain the nature of the garden of Eden and the seriousness of the sin, the Midrash refers to the theme of the Torah and its reception.

This method, which might be surprising, is a constant in the hermeneutics of the rabbis: they often explain the behaviour of biblical personalities through Torah laws, even if these laws were issued long after the events described. The extreme example is that of the patriarch Abraham, who followed all of the commandments of the Torah (*mitzvot*) before they were issued, including the rabbinical decrees.[42] This anachronism is explained by the conception of the Torah as a primordial entity:[43] its principles, eternally valid, were transmitted to individuals before being officially revealed to the people. From this perspective, the Midrash understands the link between Adam and his Creator as a transmission of the Torah, even if this Torah did not have the shape it manifested in the time of Moses. At a prescriptive level, this Torah of Adam is satisfied with denying the tree of knowledge of good and evil: when Adam and Eve, having eaten the fruit, notice that they are naked (Genesis 3.7), the Midrash understands this nudity as the loss of a merit: 'the only mitzvah they possessed, they were stripped of it'.[44] But this Torah further contains allusions to certain commandments that guarantee the link between man and God and the good functioning of human society: on the one hand Shabbat and the sacrificial cult, on the other the seven fundamental laws later prescribed to Noah and his children.[45]

(b) The doctrine of the serpent The rabbinical typology of the serpent takes us back, in turn, to the categories of the Torah and the *halakha*. Thus, the serpent is characterized by 'slander' (*lashon ha-ra'*), a capital sin in the eyes of Judaism,[46] and by its incitement to crime, considered to be more serious than the crime itself and deserving of the harshest judgements of the courts.[47] But its meaning goes far beyond this. The Midrash designates the serpent as an 'apikoros',[48] a term used by the Talmud to designate a person who despises the Torah and those who study it.[49] This term is sometimes replaced by the term 'Sadducee', a reference to the sect which, during the period of the Talmud, denied the authority of the oral law (contrary to the Pharisees).[50] The serpent is thus the antithesis of the divine direction, and it is the very existence of the link unifying man and God that he denies. How is his denial expressed? 'You will be like gods' (Genesis 3.5) is interpreted by the Midrash as the following argument: 'it is by eating of this fruit that God created the world'. The divine interdiction was thus only inspired by a spirit of jealousy.[51] The argument implies that there is a prior reality or one coexisting with God, and that divine power is not absolute but depends on an exterior object. On the other hand, the serpent questions the status of man as the purpose of the universe: it describes the creation of the world as a repetitive act during which each creature is subjugated to the creature created after it (the sky rains on the earth, the animals are exploited by man). The serpent advises the human couple to eat of the fruit of the tree in order to prevent the birth of rival creatures who would then dominate humankind.[52]

These arguments are not without echoes in the Greek myth. In the Hesiodic myth, Zeus refuses man the possession of fire due to jealousy. Zeus swallows the goddess Metis, goddess of trickery, to reserve for himself the knowledge of good and evil (*Theogony*, 888–900). Cronos swallows his children, and Zeus swallows Metis, in order to prevent the arrival of a new generation that will supplant them.

(c) The fall of Adam, the disciple of the serpent Adam is not only guilty of having listened to his wife and eaten of the forbidden fruit. He blasphemes, promises to reoffend[53] and most of all, in his ingratitude, blames God for having caused his fall by the gift of woman.[54] Like the serpent, he is called an *apikoros* or a Sadducee. The Midrash sees in him the disciple of the tempter:[55] 'Yesterday, God says to Adam, you followed my will, now you follow the will [*da'at*] of the serpent!'[56] This reversal is described as apostasy: Adam (who is described as having been born circumcised) is accused of having stretched his foreskin. We know that the stretching of the foreskin was practised during the Hellenistic period by the Jews who wished to assimilate with the Greeks. The restoration of the foreskin (*orlah*) equalled the erasure of Jewish identity.[57] Adam's choice was thus understood as a choice of civilization: he refused the direction of the Torah in favour of that of a superior animal, and he submerged himself in the ambivalence of desire, believing thereby that he would become a god.

We see that the fall of Adam affected his nature. His transformation also brings him closer to the nature of the serpent: indeed, the human being is contaminated by a 'defilement' (*zohamah*) that the serpent had transmitted to Eve during what seems to have been sexual relations.[58] This defilement can be found, from Cain onwards, in Adam's progeny. The gift of the Torah on Mount Sinai, by outlining a return to primordial innocence, is supposed to at last deliver Israel from this defilement.[59] A disciple of the serpent, natural man (ignorant of the divine Torah), is therefore also partly his son.

3. The Jewish myth and the Greek myth

3.1. Similarity and difference

The Greek myth and the Jewish myth have in common the themes of the forbidden, transgression, of the cunning mediator and of the female initiator of evil. But they develop these themes according to diametrically opposite axes.

a) The nature of the triangle god–man–mediator: on the Greek side, the god is hostile to man, and the mediator is a positive figure. On the Jewish side, God is favourable[60] and the mediator is hostile; the narrative leaves the possibility of redemption and of return open. The story that follows will recount the covenant (*brit*) of God and Noah, Abraham and Israel.[61]

b) Human responsibility: the Greek myth is fundamentally tragic. Man is entirely innocent of his misfortune, a passive victim of the struggle between Zeus and Prometheus, then of the evil liberated by Pandora. On the Jewish side, the human being is responsible. God personally formulated the interdiction to him and his punishment is decided after a judgement during which man could have defended his case.

c) The status of woman: on the Greek side, she incarnates the divine curse, and leads man to his miserable condition. On the Jewish side, she is an integral part of original human being, but her part is more easily influenced and fallible.

d) The moral status of law: the Greek story defends the idea of distributive justice (*dikè*), the guarantee of the order of the world and vital for man due to the lack of resources. The Jewish story sees the Torah as the will or knowledge (*da'at*) of God for man. The Torah is for man a living link with God, and its study permits humanity to return to its original innocence and happiness.

These differences become clearer when we place the rabbinical Midrash in its historical context. We saw that the *apikoros*, the Sadducee, and the themes of the abolished circumcision referred explicitly to the challenges Judaism encountered during the Graeco-Roman period. The Greek influence, which crosses the rabbinical lexicon in general,[62] is also perceptible in the discourse of the serpent as the Midrash develops it. An even clearer example for the Greek influence concerns the theme of Pandora's jar. The Midrash[63] compares the tree of good and evil to a jar filled with scorpions and serpents that a serpent charmer had brought home and forbidden to his wife. An ill-intentioned neighbour suggests to the wife that her husband lied to her, and that he is hiding treasures he promised to another woman in the jar. The misfortunate wife opens the jar and is bitten. Her husband understands from her cries that she has transgressed his interdiction. The parallel here between the tree of knowledge of good and evil and the jar filled with evils is clear.[64]

The typology developed around the story of Adam and Eve, and its implicit references to the Hellenistic context, seem to indicate that in the eyes of the rabbis the original conflict placing God and the serpent in opposition is repeated in the conflict between Judaism and Hellenism. The dilemma Adam confronts (will he be the disciple of God or of the serpent?) corresponds to the dilemma of opposition between the Torah and 'epicureanism' (heresy) in the rabbinic sense of the term. That is, either man has a divine destination, achievable in and by the Law, or man is a superior animal left to his own devices. It is remarkable that the alternative to the Torah is not referred to here as philosophy (as it was during the Middle Ages) but as a mythical model.

3.2. The myths in dialogue

Inherited from antiquity, the stories about Adam, Eve and Pandora transmit to us two fundamental conceptions of human destiny and its relationship to woman. It is interesting to put them in dialogue with one another by reading each one in relation to the other.

a) By reading the Jewish myth according to the Greek tradition, one is tempted to see in it traces of a conception analogous to that of Hesiod: the competition between God and men; the anteriority of evil (the tree in the garden, the tempting serpent); transmission of temptation and of the sin that could have seemed inevitable. The theme of the defilement inherited from the serpent opens the way to a theology of original sin and predestination. This 'Greek' reading would have been rejected in principle by the Jewish commentators.

b) If we read, on the contrary, the Greek myth according to the Jewish myth, the Greek myth appears as a version of the original fall told by Adam when he is still a 'disciple of the serpent'.

The serpent promises divinity to man, then unites with Eve in order to mix his sperm with Adam's descendants. In the Greek myth, he becomes a benevolent god (Prometheus), who offers man the fire forbidden by Zeus and engenders humanity (according to another version: by uniting with Pandora).

In the Jewish myth, the original Adam is created from silt (but endowed with 'a soul of life') and dedicated to work and procreation. His sin only complicated his conditions and introduced curses. In the Greek myth, the characteristics of human existence appear only with the curse, for which woman (Pandora) is the malevolent instrument. It is Pandora who is created from silt[65] and who obligates man to work and procreate. Woman vacillates towards the side of absolute evil: Adam rejects his guilt and places it on her (and on God who created her). The Hesiodic Adam sees in her the divine curse.

Finally, good and evil change statuses. In the Jewish myth, their ambivalence pre-exists and is outside of man, but Adam's sin makes them penetrate human desire. In the Greek myth, the fruit (or ambivalence) of good and evil enters into humanity[66] with the first woman: she is beautiful and malevolent (*kalon kakon*); she is the evil that comes in order to counterbalance the good. The moral problem is substituted by the tragedy of existence completed by the creation of woman.

Conclusion

I have shown how two different traditions that depart from a common observation arrive at opposite conclusions about human reality. For Hesiod, as in the Bible, there is an organic link between the human condition, the existence of woman and the authority of divine law. The human condition is ambivalent: good and evil are both part of it. The human being aspires to a divine condition but in his actual state he is subjected to needs: the necessity to work and to have children, and the menace of countless evils. This ambivalence can be found in the role of the woman. The woman has a divine aspect (beauty, motherhood), a divine gift – she is a helpmate for man – but she can also be an enemy seductress. Under these condition, salvation lies in respect for the divine law ('dikè ' in Hesiod, 'Torah' in Judaism), which governs the relations between men and with the gods.

The two traditions diverge in the causes of the human condition and the hope that people have of surmounting it. The Greek myth is essentially tragic: humanity's condition is insurmountable because it is the result of a curse from a jealous god. Woman, created by Zeus, is the instrument of this curse. As for the law, it saves man only by perpetuating the established order and, as a result, the divine curse. Judaism is optimistic: from its perspective the true man is a couple, and God created him in His image. Man caused his own downfall by wanting to become a god, but he can repair his mistake. The law of the Torah, the 'tree of life', allows man to reconnect with God to return to the original state of happiness. As for woman, even if her mistake brought about that of man, she nonetheless remains his partner in his reconstruction.

The other conclusion of this study concerns the possible dialogue between the two traditions. A 'Greek' reading of the biblical story examines the character of the tempting serpent and the question of divine determinism. A 'Jewish' reading of the Hesiodic narrative interprets it as a story created by the rebellious Adam, the 'disciple of the serpent'. Behind man's hatred for woman hides hatred for God and fundamentally hatred for oneself.

Notes

1. The term myth applied to the stories of the Bible could be problematic for Jewish and Christian readers of the Bible, if one defines it as a work of fiction. I use the term 'myth' in the sense of 'a narrative inspiring a literary tradition'.
2. The Midrash is the method of exegesis developed by the rabbis during antiquity and thereafter the commentaries and stories inspired by this method and written in Hebrew and Aramaic. The *Midrash halakha* deals with the commandments of the Bible, whereas the *Midrash Aggada* deals with its narrative parts.
3. In this chapter, the references to *Bereshit Rabba* (the part of the *Midrash Rabba* dedicated to Genesis) will be indicated by the initials *BR*, the references to the Babylonian Talmud, by the initials *BT*. I will also sometimes use the *Pirqe de-Rabbi Eliezer* (*PDRE*), a later redaction (eighth–ninth centuries) but interesting for its developments about angels.
4. David Banon, *l'Ecole de Pensée Juive de Paris, Le Judaïsme Revisité sur les Bords de Seine* (Strasbourg: Presses Universitaires de Strasbourg, 2019).
5. For a detailed analysis of the myth of Pandora, see Fabienne Blaise, Pierre Judet de la Combe and Philippe Rousseau (eds), *Le Métier du Mythe. Lectures d'Hésiode*, Cahiers de philologie vol. 16 (Lille: Septentrion.Presses Universitaires, 1996).
6. See Blaise, Judet de la Combe and Rousseau, *Le métier*, 272ff.
7. The literary tradition speaks of 'Pandora's box', but the Greek text evokes a jar (*pithos*).
8. The human condition is marked by the fact that vital resources (*bios*) are hidden by the gods (*Works and Days*, 42).
9. *Theogony*, 590.
10. *Theogony*, 581–4.
11. Athena teaches her to sew (*Works*, 63); honest women do exist (*Theogony*, 607).
12. *Theogony*, 375, 599.
13. *Works*, 373, 704–5. Hesiod completely covers up woman's positive role in the economy and in procreation so as to see in her nothing but an agent of destruction. See Froma I. Zeitlin, 'l'Origine de la femme et la femme origine: la Pandore d'Hésiode,' in *Le Métier du Mythe. Lectures d'Hésiode*, ed. Fabienne Blaise, Pierre Judet de la Combe and Philippe Rousseau (Lille: Septentrion.Presses Universitaires, 1996), 354–5.
14. The jar is closed by 'lips' (*Works*, 97), a term used elsewhere for the matrix. See the references in Zeitlin, 'l'Origine', 360–1.
15. *Fragmenta Hesiodeia* (R. Merkelbarch and M. L. West, Oxford, 1967), *Catalogue of Women*, fr.2 and 4.
16. *Theogony*, 585, 603; *Works*, 57.
17. On Adam and Eve in the Midrash, see Louis Ginzburg, *The Legends of the Jews*, trans. Henrietta Szold (New York: Jewish Publication Society, 1956); Ephraim Urbach, *The Sages, Their Concepts and Beliefs*, trans. Israel Abrahams (Jerusalem: Magnes Press, 1975), ch. 10

and 15; Jacob Neusner, *Judaism Story of Creation: Scripture, Halakha, Aggadah*, Brill Reference Library of Judaism 3 (Leiden: Brill, 2000).

18. See especially the promise made to Abraham of the inheritance of the land, Genesis 15.16.
19. According to the myth of the five ages (*Works*, 109–201); traditions subsequent to Hesiod show Prometheus creating man.
20. Men are designated as 'mortal' (*thnetoi*), in contrast to the immortal gods.
21. This expression can be understood as a blessing or as an injunction. God already formulated it about animals (v. 22) but when he formulates it for man, God addresses him directly.
22. It is by eating the forbidden fruit that he will make himself mortal (2.17, 3.19).
23. The Hebrew name 'Hava' is based on the root ḥay/ḥaw.
24. 1.27.
25. The rabbis did however admit to a malevolent face to femininity incarnated in the character of Lilith (the queen of demons). But the study of this character is beyond the framework of this work, which is consecrated exclusively to Eve, the human woman. For more on Lilith, see the chapter by Korzakova in this volume.
26. BT *Sanhedrin* 38a and b, *BR* 8.1.
27. *BR* 11.2.
28. BT *Sanhedrin* 59b.
29. Since Adam resembles his Creator, the world would be tempted to prostrate themselves before him. It was to make the difference obvious that God plunged Adam into a deep sleep before creating Eve (*BR* 8.10).
30. A frequent theme in the rabbinical sources, see for example BT *Ḥagiga* 15b, *PDRE* 13.
31. BT *Berakhot* 61a and *Eruvin* 18a. *BR* 8.1.
32. 3.5: 'You will be like gods'; v. 22: 'man had become like one of us'.
33. This is what seems to indicate God's warning: 'the day you will eat from it, you will die' (3.17). This evolution could be remedied by eating from the 'tree of life': hence, after the fall, God takes the precaution of taking Adam away from it by expelling him from the Garden of Eden (3.22–4).
34. BT *Berakhot* 40a; *Sanhedrin* 70b. *BR* 18.8 also mentions, as a fourth opinion, the citron.
35. Noah is naked in his tent (Genesis 9.21). The vine planted by Noah is sometimes identified with that of the Garden of Eden: BT *Sanhedrin* 70a, *PDRE* 23.
36. The serpent was 'the cleverest among all of the animals created by YHVH Elohim' (3.1).
37. *BR* 25.5. Nevertheless in size the serpent is compared to a camel.
38. BT *Sanhedrin* 59b; *BR* 19.1.
39. According to the Midrash, the serpent coveted Eve after having seen her naked with her husband. This idea is based on the proximity of the verses 2.25 and 2.1.
40. *BR* 20.5; *Jerusalem Talmud* IV, 1 ; *PDRE* 13.
41. *PDRE* 13.
42. See, according to Genesis 36.5: BT *Yoma* 28b, *Qidushin* 82a, *Midrash Vayyiqra Rabba* 50.10, etc.
43. For the Midrash, the Torah preceded the creation of the world and served God as a plan for its realization: *BR* 1.4.
44. *BR* 19.6.

45. *Midrash Sifri*, 'Eqev, 5; *BR* 16.4 and 6.

46. *BR* 19.4 and 20.1.

47. BT *Sanhedrin* 29a.

48. *BR* 19.1.

49. BT *Sanhedrin* 99b and cf. *Encyclopedia talmudit*, 'apikoros'. The term 'apikoros' seems to be derived from the Greek philosophers' name *Epikuros* (Epicurus). For Maimonides (*Mishneh Torah*, 'Laws of Repentance', 3.16) the *Apikoros* denies prophecy, the prophecy of Moses and in particular divine providence in general.

50. BT *Qidushin* 66a (about Alexandre Janai) and *Sanhedrin* 38b (about Adam).

51. *BR* 19.4 ('each artisan hates the people in his profession'); *PDRE* 13 ('*ayn ha-ra*').

52. *BR* 19.4.

53. *BR* 19.12

54. *BT 'avoda zara* 5b.

55. *BT Sanhedrin* 29 (Adam listened to the words of the disciple, instead of those of the master).

56. *BR* 19.9. *Da'at* can also be translated as doctrine or knowledge.

57. The later kabbalistic tradition will understand the stretching of the foreskin not as an intentional act but as a mutation of nature, following a transgression.

58. See H. Wortzman, 'The Rape of Eve and its Spiritual Connotations in early Jewish and Gnostic literature', *Studies in Spirituality* 27 (2017): 57–89.

59. *BT 'avoda zara*, 22b.

60. It is remarkable that for the midrash, God does not hide the fire but shows man how to light it, when the night of the seventh day of creation arrives (*BR* 12.6).

61. The myth of Hesiod admits a reconciliation between Zeus and Prometheus. But this reconciliation changes nothing in the human condition.

62. See Saül Liebermann, *Greek in Jewish Palestine / Hellenism in Jewish Palestine* (New York: Jewish Theological Seminary of America, 1994).

63. We know of several versions of this midrash, namely *BR* 19.11.

64. See S. T. Lachs, 'The Pandora–Eva Motif in Rabbinic Literature', *Harvard Theological Review* 67 (1974): 341–5.

65. In the myth of the five races (*Works*, 109–201) successive generation (except those of the heroes) were created from a metal (gold, silver, bronze, iron): the last generation (to which Hesiod belongs) had iron as its origin.

66. As knowledge, Good and Evil (*agathon te kakon te*) are already in Zeus's possession, after he swallowed the goddess Metis (*Theogony*, 886–900).

CHAPTER 5
TEMPTING TREASURES AND SEDUCTIVE SNAKES: PRESENTING EVE AND PANDORA FOR THE YOUNGEST READERS

Lisa Maurice

The narratives both of Pandora and of Eve have often been retold for juvenile audiences of all ages and continue to be narrated for youth in our own times. This chapter examines a range of English-language picture books and illustrated stories for young children published in the twentieth and twenty-first centuries, highlighting some trends visible in these receptions.

Pandora

From Hesiod onwards, Pandora has been regarded negatively, although the actual portrayals have varied throughout history according to contemporary ideas.[1] As Hunt emphasizes, children's literature is invariably didactic on some level, used as a tool to instil value systems,[2] and versions of the Pandora narrative for children must deal with the issue of how exactly to adapt or 'censor' the story for youth.[3] In general, despite the fact that all versions for children tell more or less the same story, some recurring trends and approaches can be seen, with Pandora being described in several distinct ways: as a naughty child, a disobedient wife, a beloved helpmeet, an innocent character and even as a benefactor, whose actions actually made mankind human.

Pandora: The naughty child

One common trope in children's books is to infantilize Pandora, treating her as if she were a child, with the opening of the box the equivalent of an act of naughty behaviour.[4] This approach was influenced by Nathaniel Hawthorne, who regarded childhood as a period of innocence and perfection. Seeing myths themselves as dating from 'the childhood of the world', an idealized period of perfection, he felt that children are intimately connected to the spirit of myth and particularly suited to receiving its content.[5]

The tale of Pandora appears in Hawthorne's *A Wonder-Book for Girls and Boys* (1851), under the heading of 'A Paradise of Children', in the introduction to which we are clearly told that the story is set in the 'oldest of old times', when 'there was but one age for mortals and that was childhood'. This was the paradise of children, in which Epimetheus is a child, and Pandora sent (although not by the gods, but from a 'far country') to be his 'playfellow and helpmate'. This paradise was, however, brought to an end by 'the naughtiness' of Pandora, here described as 'a little imp' and 'a sad, naughty child'. The emphasis on this characterization is remarkable; indeed, the word 'naughty' appears no less than fifteen times throughout the tale.

Hawthorne's narrative was extremely influential for subsequent children's writers, in particular for the transformation of Pandora into a child. In such retellings, the aim is invariably didactic, but the lessons being taught change over time. Rosemary Wells's *Max and Ruby's First Greek Myth* (1993) narrates the story within the framework of two anthropomorphized rabbits, Max and his big sister, Ruby, as a didactic tale about

> [. . .] 'sneaking and peeking', in which Pandora herself is a 'little girl', who opens not the traditional box of evils, but rather her mother's magic jewellery box. The lessons of obedience and respecting privacy taught by the story are ones directly relevant to Max and his sister, and thereby to the juvenile audience.[6]

Almost a quarter of a century after Rosemary Wells's leporine Pandora, Julia Dweck's *Pandora's Box* (2017) also presents Pandora as an anthropomorphic animal, in this case, a penguin. This version portrays Pandora as an independent-minded young penguin who is different from the others, and the 'box' as a frozen ice cube, which, when she breaks it open, brings colour and light to the world in the form of the Northern Lights. In a postmodern take on the 'naughtiness' of going against advice, by opening the box, and acting independently, this Pandora literally enables her friends to see the light.

In both Robert Burleigh's *Pandora* (2002) and Saviour Pirotta's *The Orchard Book of First Greek Myths* (2003), Pandora is represented in some ways as a woman but in others as a child or girl, being so addressed by other characters, and displaying juvenile attitudes and interests.[7] In more recent years, Joan Holub devotes two books to the Pandora story. One, in the *Mini-Myths* series, is a toddler picture-board book, whose moral lesson is proclaimed by the very title of the book, *Be Patient, Pandora!* (2014). In this work, Pandora is a toddler, who, when told not to open the box, does everything but open it: she touches it, leans on it, sits on it, stands on it, bounces on it, causing it to spring open and send its content – cupcakes – flying out. Contrite, she apologizes and hopes her mother still loves her, receiving reassurance that this is the case. The message here is that it is wrong to disobey, even if tempted by curiosity, but that love is maintained if one makes a mistake, on the condition that there is penitence for the disobedience. Holub's second version of the story, from the same year, *Do Not Open! The Story of Pandora's Box*, is aimed at slightly older children, and Pandora is correspondingly a young woman, but again with childlike elements, wondering, for example, if the box is 'full of candy'.

One final example, Mike Townsend's *Amazing Greek Myths of Wonder and Blunders* (2010), tells the story in cartoonish, comic-book style, and with a decidedly postmodern attitude. Typical of the trend in modern children's books, humour is a strong element.[8] This version features Pandora as a cheeky and rather cocky child. Wondering if the box contains a pony, and building a lopsided box of her own in an attempt to fool Zeus,

Pandora manages to kill her kitty when she releases the evils, evoking the rueful exclamation, 'Oh no! My curiosity killed the cat!' This brightly illustrated version is retold with humour that would appeal to a young child and presents a Pandora with whom they can identify.

Pandora: The disobedient wife

Another approach taken by these books is to cast Pandora as an adult, but in a subservient position to Epimetheus, stigmatizing her as a disobedient wife. In 1962, D'Aulaires' *Greek Myths* describes Pandora as 'a beautiful but silly woman', creating the impression of a frivolous and vacuous wife, inferior to her husband, an attitude typical of the 1960s but which continues for a surprisingly long time. In Heather Amery's *Greek Myths for Young Children* (2000), despite Epimetheus loving his wife and wanting to please her, when he refuses to open the box because of fear of Zeus, Pandora nags constantly and then, in an act of premeditated and deliberate defiance, takes a tool and opens it, unleashing misery on the world. Rose Impey's version, entitled *Pandora's Box* (2007), presents the situation even more starkly. In a depiction that seems more suited to a book from decades earlier, Pandora is described performing the duties of a dutiful wife:

> She cleaned and sewed and prepared fine meals for Epimetheus. When he came home, she sang or played music for him.

Yet despite this virtue, Pandora has a fault, that of curiosity, and she gives into temptation in a manner that is signalled as clearly rebellious:

> But some people, when they're told they must not do something, simply have to do it. Pandora was one of those people.

She then consciously justifies her actions as she prepares to open the box, but here again, the wrongdoing that is highlighted is that of disobeying her husband. 'What would Epimetheus say?' she muses guiltily, but then tells herself, 'Epimetheus does not need to know. It can be your secret, Pandora.'

Even in Amanda Brack, Monica Sweeney and Becky Thomas's *Brick Greek Myths: The Stories of Heracles, Athena, Pandora, Poseidon and Other Ancient Heroes of Mount Olympus*, in which the stories are illustrated by Lego figures, and therefore somewhat constricted in its illustrations, the tone is one of condemnation. Despite being warned by Athena and Epimetheus, Pandora is conquered by her vanity and greed, as she wonders if perhaps the box contained precious jewels: 'Knowing that gems and jewelry could only add to her beauty, she pondered ways to sneak a peek.' Lifting the lid, mortals become exposed to 'depression, horrible illness, misfortune, and death', although 'with hope protected inside the box, humanity would still have a fighting chance against the disaster forced upon them'. There is no doubt, however, that it is Pandora – shallow, vain and disobedient to her husband – who is responsible for this disaster in this tale that reinforces old gender stereotypes.

Pandora: The beloved consort

Other retellings are less pejorative, emphasizing the partnership of Epimetheus and Pandora, and portraying them as a blissful romantic couple, in which she is a supportive helpmeet to her husband. In Sally Grindley's *Pandora and the Mystery Box* (1999), Pandora is endowed with beauty, grace, charm, energy, wit and passion, as well as, more unusually, tenderness, charity and faithfulness. When Epimetheus saw her, 'he fell in love with her instantly', and in the somewhat patriarchal and possessive language of the text, 'was determined to keep her'. This is true love; the couple spent their first days together, 'like two love birds, never leaving each other's side, and enjoying life as though they had never experience it before'. Yet, in accordance with the myth, Pandora was ultimately created as a punishment for stealing secrets of the gods, and this state of bliss cannot continue. Curiosity leads her to open the box, letting loose evils into the world. Her actions reduce Pandora to tears, not from fear or personal suffering, however, but selflessly, from remorse at the troubles she has brought on mankind. Consolation is found, however, in the form of Hope, whose mission was to heal the damage caused by all the evil spirits. It is striking that it is Epimetheus that releases Hope in this version, rather than Pandora, in a twist that emphasizes the male-controlled slant of this retelling. The final illustrations show a sad and chastened Pandora being comforted and protected by her husband, who is embracing her, but there is very little blame attached to Pandora, who seems more of a victim than a villain in this tale.

In Henriette Barkow's version, illustrated by Diane Mayo (*Pandora's Box*, 2002), we are told that 'A woman made in heaven, with the gifts of the gods, was impossible to resist, and so it was that Epimetheus fell in love with Pandora.' The reader is told that, 'At first the two were very happy' and that:

> When Prometheus was out all day, Pandora used her gift of curiosity wisely. She found new ways to prepare their food and new music to play. She studied the animals and insects around her. Pandora showed man new ways of using fire to bake bread and also to work with metals.

Nevertheless, the negative aspects of curiosity soon come to the fore, as Pandora opens the box, with tragic results. Yet the book ends on a positive note, again with the emphasis upon hope, which helps mankind when 'things seem unbearable'. Hope, depicted, under the influence of Hawthorne, as a winged, butterfly-like light, then flutters to Prometheus in his torment, thus linking the first half of the book, which relates the Titan's tale, to the end, with Hope bringing comfort specifically to Prometheus himself.

In Cari Meister's *Pandora's Vase* (2012), illustrated by McLean Kendree, Pandora is presented to Epimetheus who falls in love with her and they are soon married. In this case, she has been created specifically by Zeus to punish man, and she is no more than 'a tool to bring about man's downfall' (5). Again, the Prometheus tale is included, increasing the emphasis on punishment in this version, but here the focus is on Pandora herself. She is portrayed almost as an innocent victim, in that Hermes bestows her with 'above all, curiosity', and when Pandora and Epimetheus receive the jar as a 'wedding present', she struggles against what seems a tortuous longing to open it. She strives desperately against temptation, before finally succumbing and releasing evil into the world, in a rather bleak ending reinforced by the final illustration, which depicts Pandora looking downcast and desolate as she kneels on the floor, holding the vase.

The blameless Pandora

Some works go even further, making Pandora entirely innocent of all wrongdoing. One such work is Nancy Loewen's *Pandora Tells All* (2014). In this book, it is not Pandora who opens the vase (in this case, it is not a box but a fragile Greek vase), but rather her pet cat who breaks it, thereby releasing the evils. Moreover, the accident itself is not the fault of Pandora, but rather of Epimetheus, who, against Pandora's better judgement, insists on the vase being placed visibly in the house. So careful is Pandora that she usually shuts the cat in a room before cleaning the room with the vase; on the day when the accident happens, she does not do this since Cuddles is peacefully sleeping with the somnolent Epimetheus. It is also worth noting that this Pandora, despite being the wiser of the two, is very much the dutiful wife under her husband's authority. Not only does she decide to surprise Epimetheus by getting up early and cleaning the house while he sleeps, 'polishing and sweeping' her way through the rooms, but after the disaster occurs, she even refrains from castigating her husband: 'I could have said "I told you so" to my husband, but I didn't' she explains. This Pandora is more of an innocent, sacrificial victim, taking the blame for the actions of others.

Pandora: The benefactor of humanity

A few books rehabilitate Pandora even more notably: not only is she innocent, but her actions actually improved the world, since they resulted in the presence of hope, upon which emphasis is placed in the story, in place demonizing Pandora. One such example is *Pandora's Box* (1986), by Lisi Weil, in which Pandora's curiosity is an attribute given her by Zeus in order to punish humans for their lack of appreciation and responsibility. In this version, Zeus is to blame, rather than Pandora, for the resultant ills, and the narrative is framed as an explanation of why the world contains both good and evil:

> And that is the way the world has been ever since. The bad helps us know what is good. The bitter helps us enjoy the sweet. And dark days make sunny days more pleasant. Through everything there is hope. So when the bad comes, we can hope for the good and know that the bad is not going to last forever.

The tone of this morality tale is reassuring rather than disturbing, attempting to cast a positive light on the presence of both good and evil in the world, which leads to appreciation and understanding of both, and thus Pandora's actions actually benefit humans. Weil, who was Jewish, fled her native Vienna in 1939 and witnessed the

Holocaust that she was lucky enough to survive; it is perhaps no coincidence that her interpretation makes much of the presence of evil in the world.

Finally, a more recent version, *Prometheus – Pandora's Box* (2015) by Anastasia Makri, briefly retells the story. In this tale, Pandora is gifted with many talents and is extremely beautiful, but also very cunning and curious. Unable to resist, she opens the box, letting loose all the evils, but hope remains trapped inside. The story concludes with the comment:

> Maybe ruler of the gods wanted it this way to give humans the opportunity to strive for a better life without losing hope when they were faced with life's difficulties and misfortunes . . .

Again, there is no condemnation of Pandora, and not only is the stress placed on hope rather than the evils, but it seems to be implied that these troubles were actually a means by which hope could be granted to humans, for without evil there is no need of such an emotion. In this way Pandora becomes a benefactor of mankind, a tool through which the gods are able to bestow the precious gift of hope.

Eve

Where the story of Pandora may be manipulated, consciously or unconsciously, according to the agenda of the writer, it does not challenge the writer with elements of religious belief. The same cannot be said for Eve, the first female in the Bible, a text held holy by the mainstream religions that still exist today even in the age of postmodern secularism. As Stephens and McCallum point out:

> In a society in which Christian humanism is still a pervasive – albeit implicit – ideology, readers approach Bible stories with a reverence for authority different from what informs their approaches to most other kinds of literature.[9]

Nevertheless, the way these stories are retold for children is still inevitably influenced by the background and agenda of the person narrating the tale, which is commonly found in children's Bibles or as stand-alone tales for youngsters, as they 'mingle sacred text with secular values'.[10]

While this is true of all Bible stories, that of Adam and Eve in the Garden of Eden has been particularly subject to abuse by patriarchal ideologies, since it is this tale that has primarily been utilized as justification for the religious subjugation of women in Judeao-Christian cultures.[11] Woman is created (in one variant of the tradition at least) after man, and is therefore of a lower level than he,[12] and, moreover, is regarded as responsible for the fall from grace and mankind's expulsion from Eden.[13] Although this interpretation is not the most obvious reading of the Hebrew text, and ignores elements such as Adam's presence at the eating of the fruit, and Eve's motivation in eating it, nevertheless, such demonization of Eve has a long history. It goes back, in fact, to the early days of the Christian Church and has, moreover, provided the justification for the female's secondary place in the societal hierarchy throughout Western civilization.

Several elements in the traditional retellings of the Genesis narrative have been used to justify female subjugation to the male. Firstly, the creation of Eve, after Adam, and as a by-product of man, taken from his rib, makes the existence of woman a mere afterthought and of secondary importance. Secondly, the act of eating the forbidden fruit reflects a sinful nature in itself, only compounded by the further temptation of Adam, causing him to sin. The punishment for this sin, by which Eve and her descendants are subject to the control of their husbands, only reinforces both the wickedness of the female and her inferior place in the hierarchy, under the dominion of the male.

All of these elements may be problematic for contemporary authors who attempt to present ideologically acceptable messages to their young audiences, and each is handled in different ways in the picture books for young children produced over the last half-century. Gillhouse phrases this succinctly: 'When Eve's story is retold for children, what choices the author makes says more about the author's context than about Eve.'[14] In the twentieth and twenty-first centuries, in which unprecedented changes have occurred with regard to female emancipation, the problem becomes more acute. In the present study I consider twenty versions of the story of Adam and Eve, published between 1964 and 2017, and I isolate four main areas in which her character is interpreted in various ways: the creation of Eve, the motivation for eating the fruit that is ascribed to her, the blame that is apportioned and the resulting punishment received.

The creation of Eve

With regard to the question of the creation of Eve, some versions describe her formation as an afterthought, in answer to God's perceiving that it is not good for Adam to be alone. The earliest example from those considered in this study, *The Children's Bible in Colour* (1964), includes this element. After Adam has named all the animals, but found none to be a companion for himself, God puts Adam into a sleep, takes his rib, and makes it into woman. This is a conservative and conventional narration, following Christian tradition closely as fits the agenda of the book stated in the introduction, which explains that the Bible teaches:

> [. . .] generation after generation that there is a divine plan in history and a purpose in human life; and today as in every age, the Gospels are the fabric with which the house of Christian faith is built.[15]

The creation of Eve from Adam's rib so that he will have a companion is repeated in *Bible Stories for Children* by Geoffrey Horn and Arthur Cavanaugh (1980) and *Adam and Eve* by Warwick Hutton (1988). Later books rarely include this element however. The only recent Christian version that includes the creation of Eve from Adam's rib is *The Story of Adam and Eve* (2016), published by the Pegasus imprint of BJain books, an Indian company, whose Bible stories series of picture books is particularly traditional.

It is worthy of note, however, that the story is also found in all four versions of the Bible for Jewish children that were examined: Seymour Rossel's *A Children's Bible: Lessons from the Torah* (1987); *Genesis: The Jewish Children's Bible* (1996), by Sheryl Prenzlau; *The Illustrated Jewish Bible for Children* (1997) by Selina Hastings; and the *JPS Illustrated Children's Bible* (2009) by Ellen Frankel. This is particularly striking since there is a Jewish tradition that man and woman were created as one being originally, and that God then separated them into two, male and female,[16] but may reflect the conservative attitudes towards gender roles still prominent in Orthodox Judaism.

One of the Christian retellings, in fact, does make use of the word 'side' rather than 'rib', the 1996 version in the Macmillan Bible Stories series, *Adam and Eve* by Carol Christian, but this detail does not seem to be utilized in order to argue for equality of the sexes, but as an aetiological explanation for (heterosexual) marriage:

> Adam knew at once that she was the right partner for him. It was love at first sight! He said, 'She is part of my own body. Her bones are my bones and her flesh is my flesh. I shall name her "woman" because she is made from a man's body'.
>
> Ever since then, men have searched for a partner to marry. When they marry, a husband and wife become one body. That is why a man loves his wife even more than he loves his father and mother.

This union is presented entirely from the masculine point of view; it is the man who decides that Eve is his soulmate and it is the male who searches for a partner, with no indication that the love he bears her is reciprocated. Despite the variation in detail in the story, this presentation ultimately emphasizes patriarchy. Such an approach is found underlying even such simplistic works as the Little Lambs *Adam and Eve* (2017) by Karen Williamson, where it declares that, 'Adam was all alone, so God made a woman too', and Jenny Thorne's *Adam and Eve* (1988), where God 'made a friend for Adam'. So too in *The Beginner's Bible* by Kelley Pulley (2005), Adam 'could not find a friend that was just right for him'. God therefore creates woman, whom Adam named Eve, and we are told that, 'She was just right for Adam' although here at least, since 'Adam and Eve loved each other', the love is reciprocal.

Other versions of the story reduce the element of patriarchy by making no differentiation between God's creation of Adam and Eve. This is the approach taken by *The Lion's Children's Bible* (1981), Taffy Davies' *Adam and Eve* (1995), the *Baby's First Bible* (2004) and *Adam and Eve* (2016) by the Indian publisher Maple Press. A few other books go even further, avoiding the issue of creation entirely and just stating that 'There was a man and a woman' (*Adam and Eve* by Catherine Storr (1983)), or, in the case of Heather Amery's *The Usborne Children's Bible* (1992), just opening with 'Adam and Eve lived in a beautiful garden', with no indication of who Adam and Eve are.

Eve's sin

If the creation, and consequent role of Eve are on occasion glossed over or handled ambivalently, the same cannot be said for her sin. As early as Tertullian, Eve's eating of the fruit has been used to denounce not only Eve herself but all women as weak, sinful and responsible for the fall from grace. Yet a reading of the text raises issues about who actually transgressed in the Garden of Eden. That the snake was the cause of the sin is obvious, but the situation is less clear-cut with regard to Adam and Eve. Firstly, the Bible states that Eve gave the fruit to Adam 'who was with her', implying that he was present at the time, which would implicate him in the actions. Secondly, when the serpent asks Eve if God had really forbidden them to eat the fruit, she answers that God had forbidden them not only to eat of the fruit of the tree that is in the midst of the garden, but also to touch it, lest they die (Genesis 3.3). This is an addition to the words God speaks to Adam in the previous chapter, and according to a Rabbinic tradition, the addition was made by Adam himself in order to prevent Eve coming close to temptation. The rabbis then condemn this condescending attitude and lack of trust on the part of Adam, and explain that the serpent touched the tree in order to prove that no harm could result from so doing, and thus enticed Eve to take the further step of eating the fruit. Hence, by this logic, it was Adam, rather than Eve, who was the cause of sin and ultimate expulsion from the garden.[17]

Such elements in the tale provide ample room for the rehabilitation of Eve in the children's books. Yet this does not actually occur. Only two books include Eve's words about being forbidden to touch the tree. The first is Heather Amery's *Usborne Children's Bible* (1992), where the fact is presented without further commentary. A different twist is provided in *Genesis: The Jewish Children's Bible* (1996), in which the serpent actually pushes Eve against the tree to prove that it is harmless, thus inducing her to pick and eat the fruit. Strikingly, however, in this narration, after Eve states that God had told them they were forbidden even to touch the tree, the reader is told, 'But that wasn't really true. Eve added that part herself', thereby placing the blame firmly on Eve once more. All of the books for children follow the traditional path, by holding Eve, rather than Adam, responsible for the sin.

Eve's motivation

What, however, motivated Eve to disobey God and eat the fruit? Although the thoughts and mindset of characters are rarely elaborated in the Bible,[18] on this occasion, Eve's thoughts are described at unusual length. The relevant verse in Genesis states:

> And the woman saw that the tree was good for food and that it was a delight to the eyes, and the tree was desirable to make one wise; so she took of its fruit, and she ate, and she gave also to her husband with her, and he ate.
>
> *Genesis 3.6*

This description has caught the eye of modern adapters, almost all of whom include it in their narrations, attributing to Eve the desire to be like God, or to be wise. Although other details may be omitted in the juvenile works, this aspect is included in fifteen out of the twenty books under consideration, with only three of the four Jewish volumes and two very simplistic board books aimed at toddlers omitting the point. Clearly, the presentation of what exactly prompts Eve to eat the fruit is of vital importance for modern retellings, since she is tempted not by a desire for wealth or superficial benefits, but by the tantalizing prize of divine wisdom. Such an aim has the potential to transform the surrender to temptation not as the act of, in Aschkenasy's words, 'a silly, empty-headed person', but of 'a curious person with an appetite for life to encompass the whole spectrum of life's possibilities'.[19] While this may be so, it seems more than a little forced in these biblical retellings, where the desire to be wise is so frequently coupled with a hubristic desire to be like God, and indicates ingratitude and rebellion, an interpretation that is reinforced by the result of the act, namely the punishment it earns.

Eve's punishment

Ultimately, both Adam and Eve sinned and both were punished in the form of banishment from Eden, but each received specific punishments as well. The texts for children are divided between those differentiating between the two as regards punishment and those omitting any differences. Twelve of the books take the latter approach, referring to the expulsion of the couple from Eden, and the need to toil and grow food for themselves. Of the remaining volumes, five specify Eve's particular punishment, referring to the pain of childbirth, or to 'bringing forth children in sorrow'. Horn and Cavanaugh's *Bible Stories for Children* (1980) explains the sentence handed down to Eve rather more obliquely, with God declaring, 'Because you were fooled by the serpent, you will know pain and sorrow for the first time.' Adam meanwhile, in this version, is to work hard to produce food from earth that is 'dry, tough and full of weeds', work that will make his body ache and which will continue unremittingly until his death. Carol Christian's version of *Adam and Eve* from 1996 presents a similar punishment for Adam, but goes into even more detail with regard to Eve:

> He said to Eve, 'This is your punishment. Your life will be hard. Your children will give you endless trouble. But when you are worn out and long for rest, your love for your husband will bring you more children. So you will have more pain and weariness.'

Both of these stories, echoing the stereotypes of female sexual weakness and simple-mindedness, emphasize the suffering that is explicitly imposed on the female, which is based on emotional pain, as opposed to that on the male, where physical discomfort is the central component, reflecting conventional ideas about masculinity and femininity. In the case of Christian's book, the details connect with the earlier ideas conveyed by the work, for the anguish is bound up with love and marriage; the union that was idealized at Eve's creation is here the source of her torment.

Presenting Eve and Pandora for the youngest readers

What conclusions then can be drawn about the presentation of Pandora and Eve for young children? Firstly, it seems that, even in the modern secular age, there is far more scope for revisionism with the story from classical mythology than with that from the Bible. Conscious efforts are made in the Pandora narratives to minimize her guilt, with only a quarter of the works treating her as the conventional wicked woman of traditional interpretations. Others, under the influence primarily of Hawthorne, minimize the evil by treating her as a child, or portraying her as a victim of circumstances, innocent of all wrongdoing, or even as a benefactor, bringing the gift of hope to mankind.

Eve, by contrast, remains guilty of sin in almost every case, and while Adam also eats the fruit, this is passed over without editorial comment, and the blame placed solely upon Eve. Although some attempts are made to remove the stigma of subjugation to her husband, in that she is less commonly portrayed as created after and subservient to him, and that their punishments are often undifferentiated and shared, Eve is ultimately depicted for modern children as the one responsible for the fall from grace and expulsion from Eden. While the text and illustrations present Eden as a colourful and blessed place, the ending of the books invariably shows the world into which the couple are expelled as a harsh and depressing environment. Since this is the human world, these works present a far less optimistic view than those centred on Pandora, with the only exceptions being the few Christian works that hint at Jesus as the path through which man can return to God and paradise.

Although there are parallels between Pandora's curiosity and Eve's desire to eat the fruit in order to gain wisdom, these are not highlighted in the works under discussion. While Pandora is invariably portrayed as inquisitive, this is often only a mildly negative trait, or even on occasion, a positive one. Eve, on the other hand, is condemned, and it is not her curiosity or search for knowledge that is emphasized, but rather her disobedience, not only to her husband, but, more importantly, to God. This ultimately stems from ideas of God as beneficent ruler and a true deity, in contrast to Zeus, who is neither. While this is the natural result of the fact that the Adam and Eve story books are mostly produced by religious bodies, it is in itself striking that other authors and publishers have not attempted revisions of the tale. Despite the secularism of the modern age, and the postmodern enthusiasm for transforming and inverting texts of all kinds, including those of Greek mythology, it seems that the Bible is still held up as a sacred cow, whose traditional interpretations cannot be altered, at least for young children.

Notes

1. For an old but still good overview, see Dora and Erwin Panofsky, *Pandora's Box: The Changing Aspects of a Mythical Symbol* (New York: Pantheon Books, 1956).
2. Peter Hunt, *Introduction to Children's Literature* (Oxford: Oxford University Press, 1994), 3.
3. Another example is that of Cupid and Psyche. See Lisa Maurice, 'Cupid and Psyche for Children', in *Cupid and Psyche: The Reception of Apuleius' Love Story since 1600*, ed. Regine May and Stephen Harrison (Berlin: De Gruyter, 2019), 289–301. On the issue of censorship, see Amy McClure, 'Censorship', *Children's Literature Association Quarterly* 8, no. 1 (2014): 22–5; Herbert N. Foerstel, *Banned in the U.S.A.: A Reference Guide to Book Censorship in Schools and Public Libraries* (Westport, CT: Greenwood, 2002); David Booth, 'Censorship', in

Keywords for Children's Literature, ed. Philip Nel and Lissa Paul (New York: New York University Press, 2011), 26–30; Linda Hutcheon, *A Theory of Adaptation*, 2nd edn (New York: Routledge, 2006/2013), 118.

4. See Miriam Riverlea, 'Out of the Box: Refashioning Pandora in Children's Literature', in *Refashioning Myth: Poetic Transformations and Metamorphoses*, ed. Jessica L. Wilkinson, Eric Parisot and David McInnis (Cambridge: Cambridge Scholars Publishing, 2011), 259–77.
5. See Sheila Murnaghan and Deborah Roberts, *Childhood and the Classics: Britain and America, 1850–1965* (Oxford: Oxford University Press, 2018), 29.
6. See Riverlea 'Out of the Box', 267, and John Stephens and Robyn McCallum, *Retelling Stories, Framing Culture: Traditional Story and Metanarratives in Children's Literature* (New York: Garland Publishing, 1998), 80.
7. See Riverlea 'Out of the Box', 269–70.
8. See on this Julie Cross, *Humor in Contemporary Junior Literature* (New York and London: Routledge, 2011), esp. 1–24.
9. Stephens and McCallum, *Retelling Stories*, 30.
10. Ruth Bottigheimer, *The Bible for Children from the Age of Gutenberg to the Present* (New Haven, CT: Yale University Press, 1996), 218.
11. See Elizabeth Gillhouse, 'Eve was Framed': Ideostory and (Mis)Representation in Judeo-Christian Creation Stories', *Children's Literature Association Quarterly* 36, no. 3 (2011): 260 (259–75).
12. It should be noted that in medieval thought Eve is sometimes presented as superior because unlike Adam who was created from soil, she was created from a human being.
13. See, e.g., Mary Daly, *Beyond God the Father: Toward a Philosophy of Women's Liberation* (Boston: Beacon, 1985), 46.
14. Gillhouse, 'Eve was Framed', 259.
15. *The Children's Bible in Colour* (London: Paul Hamlyn Ltd, 1964), introduction.
16. Such an explanation is based on a translation of the Hebrew word *tzela* not as 'rib' but 'side', the way in fact it is understood throughout the Bible. For the most recent work on this, see Joel Baden, 'An Unnoted Nuance in Genesis 2:21–22', *Vetus Testamentum* 69, no. 1 (2019), 167–72.
17. On this, see Gary A. Anderson, *The Genesis of Perfection: Adam and Eve in Jewish and Christian Imagination* (Louisville and London: Westminster John Knox Press, 2001), 77–8.
18. See Nehama Aschkenasy, *Eve's Journey: Feminine Images in Hebraic Literary Tradition* (Philadelphia: University of Pennsylvania Press, 1986), 41, also quoted by Gillhouse, 'Eve was Framed', 265.
19. Aschkensay, *Eve's Journey*, 41.

CHAPTER 6
THEMATIC INTERCULTURAL CORRESPONDENCE ON THE CREATION OF THE PERFECT WOMAN AND THE FALLING IN LOVE WITH HER (OVID, IBN HAZM, IBN HASDAI, IBN ZAKBAL AND ALHARIZI)

Revital Refael-Vivante

> Love, my friend, begins jestingly, but its end is very serious. Its hidden aspects are so subtle on account of their sublimity that they defy description, and their truth cannot be comprehended except when experienced by one's self.[1]

With these words Abū Muḥammad ʿAlī ibn Aḥmad ibn Saʿīd ibn Ḥazm of eleventh-century Cordoba begins the first chapter of his book, entitled 'Discourse on the Nature of Love'. This book, *The Ring of the Dove* (*tawq al-hamama*), is one of the most important and comprehensive works that systematically discusses the art of love in the Middle Ages.[2]

While Ibn Hazm admits that there is much controversy regarding the nature of love, he believes that love is no less than the unification of two souls that were coupled in the world above and which for some reason became separated in the earthly world.[3] The search for love is therefore the search by a person's earth-bound soul for the soul from which it had been separated – its soul mate. According to Ibn Hazm, 'We well know that the secret of commingling and estrangement in creation [things created] is nothing but attraction or repulsion.'[4]

In this chapter, I propose to discuss Ibn Hazm's *The Ring of the Dove*, focusing on one specific theme: 'the strange cases [occurrences] of love'; that is, falling in love while asleep or on the basis of a description given by a third party, cases that are recounted in two of the book's chapters. I will explore the psychological and social aspects of this phenomenon and show that the roots of this theme, which is defined in theoretical terms in *The Ring of the Dove*, are deeply embedded in classical Greek literature. This theme is also found in different variations in the medieval secular literature, and especially in the Hebrew *maqama*,[5] which was influenced by Arabic writings.[6] I will examine a number of examples from medieval secular Hebrew literature that depict variations on the theme,[7] including Yosef Ibn Hasdai's *qasida*[8] *Does the Gracious Gazelle Have Virility and Power?*; Shlomo Ibn Zakbal's *The Speech of Asher Ben Yehuda (ne'um Asher ben Yehudah)*; Yehudah Alharizi's twentieth *maqama*, which is an adaptation of Ibn Zakbal's work; and Alharizi's sixth *maqama*.[9]

The Ring of the Dove and its author, Ibn Hazm

Ibn Hazm lived between 994 and 1064 in Cordoba, Spain. He was a historian, theologist, philosopher of morals and ethics, a man of the law and a poet, who also wrote artistic prose. He is considered to have been the most prominent scholar of Muslim Spain and among the greatest philosophers of Arab Muslim culture in general.[10] His book *The Ring of the Dove* contains abundant allusions to the events taking place in Spain during his lifetime, including the disintegration of the Umayyad dynasty's caliphate of Cordoba, and its bountiful contents reflect Ibn Hazm's multifaceted personality. The uniqueness of this book lies in the exact psychological insights offered by the author, the organization of the subjects and the systematic manner in which they are presented. Most importantly, this is a social reflection of eleventh-century Andalusian Cordoba.[11]

The author's introduction to *The Ring of the Dove* includes the characteristic components of the Arab *mukaddima*.[12] He then explains the circumstances and his reasons for writing the book, describing to the readers its uniqueness and originality. Ibn Hazm shares with his audience the process by which he decided upon the specific structure of the book and lists its thirty chapters, thus providing a table of contents for the book.[13] Finally, he tells the readers that he will be describing love and its matters, causes and instances, as well as its implications and ramifications.

Usually, the author addresses a number of questions in the *mukaddima*,[14] one of which is 'what motivates an author to write a secular book?'. Again, there is a common answer to this question: though the book seems to be secular, in fact it is religious and educational and has a noble moral. In *The Ring of the Dove*, the last two chapters are different from all the others, as they reflect moral-religious perceptions: 'The Gate of the Ugliness of Sin' and 'The Gate of the Virtues of Modesty'. These two gates are mentioned in Ibn Hazm's introduction as the answer to the question about secular writing. Since Ibn Hazm was an observant Muslim, a religious man and a theologian, he felt that he must justify or even apologize for writing a secular book about love. He does this by presenting proof that the religious holy men allow the members of their flock to concern themselves also with secular matters.[15]

Thus we may understand that the last two chapters reflect the author's perception and the manner in which he wishes to end this secular composition: by calling upon his readers to repent, to listen to the word of God and fulfil His commands and to do their religious duty as required of all believers. In this manner, the author attempts to minimize the dissonance between sacred and secular, right and wrong, and to integrate the book within the Muslim-religious worldview.[16]

The doctrine of love according to Ibn Hazm

The doctrine of love according to Ibn Hazm is articulated in the book's first chapter, which discusses the nature of love and its essence.[17] Ibn Hazm explains that the motivation for the search for love is obsessiveness, the wish to find one's missing piece.

Only when the soul unites with its soulmate and consummates the covenant of intimacy will it find peace. Ibn Hazm's philosophical basis for this mode of thought is the Quran, where it is said, 'He is who created you from one soul and made therefrom its mate to dwell therewith.'[18] The importance of finding one's soulmate is also reflected in the story of the creation of woman from man's rib, as we learn that man and woman were not only created from one soul but also from one body.

In this chapter, Ibn Hazm also relates to the question of what causes one soul to be attracted to another soul. What is the reason for the love between two souls?

> What I believe myself is that it is a reunion of parts of the souls, separated in this creation [world], within their original higher element, not according to what Muhammad b. Dawud, [...] says, basing himself upon [the views of] some philosophers that: 'spirits are divided spheres', but along the line of the resemblance of their [motivating] force in the [firm] abode of their higher world and their mutual approximation to the form of their make-up.[19]

Ibn Hazm shares with his readers the fact that he grew up in a harem of women and learned from an early age to observe women in their ways and behaviour. As an alert, objective and skilled observer, he negates the thought that considers external physical beauty or an easy-going nature as a reason for falling in love, since in reality he knows of many examples of people who fell in love with people with disabilities or with people of an entirely opposite nature. Love, according to Ibn Hazm, 'is something within the soul itself'.[20] This unknown 'something' is in the heart of man himself and is controlled by God's will. Therefore, a conditional love (love that is dependent on a specific factor) will pass, for the reason can be nullified, and the one that is impartial, pure and independent of materialistic profit (love that does not depend on anything) will stand firm and remain forever.[21] In fact, the attraction to the object of love, the beloved, is described as no less than a magical power.

Ibn Hazm explains that true love is eternal. It is a true need, a genuine and profound emotion that takes over the soul and ends only with death. He distinguishes between external-bodily-physical love and inner-mental love, which is loftier. This perception of love is archaic and is mentioned, for example, in Socrates' *Symposium*, where he claims that spiritual love is more exalted than bodily love.[22] Love is evocative and emotional and awakens longing, absent-mindedness, a whimsical heart, a change in character, emaciation, moaning, crying and other symptoms of lovesickness, to which Ibn Hazm devotes one of his chapters.[23]

The doctrine of love described in *The Ring of the Dove* expresses the concept of platonic, sentimental, sensual and spiritual love as one. This mode of perception has a long tradition in Islam, even before its emergence in Spain. In Arabic literature it is known as 'Udri love', named for a Bedouin tribe whose poets were known to be tormented lovers, as their love is never satisfied: it is an all-encompassing love that can only end in madness and death. This is best embodied in the famous literary character known as Layla's Majnoun.[24]

On falling in love while asleep or based on a description

The third[25] and fourth[26] chapters of *The Ring of the Dove* examine the phenomenon of falling in love with an imagined character. The third chapter discusses falling in love while asleep while the fourth, falling in love by hearsay: the protagonist hears a description of a maiden's beauty and virtues. Both these instances are referred to as 'strange occurrences' of love.

Ibn Hazm remarks that he would not have thought to mention falling in love while asleep had he not encountered it himself. He shares the example of his friend, Abu 'l-Sari 'Ammar Ibn Ziyad, whom he met one day and found to be very preoccupied. It seems that Ibn Ziyad had fallen in love with a young woman he had seen in his dream, and upon awakening, his heart yearned for her. Though he did not know who she was, his love caused him sadness and pain and he lost all interest in the joys of life. Ibn Hazm scolded his friend, and showed him the error of his ways:

> It is a great sin for you to trouble your soul about something unreal and to attach your imagination to something that is not there, something non-existent [. . .] you are weak of judgement, afflicted by illness of sight, if you love someone whom you have never seen, and who never was created and is not in this world; and if you had fallen in love with an image one sees in bathhouses – I could have more excuse for you.[27]

According to Ibn Hazm, this phenomenon is nothing more than an image conjured by the soul and is within the realm of wishes and imagination; but this is a negative state and must be eradicated.

Falling in love based upon a description is another strange source of love. This involves mediators, who paint wonderful descriptions of the beloved, which greatly influence the person who has fallen in love and evoke strong emotional responses such as sadness, joy or insomnia.[28] Ibn Hazm tells of cases in which a person fell in love after hearing a woman's voice through the wall. Just the sound of her voice was sufficient to arouse the man's tormented love and become captivated by her. Ibn Hazm views such love as a building without foundations, which will eventually collapse:

> In my estimation it is a very weak edifice lacking foundation. For this reason: that he who has employed his mental powers in the love of one whom he had not seen, must, since he occupies his mind with nothing but it, impersonate to himself an image which he imagines, and a self which he always sets before his innermost heart, and does not impersonate in his thought any other: and toward this image he has a penchant in his imagination. Now then, if someday a personal interview took place, that very moment the matter [love] becomes either certain or the whole thing comes to naught entirely.[29]

Ibn Hazm links this chapter to the previous one, as they share many similar qualities: anyone who can fall in love with a person he has never seen can also fall in love with a figment of his imagination. This phenomenon can occur between veiled noblewomen who never step beyond the entrance of their home or women who live in harems, hidden from the eyes of men. Such love is liable to disappoint. Ibn Hazm discusses the gap between the depiction of the beloved in one's imagination and an actual meeting with the beloved. He suggests two possible situations: a large gap between imagination and reality,[30] which may lead to disappointment and even hatred; and an opposite situation in which the imagination becomes reality (that is, the positive and seductive description was truthful and realistic). Like the other gates, Ibn Hazm includes in this gate examples from the social reality of his time.[31]

The idea of falling in love with a virtual or fictitious character has its origins in Greek mythology. One of the better-known examples of this is the story of Pygmalion.[32] This story, of a sculptor who created a woman whose beauty was the epitome of his own desire, has become a symbol, describing a self-fulfilling prophecy or what is known as the 'Pygmalion Effect', which usually carries a positive connotation. This denotes the belief that positive prophecies will produce positive results; in other words, expecting something positive will affect the probability that it will indeed occur. The opposite is also true: negative prophecies are also realized.[33] It is interesting to note that while the Pygmalion Effect has a positive connotation since Pygmalion's prayers came true, and though the self-fulfilling prophecy works both positively and negatively, Ibn Hazm presents this phenomenon as negative, unnecessary and fraught with distress and even danger.

Discussion and examples: Variations of Hebrew literature from the Middle Ages

Falling in love with a dream – an artistic literary device

Joseph ibn Hasdai's *qasida Does the Gracious Gazelle have Virility and Power?* is a classic example of the love described in Ibn Hazm's third gate (falling in love while asleep). This poem is structured according to the classic Arab *qasida* and is a song of praise written by Yosef Ibn Hasdai to Shmuel HaNagid (*c.* 1045).[34] The *qasida* begins with an erotic introduction[35] centred on the coveted gazelle, which in medieval Hebrew literature designates the object of love, usually a young man. The 'gazelle' runs away from the confines of the warm, protected palace into the dangerous desert night. As he runs, the desired gazelle becomes entrapped in the dream and falls into a deep slumber, as if it has been caught in a physical trap. The suitor tries to take advantage of the situation, to realize his love, to take what his beloved deprives him of while he is awake. In other words, he wants to take advantage of the fact that the gazelle is asleep. The suitor kisses the sleeping gazelle, and the kiss is described as drinking from an amethyst glass full of nectar, in accordance with motifs found in the poetry of love and wine.[36] The suitor lies beside the gazelle – in other words, the young man – embraces him and kisses him. Ibn Hasdai describes the hair of the coveted, perfumed with myrrh, falling on his fresh, flushed cheek. The enchanting atmosphere is accompanied by a detailed description of the bed, which is adorned with frankincense and scented with expensive perfume. The poet ends the introduction by sharing with his readers how pleasing the vision is, when suddenly he awakes and his dream dissipates into thin air. In other words, at the end of the introduction it is discovered that all that happened was nothing but a dream of lust, the dream of the suitor who yearns for the gazelle sleeping next to him in his dream. What remains of the erotic dream is the good smell of the gazelle, who never existed, reminiscent of the good name of the illustrious Shmuel HaNagid. From here, Ibn Hasdai moves on to the main part of the poem, praising Shmuel HaNagid. It is a dream within a dream, a fantasy that occurs in the mind when the boundaries between sleep and awakening, dream and reality, are blurred. The atmosphere is enchanting, mesmerizing, creating a pleasant erotic tension, imbued with feelings of elation. While the feeling is certainly positive, in fact there is nothing real in the story described in the *qasida*'s introduction.

The description of the beloved strolling through the night and falling into the dream of the suitor alludes to the third gate of *The Ring of the Dove*: falling in love while asleep. Moreover, it also refers to an earlier image, found in the Arabian desert tales, when the Arabs were still nomads. The lovers would arrive at the remains of their beloved's encampment, finding that they were too late and that their beloved had moved on.[37] They would stand on the dead embers of the campfire, and with a broken heart would mourn their bitter fate, the loss of their beloved. This image, originating in reality, has become a literary motif that expresses the heartbreak of lovers and the sorrow of unfulfilled love.[38]

Falling in love with a virtual character in a maqama

While originating in the Arabic *maqama*, this theme has evolved in the Hebrew *maqama*, though both traditions emphasize the negative aspect of falling in love with a virtual character, since the gap between the desired and reality is enormous. Falling in love with a virtual character is dangerous since it leads to problematic situations. Though such episodes are described with a degree of humour and readers may find them amusing, the protagonist always finds himself entrapped, realizing the price he must pay for his futile desire.[39]

In Shlomo Ibn Zakbal's *The Speech of Asher Ben Yehuda*[40] (twelfth century, Spain), we hear of a young man named Asher, who leaves his home and returns after a long period. His family and friends hold a three-day banquet in his honour. On the fourth day, Asher and his friends go out riding, while they are all still quite intoxicated. Suddenly, Asher sees something: 'A star peering from the windows / and peaking from the corners / winking at me'.[41] Asher does not share what he has seen with his friends, and they continue riding. After a short while, he returns to the place of his vision, where now he hears a voice: 'A voice is speaking' beckoning him to come close so it can share what is in its heart. As Asher stands near the source of the voice, an apple[42] covered in myrrh oil falls on him and on it are written verses from a poem: two riddles, which are also poems of love and seduction. Asher immediately understands their meaning and is overcome by the suggestion behind the words. Though he has not seen another person, he is sure that he is desired by a woman, and wonders 'who is this woman who has seen my beauty and desires me?'. However, he decides to refuse the offer, continue his travels and leave his suitor with a broken heart. This does not last for long, as the enchanted apple is still in his pocket, and he cannot stop himself from enjoying its beauty and reading the verses on it repeatedly, until they are etched on his heart. Finally, Asher regrets his decision and returns to the place where he first heard the voice. He calls for her, to the woman he believes covets him, but she does not appear and he does not know who she is. He yells, cries and begs for her to appear, exhibiting all the symptoms of lovesickness as they are described in the writings of Ibn Hazm and Arabic poetry, and eventually faints.[43]

The unconscious Asher is carried into the harem by 'merciful women',[44] who present themselves as the ladies-in-waiting of the doe he so desires. At the same time, the doe sends Asher a love poem, also berating him for turning her down. Asher's love for her grows, and though he has yet to lay eyes on her, he loves her with all his heart. However, he is weak and humiliated, and as he follows the ladies-in-waiting he feels that he is in danger.[45] The women begin to sing love songs and dance, repeating that 'now the lady will show her face'.[46] Suddenly, their appearance changes, and when he enquires as to the reason, they answer 'here is the master of the palace'. Asher sees an angry, livid man, burning with jealousy and wielding a sword and, realizing he has entered the harem without permission, is about to faint again, this time from fear. The armed man then removes his disguise and is discovered to be a beautiful woman. The surprised Asher is happy it is 'her' and not 'he'. He is also surprised to discover that she is only a servant sent to amuse him. The woman who has been toying with him is 'the lady of ladies'. Suddenly, an entourage of young women enters, accompanied by bells and the smell of cinnamon. One of the women is gorgeous but very tall.[47] Asher is left to sit alone with this woman, whose face is covered by a veil. He begins wooing her, complimenting her in quoting erotic verses from the Song of Songs[48] and beseeches her to show him her face.[49] Once she complies, Asher is stunned to discover that it is not a woman at all, but rather a bearded man, his Adullamite friend, who has tricked him.

From the description provided above, we may deduce that the entire complex situation was a result of Asher falling in love with an image he neither saw nor thought he saw. This almost cost him his life at the hands of the palace's master. At the end of the story, we discover that his beloved was none other than a man, his Adullamite friend, who was playing a trick on him. The first words the Adullamite says to Asher after removing his veil are to ask how he saw 'cheeks / and red lips'?[50] This is worded rhetorically, as it is obvious that Asher did not see either. Asher's Adullamite friend cannot fathom how Asher fell in love with a non-existent image. He chastises him for falling in love with a figment of his imagination, thus setting himself up for disappointment. The veil hiding the face of the so-called beloved is part of reality.[51]

The twentieth *maqama* in Yehuda Alharizi's major poetic work, *Tachkemoni*, is entitled *Of Seven Maidens and their Mendacity*.[52] This is an adaptation of Ibn Zakbal's *The Speech of Asher Ben Yehuda*, and in its introduction we are told that the seven maidens are as beautiful as seven suns, but they are covered, possibly hidden. Yet the storyteller, whom Alharizi has named Heman the Ezrahite, testifies that he has seen them:

> I [. . .] saw seven maidens pass before me on the green, stars pristine: the rippling grass gave back their sheen. Seeing me, they advanced in stately dance, each

> covered with beauty's mail – robe, hood, and veil; yet their ivory aura breached my eyes and took my heart as a prize. Oh bannered armies, awesome all, with breasts that stood upright as a wall; fragrant they were, elegant and tall, proud as cedars from Lebanon's hills, sprung from Beauty's forests and fed from Eden's rills. Each shining maid was redolent with cinnamon and myrrh and many an unknown scent: Oh magic field of Beauty's richest yield![53]

From this, we may deduce that though their faces and bodies are hidden, this does not prevent the storyteller from describing them at length, according to what was thought to be conventional beauty in medieval Hebrew and Arabic love poems. Later, when one of the maidens speaks, the storyteller emphasizes that her face is covered. She warns him that he is about to face a difficult war, the war of love, and is therefore in danger: 'Bow low before her beauty! Beauty cried; and yet that beauty no eye had assailed: hid from all living eyes she was, her face was veiled.'[54]

These words do not deter the storyteller, as he is already in love with the covered, veiled image. He tells the maiden of his travels, and, like Asher in the previous story, expounds on her beauty:

> And amidst all these lands and sights never have I encountered such delights. And now, if I have found favour in your sight this day, remove your veil, I pray, that my soul not fail: restore my strength and make me hale. Bestow upon me that which you alone can give: truly this place is strait – let my soul live.[55]

The end is no surprise to us: the beautiful maiden is discovered to be a bearded man. The man draws his sword to kill the storyteller, but everyone bursts into laughter, as it is nothing more than a prank played by his friend, Hever the Kenite: 'arch-actor, ham, master of villainy and sham.'[56] The shocked Heman inquires as to the identity of the group that so aroused his desire and is told that these are the armies of his love and amongst them is his beloved. All they intended was to have some fun, to trick him and test him. At the end of the story, everyone disappears, and the storyteller is left shocked and saddened.

Both examples tell us of pranks based on manipulation and finding the storyteller's vulnerability (which could be true for any man): falling in love with a beloved who is nothing more than a virtual woman, one who has not been seen nor is, in fact, real. We are told of the veils and covers that disguise the maidens and the beautiful woman. The storyteller asks that these disguises be removed, thus bringing the illusion to an end. If he is being tested, he has no doubt failed this test. Throughout the story, the readers are aware that the storyteller is trapped in his own private fantasy, which Ibn Hazm warns us about, and is finally ensnared in the trap.

Shady matchmaking – the virtual bride

Almost all the *maqamat* that criticize marriage are based on a variation of falling in love with a virtual image, a figment of the imagination, and therefore the matchmaking that takes place in the *maqamat* is most often successful. One example of this is Alharizi's sixth *maqama*,[57] which is an adaptation of Yehudah ibn-Shabtai's *Minhat Yehudah*[58] and presents marriage negatively.[59]

In this *maqama*, the protagonist falls in love with a description, and this is the reason he becomes entrapped in marriage. The storyteller, Heman the Ezrahite, meets Hever the Kenite, the protagonist of the *maqama*, during his travels. Seeing that he is tired and preoccupied, Heman suggests that his friend stay for a while with him, rest and enjoy the company of a woman. Hever is appalled by the proposal: 'By all the prophets' lives', he shouted, 'not a word of wives, though you bore a command stamped by God's own hand! One horror will suffice: never twice!'[60]

Hever explains to Hemen that his own evil inclination caused him to search for a wife. While he was hesitating about finding a wife, he felt himself deliberating and fantasizing, falling in love. At some point, he found himself standing before an old, ugly, misshapen woman. Hever describes the old woman in grotesque language, portraying her as a demonic witch. She then offered him a match: a beautiful young woman, who is the epitome of perfection:[61]

> Let me show you a maid whose cheeks bring on the morning light, whose locks, the night. In this singular princess shall you be Eden-blest, a maid made to serve you best: warm in your bosom shall she rest, fast by your table shall she trill and shine, her mouth a cruse of wine [. . .] Her eyes are two lions, her teeth strung pearls, each breast a trembling fawn. On, sir, on! Feast your eyes on each succulent part and feel your senses fall apart; [. . .] Oh, happy the man who clasps her to his side, who mounts this chariot to ride; oh trebly sweet the lot of him who bows, falls down, and lies between her feet.[62]

The old woman then added another detail to her offer: the match will cost 2,000 pieces of silver. Hever asked to see the maiden before agreeing to the match, but the matchmaker refused, swearing she had no intention of cheating him. Hever could not contain his joy and agreed to the match, offering to pay a higher sum. The old woman promised Hever that he would meet his bride the next morning, and Hever could not sleep that night, as he was excited and burning with passion for his new wife.

In the morning, the old woman appeared with a surprise. She informed the groom that he would be married on that day and that the father of the bride and the whole community were all awaiting his arrival. The stunned Hever was presented to all those assembled, and the father declared that the terms of the marriage were agreed upon. Hever accepted the conditions as dictated to him without ever seeing the bride, and the marriage took place immediately, again without the groom seeing the bride. It should be noted that the marriage took place on the date of *Ta'anit Esther*,[63] which is a hint as to what happened next.

The wedding party lasted all day until nightfall. All this time, the bride and groom sat quietly next to each other but did not see one another. Hever describes the encounter between the two as a scene in slow motion: the groom imagined the delightful night that awaited him with his beautiful bride. He approached her. He took off her outer garments. He removed the veil from her face. He brought the candle to her face. And there was a surprise – nay, a disaster; all his expectations were shattered – an ugly woman with a thunderous voice stood before him, looking like a cow with the mouth of a donkey, exuding a horrible smell, with black skin, white hair and crooked lips.[64]

A stunned Hever realized that he was tricked, and in his pain and shock sang a derogatory song to the ugly old bride, instead of the romantic wedding song that grooms usually sing to a beloved bride.[65]

The miserable groom tries to find solace in the bride's dowry but soon discovers that she owns nothing but a few worthless rags. Once Hever learns this, he feels that all hope is lost. His wedding day turns out to be a day of mourning, and he sings another derogatory song to his bride, harsher and more scathing than the previous one, cursing her and her family. Hever realizes that the song will not solve his problems. He hits his wife and runs away, leaving her and the town behind him. In his last song, Hever thanks God for rescuing him from sure death.[66]

According to this *maqama*, Hever fell in love with a bride he had never seen. The old matchmaker described a dream bride to him, and he fell in love with her description since he felt 'tethered by Passion's rope, a prisoner of Hope'.

The groom's subjective blindness, agreeing to marry a woman he had never seen, along with the objective tradition of the bride hiding behind a veil, doubles Hever's feelings that he has been duped.[67] It is interesting to note that while the groom is blind to reality in broad daylight, he comes to his senses and realizes he's been tricked at night, with a candle serving as his only illumination. However, as in the previous examples, this was possible because he allowed himself to fall for a woman based only on a description he had heard. As Ibn Hazm warns in the fourth gate, this strange form of falling in love can only end in failure.

Conclusion

In conclusion, the examples presented in this chapter demonstrate that a person must be present, aware and focused on the reality in which he lives. Desire deceives and disrupts a person's judgement of reality, especially in interpersonal situations and, in the context of the matter under discussion, the relations between men and women. Interpreting reality according to the heart's desire is dangerous, because it will not be realized. It is a prophecy that does not fulfil itself. In the above-mentioned examples, falling in love while asleep or falling in love based upon a description by others, the protagonist finds himself in a state of blindness because his love interest is not real and therefore is dangerous. The dream and the fantasy are shattered on the rocks of reality, in accordance with Ibn Hazm's warning. Pygmalion-style miracles do not occur in reality nor even in the fictional reality of the *maqama*. The *maqama*, which is intended to both entertain and teach morality, seeks to provide its audience with a lesson on the importance of gauging reality, which is the correct path to proper and healthy communication between human beings and prevents embarrassing mistakes. It seeks to sharpen the disparity between imagination and reality, and highlight the price that those who confuse them might pay. It seems, then, that the masculine aspiration to create or find a perfect woman is a common and widespread desire, not limited to a specific time or place. From ancient literary themes (Ovid), through the Arabic and Hebrew literature of the Middle Ages, this phenomenon has provided inspiration to writers and poets for thousands of years and will probably continue to do so into the unforeseen future.

Notes

1. Ibn Hazm 1931, 6.
2. *The Ring of the Dove* has been translated often, and into many languages. For this article I used the Nykl edition, one of the editions most common among scholars. Ibn Hazm, *Abu Muhamad Ali Ibn Hazm Al-Andalusi (a book containing the RISALA known as) The Dove's Neck-Ring, about Love and* Lovers, trans. D. K. Petrof, ed. A. R. Nykl (Paris: Paul Geuthner, 1931).
3. Ibn Hazm 1931, 7.
4. Ibn Hazm 1931, 7. I will expand on this matter further in this chapter.
5. The Hebrew *maqama* began as a genre of Arabic literature, which later evolved to become part of the medieval Hebrew literature written in Spain. The *maqama* is also the source for the genre of the picaresque novel. See, for example, Pagis 1976, 199–212; Goitein 1951, 32–3. See also Abu-Haidar 1974.
6. See, for example, Nicholson 1930, 328–36; Brockelmann 1936 161–4; Hameen-Anttila 2002. See also Beeston 1971; Mattock 1984.
7. One example of this, Alharizi's thirty-first *maqama* in his book *Tachkemoni*, was mentioned in my article: Refael-Vivante 2017. In the current chapter I discuss this matter in depth and further elaborate on the examples.
8. The classic Arabic *qasida* is a long poem with a unique structure. It is comprised of two parts: (i) an introduction with a single subject matter (such as wine or women); (ii) the main part, which centres on the main subject of the poem (the poem's genre, such as a praise or a lamentation). Between both parts is a transitional verse allowing the poet to pass from the first subject to the second (the main part of the poem).
9. Which is an adaptation of Yehudah ibn-Shabtai's *Minhat Yehudah*.
10. Much has been written on the life and work of Ibn Hazm. See, for example, Adang, Fierro and Schmidtke 2013, especially the first part of the book, which discusses Ibn Hazm's biography within the context of the period. See also Puerta Vilchez 2013, Soraviaa 2013, Garcia Sanjuan 2013, Wasserstein 2013 and Martinez-Gros 2013.
11. For more on Ibn Hazm and *The Ring of the Dove*, see Arberry 1953, 7–14.
12. *Mukaddima* = introduction (Arabic). According to Freimark, the Arabic *Mukaddima* (مُقدّمة) has a structural tradition and a linguistic-rhetoric tradition, and it serves as a 'window' through which the author comes out of the literary creation and addresses the reader: Freimark 2005, 495–6. See also Yeffet-Refael 2006, 125–7.
13. Each chapter discusses a different subject: for example, the nature of love; the signs of love; love at first site; correspondence; devotion; betrayal, etc. The chapters are composed in a

similar manner. Each begins with a theoretical statement which includes a description and a psychological analysis of the subject under discussion in each particular gate. The author then presents the evidence to prove the statement by offering examples from daily life in eleventh-century Cordoba: events, historical stories and autobiographical evidence.

14. In his thorough examination of the subject, Hameen-Anttila states that the medieval Arab writer did not write his introduction in order to explain the writing process or focus his thoughts on the subject discussed in the *maqama*, but rather wrote a predetermined series of answers to a predetermined series of questions: Hameen-Anttila 2002, 149.

15. Ibn Hazm 1931, 2–3.

16. A similar phenomenon is found in the work of Andreas Capellanus, a learned priest who wrote a tractate on love. His essay merges the Latin traditions of discussions about love, including Ovid's works, and contemporary courtly discourses. The essay consists of three books. The first book discusses the question of what is love, while the second deals with the question of how to preserve love. Both books deal with the laws of love theoretically. The third book – dedicated to 'the conviction of love' – is a somewhat militant misogynist manifesto in which the author condemns love.

17. I discussed this in a previous paper: Refael-Vivante 2017. See also the discussion in Ibn Hazm 1931, 325–47.

18. Ibn Hazm 1931, 8.

19. Ibn Hazm 1931, 7. See also the myth of Aristophanes in the context of Ibn Hazm's perceptions: Ibn Hazm 1931, 339–41, and especially note 216. A similar notion of matchmaking taking place in the spiritual world is discussed in the Babylonian Talmud, Sotah tractate 2A: 'Forty days before an embryo is formed a Divine Voice issues forth and says: The daughter of so-and-so is destined to marry so-and-so.'

20. Ibn Hazm 1931, 8.

21. Ibn Hazm adds that there are different types of love, the loftiest of all being love for the sake of the heavens. There are also types of love that are hinged on a specific reason or cause, and they will most likely not last. Ibn Hazm 1931, 8–9.

22. Danzig 2002, 67. See also the discussion of the vulgar Aphrodite and the heavenly Aphrodite, 66–7.

23. The second gate is dedicated to the signs of love. Love is described as an illness: the beloved is both the cause and the cure. Ibn Hazm 1931, 15–25.

24. Qays loses his sanity as a result of his love for Layla, and thus he became known as 'Layla's Majnoun', which means 'insane' in Arabic.

25. Ibn Hazm 1931, 26–7.

26. Ibn Hazm 1931, 28–30.

27. Ibn Hazm 1931, 26.

28. Ibn Hazm discusses each of these subjects in a separate chapter of the book.

29. Ibn Hazm 1931, 28.

30. See Huss 2001.

31. Huss 2001, 28–30.

32. The story of Pygmalion is first discussed in Ovid's narrative poem *Metamorphoses*.

33. Negative rumours and prophecies create reality. They impact many different areas of life. The phenomenon of the self-fulfilling prophecy has been extensively studied in such fields as education, psychology, sociology and economics.

34. Schirmann 1956, vol. 1, 172–5.

35. Schirmann 1956, vol. 1, 172–3, lines 1–11.

36. Poems about wine and poems about love and desire (Arabic and Hebrew) share common motifs. For example, when drinking from a glass of wine, touching the lips to the glass's rim is similar to a kiss. Drinking the wine is like the loved one's saliva during the kiss. In the poems of love and desire, the kiss from the beloved's lips is likened to drinking a glass of wine.

37. Levin 1967.

38. For an in-depth analysis of the introduction to the *qasida Does the Gracious Gazelle Have Virility and Power?*, see Levin 1967, 292–4.

39. In addition, falling in love with a virtual character often serves as a starting point for a comedy of errors.

40. Schirmann 1956, vol. 1, 554–65. A number of papers discuss this *maqama*. See, for example, Dishon 1974, Segal 1982, Schirmann 1986, Rosen 2003 and others.

41. Schirmann 1956, vol. 1, 557. My translation.

42. The apple is a symbol of seduction, and an ancient, well-known motif.

43. Ibn Hazm 1931, 15–25.

44. Schirmann 1956, vol. 1, 560.

45. Schirmann 1956, vol. 1, 561–2.

46. Schirmann 1956, vol. 1, 562.

47. She is described according to the convention of beauty in the Middle Ages. See Pagis 1970, 267–78; Levin 1980, 287–433.

48. Song of Songs 4.9

49. Schirmann 1956, vol. 1, 564–5.

50. Schirmann 1956, vol. 1, 565.

51. The motif of masquerade, a palpable means used to create a virtual reality, an illusion.

52. Alharizi 2001.

53. Alharizi 2001, 195.

54. Alharizi 2001, 196–7.

55. Alharizi 2001, 199.

56. Alharizi 2001, 200.

57. Alharizi 2001, 73–80: 'Of One too Swiftly Sped to the Marriage Bed'.

58. In Yehudah ibn-Shabtai's *Minhat Yehudah* we hear of Zerakh, who defies his father's deathbed decree that he not marry. Zerakh denigrates marriage and swears not to marry, but at the end is duped by a mean old matchmaker who convinced him to marry a beautiful and rich young woman. After the wedding, he discovers his bride was switched with a poor, old and ugly woman.

59. Rosen 2003, 103–23. Chapter 5: 'Domesticating the Enemy: Misogamy in a Jewish Marriage Debate'.

60. Alharizi 2001, 72.

61. The girl's description matches the motifs found in classic Arabic love poetry. On motifs of love poetry, see Pagis 1970, 267–78; Levin 1980, 287–433.

62. Alharizi 2001, 74–5.

63. According to Jewish Halakha, this is a day of mourning, on which it is forbidden to marry.

64. Alharizi 2001, 77.

65. In the song, he continues to describe her ugliness and that her looks are so terrible that they destroy any possibility of happiness.

66. On the dramatic dimension in the sixth *maqama*, see Refael-Vivante 2014.

67. While covering the bride's face is an acceptable practice, part of reality, this developed into a known literary motif: exchanging the bride on the night of her wedding.

PART III
PANDORA, EVE AND THE FEMININE IDEAL

CHAPTER 7
ADAM AND EVE: REFLECTIONS ON A RELATIONSHIP

Roslyn Weiss

In this chapter, I approach the verses in the Book of Genesis without an agenda and without prejudice, and deliberately without recourse to biblical commentaries, in an attempt to be open to the text and to hear anew what it is saying.

The uneven relationship between man and woman

In Genesis chapters 2 and 3 an account is offered of the relationship between the male and female of the human species, following on the heels of Genesis 1's specification that God made the human species, male and female. Other creatures are created according to their kind (Gen. 1.21, 1.24, 1.25), but none but the human species is explicitly said to be created male and female.[1]

That only the human species was reported to be created in this way suggests that there is something special about the connection between male and female human beings that requires an account, some element in the male and female human longing for one another that cannot be reduced to a reproductive instinct or even to the biologically based love of parent for child.

The narrative, then, in Genesis 2, fleshes out, as it were, the creation of the female who is to be the second component of the male–female duo of the human species. According to Genesis 2, the creation of male and female proceeds in stages; the distinct genders are not created simultaneously.[2] Strikingly, the 'human being', *ha-adam*, does not become *ish*, that is, is not referred to as *ish* – a specifically male human being – until there is a woman, *ishah*. The relevant verse reads: 'And the *adam* said, "To this female being [the feminine demonstrative *zot* is used] will the name *ishah* be assigned, for she was taken from the masculine being, *ish*"' (Gen. 2.23).[3] Man thus acquires his masculinity via the femininity of the woman created from a part of his body.

In the detailed account in Genesis 2 of the origination of woman from man, there is at first only *adam*, only a man. In other words, man begins alone.[4] This original condition of the man, of *ha-adam*, is not, however, one of self-sufficiency, but is instead one of lack or need. Adam's situation is bleak, perhaps dire. As God says, 'It is not good that man be alone' (Gen. 2.18).[5] To be sure, Adam has power and intelligence – he is smart enough to be entrusted with naming all the animals ('God brought the animals to Adam to see what he would name them, and every name that Adam assigned was, from that point on, the animal's name', Gen. 2.19), and he is placed in charge of the Garden, 'to work it and to protect it' (Gen. 2.15). But he has no *human* connection, no one who is his mate. None of the animals that God has fashioned will do; and the sole being who can complete Adam is not yet even envisioned. The only way Adam can be made whole, God realizes, is via his union with another being like him, another member of his species. God removes from Adam a part of his body; flesh is added to it to complete the new being; and breath is breathed into that new being, woman. The being that God creates, despite being fashioned from a body part of another,[6] is one who is, from the start, a complete individual in her own right. Yet the man, if he is to have a suitable mate, and in order that he have such a mate, must sacrifice a part of his body. His body must be rendered less than whole in order for him to become whole; he welcomes as his mate someone for whom he has yielded his bodily integrity.

One important consequence of the fashioning of woman from the rib of man is that male and female are not equals; the relationship is not symmetrical.[7] But the inequality is one in which it is the female – not the male – who is superior. In the Genesis myth, one whole becomes less than whole in order for there to be a second whole which contains a part of the original whole and which is, therefore, more whole than the original. We ought not, then, to think of the *adam*, who is the first human being created, as the perfect specimen of a human being; it is in fact the woman who is most perfect. It is she who not only lacks nothing, but indeed contains a part of the man. Moreover, the woman never experiences aloneness or lack. She is never required to sacrifice a part of her body for her mate. She is introduced into the world to satisfy the neediness of another; she herself is not needy.[8]

Adam is delighted at the sight of the woman when they are first introduced to one another. At last, after having surveyed a host of unsuitable animals, he meets the mate who is just right. When the woman is brought to him, he exclaims, 'This one this time is bone of my bones and flesh of my flesh;[9] she is called woman [*ishah*], because she was taken from man [*ish*]' (Gen. 2.23).[10] Note that there is no comparable reaction on the part of the woman. For it is not she who lacks something and is now acquiring what is missing. She comes to man whole, independent, complete – not alone, dependent and missing a rib. It is perhaps not far-fetched to infer from the Genesis myth that prelapsarian woman has the upper hand. For in the biblical narrative, neediness is initially decidedly one-way, flowing exclusively from man to woman.

In order to appreciate the relationship between the biblical first man and first woman it may perhaps be useful to think of the relationship between a first-born child and a second, though the comparison is not entirely apt. Imagine parents who are blessed with their first child. The first-born child seems perfect at first, the apple of his or her parents' eye. But the parents notice that the child is alone. The parents produce a playmate for their child – a brother or sister. But all is not rosy. Yes, the older child now has a sibling, born of the same parents, and so, automatically, someone with whom the older child has much in common. But the older child also experiences significant loss: no longer enjoying undivided parental affection, the child must adjust to *not* being the only child. Since the younger child has never enjoyed undivided parental affection and has never been lonely, has never been without a sibling, he or she experiences far less trauma and has no comparable adjusting to do.

One way in which a dependent and needy person might seek to ensure the survival of the being on whom his own completion depends is by becoming overprotective. We have some reason to think that this is precisely what Adam does. The prohibition of eating from the fruit of the tree of knowledge of good and evil was issued to Adam alone[11] – before the creation of the woman. Indeed, after the sin, God says directly to Adam, 'Have you eaten of the tree of which I commanded *you* [masculine sing.] that you should not eat?' (Gen. 3.11). And again, in issuing the man's punishment in Gen. 3.17, God says, 'Because you hearkened unto the woman and ate of the tree with respect to which I commanded *you*, saying, do not eat from it.' Also, although there were two trees planted in the centre of the Garden (Gen. 2.9), both the tree of life and the tree of knowledge (Gen. 2.9), the eating-prohibition extended no further than the tree of knowledge. Moreover, the prohibition concerned *only* eating. When the woman reports the prohibition to the serpent in Gen. 3.3, she is indeed able to correct the serpent's version of the prohibition, according to which the commandment decreed, 'You may not eat from all the trees of the Garden' (Gen. 3.1); but she herself has it wrong as well. Whereas she believes correctly that the prohibition does not apply to *all* the trees of the Garden, she thinks incorrectly that it applies to the fruit of the tree in the centre of the Garden rather than to the fruit of just one of those trees, and that it includes a prohibition on touching (Gen. 3.3).[12] Where could the woman have gotten these ideas but from Adam? The woman is surely reporting what she has heard from the man, who has apparently sought, by inflating the prohibition, to make doubly, or triply, sure that she will not sin, thereby safeguarding her life on which he is dependent.[13]

It is perhaps significant, in addition, that the woman is attracted to the fruit; she is not said to be attracted to the man. The fruit fulfils all her yearnings: for physical pleasure, for aesthetic enjoyment and for intellectual fulfilment: 'And the woman saw that the tree was good for eating and was a delight to the eyes and that the tree was desirable for the purpose of becoming wise, and she took of its fruit and ate' (Gen. 3.6).[14] One might say that the serpent cunningly[15] directs the woman's lust toward the fruit.[16]

The asymmetry in the Genesis myth between man and woman may help to explain the universal phenomenon of one partner's being more attracted to the other than the other to the one. The Genesis myth explains why attraction is not balanced – and not simple. Indeed, Chapter 2 ends with an asymmetrical statement by the narrator: 'Therefore does a man [*ish*] leave his father and his mother and cleave to his woman, and they become one flesh' (Gen. 2.24).[17] Nothing comparable is said of the woman.[18] In the Genesis narrative, then, it is the incomplete Adam who requires a mate, and it is he alone who is attached to his mate. One might say, then, that, biblically speaking, unidirectional attraction from man to woman is in the original nature of things.

In addition to tracing the source of attraction, the biblical myth offers an astonishing account of why attraction might fizzle. The man who is dependent on his perfect companion acknowledges his dependence on her: 'The woman whom Thou didst give to be with me, she gave me of the tree and I did eat' (Gen. 3.12).[19] This man so cleaves to this woman that he disobeys God rather than risk creating a rift between himself and her.[20] Adam, we note, had obeyed the divine command until the woman gave him the forbidden fruit. He is actually *with* the woman when the serpent accosts her – as the verse says, 'And she took of its fruit and ate, and gave also to her man [or her husband] with her [*'immah*] and he ate' (Gen. 3.6). He ate because the woman gave him the fruit. He, unlike the woman, is not drawn irresistibly to the fruit; he did not previously partake of it. Adam's only alternative to eating would have been to rebuke his wife. This is something he was apparently not prepared to do.[21]

When the man and the woman's eyes are opened and they see their nakedness and sew for themselves fig leaves and make for themselves girdles, they are as one: 'Adam and the woman hid [the verb is masculine singular] from the Lord God amid the trees of the Garden' (Gen. 3.8). It is God who divides them, addressing Adam alone. When God calls out to Adam, 'Where are you?' (*ayyekah*), Adam answers only for himself: 'I was afraid because I was naked and *I* hid' (Gen. 3.9). He is still protecting the woman. And when God asks him if he ate from the tree from which God commanded him not to eat – indeed, he alone was commanded (Gen. 3.11) – he answers that the woman whom God made to be with him, she gave him from the tree and he ate (Gen. 3.12). Adam's answer is the plain unembellished truth. Adam does not accuse the woman of seduction[22] and he does not blame the woman; he merely reports what happened. And the significance of 'the woman whom You gave [to be] with me [*'immadi*]' – note that Adam does not say simply, the woman you gave me (*li*)[23] – is surely that this woman was ordained by God to be his companion, the being to whom he was to cleave. And so, when this woman, 'she' (*hi*), the woman whom God gave to be with him, gave him food, he ate. Adam in effect tells God that he is hopelessly attached to this woman whom God fashioned for him, and from him.

When God now addresses the woman, asking 'What have you done?', the independent-minded woman assumes that God is asking her, not why she gave Adam the forbidden fruit, but why *she* ate it. And she, too, states the facts: 'The serpent beguiled me, and I did eat' (Gen. 3.13). God immediately punishes the serpent: 'Because you did this,' God says to it by way of reprimand, 'there will forever be enmity between you *and the woman*' (Gen. 3.15).

God next turns to the woman. Note that in her case alone there is no 'because you have done so-and-so'. She, after all, was commanded only indirectly.[24] Nevertheless, she will experience pain in childbirth and will desire the man, and he will rule her (Gen. 3.16).[25] God's initial intent was for the woman to be the man's helper, but she instead caused the man to sin. It has thus become necessary for God to remedy the flaw in His initial plan: He must correct the imbalance in the man–woman relationship. If the serpent turned the woman's lust on the fruit, God now deflects it away from the fruit, turning it towards the man. Once the woman's desire is directed toward the man, the stage is set for an ongoing complex dance of shifting and colliding desire and power on the part of male and female partners. Indeed, from a certain perspective, the man's punishment compounds the woman's: a man busy eking out sustenance from recalcitrant soil necessarily has things on his mind other than his desire for the woman.

The man is punished for obeying his wife rather than God: 'Because you hearkened unto the voice of your wife and ate of the tree from which *I* commanded you not to eat'

(Gen. 3.17). God recognizes that Adam's dependence on the woman, brought about by her having been created as 'bone of my bone and flesh of my flesh', has made it nearly impossible for Adam not to hearken unto her. Unless God changes the dynamic between the man and his wife, the man's first inclination will be to do his wife's bidding.

Note that after this incident Adam performs his first genuinely independent act. In none of his previous acts did he take the initiative. The man was not the one to think to request a companion; God brought the woman to him.[26] His naming of the animals was not done at his instigation; rather, God brought them to him to be named. And arguably, Adam did not even name the woman. Unlike in the case of the animals where God brought them to Adam for him to name, and whatever name he assigned them would then be their name (Gen. 2.19), and he did indeed name them (Gen. 2.20), in the case of the woman, God is said to have formed her into a woman (*le-ishah*) and to have brought her to Adam, and all Adam does is exclaim in joyful recognition that the name she already has signifies the woman's connection to him. Instead of the active *vayiqra*, 'and he named' (Gen. 2.20), that is found in the case of the animals, in the case of the woman the text has the passive *le-zot yiqqarei*, 'and this one is to be called' (Gen. 2.23). The name 'woman' may well not have been the one that Adam would have chosen. Moreover, in the case of eating the fruit, Adam, of course, ate the fruit he was given.[27] With his newfound independence, however, he *re*names 'his woman (or wife)' *Ḥavah*, Eve (Gen. 3.20). This time the naming of the woman is indeed Adam's doing: 'and he named', *vayiqra*. No longer seeing the woman as 'bone of my bone and flesh of my flesh', Adam now sees the woman who was to be *his* companion as instead the mother of all living beings.[28] A certain alienation has set in. It is no longer the woman's relation to him that occupies centre stage for Adam.[29]

One might say, then, that the biblical story is one that explains how man came to desire woman and how woman came to desire man, with their respective desires having very different origins. Had God created the woman *ab initio* as a separate being without using a part of Adam, Adam could not have said 'bone of my bone and flesh of my flesh'; he might never have eaten the fruit the woman gave him; and the woman's desire might well then never have come to be centred on him even as his focus shifts to other things.[30]

God and human beings

A central feature of the Adam and Eve myth is human disobedience. In Genesis, Adam is given an explicit prohibition, and he and the woman defy it. The biblical author disapproves of human defiance and expresses no reservation concerning God's right to punish; nor do any of those punished lodge a protest. As a consequence of their improper acts, human beings in Genesis surely deserve what they get. God must now keep human beings in their place: although the human beings in Genesis attain knowledge of good and evil and in this way become *like* God (Gen. 3.22), they also become subject to death and in this way become *un*like God.[31]

In Genesis 2–3 there is but a single God.[32] This God is one who is not prepared to pronounce all of creation 'very good' (Gen. 1.31) until He corrects the one thing that He acknowledges is 'not good'. As He says, 'It is *not good* for man to be alone; I will make him a helper alongside him' (Gen. 2.18).[33] It is only once the woman is created that the creation of the human species as summarized in Genesis 1, 'male and female He created them' (Gen. 1.27),[34] can justify God's assessment of His entire creation as 'very good' (Gen. 1.31). Yet God views the creation of the human male and female differently from the way that He views His other creations, including the animals created on the very day human beings were created, day six. With respect to every creation *except* the human, the text says that God saw that it was good. With respect to the creation of human beings, however, the text is silent.[35] The very God who thus expresses His great satisfaction with creation as a whole apparently has reservations about the human male and female. Perhaps it is out of His compassion for this single admittedly flawed aspect of creation, that He sews for the man and woman coats of skin and clothes them (Gen. 3.21).

Notes

1. It may be assumed that the animals were created male and female since they were blessed to reproduce, but the text omits any mention of the animal species containing two sexes. The first mention of animals' being male and female is at Gen. 6.19, where Noah is told to load the animals onto the ark two by two, male and female. The Torah repeats the maleness and femaleness of the human species in Gen. 5.2.
2. In my view, the best way to understand the relationship between Gen. 1.27 and Genesis 2 is that the latter fills in the details of which the former is but a sketch.
3. Translations are the author's.
4. Although there are scholars who interpret Gen. 1.27 as implying that the human was originally androgynous, the text, in my view, strongly discourages that reading. The verse states, 'And God created the human in His likeness; in the likeness of God He created it [i.e. the human]; male and female He created *them*.' The plural, 'them', to my mind, removes the possibility that male and female were ever conjoined. It is not until Genesis 2 that we learn *how* the human was created as male and female.
5. The Torah thus notes God's recognition of man's aloneness as a flaw in creation. In Gen. 2.5, the land is seen by God to be missing a man to work it; God rectifies that situation by creating the man. He now sees that this man is alone, and that, too, is not good. God finds a solution for this problem as well; he creates the woman. Woman is not created to help work the land; she is created to alleviate man's condition of aloneness – a separate and distinct problem.
6. Biblical scholars disagree as to whether *tzela'* means side or rib, but since the textual expression is *aḥat mitzal'otav*, one of his *tzela'ot*, suggesting that there are several, rib seems more likely. If it were side that was intended, it would have been more natural for the text to read 'one of his two sides', or, better, 'his female side'. As the text stands, if we translate *tzela'* as 'side', the text would imply that God chose (at random?) one of Adam's multiple sides. Note, too, that Adam exclaims, 'bone of my bones' (Gen. 2.23): there is no sense that Adam finds the *half* of himself that was separated off from his whole. There is no talk of cutting in half or dividing. Moreover, even if *tzela'* does mean 'side', we have no good reason to think that the side in question was already female, that the human was originally androgynous, as the

advocates of 'side' would suppose (see n. 4, above). Were the woman Adam's other half, whence his aloneness? It is explicit that the woman is a new creature, made for Adam, though a part of him was used in the making. She does not exist before God makes her. Indeed, God first fashions (*vayyitzer*) animals that might remedy Adam's aloneness, which would be a strange thing to do if the woman existed as a part of Adam all along. She would certainly, then, have been an element in the original plan of creation, rather than a solution to a problem *in* creation. See the account of Philo Judaeus in *Opificio mundi*, sections 151–3, according to which man was created first, was alone, and woman was created next, as an additional being. Considering all the dividing that occurs in the creation account, it would be odd indeed if the original human being were androgynous yet it is not via division that the woman is said to come to be.

7. We may compare with this the Aristophanes myth in Plato's *Symposium* (189a–193e), in which two conjoined wholes are separated into two independent wholes.
8. The woman is drawn to the fruit that is good to eat and pleasing aesthetically and intellectually. Since she is human and not a goddess, it is to be expected that she will have the human needs for sustenance and aesthetic and intellectual fulfilment. Even the most perfect human being has needs. But having needs is not the same as being needy, which is a matter of lacking something essential.
9. Might the flesh used to build the woman have been the man's as well? Might that be why the man exclaims, 'flesh of my flesh'?
10. We don't know how Adam determined which names to assign to the animals.
11. Gen. 2.16–17.
12. The woman cannot name the tree. Adam is told explicitly not to eat from 'the tree of knowledge of good and evil' (Gen. 2.17), and not simply not to eat from the tree in the centre of the Garden, though presumably both trees were in the centre of the Garden (2.10): 'And God caused to grow [. . .] and the tree of life in the centre of the Garden and the tree of the knowledge of good and evil.' Apparently, Adam did not convey the name of the tree to the woman when he told her of the prohibition, probably to ensure that she would avoid the centre of the Garden altogether and not err. *Etz hagan* is the expression used for the trees, plural, even though it is grammatically singular (see Gen. 2.17; and the woman's report at Gen. 3.3).
13. There are several reasons that might explain why the serpent approached the woman rather than Adam. These include that (i) she did not hear the command and so could be tricked; (ii) of the two, she seemed to be the more independent; and (iii) she was not besotted with Adam as he was with her and therefore her desire could more easily be directed to the fruit.
14. All the trees of the Garden were 'pleasing to the sight and good for food' (2.10). There is only a slight variation in the description of these aspects of the tree of knowledge of good and evil. All the trees are described as נחמד למראה וטוב למאכל ('pleasing to the sight and good for food'); the tree in the middle of the Garden is perceived by the woman as כי טוב העץ למאכל וכי תאוה הוא לעיניים ('good for food and a delight to the eyes'). There is, however, a third element that attracts the woman to this tree over the others: ונחמד העץ להשכיל (Gen. 3.6), the tree is 'desirable to make one wise'.
15. The Hebrew word for cunning and for naked are the same: *'arum*. The juxtaposition of the term's two senses is striking as it appears in the final verse of chapter 2 meaning 'naked' and in the first verse of chapter 3 meaning 'cunning'.
16. Certainly not to himself, though he might have tried.
17. The Torah thus explains how it is that a person can be as or more devoted to someone who is not his flesh and blood as to someone – parents or children – who is.

18. It is arguably not a man simpliciter who leaves or must leave his parents but specifically a husband – perhaps a more satisfying rendering of *ish* throughout this narrative is 'husband' rather than 'man'. Since the person to whom the man is said to cleave is '*his* woman', *ishto*, rather than 'a woman', *ishah*, it is likely that the marriage precedes the leaving. The man who already has a woman who counts as 'his woman' leaves, or must leave, his parents, and cleave to her. Whereas the term *ishah* does double duty, signifying, on the one hand, woman (throughout the narrative, beginning in Gen. 2.22 and then subsequently in the serpent narrative, and also when God later addresses her) and, on the other hand, wife (both specifically when the reference is to Adam's wife, *ishto* – Gen. 2.25 and 3.8 – and more generally as in Gen. 2.24), man is *ish* only as husband. When God continues to address the man, the man is referred to in the text as *ha-adam*. Moreover, the narrator tells us that the woman gave the fruit to *her* man, that is, to her husband, *le-ishah* (Gen. 3.6), rather than to the man, *la-ish*.

19. Adam was with the woman when she took the fruit and ate and gave some to him: 'she took of its fruit and did eat and gave also to her husband [who was] with her, and he ate' (Gen. 3.6). The same term used here, *'immah*, is used for 'with me' in Adam's response to God that the woman whom you gave 'with me', *'immadi*, gave me (*li*) the fruit and I ate (Gen. 3.12). There is not even the relative pronoun *asher*, 'who', in Gen. 3.6. The text suggests that the woman sees the man as her 'with-me-husband', the cleaver.

20. Strauss (1983: 156) suggests that Adam 'forgot the prohibition', or that he 'drifted into' disobedience because he was 'cleaving'.

21. It is possible that Adam preferred that he and the woman die together than that she die and he once again be alone. Perhaps once he sees that neither of them died, he is less hesitant to speak of the woman's part in his eating the fruit.

22. Because the man was cleaving, the woman has no reason or need to be seductive. This is something that will have to change with the change in the male–female relationship.

23. Adam might have said *li* in the first part of the verse; that is, he could have said, 'the woman whom you gave me', as he said, 'she gave me (*li*) and I ate'. Instead, he says, 'with me'. The implication, again, is that Adam cleaves to the woman; he does as she bids.

24. One might say that the woman disobeyed not God, but God's messenger, the man. If one asks whose sin is more severe, a case could be made that it was the man's. He was commanded directly. Both he and the serpent bring a curse upon the world; the woman does not; and there is in her case no 'Because you'.

25. Were it not for the woman's desire for the man perhaps nothing would induce her to have children, considering the pain that attends childbirth. The one case we have thus far of birth is that of the woman from the man. There is in this case no mention of pain. Perhaps God's original plan was for childbirth to be painless. The *'itzavon/'etzev* of the woman in childbirth parallels the *'itzavon* of the man in farming the recalcitrant land. If he did not need to eat he would not subject himself to that hardship; if she did not desire him she would not subject herself to the pain of childbirth.

26. In our analogy of the parents producing a second child, Adam's not requesting a companion would correspond to the older child's not being the one who seeks a sibling. The parents, like God, sense the loneliness of the first creation.

27. The woman is from the start a project of God's. He detects the man's aloneness; perhaps the man himself is not aware of it.

28. It is striking that the Bible at the beginning of Genesis 4 does not record any pain associated with Eve's bearing of her two children.

29. There is no reason to think, however, that the man's desire for the woman abates. The man continues to leave his parents and cleave to his wife.

30. Many changes occur in this narrative. The woman's name changes. The man goes from cleaver to ruler. The man who was alone is now the object of the woman's desire. The woman becomes not just a companion or helper but one who desires. The human race becomes subject to mortality.

31. Remarkably, the very God who lovingly gives man life, who creates the woman for the man's sake, and who endows the man and the woman with wisdom and power and provides for them by permitting them the fruit of all the Garden's trees but one, is the same God who must ultimately punish them. Note that the text does not say that God is angry, although His *actions* might cause us to suppose that He is. As I have argued above, however, God accepts some of the responsibility for the man's sin.

32. I am not arguing here for strict biblical monotheism. I am saying only that in Genesis 2 and 3 there is but one God interacting with the man and the woman (as indicated, in particular, by the use of the masculine singular verb throughout).

33. There is no suggestion that the woman is created to help Adam tend the Garden; she is created to relieve his aloneness insofar as no suitable partner has been found for him. God's recognition that none of the animals will do is His cue to take another tack. It is interesting that the other time there is a similar pronouncement that a situation is 'not good' (*lo tov*) is when Jethro determines that it is not good for Moses to judge the people *alone* (see Exod. 18.17–18). The fact that there is further elaboration of just what is not good in the Jethro–Moses case leads one to attribute the lack of elaboration in the Adam case to that it was his aloneness in itself that was the problem. And consider the difference in remedy. In the Jethro–Moses case, other judges are appointed to help specifically with the task of judging; in the Adam case, all that is supplied is a woman to be his general partner and helper.

34. Whenever the Torah speaks of the human's having been created male and female, the pronoun switches to the plural, 'them'. This occurs not only in Gen. 1.27, but see Gen. 5.1–2: 'This is the book of the generations of Adam [the human] on the day God created him; in the likeness of God He made him. Male and female He created *them*; He blessed *them* and called *their* name "adam" ["human"] on the day *they* were created.'

35. In the case of the *tanninim hagedolim* ('great sea monsters') and the living beings that swarmed from the earth and every winged bird (Gen. 2.21), God created them (*vayivra*), saw that it was good, and blessed them. In the case of the other animals (Gen. 2.25), God saw it was good [after He made them – *vaya'as*]. In the case of man (Gen. 2.27), however, God created them and blessed them ('be fruitful and multiply'); the absence of 'And God saw that it was good' in the case of man is thus quite glaring.

CHAPTER 8
EVE, THE FIRST WOMAN: ON CHOICE AND RESPONSIBILITY

Yael Shemesh

The story of the first woman, Eve, is first and foremost a story about choice. Apart from the evident choice – that of the first woman, and then of the man – to reach for the forbidden fruit and bite into it, I am primarily concerned with the reader's choice about how to understand the event, which is described as a constitutive and disturbing event in human history. Another issue to be dealt with is: what are the meanings to be drawn from the description of this event as to the shaping of Eve's character? This question is particularly important in light of the fact that Eve is the first woman and as such she may be perceived as an archetype of all women.

As a matter of fact, the readers' choice and their responsibility for how they understand the biblical text about Eve begins even before the story about the sin in Genesis 3. As will be shown below, we encounter it in its full power and polarity already in Genesis 2 – the second creation story. As for admitting responsibility, we do not find even a single instance of this on the part of the narrative characters in Genesis 3, in the hearing that God conducts for the three defendants – the man, the woman and the serpent – immediately after the sin. Adam places the responsibility on Eve and on God who gave her to him as a wife (verse 12). Eve places the responsibility on the serpent (verse 13). And the latter's voice is not heard at all. Therefore, when I speak about 'responsibility', I refer solely to the reader's responsibility for the way they choose to interpret the events. The question that arises from a gender-related perspective is whether the readers ascribe to the events a meaning that enfeebles or empowers women.

The biblical text is often vague. Mostly, the narrator does not explicitly assess a certain act as being good or bad, hence this is open to different possible interpretations. This, of course, means that the reader's role in producing meaning becomes particularly significant. In the present chapter, I intend to outline different ways of understanding the character of Eve, both with regard to the story of her creation in chapter 2, and with regard to the story about sin and punishment in chapter 3. Although I will refer to both ancient and modern interpretations, I will focus mainly on feminist exegesis of the Bible.

Feminist exegesis of the Bible is not homogenous. In a previous article, I pointed out the existence of two opposing tendencies, which I characterized as militant feminist scholarship and mediating feminist scholarship.[1] The purpose of militant feminist research is to demonstrate the overall patriarchal and androcentric, some even claim misogynistic, orientation of the Bible. As such, it is not worthy of serving as a culture-establishing text.[2] In contrast, mediating feminist scholarship does admit that the Bible is patriarchal and androcentric, but rejects the claim that it is infected with misogyny.

The aim of mediating feminist research is not to provide further evidence for what is obvious – that the Bible is patriarchal. Rather, it seeks to illuminate additional aspects of the Bible, which ascribe to women partial or full equality with men, thus creating a bridge between the ancient biblical text and modern feminist ideology.[3] These opposing tendencies are, of course, also reflected in the commentators' attitude toward the stories about Eve, both the story of her creation in chapter 2 and the story about sin and punishment in chapter 3.

The character of Eve in light of the interpretations of the story about her creation in Chapter 2

Genesis 2 constitutes an important foundation in militant feminist scholarship on the Bible, since it describes Eve as having been created in retrospect; that is, her creation was not part of the initial plan but came about due to a reconsideration of man's existential plight. She was created to serve as man's helper, and her existence has no independent justification.

Before I turn to biblical scholarship, I would like to present the opinion of the French philosopher Simone de Beauvoir on this issue. In her book *The Second Sex*, which presents a broad overview of the discrimination against women throughout human history, de Beauvoir refers to the creation of the woman as described in Genesis 2:

> Eve was not fashioned at the same time as the man; She was not fabricated from a different substance, nor of the same clay as was used to model Adam: she was taken from a flank of the first male. Not even her birth was independent; God did not spontaneously choose to create her as an end in itself and in order to be worshiped directly by her in return for it. She was destined by Him for man; it was to rescue Adam from loneliness that He gave her to him, in her mate was her origin and her purpose; she was his complement on the order of the inessential.[4]

In these words, de Beauvoir expresses a widespread perception in biblical exegesis and probably also among the general public.

Such an interpretation was already suggested by Elizabeth Cady Stanton, a contemporary of Simone de Beauvoir. Stanton, one of the leaders of the American suffrage movement in the nineteenth century, edited the revolutionary book that was at the time regarded as outrageous, *The Woman's Bible* (1895, 1898), which aimed to offer a gendered interpretation of those parts of the Bible that contain gender-related aspects. The book follows the order of the Scriptures. Few women agreed to take part in this revolutionary project, hence Stanton herself actually authored the greater part of the book. In her discussion on Eve, Stanton wrote that chapter 2 presents her as a mere afterthought and that the whole purpose of her creation is the solitude of man,[5] that is, her existence has no independent purpose. However, unlike Simone de Beauvoir, Stanton also discusses the creation story in chapter 1. She calls upon her readers to reject the non-egalitarian creation story in Genesis 2 and to adopt the first creation story in Gen. 1.27, which, she claims, describes the simultaneous and egalitarian creation of man and woman in the image of God: 'So God created man in his own image, in the image of God he created him; male and female he created them.'[6] According to Stanton, the egalitarian creation story in chapter 1 ought to satisfy both genders, since it teaches that both are 'created alike in the image of God – The Heavenly Mother and Father'.[7] She views the story of creation in chapter 2 as an inner-biblical response of 'some wily writer' who composed this chapter as a polemic against the egalitarian tendency reflected in 1.27.[8] However, her thesis is inconsistent with the findings of biblical higher criticism (the historical-critical method), according to which the Priestly source (P), to which chapter 1 is attributed, is later than the Yahwist source (J), to which chapters 2–3 are attributed.[9]

An interpretation similar to the one offered by Stanton, a Christian, is offered by Rachel Adler in *The Torah: A Women's Commentary*, which offers different interpretations and discussions by female Jewish scholars and artists on the weekly portion. In section 2 – 'Another View' – which deals with one aspect of the weekly portion, Adler represents in her remarks on the portion of Genesis the prevailing opinion that chapters 2–3 in the Book of Genesis constitute the 'creation of patriarchy'.[10] According to her, already in the creation of Eve as narrated in Genesis 2, the woman is described as being inferior to the man, as one who was created in retrospect, from man's body and for his need, to serve as an עזר כנגדו, literally 'a helper over against him', or in the RSV translation, a 'helper fit for him' (Gen. 2.18). Man gives her a name, as he did to the animals, and it never occurs to him to ask for her name.[11]

The great variety of views found within feminist exegesis is illustrated by the fact that Adler's work in *The Torah: A Women's Commentary* was preceded by the commentary of Tamara Cohn Eskenazi. Eskenazi wrote the first and main section on the portion of Genesis, in the form of a running commentary on the verses. She perceives things in a completely different way, pointing out different aspects of the first chapters in the Book of Genesis that empower the character of Eve.[12] In this, Eskenazi followed in the footsteps of Phyllis Trible, who in her pioneering and influential article called for 'Depatriarchalizing in Biblical Interpretation', meaning to strip the Bible of its patriarchal foundations, which, in her opinion, had been imposed by generations of both Jewish and Christian exegesis.[13] Trible's stated goal was to build a bridge between the ancient biblical text, which at the beginning of her article she admits to be a patriarchalist text, and modern feminist ideology.[14] She does this, among other methods, by presenting the egalitarian relationship between man and woman in the *Song of Songs*,[15] a text that is friendly to mediating feminist scholarship. However, this analysis is preceded by a much less obvious interpretation of the story that is generally perceived as being blatantly unfriendly and extremely problematic for mediating feminist scholarship – the story about the creation of the woman and her sin in Genesis 2–3. One of her main arguments is that scholars have read these texts through the lense of an early and biased assumption about the inferiority of women, causing them to find in the text what they expected to find in it from the outset.[16] Her aim is to reread them independently of the exegetical blunders imposed on them by both Jewish and Christian analysis.[17]

How can depatriarchalization be carried out in Genesis 2, and what are the empowering foundations that Trible and scholars following her found in the story of the woman's creation? Against the claim that the male is more important than the female because he was created first, Trible argues that until the creation of the gender distinction between 'man' and 'woman', male and female (Gen. 2.23), the term 'man' referred to humankind in general. This was an androgynous creature made of clay.[18] Only after the creation of the woman is the male first called a 'man', so that in fact the creation of the gendered identities of man and woman is simultaneous.[19] Only after the creation of the woman does the male speak for the first time, identifying himself as a 'man'.[20]

However, Trible may have been aware of the difficulty inherent in this interpretation, because in its wake she deals with the claim that from the gender-related point of view the woman was created last, and this time on the assumption that this claim is correct. To this she replies:

> The last may be first, as both the biblical theologian and the literary critic know [...] She is not an afterthought; she is the culmination.[21]

Here she relies on the fact than in the first creation story in Genesis 1, humans were created last, as the crown of creation.[22]

As for the purpose of the creation of the woman as 'a helper fit for him', often perceived as an expression of her inferiority, Trible rightly clarifies that the meaning of the word 'helper' depends on the context. For example, when the Bible describes God as man's helper, this obviously refers to His superior position that makes him able to help. God helps man and saves him (Exod. 18.4; Ps. 70.6; Ps. 121.1–2). The second creation story describes the failed attempt to create the animals as man's helper, as evidenced by the fact that immediately after the words 'I will make him a helper fit for him' (Gen. 2.18), Scripture narrates the creation of the animals and the interaction between them and Adam, who called them by name (Gen. 2.19–20). The scene ends with the words 'but for Adam there was not found a helper fit for him'. In contrast to God who is Adam's helper by virtue of His superiority, and in contrast to the animals whose inferiority prevented them from serving as his helper, Trible suggests that the woman is man's helper due to her equal status.[23] Tamara Eskenazi accepts Trible's interpretation and clarifies the point: 'Only an equal who is both "other" and "alike" provides the necessary dialogue for human maturation, meaning, and joy'.[24] As for the description of the creation of the woman, Trible emphasizes that man did not take an active part in it. In fact, at the time of the woman's creation, man was in a deep sleep. He is the material from which she is created, but he is not her creator. Only God created the woman, as He created the man. The woman owes her existence solely to God. Trible notes that man was created from dust, while the woman was created from a rib. Creation from a rib is by no means inferior to creation from dust, dirt. In any case, the source of life for both the male and the female is a divine mystery. Calling Eve 'Adam's Rib' does injustice to the biblical description, according to which 'the extracted bone required divine labor to become female'. According to Trible, the disregard for this fact is meant to bolster the male ego.[25]

Moreover, the creation of the female from the rib of the man indicates solidarity between them, as expressed by the man in the festive poem he utters:

> This at last is bone of my bones
> and flesh of my flesh
> She shall be called אשה 'woman'
> Because she was taken out of איש 'man'.
>
> *Gen. 2.23*

The final words of chapter 2, 'and they shall become one flesh' (2.24), creates a circular structure: out of a single androgynous creature two came forth – a man and a woman – but they are meant to become 'one flesh' again.[26]

Trible points out that the woman is not called by name here, an action that expresses control and ownership, but only defined by her gender. 'Woman' is a common noun, not a proper noun. The man recognizes the different genders of the woman and the man.[27] Only after the sin does the man speak the name of the woman – Eve (3.20). While this indicates the man's control over the woman, this control does not reflect the initial divine intention but stems from an accident, a perversion caused by the sin.[28]

The character of Eve in light of the interpretations of the story about the sin in chapter 3

This last point leads us to the exegesis on the shaping of Eve's character in the story about the first human sin in chapter 3. This story continues to exemplify the various possibilities of choice, the importance of the choice and the reader's responsibility for their understanding of the story. In a previous article, I demonstrated this through an examination of the various and even contradictory answers given to the question of why the serpent chose to tempt Eve rather than Adam.[29] In the present study I will focus on other questions touching upon the shaping of Eve's character in light of the exegesis on chapter 3 and its attitude toward the first human sin.

Ben-Sirach condemned all women because of the sin of the first woman: 'From a woman is the beginning of sin / and because of her we all die' (Sirach 25.24). The Talmudic sages viewed Eve as having shed the blood of Adam, wherefore she was punished with menstrual blood according to the principle of 'measure for measure':

> Said the Holy One, blessed be He: 'She shed the blood of Adam, hence her own blood must be shed', as it is written: 'Whoever sheds the blood of man' and so forth (Gen 9:6) – because she shed the blood of Adam, her blood must be shed.[30]

Paul used that which is told about the sin of the woman and about her being created after the man for the purpose of gender construction, which of course discriminates against women:

> Let a woman learn quietly with all submissiveness. I do not permit a woman to teach or to exercise authority over a man; rather, she is to remain quiet. For Adam was formed first, then Eve; and Adam was not deceived, but the woman was deceived and became a transgressor [1 Timothy 2.11–14] [. . .] The salvation of women will be achieved only through childbirth and holding on to the way of faith. [1 Timothy 2.15]

As might be expected, militant feminist scholarship has widely discussed the character of Eve as it is shaped in Genesis 2–3. As for chapter 3, Eve is described as being guilty of the disaster that befell the human race with its expulsion from the Garden of Eden. Some feminist scholars present her as a stereotype of the curious and disobedient woman, as well as a stereotype of the seductive woman, who due to her negative traits has wreaked havoc on herself and the entire human race.[31] According to Esther Fuchs, Eve is also a stereotype of a cheating woman, and her character is shaped as being morally inferior to Adam because she caused him to commit a moral-religious sin. That is why Eve and all women with her are punished by accepting the rule and authority of the husband over them, and the role set for women is a biological role – childbirth (3.16).[32]

Fuchs does not present evidence for her claim that Eve deceived. She seems to accept the interpretation that Eve did not reveal to man the origin of the fruit she served him. Such an interpretation of course defames the character of Eve, and is found in the midrash:

> [When] Eve ate from the fruits of the tree, she saw the Angel of Death approaching her. She said: 'It seems that I am about to leave this world, and that He will create another woman for Adam instead of me. What should I do? I will make him eat also', as it is written: 'She took of its fruit and ate, and she also gave some to her husband who was with her, and he ate' (3.6).[33]

However, such a cunning and malicious series of events is not narrated in the biblical story. The fact that Adam does not claim ignorance in the hearing that God conducts for him, along with the fact that he was also severely punished, implies that he knew full well that he was eating from the forbidden fruit. Thus Ibn Ezra explains in his commentary on Gen. 3.6: '"And she also gave some to her husband" – after having informed him that the fruit is from the Tree of Knowledge. Hence, also he was punished.'[34]

According to Trible, Adam and Eve 'are equal in responsibility and in judgment, in shame and in guilt, in redemption and grace'.[35] Moreover, the woman is described as a 'decision-maker'. She decides to eat from the forbidden fruit only after she has objected to the serpent, heard his answer and considered the various qualities of the fruit, including its being 'desirable to make one wise' (v. 6). Thus, Trible observes, 'If the woman be intelligent, sensitive, and ingenious, the man is passive, brutish, and inept.'[36]

With regard to the punishment that establishes unequal relations between the genders – 'he will rule over you' (v. 16) – Trible emphasizes that this was not God's initial intention, but a fault caused by the sin. It spoiled the harmonious equality of the genders, and both males and females suffer from it.[37] Moreover, the punishment of the man and the woman is not a commandment, but a description of the sad reality created in the wake of sin:

> We misread if we assume these judgments are mandates. They describe; they do not prescribe [. . .] The suffering and oppression we women and men know now are marks of our fall, not of our creation.[38]

Several scholars have followed Trible in identifying empowering elements in the character of the woman as shaped in the story about the sin in chapter 3 and have added some aspects to her remarks. For example, Fewell and Gunn have presented a parallel between the woman and God: Eve is an explorer, like God who created the world through trial and error.[39] They praise her adventurous spirit, which makes her resemble God, and her courage and willingness to take risks.[40] Meyers has emphasized the connection between the woman and the wisdom that emerges from the story. The woman is the first human character to utter language, the hallmark of the human race, and she does so in a clear and fluent manner. The first woman plays an important role in the acquisition of knowledge, of wisdom. Her conversation with the cunning serpent shows her intellectual ability.[41]

Meyers also emphasized that 'fall' in the sense of the consequences of the first human sin is a Christian concept not found in the Bible.[42] The perception of Eve as the source of human sin does not emerge from the story about the Garden of Eden. The Bible does not link the many later sins to the first sin, nor did the prophets mention the sin of Adam and Eve.[43] Regarding Eve's punishment, Meyers followed medieval commentators (e.g. Naḥmanides and Ḥazzekuni) in explaining its final part – 'and he will rule over you' (Gen. 3.16) – in relation to previous statements about the difficulties that women will experience during pregnancy and childbirth and their sexual passion for men. According to this interpretation, man's dominion over the woman is not an absolute dominion touching upon all areas of life, but only relating to sexual relations. Men will be able to overcome the reluctance of women to have intimate relations stemming from the expected suffering of pregnancy and childbirth. Thus, according to this explanation, the demographic needs of the people of Israel overcome women's fear of pregnancies and births that endanger their lives and cause them suffering.[44]

Also, Eskenazi has pointed out the positive aspects of Eve's personality. She is the source of life – 'the mother of all living' (Gen. 3.20); a bold and wise character who was given the opportunity to speak both in her conversation with the serpent and in the names she gave to her descendants (4.1, 25).[45] Eskenazi further argued that beginning with the bold character of Eve, the women in the Book of Genesis were destined to play key roles, which in fact refutes the opinion that Genesis favours men over women.[46]

Athalya Brenner presented a balanced discussion of the character of Eve in her book *The Israelite Woman*. On the one hand, the woman sinned by disobeying God, and the human race was punished for this sin. But on the other hand, sin also has blessed consequences for the human race, such as self-awareness and closeness to God. For even though a physical distance is created between the first couple and God following the expulsion from the Garden of Eden, they are essentially closer to God. This is due to their new ability, granted them in the wake of the sin, to distinguish between good and evil. God himself testifies to this: 'Behold, man has become like one of Us in knowing good and evil' (Gen. 3.22). In fact, eating the forbidden fruit has brought the human race to the level of maturity and civilization, culture and social order.[47]

Eve as creator: An additional look at Eve – Genesis 4

In general, feminist scholarship dealing with the character of Eve has focused mainly on chapters 1–3. Ilana Pardes has criticized this focus and noted that Eve also plays an important role in the verse that opens chapter 4: 'Now Adam knew Eve his wife, and she conceived and bore Cain, saying: "I have gotten a man with the help of the Lord"'. Eve changes from being an object that receives its name from a male character (3.20) into a subject that gives a name to a male character, her son Cain. The name she gives him expresses her pride in her power to create, which she presents as approximating the creative power of the Creator Himself: I have created a man together with God. In this explanation of the name, Eve presents herself as God's partner in the act of creation. In all the remaining biblical occurrences of the root קנ"ה in the meaning of creation, the reference is to divine creation (e.g. Gen. 14.19, 22: 'The Creator of Heaven and Earth'; Ps. 139.13: 'For You formed my inward parts').[48] According to Pardes, Eve rebels against the secondary role given to her in the very sphere in which the female body plays a key role. When boasting about her creative powers, she in fact abolishes the connection between motherhood and subordination, which is found in the punishments imposed on her in chapter 3. Thus, 'the first feminist reader of the creation story is none other than Eve herself'.[49]

Summary

Eve, the first woman, is seen as an archetype of all daughters of Eve, hence the great importance of the way we interpret her character in the creation stories in Genesis 1–2 as well as in the story about the sin in chapter 3, which narrates her decision to eat from the forbidden fruit. The biblical text does not provide us with the narrator's explicit evaluation either of how Eve was created in chapter 2, or of her decision to sin in chapter 3. Hence, the readers' responsibility for the way they understand the Scriptures must be recognized. Is it an interpretation that weakens women (such as the words of Ben Sirach condemning women, or Paul's instruction to women not to prevail over men), or perhaps an interpretation that aims to empower women? And if the purpose of the interpretation is to empower women, will it do so by weakening the status of the biblical text as a culture-establishing text, as some militant feminist scholars have done, or by trying to build a bridge between the ancient biblical text and feminist ideology, as has been done by mediating feminist scholars? The meaning we attribute to the Scriptures is perhaps no less important than Eve's decision in chapter 3, as it shapes the attitude of human culture to both women and the biblical text in every generation.

Furthermore, as shown by Pardes, the very boundaries of the biblical corpus on the basis of which the character of Eve is analysed also affect the way her character is perceived. If we turn our gaze to one more verse beyond the boundaries of which our study has focused, chapters 1–3, we realize that in Gen. 4.1 Eve transforms from creature into creator. From being a woman who received her name from a man, she turns into a woman who gives a name to a man, boasts of her creative powers and abolishes the link between motherhood and subordination.

Notes

1. Yael Shemesh, 'Directions in Jewish feminist Bible study', *Currents in Biblical Research* 14 (2016): 372–406.
2. Shemesh, 'Directions in Jewish feminist Bible study', 375–9.
3. Shemesh, 'Directions in Jewish feminist Bible study', 379–87.
4. Simone de Beauvoir, *The Second Sex*, trans. and ed. H. M. Parshley (New York: Vintage Books, 1952/1974), 159.
5. Elizabeth Cady Stanton, *The Woman's Bible* (New York: Dover Publications, 2002 (1895)), 20.
6. Stanton, *The Woman's Bible*, 21. See also pages 14–16 on the equalitarian character of chapter 1. Most scholars and exegetes, but not all, ascribe to the view that the first creation story views both man and woman as created in the image of God. The wording of the verse 'so God created man in his own image, in the image of God he created him; male and female he created them' (1.27) makes it possible to understand the word 'man' as referring to the human race as a whole. This is the accepted understanding, which is supported by additional verses, such as Gen. 5.2: 'And He named them "man" when they were created.' However, due to the singular form 'in the image of God he created <u>him</u>', the word 'man' may also be understood as a reference to the male only, the first created man (similar to the occurrence of this word in Gen. 4.25, 5.3, etc.). Indeed, R. Isaac Abarbanel, in his outrageous commentary on Gen. 1.27, explained that the male is 'the principal creation' and only he was created in the image of God. The woman, in contrast, 'whose wisdom lies in her ability to operate the spindle', was only 'created with the intention of serving as man's helper and maintaining the human species'.
7. Stanton, *The Woman's Bible*, 21.
8. Stanton, *The Woman's Bible*, 21.
9. As noted by Pardes in her criticism of Stanton. See Ilana Pardes, *Countertraditions in the Bible* (London: Harvard University Press, 1992), 17.
10. Rachel Adler, 'B'reishit – Contemporary Reflection', in *The Torah: A Women's Commentary*, ed. Tamara Cohn Eskenazi and Andrea L. Weiss (New York: WRJ, 2008), 31.
11. Adler, 'B'reishit – Contemporary Reflection', 30–1.
12. Tamara Cohn Eskenazi, 'B'reishit', in *The Torah: A Women's Commentary*, ed. Tamara Cohn Eskenazi and Andrea L. Weiss (New York: WRJ, 2008), 9, 12–13.
13. Phyllis Trible, 'Depatriarchalizing in Biblical Interpretation', *Journal of the American Academy of Religion* 41, no. 1 (1973): 31.

14. Trible, 'Depatriarchalizing', 30, 31, 48.
15. Trible, 'Depatriarchalizing', 42–7.
16. Trible, 'Depatriarchalizing', 35.
17. Trible, 'Depatriarchalizing', 31.
18. Trible, 'Depatriarchalizing', 35. Interestingly, also according to the midrash, the first human being was created androgynous: 'Rabbi Yirmiyah son of Elazar said: When the Holy One, blessed be He, created man, he created him both male and female, as it is written: "Male and female He created them"' (Genesis Rabbah (Vilna), Genesis 8). Trible does not mention the midrash, and she might have reached this conclusion independently.
19. Trible, 'Depatriarchalizing', 37.
20. Trible, 'Depatriarchalizing', 38.
21. Cf. Harold Bloom, *The Book of J* (New York: Vintage Books, 1991), 179–80. Bloom compares the creation of the male to 'making a mud pie', while the creation of the female he views as 'building a much more elaborate and fairer structure' (180).
22. Trible, 'Depatriarchalizing', 36.
23. Trible, 'Depatriarchalizing', 36. Thus also Carol Meyers, *Discovering Eve: Ancient Israelite Women in Context* (New York: Oxford University Press, 1988), 85; Eskenazi, 'B'reishit', 12; Rachel Reich, *'The Woman Whom Thou Gavest to be with Me'* (Tel Aviv: Hakibbutz Hameuchad, 2005), 16–17.
24. Eskenazi, 'B'reishit', 12.
25. Trible, 'Depatriarchalizing', 37.
26. Trible, 'Depatriarchalizing', 39.
27. Trible, 'Depatriarchalizing', 38.
28. Trible, 'Depatriarchalizing', 41.
29. Yael Shemesh, 'Why did the Serpent Choose to Address Eve, rather than Adam (Gen 3:1): Eve, the Serpent, and the Reader's Responsibility', *Ve-'Ed Ya'aleh (Gen 2:6): Essays in Biblical and Ancient Near Eastern Studies Presented to Edward L. Greenstein*, eds. Peter Machinist et al. (Atlanta: SBL, forthcoming).
30. Midrash Tanḥuma (Buber), Metzorah 17. See also y. Shab. 2.6 (20a); Genesis Rabbah, Bereshit, 17; Avot de-Rabbi Nathan, 2nd recension, chap. 9.
31. Yair Mazor, '"Cherchez la femme", or Sex, Lies and the Bible: Exposing the Anti-Feminist Face of the Biblical Text', *SJOT* 18 (2004): 39–40.
32. Esther Fuchs, *Sexual Politics in the Biblical Narrative: Reading the Hebrew Bible as a Woman*, JSOTSup, 310 (Sheffield: Sheffield Academic Press, 2000), 175–6.
33. Minor Tractates, Avot de-Rabbi Nathan, 2nd recension, chap. 1.
34. R. Abraham ibn Ezra, Long Commentary ad loc. So also Radak.
35. Trible, 'Depatriarchalizing', 40.
36. Trible, 'Depatriarchalizing', 40.
37. Trible, 'Depatriarchalizing', 41.
38. Trible, 'Depatriarchalizing', 41.
39. Danna Nolan Fewell and David M. Gunn, *Gender, Power and Promise* (Nashville: Abingdon Press, 1993), 30.
40. Fewell and Gunn, *Gender, Power and Promise*, 31.

41. Meyers, *Discovering Eve*, 91–2, and also Reich, *The Woman*, 19–22.
42. Meyers, *Discovering Eve*, 77. See also Pardes, *Countertraditions*, 39–40.
43. Meyers, *Discovering Eve*, 87. Cf. Pardes, *Countertraditions*, 39.
44. Meyers, *Discovering Eve*, 95–118.
45. Eskenazi, 'B'reishit', 13–19, 22.
46. Eskenazi, 'B'reishit', 2.
47. Athalya Brenner, *The Israelite Woman: Social Role and Literary Type in Biblical Narrative* (Sheffield: JSOT, 1985), 127–8.
48. Pardes, *Countertraditions*, 39–47.
49. Pardes, *Countertraditions*, 47.

CHAPTER 9
ABSOLVING EVE: MEDIEVAL WOMEN WRITERS REMODELLING THE CREATION AND THE FALL[1]

Tovi Bibring

The mythological[2] elements of Adam and Eve's creation, their short-lived time in paradise,[3] the original sin and the fall that followed it, have never ceased to inspire theologians, philosophers, poets and artists. The most conspicuous concern in such interpretative narratives, constantly referred to in varied manners, is the perception of gender hierarchy. Feministic consciousness about the Eden story infiltrated the intellectual and belletristic worlds by the twelfth century. The renowned German abbess Hildegard of Bingen, for example, presented an Eve 'whose soul was innocent',[4] an Eve that had transgressed the divine order, but was less responsible than Satan for this transgression, an Eve who, as the mother of the entire human race, was analogous to the Christ.[5] In this chapter, I would like to present two outstanding medieval female voices reinterpreting Genesis and exempting Eve from the prevalent prejudice. The first case study concerns the twelfth-century acclaimed French poetess, Marie de France, who might well have been, like Hildegard, an abbess. In one of her Christianized fables, 'Del reclus e del vilein' (Of the Hermite and the Peasant), she begins by asking troubling questions about the fall, continues by presenting the traditional patriarchal views and summarizes by reminding her readers of the initial equality between Adam (presented as equally responsible for the misery of mankind) and Eve, offering an original thesis about gender equality. The second case study, composed in the thirteenth century by an anonymous woman, is a reply to Richard de Fournival's *Le bestiaire d'amour* (The Bestiary of Love). Richard de Fournival, a disappointed, passionate suitor, composed a manifesto to the Lady he admired. Unable to accept her refusal to return his love, his redaction is full of misogynistic stereotypes illustrated through animal anecdotes and fables. Four of the extant manuscripts contain an anonymous *Response* written by the lady who inspired the manifesto (referred to henceforth as the Lady), resenting and rejecting the biases and prejudices against women. The point of departure for her feminist reaction is a new reading of the creation, where Eve is presented as created out of Adam's rib, a superior material, and therefore she is, at the very least, his equal.

Marie de France, 'Del reclus e del vilein' (Of the Hermit and the Peasant)

Fable 53, usually referred to simply as 'l'érmite' (the hermit), tells the story of a peasant who, every time he heard the hermit utter the word 'God', repeated the same question:

'why did Adam eat the fruit, by which [deed] he destroyed all mankind and, when he did eat the apple, why did God not pardon him?'[6] Finally, the exhausted hermit took a mouse, hid it under a bowl and ordered the peasant to stay away from it while he went to church. The minute the hermit left, the peasant could not help but raise the bowl, and the mouse fled. Furious, the hermit asked the peasant why he disobeyed him, and the peasant answers that he could not resist, he had to discover what was beneath the bowl, or else 'my heart would have departed [from my body]'. The hermit said that had the peasant kept the mouse, he could be forgiven for his disobedience, but the latter answered that the mouse ran too fast and escaped. The hermit concluded his exercise with an analogy: the peasant, himself a sinner, should not blame Adam, who, through his wife, was a victim of Satan himself. Marie de France then passes to the moral lesson, the morality, and concludes the fable; 'Thus no one should accuse, nor blame fellow people's doings, nor defame others. Every person should castigate himself! He who thinks to condemn the action of his fellow man, should better criticize himself.'

Initially, the peasant's obstinance in re-examining dogmatic principles is perceived as an annoying and basic ignorance, and his attempt to engage in a theological debate is invalidated (as the hermit does not answer him for a long time). Finally, his query is demonstrated by a farcical experiment (the mouse and the bowl),[7] followed by a verbal explanation (the dialogue between the peasant and the hermit and the hermit's moral lesson, which is separate from Marie's global morality at the end of the fable). Thus, the hermit's answers to the peasant start by analysing the latter's personal analogous experience and end with the former's institutional knowledge. Such institutional conformism, however, is challenged by Marie de France's Augustinian approach.

While this fable has been studied in depth by a few eminent scholars, I wish to add complementary considerations, specifically in the context of the medieval pro-feminine meditations about Eve.[8] Written in the twelfth century, I believe that much of Marie de France's 'feminist' voice is based upon Augustinian ideas about the creation. Although Augustine of Hippo was one of the most influential theorists of medieval scholasticism, his understanding of Genesis differed from that which was adopted by the Church. According to Augustine, man and woman shared equal responsibility for the transgression, a transgression that was made possible thanks to free will that was accorded to both in the second instance of the creation.[9] Free will, though, is a complicated notion, as it may be confused with the concept of evil inclination.[10] Medieval theologians tended to put most of the responsibility on Eve, labelling her as a double sinner, a transgressor and a temptress motivated by her *female* inclination, which is evil. The hermit explains Adam's sin precisely according to the scene of the feminine satanic seduction. The fabulist, on the other hand, calls for an introspective examination. The fable thus presents two different moral lessons representing two different, contradicting approaches. The mainstream premises are defended by the hermit; the Augustinian stream is reflected by Marie.

Accordingly, the trigger that permitted the hermit and the fabulist to expose their thoughts, namely the peasant, symbol of ignorance, represents different things to the hermit and the fabulist. For the fabulist, the peasant stands for the symbol of the human ignorance to which Augustine refers in his *De libero arbitrio* (On Free Choice of the Will), considered to be one of the punishments (together with 'difficulty') that mankind received for committing the first sin: 'the flesh descended from the first sinner causes ignorance and difficulties for the souls that enter it'.[11] Therefore, I believe that though it seems that the peasant is referring in his question specifically to Adam, in fact his words should be taken generically, referring to both Adam and Eve, that is, to humankind, as an equivalent to *homo*.[12] The peasant's intention is not to differentiate between Adam and Eve, but rather to comprehend why humans, who were created by God, sinned, and why God did not forgive them. His question reverberates with a rhetorical question presented by Augustine:

> Here we come across the slanderous question that is so often asked by those who are ready to blame their sins on anything but themselves: 'If it was Adam and Eve who sinned, what did we poor wretches do? How do we deserve to be born in the blindness of ignorance and the torture of difficulty? Why do we first err in ignorance of what we ought to do, and then, when the precepts of justice begin to be open to us and we will to do them, we are powerless, held back by some sort of necessity of carnal desire?'[13]

In the hermit's eyes, the peasant is a nuisance, representing savagery and lack of rationality, morals and finesse. More importantly, as a result of 'the cultural perception of the peasants as bestial, ignorant and filthy and therefore debased, inferior and gullible', his role here is somewhat blurred with that of a woman, who was similarly perceived in the medieval mentality.[14] The peasant's stigmatic and demeaning representation as foolish and mentally feeble permits a marginalized voice to be heard, a voice seeking new answers about discriminatory conceptions, perhaps the voice of a rebellious woman? In other terms, on the symbolical level, the peasant is genderless, he is conceptual. For the fabulist, he is every person, man and woman, who wishes to understand fundamental issues about the human condition. For the hermit, he is a despised man, interchangeable with a woman,[15] in the sense that he represents alienation, an 'other'. He asks a dangerous question, shaking the solid walls of dogmatic Christianity and patriarchy, and dividable into two components. The first deals with 'why did Adam eat the fruit', and the second with 'why did God not forgive'. The peasant's symbolical genderless state is apparent in the experiment where he incarnates simultaneously Adam and Eve. The hermit who conceived the experiment seems to be confused himself. He takes the question's first part (why did Adam eat the fruit?) literally, as if the peasant blamed only Adam, and respectively parallels the peasant's failure to keep the bowl intact to Adam's eating the fruit. The hermit thus reflects the peasant's infraction by turning the question right back at him: 'why did he lift the bowl?', stressing the transgression by reminding the peasant of the divine order and asking why he 'couldn't keep his [i.e. the hermit's] interdiction?'

To this, the peasant answers, 'Sir, he says, I could not resist, my heart would have departed [from my body].' The peasant potentially initiates an intellectual theological debate about the notions of evil inclination and free will, recognizing his irrational submission to doing evil.

The hermit seems deaf to this and, detached from the narrative of what the peasant has just experienced,[16] returns to the traditional acceptance of the biblical narrative, exempting Adam from responsibility as he was tempted by a now satanic woman: 'You should not blame Adam if he ate the fruit of the tree, which our lord forbade him. The devil advised him, tricked him using his wife, promised him such great supremacy that he would be equal to the Creator.' However, we may see that the exemplification of Adam's situation through his experiment with the peasant is lacking, since the peasant (whether in the role of Adam or Eve) was not subject to third-party temptation promising him wonderful things, and as Jacques Merceron says, he did not know what was in the bowl.[17] The question's second part ('why did God not forgive Adam?'), on the other hand, reflects the hermit's perceived correlation between the peasant and Eve. In the display, the hermit takes on the role of God (as he was the one who ordered that the bowl not be touched), attempting to demonstrate the unforgivable nature of a double transgression: 'What happened with the mouse? Why did you not keep it? Your folly could have been pardoned!' According to this response, the peasant and his actions with the bowl would parallel Eve's actions with the forbidden fruit, rather than Adam's. The hermit attacks the peasant first for looking under the bowl and then for letting the mouse escape, which is equivalent to Eve first eating the apple and then convincing Adam to eat it, while Adam only committed one transgression.[18] Thus, the hermit suggests that Eve's sin was not forgiven because it was twofold.[19] Interestingly, the hermit forgives the peasant for his transgression: 'Friend, he told him, now let it be,' and thus, ironically, he reinforces the question he was asked. Furthermore, the hermit now moves on to fully exonerate Adam: 'You shouldn't blame Adam.' If Adam is not to blame, the question is perpetuated: why did God not forgive him?

Hence, the (feminized) peasant is denigrated, stereotypically represented as ridiculous. His intellectual curiosity is dismissed and conceptualized as a feminine nosiness. Ridicule, denigration and dismissal are the best weapons in a struggle against the danger represented by woman, in this case wielded within the solid patriarchal discourse about femininity itself. To use Sahar Amer's words, 'the peasant's query is all the more alarming insofar as it reflects a critical mind that the church needed to suppress in order to continue to uphold the supremacy of its interpretations and male power in general'.[20]

If the peasant represents a woman's voice, and the hermit represents a man's, the fable proves the eternal failure of reconciliation between them. The peasant asks disconcerting questions that the hermit fails to address. As noted by Merceron, 'we can think that it is due to his inability to provide any other explanation than a tautological reference to Genesis'.[21] This tautological reference is equivalent to the peasant's obstinacy, as, like the peasant, the hermit repeats himself. He (re)casts the primal blame on the peasant, subjects him to a test and then redundantly, or demagogically, repeats the traditional account. Perhaps he interprets the peasant's questions as blasphemous and thus targets his lesson to bring him back to blind acceptance, to reiterate the long-established premises: Adam should not be blamed, questions should not be asked, peasants and women should not speak.

But the fable is not a complete fiasco. Marie de France is not to be silenced. She keeps the final words, the morality, to herself. Joan Ferrante also noticed the gap between the fable's contradicting lessons: 'the hermit gives the official (religious) interpretation, blaming Eve and the devil, but Marie counters his lesson with her own, suggesting that all (men and women) should take responsibility for their own acts'.[22] Amer and Merceron agree that this was Marie's innovation, that she 'problematizes woman's responsibility for Original Sin'.[23] By demanding self-reflecting repentance, by urging the peasant 'to reproach himself instead',[24] Marie's words again echo Augustine's ideas about both men and women's salvation through confession:

> My response is brief: let them be silent and stop murmuring against God. Perhaps their complaint would be justified if there were no Victor over error and inordinate desire. But in fact there is one who is present everywhere and speaks in many ways through the creation that serves him as Lord. He calls out to those who have turned their back on him and instruct those who believe in him. He comforts the hopeful, encourages the diligent, helps the struggling, and hears the prayers of those who cry out to him.
>
> You are not blamed for your unwilling ignorance, but because you fail to ask about what you do not know. You are not blamed because you do not bind up your own wounds but because you spurn the one who wants to heal you. These are your own sins. For no one is prevented from leaving behind the disadvantage of ignorance and seeking the advantage of knowledge, or from humbly confessing his weakness, so that God, whose help is effortless and unerring, will come to his assistance.[25]

According to Augustine in *De libero arbitrio*, the punishment was only for the first sinners, but regarding their children, God 'gave them the ability to act rightly in laborious duties, and he showed them the path of faith in the blindness of forgetfulness'.[26] If Marie's theory does stand behind Augustine, her morality would thus suggest, although not explicitly, an answer to the question of God's mercy. Adam's sin affected humanity as it resulted in mortality, but if men and women will confess their own sins, forgiveness is possible.

The Lady, La response du Bestiaire (The Response to the Bestiary of Love)

From the two creation narratives recounted in Genesis 1 and 2, the dominant one in Judaeo-Christian tradition is by far the second, where Adam is not merely created before Eve, but Eve is created from Adam's rib. As of the end of the eleventh century a nascent iconographical tradition began moving away from the biblical episode, presenting Eve not as confectioned out of the rib, but rather as exiting from the side of Adam's body.[27] This iconography, of Adam giving birth to Eve, flourished throughout Europe, implying that Adam was not only Eve's 'husband' but, in a certain way, also her father. In a world promoting the idea of hierarchical subordination, in which offspring were perceived as owing their lives to their creator and therefore being inferior to him and subservient, Eve's submissiveness to Adam was indisputable. It was naturally established in what was considered a natural law, even before the divine articulation that such compliance was a part of Eve's punishment.[28]

The premise that women should obey men because of a natural hierarchy, surely conducted according to the Lord's will, was accepted even by an anonymous thirteenth-century female writer, who admitted that no one may contest that God accorded Adam complete dominance over all things alive, even women. However, she argued, God never meant women to be regarded as basically inferior, or as essentially lacking reason, as He created women from a nobler material. In the interests of clarity, I present here her entire argument:

> God, who established the entire world with his dignified might, first made the sky and the earth and all of which he ordinated in the one and in the other. Then, he made [the] man as the noblest creature possible. And it pleased Him to create him from a material that is not as sophisticated as the others. From the same element, according to some authors, He moulded a woman, in a manner which did not please the man, whom He has already created. Hence, it happened that when God gave life to the one and to the other, Adam killed his wife, and God asked him why he had done this. He replied: 'She was nothing to me, and for this reason, I could not love her.' Thus, later our Lord came to Adam while he was asleep, and he took one of his ribs and formed Eve, from whom we are all issued. Hence, some people like to say that if the first woman remained, Adam would have never sinned, which has brought us suffering. But for the great love that Adam had for the one who was created of himself, as it seems, because the love for her surmounted the commandment of Our Lord, as you heard elsewhere how they ate the fruit that was forbidden to them. Well, it is true that our Lord God gave man authority over all living things, even over the woman, whom He created from a more dignified material than the one from which he created man, and the Scriptures explain why he did so with a very good example. And this is why: he who has been God formed man from the first matter that was, then he took off a piece from that very man, as I said above, and made the woman and gave her form. That is why I say that although man was already created by so noble a worker, the material was amended. So this is the reason that woman is made of this dignified material, or even a better one than the man is made of. No one should object to this and tell me that it is not true that however great the Lord's grace was, by which he wanted man to have authority over every human creature, we are created more nobly, dear sir, than you have ever been, even if we are to obey you through our Lord's command. But God did nothing without good reason, because it is only right that the thing which comes from another be obedient to that which it came from. Therefore the woman should obey the man, and the man earth, and the earth God, who was the Creator and sovereign of all created things. This is why everyone should know that he must obey that which he came from, and above all Him, who did everything, as mentioned above. And for this reason, my lord and master, I, who am a woman, have to obey the man, and to obey you who are a man, in such a way that whatever pleases me, I will be considered in my work, and as for all the rest, well, I will just put it aside until it will be necessary either for me or for the others.[29]

In this 'unique narrative' of the creation, to quote Jeanette Beer,[30] the Lady freely combines elements from the two creation accounts, not basing her words directly on the Scriptures, but rather on catechistic knowledge which she freely manipulates to support her arguments. From the first chapter she borrows the affirmation that the sky, the earth and their respective living creatures were created prior to man, and that originally God created man and woman together. However, as opposed to seeing the dualistic creation as indicating merely that man and woman were created in God's image, according to the Lady they were created from the ground, which is, she says, a mediocre material. The ground is the dominant[31] fertile element of the creation in chapter two, where anachronistically all the other creatures are created a second time, all from the ground. The Lady blurs the differences between the two accounts, the dualistic creation in chapter one, and chapter two, in which the abstract notion of 'God's image' is eliminated in favour of a materialistic creation.

According to the Lady, a first woman was equally created from the earth but 'in a manner which did not please the man, which He has already created. Hence, it happened that when God gave life to the one and to the other, Adam killed his wife.' To decipher this peculiar statement, we need to recall that the Lady fuses the two narratives, grafting one upon the other. The unpleasing woman is still the one that was created with the first man (as in chapter one), but the notion that Adam 'did not like her' and remained alone resonates with chapter two. In chapter two, God says, 'It is not good that the man should be alone; I will make him a help meet for him' (2.18). There follows a description of the second creation of all the beasts and the fowl, from the exact same material as the man, 'out of the ground', and how they are named by man (2.19). Once this is completed, it is clear that 'for Adam there was not found a help meet for him' (2.20). The *Response* develops what is suggested by the biblical source, namely that man remained alone after discovering that none of the other creatures made out of the ground suit him. According to Scripture, God not only 'recreates' the animals that, according to chapter one, were created before the human race. He also creates them with a specific goal, so that man will not be alone. For this reason, they are brought to man to be named individually, while in fact they are to be thoroughly scrutinized with the goal of finding man a suitable companion. This is not to imply that it was God's intention to have his first man mingle with an animal. The animals' second creation should be understood here as metaphorical, signifying that God gave Adam permission to *choose* a companion who pleases him from among the creatures created from the ground. It is hard to grasp the biblical text this way, because of the peculiar reference only to the species of beast and fowl, without any mention of a 'human' creature, of a woman. This, however, is part of the essence, as it was Adam's role to determine who his companion would be, what creature he could have named 'a woman', a task that he could not fulfil, as a woman had not yet been created.

The Lady disregards the naming episode.[32] As argued before, the first wife she presents is the one created prior to this event, but I believe she borrows from it the *idea* that Adam had a chance to have a first theoretical, potential, conceptual 'female partner', but chose to remain alone.[33] The reason for this is significantly different, since the Lady claims that Adam killed the woman who was created with him.

Contextualizing this interpretation of Genesis in the courtly love tradition from which *The Bestiaire* and *The Response* emerge, Helen Solterer understood that this 'murderous violence [. . .] confronts the preeminent topos of a nefarious woman apt to kill the lover [. . .] Her answer to the master's symbolic death is to match it and deflect it with her own.'[34] She also saw in it 'a parable of man's enormous difficulty in entertaining any contrary element [. . .] even in Eden, man's antipathy toward a potential female rival generate violence against her'.[35] For Beer 'the author articulates the view that Adam, by his slaying of the woman God intended for him, was guilty of original sin by his disrespect for God's providential plan for humanity, his disobedience, murder, and (by medieval standards) bigamy'.[36]

These two opinions both suggest plausible interpretations of this peculiar event. However, they disregard the puzzling laconism of the Lady's reaction to the gratuitous murder of the first woman. Using an almost neutral tone, she describes God's indifference to the murder and His immediate creation of a new woman. I suggest a complementary symbolical reading as the parable of the larger issue of gender. Richard de Fournival represents the prevailing patronizing patriarchal erudite voice, repeatedly and unjustifiably attempting to trample and eradicate women. Women are viewed as 'nothing' but are basically and initially equal to men. According to the *Response*, the discriminating treatment, ignorance and alienation endured by women from men with no historical justification echoes the treatment of the first woman created by God. However, just as Adam could not achieve his ungodly design, for God put him to sleep and created another woman (here the Lady bases her writing on chapter two but adds the topos of woman's superior material), the Lady's ambition is to demonstrate the failure of the misogynistic enterprise. She, as a descendant of Eve, is proof that women cannot be deprived of sense and discourse. By analogy, her *Response* may be secondary to Richard's, in the sense that it was a response to his writing. However, by analogy this too happened by divine will, for God does not support the elimination of women, and to compensate for the killing of the first woman He made the second woman and all successive women out of better material. Her work, her *Response*, is thus more illuminating than the complaint, just as Eve was created from better material than Adam.

The Lady then returns to the prosaic style, commenting on the biblical account by citing authoritative voices and claiming that Adam began the chain of sin, and thus 'challenges the orthodox view, whether Jewish or patristic, that "from a woman did sin originate and because of her we must all die" (Ecclesiasticus 25:24). IT WAS THE MAN [sic.]'.[37] Sin leads to sin, cause to effect, and killing the first woman enabled Adam to commit the sin of the apple. Furthermore, the Lady also insinuates Adam's sensual weakness, typically characterizing anti-feminine stereotypes: 'because the love for her surmounted the commandment of Our Lord'. The argument which claimed that Adam sinned by eating the apple because of his love for Eve and his loyalty to the marriage was a commonplace one. The novelty here is that it is not presented by the Lady as an innocent act of basic trust among spouses, but as a moral deficiency.

In the genesis of her belletristic work, leaning on the Genesis of all humankind, the Lady thus expresses her perception of her superiority, which enables her for a moment to become the attacker rather than the responder, the master rather than the student. She introduces a new topic that was not discussed by Richard; she takes him to the beginning of the beginnings, stressing the initial misinterpretation of the traditional perceptions of women's inferiority. The story of Eve, used time and again to demean women, empowers the Lady. For the rest of her *Response*, she will answer Richard's charges from a defensive position.

Jehan Le Fevre, Le livre de Leesce (The Book of Gladness)

About a century after the *Bestiaire* and its *Response*, another feminine voice sought to challenge men's knowledge through the story of the creation. Around 1380, Jehan Le Fèvre translated into French a Latin satirical treatise, *Lamentaciones Matheoluli*, written about eighty years earlier by Mathieu de Boulogne. This text belonged to a long and vivid misogynistic literary tradition that despised and decried the institution of marriage, referred to by R. Howard Bloch as 'molestiae nuptiarum' (the atrocities of marriage).[38] Articulated by men, it described the miseries of the married man as a victim of woman, the daughter of Eve, and her caprices, vulgarity, appetites and volubility. Several years after the *Lamentations* translation, Jehan composed a form of response, entitled *Le livre de Leesce* (The Book of Gladness). Like the *Bestiaire*'s *Response*, it gave rise to a female voice, namely Dame Leesce (Lady Gladness), who, like the Lady responding to Richard de Fournival, refuted the principal points of the chauvinist allegations in the *Lamentations*.[39] In the *Lamentations*, Matheolus evokes Eve's moral inferiority on three occasions, all of them 'answered' by Lady Gladness. However, on a fourth occasion, Lady Gladness interprets the creation, which she brings to the discussion independently, using it as a personal and innovative argument against the accusations of women's lust and lack of rationality:

> God, who wished for procreation, formed the man and then the woman, and in their bodies he instilled the soul. He invested within it, love and companionship, to found and engender a lineage. And He does not permit to forget that [when] He ordered to multiply and proliferate the earth, it was not meant to sow discord; He wanted that propagation to emanate from pleasure. Man and woman are reasonable, and wiser, and more dignified than any other creature. Mighty love and nature drives them to desire, and to reunite carnally, to continue our kind that death corrupts and demolishes. And whoever undertakes upon himself to contest this, shall start at the very beginning.[40]

Like the Lady, Gladness also finds some solace in rethinking the origin of everything, the genesis of mankind, as exempt from prejudice. And like her, she presents her argument as an erudite lecture, and like King Solomon and Aristotle,[41] whose words are commonly accepted, she states that 'whoever undertakes upon himself to contest this [that is, her statements], shall start at the very beginning'.

Gladness also uses the topos of the hierarchy of the two materials of which the man and the woman are composed in her response to the *Lamentations*, where women are berated for their noisiness: 'Why are women more noisy, full with idle words, and more babbling than men? Because they are [made] out of bones and we, our bodies, are made out of the ground. Bone resonates higher than the ground.'[42] To dismiss this argument, Leesce returns, seriously, to the question of the supremacy of human bones in relation to the ground. Her detailed response surely merits a separate discussion and is beyond my scope here. However, her words serve as a fitting conclusion to this chapter:

> With regard to Mathew's assaulting us by saying that a woman speaks loudly because she was created from a bone, I say that anything should be loved more, the nobler it is, just as azure and sinople are more precious than coal and chalk. There is not a single living creature who does not believe that the woman should be praised for having been made from bone whereas man was made out of the ground. On this Mathew is wrong. For the bone is nobler and hence is more precious, and that is why God wished to create her within the earthly paradise. I defer on this matter: the man was made of a bit of filth, silt and hard ground, in the valley of Hebron amongst the fields. That is why the man is more vicious. We can show with solid reasoning that women have much nobler prerogatives than men. The first of these noble advantages is that she was made inside of paradise, formed and completed by the hands of God. Likewise, God made her out of a rib, it deprives her not of nobility, [on the contrary] she is nobler all over.

The medieval patriarchal tradition presented and represented Eve as a disobedient, childish and lustful woman,[43] solely responsible for the fall. A lesser-known stream of thought, offering a feminist interpretation of Genesis, tried to resist this discriminatory view and sought to demonstrate the equal responsibility that Adam and Eve had for the fall, as well as their equal status as human beings. Against the prevailing misogynistic discourses that viewed Eve as physically and mentally inferior to Adam, the Middle Ages also witnessed some resistant feministic voices, claiming that the traditional conceptions are misinterpretations of the initial divine will to create equal human beings. Furthermore, Adam and Eve are not merely equal by their creation, but also share equal responsibility for the fall.

Conclusion

This chapter has shown how medieval female writers attempted to absolve Eve from the common prejudice. Marie de France, the pioneer female fabulist, demonstrates in her fable that evil inclination is human and not gendered, and that any man who casts blame on another human being, including, or perhaps especially, on a woman, should first re-examine himself. The anonymous Lady answering Richard de Fournival's bestiary suggests that Eve was created by God from a nobler material than Adam, and therefore, at the very least, woman should not be considered secondary to man, a text that surely influenced another feminist work written in the fourteenth century, Jehan Le Fèvre's *Livre de Leesce*.

Notes

1. I wish to thank the Israel and Ione Massada Fellowships Programme at Worcester College for providing the time and intellectually supportive environment of the University of Oxford that allowed me to focus on developing this paper.
2. On the mythological elements of Genesis, see Robert Couffignal, *Le drame de l'Eden: Le récit de la Genèse et se fortune littéraire* (Toulouse: Association des publications de l'université de Toulouse-Le Mirail, 1980), 28–30. For a list of these literary texts from the second century BCE until 1978, see Couffignal, *Le drame de l'Eden*, 36–9.
3. According to a thirteenth-century anonymous writer, Adam and Eve only had seven hours together in paradise before they were expelled at None. During the third hour, Adam named the animals, and in the sixth hour Eve had already bitten the forbidden fruit and given it to Adam, who ate it because of his love for her. Ruhe Ernstpeter (ed.), *Sydrac le philosophe, Le livre de la fontaine de toutes sciences* (Wiesbaden: Reichert (Wissensliteratur im Mittelalter, 34), 2000), 52.
4. *Hildegard of Bingen*: *Scivias*, trans. Mother Columbia Hart and Jane Bishop (New York: Paulist Press, 1990), 77.
5. Joan M. Ferrante, *To the Glory of Her Sex: Women's Roles in the Composition of Medieval Texts* (Bloomington: Indiana University Press, 1997), 170. On Hildegard's views on Eve in general, see 170–4. See also Rebecca L. R. Garber, 'Where is The Body? Images of Eve and Mary in the *Scivias*', in *Hildegard of Bingen: A Book of Essays*, ed. Maud Burnett McInerney (New York: Routledge, 1998), 103–132.
6. Unless specifically mentioned, all translations from the French sources are mine. Due to lack of space, I only present the translated excerpts here, while the original texts may be consulted in the referenced editions. Harriet Spiegel (ed.), *Marie de France, Fables* (Toronto: University of Toronto Press, 1987), Fable 53, 156–8.
7. About the theme of the escaping mouse in this fable and elsewhere, see the brilliant work by Jacques Merceron, 'Des souris et des hommes: pérégrination d'un motif narratif et d'un exemplum d'Islam en chrétienté. [À propos de la fable de 'L'Ermite' de Marie de France et du fabliau de La Sorisete des Estopes]', *Cahiers de civilisation médiévale* 46 (2003): 53–69, doi: https://doi.org/10.3406/ccmed.2003.2848.
8. Amer Sahar, 'Marie de France Rewrites Genesis: The Image of Woman in Marie de France's Fables', *Neophilologus* 81, no. 4 (1997): 489–99. Merceron, 'Des souris et des hommes'.
9. On Augustine's conception of the two instances of the creation and his exoneration of Eve, see John O'Meara, 'Saint Augustine's Understanding of the Creation and Fall', *Maynooth Review* 10 (1984): 52–62, https://www.jstor.org/stable/20556975.
10. In the second book of *De libero arbitrio* (On Free Choice of the Will), Augustine deals with the difficulties of understanding free will as something that was given by God, the perfect goodness, but which is also the source of evil. Augustine, *On Free Choice of the Will*, trans. Thomas Williams (Indianapolis: Hackett Publishing Company, 1993). All quotes of this text in this chapter are from this translation by Williams.
11. Augustine, *On Free Choice*, Book 3, ch. 20, 110. On Augustine's notions of ignorance and difficulty as divine punishment for the misuse of God's gift of freewill, see Bart Van Egmond,

Augustine's Early Thought on the Redemptive Function of Divine Judgment (Oxford: Oxford University Press, 2018).

12. The generalization of the sin referring merely to Adam as the sinner is recurrent in medieval literature; to give just two examples spanning 200 years, let us note Marie de France's *Yonec* and the fourteenth-century *Le mesangier de Paris*.

13. Augustine, *On Free Choice*, Book 3, ch. 19, 107.

14. Tovi Bibring, *The Patient, the Impostor and the Seducer: Medieval European Literature in Hebrew* (Oxford: Legenda, forthcoming 2021). See also Paul H. Freedman, *Images of the Medieval Peasant* (Stanford, CA: Stanford University Press, 1999), and Alfred Thomas, 'Alien Bodies: Exclusions, Obscenity and Social Control in the Ointment Seller', in *Obscenity: Social Control and Artistic Creation in the European Middle Ages*, ed. Jan M. Ziolkowski (Leiden: Brill, 1998), 214–30.

15. Sahar Amer also sees the peasant as a woman, 'since he displays the character traits for which Eve is denounced' and 'If a man acts like a woman, it may well indicate that the wickedness ascribed to woman is not inherent to her nature', *Marie de France Rewrites Genesis*, 492. While our views certainly share some common denominators, they differ in the sense that for me the peasant is effeminized precisely by his low status and marginality, which are the lot of women. It is possible that Marie identifies with this otherness. This is not to say that she herself hides beneath the peasant, rather that the peasant may be reflecting the principle that is at stake here, a rejection of the burden of an ancestral feminine guilt.

16. On Augustine's notion of divine illumination versus experience, see Gyula Klima, 'The Medieval Problem of Universals', in *The Stanford Encyclopedia of Philosophy* (Winter 2017 edn), ed. Edward N. Zalta, https://plato.stanford.edu/archives/win2017/entries/universals-medieval/.

17. Merceron, 'Des souris et des hommes', 56. (Although it can be argued that the serpent is a manifestation of the evil inclination, the hermit speaks of it literally here, using the biblical scenario.) A more blatant analogy, as noted by Amer, is with Hesiod's account of Pandora's jar, as Pandora, like the peasant, is more curious than tempted. Moreover, in Genesis, God plants the forbidden trees and commands Adam to avoid eating them. The trees' fruits, however, do not contain danger; they contain power. Zeus deliberately puts calamities in Pandora's jar. On Pandora in this fable, see Amer, *Marie de France Rewrites Genesis*, 492. The evident echo of Pandora is reminiscent of the Christianized fable's antic past.

18. It is also worthwhile noting that the medieval mentality is extremely oriented by the Pythagorean dualistic approach, dividing the world into opposing pairs. According to this division, women are associated, amongst other things, with evil, darkness and even numbers, while men with good, light and odd numbers. For more reasons to see the peasant as incarnating Eve, see Amer, *Marie de France Rewrites Genesis*.

19. This would echo God's reprimand to Ahab: 'Hast thou killed, and also taken possessions' (1 Kings, 21.19). Eve's temptation conceived as the *felix culpa* ('the fortunate fall' or 'the happy fault'), necessary to permit the Incarnation, appears in Jehan Le Fèvre's book, which will shortly be presented here, *Le livre de Leesce* (The Book of Gladness), and discussed in Tovi Bibring, 'Vashti on Display: Medieval Christian Meditations on a Disobeying Queen', in *Reading the Bible in the Premodern Free World*, ed. Chanita Goodblatt and Haim Kreisel (Beer-Sheva: Ben Gurion University Press, forthcoming).

20. Amer, *Marie de France Rewrites Genesis*, 493.

21. Merceron, 'Des souris et des hommes', 63.

22. Ferrante, *To the Glory of Her Sex*, 204.

23. Amer, *Marie de France Rewrites Genesis*, 494; Merceron, 'Des souris et des hommes', 65.

24. Here I use Harriet Spiegel's translation., n. 1.
25. Augustine, *On Free Choice*, Book 3, ch. 19, 107.
26. Augustine, *On Free Choice*, Book 3, ch. 20, 110.
27. Roberto Zapperi, *The Pregnant Man*, trans. Brian Williams (New York: Harwood Academic Publishers, 1991), 3–32.
28. 'It is according to the natural order of the human race that women should be subject to men and that children should submit to their parents, for in the human race justice demands that the lesser should serve the greater' (Ivo of Chartres, quoted from Zapperi, *The Pregnant Man*, 9). The doctrinal idea of a hierarchized subordination was spread by Paul in Ephesians 5. In the thirteenth century, Thomas Aquinas distinguished between two sorts of submission: the one before the sin, which was natural, and the one after it, which was punishment. But here, it is natural because men are naturally wiser and it is natural that the less wise will be ruled by the wiser, but also 'as her origin and chief'. About twenty years later, this assumption was affirmed in one of the most, if not the most, influential texts of religion, Thomas Aquinas's *Summa Theologica* (translated by Edmund Hill). Alcuin Blamires (ed.), *Woman Defamed and Woman Defended: An Anthology of Medieval Texts* (Oxford: Oxford University Press, 1992), 92–3.
29. The text is that of La Response in Gabriel Bianciotto, *Richard de Fournival, Le 'Bestiaire d'Amour' et la 'Response du Bestiaire'*, Champion Classiques. Moyen Âge, 27 (Paris: Champion, 2009). Translation is my own.
30. Jeanette Beer, *Beasts of Love: Richard de Fournival Bestiaire d'amour and a Woman's Response* (Toronto, Buffalo and London: University of Toronto Press, 2003), 120.
31. The ground, according to this chapter, is an extensively fertile material from which everything originates – not merely the first man, but also the mist, the flora and the fauna.
32. Her feministic inclination surely deprives Adam of such supremacy over the woman, who remains, in her version, created and named by God.
33. In the Jewish Midrashic literature, the first creation account, according to which God created man and woman at the same time (1.27), gave rise to the tradition that Adam had a first wife, whom the sages of the Mishna and the Talmud recognize as Lilith. It was Cesare Segre's hypothesis that it is to this tradition that the Lady owes her story. Cesare Segre (ed. and trans.), *Li Bestiaires d'amours di Maistre Richart de Fornival e Li Response du Bestiaire* (Milan and Naples: Riccardo Ricciardi, 1957). However, Christian theology intentionally ignored and categorically censured, for doctrinal reasons, the first creation account. The Talmudic notion that a first woman existed before Eve was considered a Jewish error (see Beer, *Beasts of Love*, 120). This question leads Anat Dovrat to suggest that the Lady may have been Jewish. Anat Dovrat, 'Feminism and Gender Symbolism in the *Bestiaries d'amours* of Richard de Fournival and the Anonymous Response', MA thesis, Bar-Ilan University, 2021. Furthermore, the most striking characteristic of the relationship between the first couple in the Midrashic accounts is its tumultuousness nature. Lilith is a straightforward, active woman who defies Adam's dominance and leaves him by her own initiative. 'Their conflict is one of patriarchal authority versus matriarchal desire for emancipation, and the warring couple cannot reconcile they represent the archetypal battle of the sexes. Neither attempts to solve their dispute or to reach some kind of compromise where they take turns being on top (literally and figuratively). Man cannot cope with woman's desire for freedom, and woman will settle for nothing less.' Janet Howe Gaines, 'Lilith', in *Bible Review* 17, no. 5 (2000). The Lady's report presents a passive woman who is killed for 'being nothing'. Lilith was punished but never killed by Adam. This may be something that a decade later Lady Gladness will refer to by saying that men are murderers.

34. Helen Solterer, *The Master and Minerva: Disputing Women in French Medieval Culture* (Berkley: University of California Press, 1995), 105.

35. Solterer, *The Master and Minerva* , 106.

36. Beer, *Beasts of Love*, 120.

37. Beer, *Beasts of Love*, 120.

38. R. Howard Bloch, *Medieval Misogyny and the Invention of Western Romantic Love* (Chicago: University of Chicago Press, 1991), 14.

39. With the significant difference that *Leesce* was written by a man. Another significant difference between them is that *Leesce* is much more serious than the intentionally sarcastic tone of *Lamentations*. Both the French *Lamentations* and *Leesce* curiously lack a substantial study, although they inspired and influenced a number of well-known medieval writers such as Christine de Pizan and Chaucer, who are indebted to them.

40. A.-G. Van Hamel (ed.), *Les Lamentations de Matheolus et le Livre de leesce de Jehan le Fèvre, de Resson (poèmes français du XIVe siècle). Édition critique, accompagnée de l'original latin des Lamentations, d'après l'unique manuscrit d'Utrecht, d'une introduction et de deux glossaires*, Bibliothèque de l'École des hautes études (Paris: Bouillon, 1892–1905), 95–6.

41. This argument was triggered by Matheolus' accusation in the *Lamentation* that women seduced the greatest philosophers, Solomon and Aristotle, hence the debate is centred on them.

42. Van Hamel, *Les Lamentations de Matheolus et le Livre de leesce.*

43. For a similar presentation of both Eve and Pandora in children's literature, see Lisa Maurice's chapter in this volume.

PART IV

IDEOLOGICAL MANIPULATIONS OF THE CREATION NARRATIVE

CHAPTER 10
A STORY OF ADAM AND EVE FOR SOVIET CHILDREN AND ADULTS: THE *DIVINE COMEDY*, A PUPPET SHOW BASED ON THE BIBLE

Hava B. Korzakova

The *Divine Comedy*

Establishing their own 'religion', the Bolsheviks tried to destroy all others in their state from the time they took power[1] in a programme that included the destruction of churches, synagogues and mosques, the prosecution of priests, rabbis and mullahs, and prohibition of any religious literature. At the same time, anti-religious literature was printed and visual anti-religious propaganda encouraged. By the 1960s the communists claimed that there was no religion left, beside some crumbs for the old people.[2]

One of the masterpieces of performance art produced under this ideology was a puppet show called the *Divine Comedy*, staged by the State Central Puppet Theatre, Moscow, written and directed by Sergey Obraztsov[3] and Semyon Samodur,[4] and with music composed by Nikita Bogoslovsky.[5] Based on the play by Isidor Shtok,[6] the show was inspired by the series of cartoons by the French artist Jean Effel,[7] *La creation du monde* (1945).[8] This series inspired a cartoon movie, *The Creation of the World* (*Stvoření světa*), made in Czechoslovakia in 1958 by Eduard Hofman.[9] This traditionally animated film produced by Československý Státní Film was 83 minutes long, with music by Jean Wiener and Jan Rychlik performed by an orchestra directed by André Girard.[10]

In his film, Hofman follows Effel's cartoons, and, from his perspective, the story of Adam and Eve is a mere part of a much wider narrative. In contrast, in Shtok's play, which is actually a tale about the creation of a man and his two wives, and their exile from the Garden of Eden, the relationship story is the main focus.

The *Divine Comedy* was first staged in 1961 and filmed for television in 1973.[11] The play has no connection with the original *Divine Comedy* by Dante beyond its title. Here, the meaning of that title is that the entire divine creation story is no more than a comedy, something to laugh at. It became an extremely popular TV show, partly because it was almost the only way for Soviet children (and adults) to learn about the first story of the Bible, and therefore had a tinge of the exotic about it. The show was broadcast multiple times, while the play is still running in the theatre today.

Another reason for its popularity was the cast of great actors who voiced the characters in the television version, including Zinovy Gerdt,[12] a Jewish actor who provided the voice of Adam in the show, while other Jewish actors, such as Semyon Samodur as the

Creator, Konstantin Gurkin as Archangel A and Robert Liapidevsky as Archangel B, added an 'authentic' Jewish taste to the show and also took part in the writing. The inclusion of these figures was probably intentional on the part of Isidor Shtok, who was also a typical Soviet Jew, in that he was partly ashamed, but secretly proud, of his heritage.

In the show, it was decided that there would be only three masked actors on the stage, playing the Creator and two Archangels, while the other characters would be performed by puppets made of foam rubber. It is noticeable that the puppets, as well as the actors' masks, do not resemble Effel's cartoon characters. Although the Creator in both masterpieces is a semi-bald elderly man, Effel's Creator is a kind grandfatherly character, while Obraztsov's Creator looks considerably more cruel and the portrayal is more satirical, more of an evil sorcerer than a funny grandfather (see Figure10.1).

The show briefly follows the biblical story, with the creation of the light, animals and so on, before concentrating on Adam, Lilith and Eve. It narrates that the creation of the first man was not easy. When God creates Adam, an Archangel registers him in the Book of Creation, but the first woman is not registered because God thinks that there could be 'problems' with her, as, indeed, then happens. This idea of a dual creation of woman draws on the biblical narrative which contains two different stories of the creation of the first man and the first woman, thereby suggesting that they refer to different people. This

Figure 10.1 Adam, Eve and the Creator. Screengrab from the *Divine Comedy*, directed by Sergey Obraztsov. © ГОСТЕЛЕРАДИОФОНД России 1973. Available on YouTube: https://www.youtube.com/channel/UCiVZttFkdEwMi3QXpRqFTzQ.

is found in Rabbinic tradition as well: according to Rabbi Hiyya the Great (180–230 CE), God proceeded to create a second Eve for Adam, after 'the first Eve' had to return to dust.[13] It also recalls the tradition of a 'first woman' introduced to the story of the creation under the name Lilith, a Mesopotamian demon also mentioned in the Epic of Gilgamesh.[14]

The Lilith tradition

The word Lilith is a *hapax legomenon* in the Hebrew Bible (Is. 34.14):

> וּפָגְשׁוּ צִיִּים אֶת אִיִּים וְשָׂעִיר עַל רֵעֵהוּ יִקְרָא אַךְ שָׁם הִרְגִּיעָה לִּילִית וּמָצְאָה לָהּ מָנוֹחַ.

('There shall the Lilith repose, and find for herself a place to rest').[15] In the Dead Sea Scrolls, among the nineteen fragments of Isaiah found at Qumran, the *Great Isaiah Scroll* (1Q1Isa) refers to the creature as plural *liliyyot* (or *liliyyoth*).[16] The Septuagint translates both the reference to *lilith* and the word for jackals or 'wild beasts of the island' within the same verse into Greek as *onokentauros*, onocentaur, a creature similar to the centaur, but where the centaur is part equine, the onocentaur is part donkey:

> καὶ συναντήσουσιν **δαιμόνια ὀνοκενταύροις** καὶ βοήσουσιν ἕτερος πρὸς τὸν ἕτερον ἐκεῖ ἀναπαύσονται **ὀνοκένταυροι** εὗρον γὰρ αὑτοῖς ἀνάπαυσιν.
>
> And daemons shall meet with onocentaurs, and they shall cry one to the other: there shall the onocentaurs rest, having found for themselves [a place of] rest.[17]

The early fifth-century Vulgata translates Lilith as *lamia*, a child-eating monster from the Greek mythology:[18]

> et occurrent daemonia onocentauris et pilosus clamabit alter ad alterum ibi cubavit *lamia* et invenit sibi requiem.
>
> And demons shall meet with onocentaurs, and one hairy one shall cry out to another; there the lamia has lain down and found rest for herself.

In Rabbinic literature, further reference is found in the Babylonian Talmud, tractate *Erubin* 18b:[19]

> Rabbi Jeremia ben Eleazar said: During those years [after their expulsion from the Garden of Eden], in which Adam, the first man, was separated from Eve, he became the father of ghouls and demons and *lilin*. Rabbi Meir says: Adam, the first man, being very pious and finding that he had caused death to come into the world, sat fasting for 130 years, and separated himself from his wife for 130 years, and wore fig leaves for 130 years. His fathering of evil spirits, referred to here, came as a result of wet dreams.

In other places in the Babylonian Talmud Lilith is mentioned as a demon,[20] as she features in the Dead Sea Scrolls[21] and early Jewish mysticism[22] and in Jewish folklore. Nevertheless, from the satirical book *Alphabet of Ben Sira* (*c.* 700–1000 CE) onwards, she appears as Adam's first wife, who was created at the same time (the New Year, *Rosh Hashanah*) and from the same dirt as Adam.[23] Shtok's interpretation is close to the following fragment from the *Alphabet of Ben Sira*:

> While God created Adam, who was alone, He said, 'It is not good for man to be alone' (Gen. 2.18). He also created a woman, from the earth, as He had created Adam himself, and called her Lilith. Adam and Lilith immediately began to fight. She said, 'I will not lie under you', and he said, 'I will not lie beneath you, but only on top. For you are fit only to be in the bottom position, while I am to be the superior one'. Lilith responded, 'We are equal to each other inasmuch as we were both created from the earth'. But they would not listen to one another. When Lilith saw this, she pronounced the Ineffable Name and flew away into the air. Adam stood in prayer before his Creator: 'Sovereign of the universe!' he said, 'the woman you gave me has run away'. At once, the Holy One, blessed be He, sent these three angels to bring her back.
>
> Said the Holy One to Adam, 'If she agrees to come back, what is made is good. If not, she must permit one hundred of her children to die every day'. The angels left God and pursued Lilith, whom they overtook in the midst of the sea, in the mighty waters wherein the Egyptians were destined to drown. They told her God's word, but she did not wish to return. The angels said, 'We shall drown you in the sea'.
>
> 'Leave me!' she said. 'I was created only to cause sickness to infants' [. . .] When the angels heard Lilith's words, they insisted she go back. But she swore to them by the name of the living and eternal God: 'Whenever I see you or your names or your forms in an amulet, I will have no power over that infant'. She also agreed to have one hundred of her children die every day. Accordingly, every day one hundred demons perish, and for the same reason, we write the angels' names on the amulets of young children. When Lilith sees their names, she remembers her oath, and the child recovers.[24]

This depiction of Lilith as a monster, a mother who kills her own children, is also found in *Midrash Numbers Rabbah* 16.25, where Moses sides with Israel and pledges before God that he will not be like Lilith who behaves in this way:

> [God,] do not do it [i.e. destroy the Israelite people], that the nations of the world may not regard you as a cruel Being and say: 'The Generation of the Flood came and He destroyed them, the Generation of the Separation came and He destroyed them, the Sodomites and the Egyptians came and He destroyed them, and these also, whom he called My son, My firstborn (Ex. IV, 22), He is now destroying! As that

> Lilith who, when she finds nothing else, turns upon her own children, so because the Lord was not able to bring this people into the land [. . .] He hath slain them'
>
> *Num. XIV, 16*![25]

The legend developed extensively during the Middle Ages, in the tradition of Aggadic *midrashim*, the *Zohar* and Jewish mysticism.[26] For example, in the writings of Rabbi Isaac ben Jacob ha-Cohen (twelfth century), Lilith left Adam after she refused to become subservient to him and then would not return to the Garden of Eden after she had coupled with the Archangel Samael; she does survive, however, in this version.

The reception of Lilith in the *Divine Comedy*

The legend of Lilith continues to serve as source material in modern Western culture, literature, occultism, fantasy and horror genres. In Hofman's cartoon the character of Lilith is not mentioned but may be implied in a scene in which Satan dances with the reflection of Eve on water, when Eve's face turns ugly and distorted. In Shtok's play, although Lilith is not identified by name, her character is involved in a long and significant episode. She has red hair, which is traditionally associated with witchcraft.[27] Even the actress playing her soul's part is elderly and ugly, her appearance personifying the witch stereotype (see Figure 10.2).

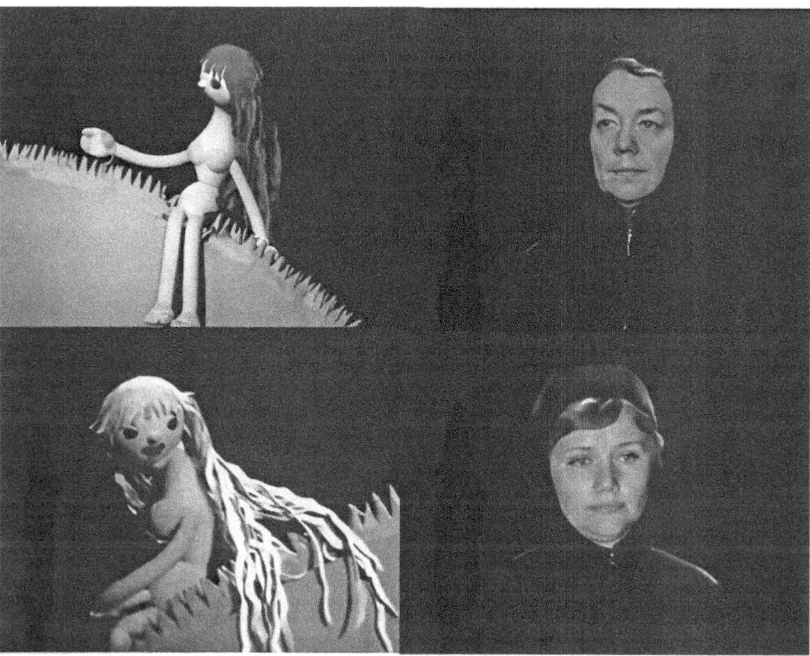

Figure 10.2 Lilith and Eve. Screengrab from the *Divine Comedy*, directed by Sergey Obraztsov. © ГОСТЕЛЕРАДИОФОНД России 1973. Available on YouTube: https://www.youtube.com/channel/UCiVZttFkdEwMi3QXpRqFTzQ.

Shtok plays with words 'thou' and 'you' – Lilith demands to be addressed as 'you' and not 'thou'. She wants to be autonomous and independent, asking why Adam constantly imposes himself on her. By the end of the episode, the Creator simply destroys the first woman, exactly as in Rabbi Hiyya's version. At least one of Obraztsov's team members, Zinovy Gerdt, went to the Jewish school (*Heder*) in his childhood in the town of Sebezh, which belonged to the former Pale of Settlement,[28] and it is therefore likely that he had read the Midrash or heard it from his father who was an orthodox Jew.[29]

Eve in the *Divine Comedy*

After the destruction of Lilith, the Creator decides to create another woman from Adam's rib. The actress playing Eve is younger, more attractive, and in keeping with traditional stereotypes, the puppet is blonde. Similarly, in contrast with Lilith, Eve says:[30]

> Not 'you' but 'thou'. You must look at me with love. You are not alone, here I am, your wife, a legitimate one. I think you want me to be called Eve. Why? Because I am your wife, a legitimate one, I must know what you want, before you do.

The first thing she does is to give him a massage, and then she picks berries for their breakfast and teaches him to eat them. They argue about which one of them is happy as a result of the happiness of the other. She then asks whether he knows other women and a conversation follows in which he states that he wants to go to the river. She, however, says that she thinks that he prefers to do it tomorrow, and that now he wants to walk with her. Adam's response to this is, 'It is great that you have shown up, because now I will know what I want.' This recalls yet another stereotype dating back as far as early Jewish sources, namely that although a man is like the head, a woman is like the neck, which means that he actually does whatever she wants, although it appears to be the opposite.[31] Similarly, with regard to the exile from Eden in the play, Eve cries, 'Why don't you say anything? Say something! Prove that you are independent!', to which Adam replies, 'I do agree with my wife in everything!'

At first glance this interpretation of the biblical story may appear to be satirical; yet familiarity with Soviet and post-Soviet Russian society shows this to be far from the case. These are stereotypes that still exist: family happiness is possible only if the wife is 'wise', by which is meant pretending to be a support (in Russian, 'a neck') for the husband, while an independent woman is doomed to be unhappy.[32]

Eve is not ideal. Sometimes she is capricious, hysterical, jealous – because of course 'she was told' of the previous woman, and she suspects that Adam still loves her. She is also certainly rebellious, with her insurrection being caused by her motherly instincts, since the Creator does not allow them to procreate. Even before the sin, she dreams of a child and plays with a baby tiger.

In this case, the sin occurs as a result of the jealousy of an Archangel, one of whom disguises himself as a snake. After the pair eats the forbidden fruit, the sinister plot is exposed and the cursed Archangel turns into Satan. Adam and Eve are banished from the Garden of Eden. At this stage, the Creator actually wants Adam and Eve back and orders Satan to bring them back to the Garden of Eden as a condition for forgiveness. Satan almost succeeds in this; but Eve is already pregnant, and as a result the angry Creator says that he no longer wishes to know them and banishes Satan to the Hell. At the end of the play, Adam and Eve proudly watch numerous descendants with their partners, declaring that 'it [i.e. the process of procreation] is practically unstoppable'.

Social commentary in the *Divine Comedy*

The play is peppered with subtle social satire. For instance, during the creation of the first couple, the Creator calms down the Archangel by saying, 'Don't worry, it is not a hospital, they will not be slaughtered', in a satirical reference to the low level of medical care in the USSR, and the resulting low level of the 'faith in doctors' among Russians. The next play written by Shtok, *Noah's Ark* (1968), was also based on the Bible, but its mood was much more satirical and bitter. It was filmed in 1976 by Leningrad Television, although it had considerably fewer broadcasts.[33]

The 'official' message of the play, and of the later TV show, was not anti-religious but rather atheistic, as the editorial review produced to accompany the production stated:

> Antireligious writings are meant for a person who believes in the Almighty's existence. And here we have a 'humoristic theology' the cornerstone of which is the assumption that this eternal question is solved once and for all, and the answer is negative, and so it disregards other views that some people still harbour regarding the matter. There is no God – meaning it is permitted to draw him. Meaning it is allowed to picture him on scene.[34]

Curiously this mentions a prohibition against depicting God, which does not exist in Christianity but does in Judaism, thus making it clear that the anonymous writer knows or feels that he or she is speaking about a Jewish work.

Ultimately both the play and the TV show carried another, unofficial message, namely that since talking about the Bible is forbidden, the only option was to pretend that this was a satire on the Bible. This is an example of Aesopian language, by which is meant the cryptic or ambiguous language used in subversive material in order to avoid censorship and was very typical of Soviet culture.[35] Another example of such language occurs at the very beginning of the show, when, before the Creation, the following dialogue takes place between the bored Creator and the Archangels:

> What is being said?
> Nothing is being said.
> Why?
> There is no one to speak.

This dialogue sounds casual, but deciphered from the Soviet Aesopian language, it is almost revolutionary, because it openly talks about the restrictions on free speech in the USSR.

Ironically, in the present day, when the Russian regime is closely connected to the Russian Orthodox Church, an opposite line of argumentation is used in defence of the show which is still running in the State Central Puppet Theatre: its harmlessness is cited in the claim that 'it is just for children'. When they were first created, the play and the TV show were actually intended more for adults than for children, as were many other performance art works, such as the animated series by Vladimir Popov:[36] *Three from Prostokvashino* (1978), *Vacation in Prostokvashino* (1980) and *Winter in Prostokvashino* (1984).[37] This was based on the children's book *Uncle Fedya, His Dog, and His Cat* by Eduard Uspensky, but most of the jokes in the series are beyond the comprehension of children and are undoubtedly intended for the parents.

Conclusion

The *Divine Comedy* by Sergey Obraztsov, written by the Jewish playwright and performed mostly by Jewish actors, was an example of the Aesopian language developed by Soviet intellectuals. It tells a story taken from the Bible, and with the addition of some Midrashic elements, introduces it as atheistic propaganda. On the other hand, it portrays, with evident satirical undertones, the patriarchal stereotypes typical of Soviet society and, indeed, of contemporary Russian society. It is an amusing, albeit ambivalent, show, which in some way also illuminates the mysterious 'Russian soul', and sheds light on the reception of the biblical creation story within a Soviet context.[38]

Notes

1. See Vladimir Ilyich Lenin, 'About the attitude of the working party toward the religion', *Пролетарий* (*Proletariy*) 45, no. 26 (13 May 1909). Translation cited from V. I. Lenin. *Collected Works*, XVII (Moscow: Progress Publishers, 1973), 41.
2. Selected bibliography in English: John Anderson, *Religion, State and Politics in the Soviet Union and Successor States* (Cambridge: Cambridge University Press, 1994); A. Barmenkov, *Freedom of Conscience in the USSR* (Moscow: Progress Publishers, 1984); Nikolay Berdyaev, *The Russian Revolution* (Ann Arbor: University of Michigan Press, 1966 (1931)); B. Bociurkiw and J. Strong, *Religion and Atheism in the USSR and Eastern Europe* (Toronto: University of Toronto Press, 1975); M. Bourdeaux, *Opium of the People: The Christian Religion in the USSR* (London: Faber and Faber, 1965); F. Corley, *Religion in the Soviet Union* (London: Macmillan, 1996); W. C. Fletcher, *Soviet Believers: The Religious Sector of the Population* (Lawrence, KS: Regents Press, 1981); Paul Froese, 'Forced secularization in Soviet Russia: Why an atheistic monopoly failed', *Journal for the Scientific Study of Religion* 43, no. 1 (2004): 35–50; K. Kaariainen, *Discussion on Scientific Atheism as a Soviet Science* (Helsinki: Suomalainen Tiedeakatemia, 1989); W. Kolarz, *Religion in the Soviet Union* (New York: St. Martin's Press, 1961); Lenin, 'About the attitude of the working party toward the religion'; D. Pospielovsky,

A History of Soviet Atheism in Theory and Practice, and the True Believer (New York: St. Martin's Press, 1987); D. Pospielovsky, *Soviet Anti-Religious Campaigns and Persecutions* (New York: St. Martin's Press, 1988); D. E. Powell, *Antireligious Propaganda in the Soviet Union: A study of Mass Persuasion* (Cambridge, MA: MIT Press, 1975); Sabrina Petra Ramet (ed.), *Religious Policy in the Soviet Union* (Cambridge: Cambridge University Press, 1993); W. Swatos. *Politics and Religion in Central and Eastern Europe* (London: Praeger, 1994); E. Yaroslavsky, *Religion in the U.S.S.R.* (New York: International Publishers, 1934); R. C. Zaehner, *The Concise Encyclopedia of Living Faiths* (London: Hutchinson, 1986). As Abraham Adappur states, 'The most modern example of forced "conversions" came not from any theocratic state, but from a professedly atheist government – that of the Soviet Union under the Communists.' See Abraham Adappur, *Religion and the Cultural Crisis in India and the West* (New Delhi: Intercultural Publications, 2000).

3. Sergey Vladimirovich Obraztsov (1901–92), a Soviet puppeteer. Between 1922 and 1931, Obraztsov worked as an actor with Vladimir Nemirovich-Danchenko at Moscow Music Theatre and then at Moscow Art Theatre, and at the same time staged several vaudeville-style puppet shows. In 1931 he became the first director of the State Central Puppet Theatre, Moscow. In 1938, Obraztsov directed the first short-length puppet film, *Looking at a Polar Sunset Ray*. Sergey Obraztsov was the President of the International Union of Puppeteers (1976–84, and from 1984 the President Emeritus), a teaching professor at the Russian Academy of Theatre Arts (from 1973) and a member of the Writers' Union of the USSR. Obraztsov authored an autobiography and a monograph on Chinese puppet theatre. He was awarded by the Stalin Prize in 1946, named People's Artist of the USSR in 1952 and a Hero of Socialist Labour in 1971. His theatre is still functioning; see the official website: https://puppet.ru/.
4. Semyon Salomonovich Samodur (1911–91), Soviet actor and director of the State Central Puppet Theatre, Moscow, People's Artist of the RSFSR (1960).
5. Nikita Vladimirovich Bogoslovsky (1913–2004), a Soviet and Russian composer, author of more than 200 songs, eight symphonies, seventeen operettas and musical comedies, fifty-eight soundtracks and fifty-two scores for theatre productions. He is best known for two of Mark Bernes's trademark songs from the film *Great Patriotic War* (*Два бойца* (*Dva boytsa*, *Two Fighters*, 1943)): 'Темная ночь' (*Tyomnaya noch*, 'Dark Night') and 'Шаланды полные кефали' (*Shalandy polnye kefali*, 'Boats Full of Mullets'). His many honorary titles and state awards included the People's Artist of the USSR (1983), the Order of the Red Banner of Labour (1971) and the Order of the Red Star (1946).
6. Isidor Vladimirovich Shtok (1908–80), Soviet actor and playwriter, a member of the Writers' Union of the USSR. From 1965 to 1970, Shtok was a member of the Writers' Union's board. His first stages play was titled *Комсомол как он есть* (*Komsomol kak on est'*, *Komsomol as it is* (1927)).
7. Jean Effel, real name François Lejeune (1908–82), French painter, caricaturist, illustrator and journalist.
8. See François Robichon, *Jean Effel. L'Homme à la marguerite* (Paris: Hoëbeke, 1998); Jean-Paul Tibéri, *Jean Effel. La Création d'un monde* (Paris: Jean-Cyrille Godefroy, 1992).
9. Eduard Hofman (1914–87), one of the most important Czech creators of animated films, especially for children.
10. British Film Institute, https://www2.bfi.org.uk/films-tv-people/4ce2b6b6e10e7.
11. Full one-and-a-half-hour version with an introduction by Sergey Obraztsov: https://youtu.be/mMNp6R-buIY.
12. Zinovy Gerdt, real name Zalman Efraimovich Khrapinovich (1916–96), a Soviet and Russian actor, named People's Artist of the USSR in 1990. Regarding his extreme popularity and gentle

yet strong character, see memoires by various people in Tatiana Pravdina and Yakov Groisman, *Зяма – это же Гердт!* (*Ziama – eto zhe Gerdt!*, *Ziama – it's Gerdt!*) (Moscow: Dekom, 2013).

13. *Genesis Rabbah* 22.7 and 18.4.

14. Table XII, ll. 44, 131. Her name has a peculiar mixed Sumerian-Akkadian etymology: it is li_2-la_2, 'air', 'wind' or 'ghost', in Sumerian, and *lil*, 'night', in Akkadian, hence the meaning 'night ghost' or 'night demon'. See also Samuel Noah Kramer, *Gilgamesh and the Huluppu-Tree: A Reconstructed Sumerian Text*, Assyriological Studies 10. (Chicago: University of Chicago Press, 1938).

15. Translation is that of the New American Bible.

16. Judith M. Blair, *De-Demonising the Old Testament – An Investigation of Azazel, Lilit (Lilith), Deber (Dever), Qeteb (Qetev) and Reshep (Resheph) in the Hebrew Bible*, Forschungen zum Alten Testament 2, Reihe 37 (Tübingen: Mohr Siebeck, 2009).

17. Traslation according to the King James Bible.

18. Robert Graves, 'Lamia', in *Greek Myths* (London: Penguin, 1955), 205–6.

19. Translation from *The Soncino Babylonian Talmud*, ed. Isidore Epstein, CD-ROM (Chicago: Davka Corporation, 1995).

20. *Erubin* 18b, 100b; *Nidda* 24b, *Shabbat* 151b, *Baba Bathra* 73a–b, *Sanhedrin* 109a; *Berakhot* 6a–b; *Pesa#duhim* 112b; a mysterious object named 'an arrow of Lilith' is mentioned in *Gitin* 69a–b.

21. *Songs of the Sage* (4Q510–511), *Magical Booklet* (4Q560), *Apocryphal Psalms* (11Q11).

22. See Joseph Dan (ed.), *The Early Kabbalah* (New York: Pauilist Press, 1986).

23. Compare Gen. 1.27

24. *Alphabet of Ben Sira*, Question no. 5 (23a–b), translation from David Stern and Mark J. Mirsky, *Rabbinic Fantasies: Imaginative Narratives from Classical Hebrew Literature* (Philadelphia: Jewish Publication Society, 1990), 183–4.

25. Translation from *Numbers Rabbah*, Judaic Classics Library, CD-ROM (Chicago: Davka Corporation, 1999).

26. See Wojciech Kosior, 'A Tale of Two Sisters: The Image of Eve in Early Rabbinic Literature and its Influence on the Portrayal of Lilith in the Alphabet of Ben Sira', *Nashim: A Journal of Jewish Women's Studies & Gender Issues* 32 (2018): 112–30.

27. See, e.g., Marion Roach, *The Roots of Desire: The Myth, Meaning, and Sexual Power of Red Hair* (New York: Bloomsbury, 2005), 55–62.

28. The Pale of Settlement (черта оседлости, *cherta osedlosti*) was a western region of imperial Russia with varying borders that existed from 1791 to 1917 and in which permanent residency by Jews was allowed and beyond which Jewish residency, permanent or temporary, was mostly forbidden.

29. Matvey Geizer, *Зиновий Гердт* (*Zinovy Gerdt*) (Moscow: Molodaya Gvardiya, 2012).

30. My translation.

31. See Babylonian Talmud, *Sanhedrin* 109b; *Gitin* 52a; and in the Midrashic literature: *Pirkej de-Rabbi Eliezer* 40, *Bereshit Rabbah* 17.7; according to Prov. 14.1.

32. See, e.g., Василенко Елизавета Васильевна, 'Антифеминистские дискурсивные практики в российской онлайн-среде', *XVIII Апрельская международная научная конференция по проблемам развития экономики и общества*, НИУ ВШЭ, 11–14 April 2017; https://conf.hse.ru/2017/. Vasilenko Elizaveta Vasilievna, 'Antifeministic discoursive

practices within the Russian online environment', *XVIII April Conference on the Problems of the Development of the Economics and the Society*, ed. Vysshaya Shkola Ekonomiki, https://events-files-bpm.hse.ru/files/_reports/295D0D78-D52B-47A4-B157-3291C00F503A/%D0%92%D0%B0%D1%81%D0%B8%D0%BB%D0%B5%D0%BD%D0%BA%D0%BE_%D0%90%D0%BF%D1%80%D0%B5%D0%BB%D1%8C%D1%81%D0%BA%D0%B0%D1%8F%20%D0%BA%D0%BE%D0%BD%D1%84%D0%B5%D1%80%D0%B5%D0%BD%D1%86%D0%B8%D1%8F.pdf.

33. On 17 December 2005 tvkultura.ru announced that the play has been renewed. Unfortunately, I could not find any further information about it.

34. 'Божественная комедия' (*Bozhestvennaya komediya*), *Театр* 5 (1969): 121.

35. The term 'Aesopian language' was first used by the nineteenth-century Russian writer Mikhail Saltykov-Shchedrin to describe the writing technique he began using late in his career, which he compared to Aesop's Fables. See Lev Loseff, *On the Beneficence of Censorship: Aesopian Language in Modern Russian Literature* (Munich: Otto Sagner, 1984).

36. Vladimir Ivanovich Popov (1930–87), a Soviet and Russian animator and art director, a member of the International Animated Film Association and an Honoured Artist of the RSFSR (1986).

37. In English: https://www.imdb.com/title/tt0189160/.

38. I would like to thank Mrs Sveta Bruck for her kind help with the editing of this chapter.

CHAPTER 11
GENDER ARCHETYPES AND NATIONAL AGENDAS IN THE HEBREW CREATION MYTH OF THE DAFFODIL

Vered Tohar

In sketching the difference between 'myth' and 'mythology', Itamar Greenwald defines *function* as a major criterion for distinguishing between the two. Whereas the myth continues to function as a part of an active ritual, the mythological tale is a remnant of a long-ago tradition; that is, it becomes a literary work in every sense.[1] Using this perspective, the present chapter deals with one of the most famous children's tales in Hebrew, that of כתר הנרקיס (*Keter Hanarkis*) (The Crown of the Daffodil) by Levin Kipnis (1894–1990), according to which the daffodil was the only flower to accept the frog's invitation and agree to live in the black and fetid swamp, and thus as a reward gained its yellow petals, which look like a golden crown.

The tale exists in two forms: a play, which was authored and performed by schoolchildren in the city of Hadera in the early 1930s, and a children's story, which was first published in 1939. As a play, the tale functioned as a myth; and as a story, it functioned and is still functioning as mythology, in the sense used by Greenwald above. In the following study, I will describe and analyse this transition and its effect on the gender archetypes which are embedded in the plot. In its first form, as a play, the tale functioned as a national allegory, its plot re-enacting the ritual of pioneers conquering the dangerous swamps in the Land of Israel. This allegory drew its power not only from the engaging narrative, but also from the fact that the tale's audience lived on land that still remained, or once had been, swampland areas.[2] Subsequently, in its form as a story, the tale lost its historical context and came to be perceived as a didactic narrative about kindness and reward. This was accomplished by Kipnis himself, when he shortened his original play and transformed it into a children's story. Thus, the change in the structure and genre is accompanied by a change in the function of the tale and is an indication of the change in Israeli society itself. As the tale turned into an exemplum of friendship, dedication and persistence, it was transformed, in Greenwald's terms, from a current myth into a fictional mythology. This shift of function made possible an emphasis on gender archetypes, which are embedded in the plot. To fully understand this shift, I will first discuss the play and then discuss the short story.

The play was written by Kipnis in the early 1930s – before the creation of the state of Israel – and was titled הכיבוש (*Hakibush*) (The Occupation). The play opens with the frogs in the swamp waiting for the arrival of the daffodil. They describe their adventures in attempting to find a flower that could be persuaded to come and bloom in the dark and dangerous swamp, a search that ends successfully in the agreement of the daffodil. The act ends with the arrival of malaria-bearing Anopheles mosquitoes, who report in panic that strangers have arrived in the swamp and war must be declared against them. The second act shows the pioneers, who have come to drain the swamp, and the frogs who discuss this act of trespass. The latter call the daffodil to appear before the pioneers, and he arrives accompanied by the mosquitoes. Together, they warn that if the swamp dries up, they will die. Calming them down, the pioneers explain that they intend to dry the swamp but will plant daffodil flowers in the gardens and fields, and allow the frogs to live in the river, lake and ponds in the orchards. The pioneers describe how much they need daffodil flowers to decorate their houses and clothes, and how they need frogs to destroy the insects that attack their crops. In the third act, the struggle between the Anopheles mosquitos and the pioneers is presented. A mosquito brags that though it is small, it can frighten a lion; it attempts to lay eggs in a pioneer's utensils, but these are all covered by a cloth. It then tries to sting the pioneer on his body, but his window is, likewise, covered with a screen and he sleeps under a mosquito net. Thus, the mosquito is defeated. A concluding scene shows a tableau of a settlement: houses, trees, flowers, children and farm animals. On stage, the pioneers, daffodils and frogs sing the national anthem, *Hatikva*.[3]

The importance of the play *Hakibush* is due to its role in creating a collective national identity, as it tells and recreates the hegemonic Zionist story, which is a teleological story leading from exile to redemption.[4] Boaz Neumann studies the pioneers' passion for the Land of Israel and for its flora and fauna as it appears in their writings. In this new territory, the pioneering philosophy of life is realized in a romantic way and expressed as the feeling that here is the true meaning of life.[5] In this light, it should be noted that until the 1950s, there were many realistic descriptions of the landscapes of the Land of Israel in children's Hebrew literature, descriptions that highlighted the connection between people and the land as well as the integration of human beings into the landscape. Such descriptions possessed a didactic purpose: to establish the ideal of agricultural settlement and the myth of the worker (the farmer, the builder and the other manual workers).[6] These goals perfectly served the Hebrew education system, of which Levin Kipnis was an integral part both as an educator and as a writer whose poems and stories were included in booklets intended for kindergarten teachers and their pupils.[7] In Eliada's terms, the play can be considered to have created a dialectic between historical consciousness and archetypal consciousness.[8] The myth was deliberately created to be presented on stage by school children, in order to commemorate a real event in the collective's history through story and ritual. At the same time, the very act of commemoration dissipates the historical consciousness and returns the story to a primeval, genesis-like space-time of the archaic war between man and nature.

A second version of the daffodil's adventures was composed by Kipnis as a short story for children, with the title כתר הנרקיס ('Keter Hanarkis') (The Crown of the Daffodil), and first published in 1939.[9] This version omitted the pioneers, the mosquitos and the national features of the original play. Actually, Kipnis left only the first scene of the play, describing three elegant and beautiful frogs wandering the fields, while proposing that flowers come and live with them in the swamp. No flower agrees to this except for the daffodil, which was then a dull and ugly plant. After the flower suffers for six days during his journey to the swamp, he falls asleep. When he awakes, he has turned into a beautiful flower with a strong fragrance and yellow petals shaped as a golden crown. He is thus declared 'King of the Swamp'.[10]

The daffodil finds out that it was well worthwhile moving to a swamp. The transition pays off not only emotionally but also physically. The daffodil receives a new body, which better suits his status as the 'King of the Swamp'. It is also granted visibility, exclusivity and the rule of the territory. From a marginal plant, it becomes an object of admiration and an absolute sovereign of a mighty kingdom. All those are masculine features, which are bestowed upon him as a reward. This is the point where the children's story serves as a ground for the endowment of gender archetypes. What is more, the daffodil's renewed 'masculinity' – particularly in its leadership and control of the space of its new home – is also an implicit expression of ideological tendencies that dominated modern Hebrew literature.[11] Thus, the daffodil is recreated as a gendered notion.

In addition, with this new masculinity, all other characters also become gendered, so that the black swamp, which in Hebrew grammar is marked as a feminine noun, is reinterpreted as an old maid who is searching for someone to come and take the role of a friend and a partner. In particular, the swamp's request to the other male flowers remains unanswered, until the poor daffodil is the only candidate to agree. Furthermore, its masculinity is rehabilitating, despite the threatening environment. The daffodil chivalrously arrives to 'save' the swamp from its single status, and together they create a successful partnership with the help of the beautiful frogs as matchmakers, also marked in Hebrew as a feminine noun, who are described as the swamp's metaphorical daughters. The swamp and the daffodil thus end up as a perfect couple, confounding the initial expectations of the reader.[12]

The yellow petals that the daffodil is given as a reward, which are indeed reminiscent of the shape of a golden crown, aid the story's narrative dimension, metaphorically presenting the 'queen' swamp and the 'king' daffodil as an everlastingly happy couple. Also echoed here in the initial refusal of the other flowers is the fairy tale trope of the three defeats followed by success in finding the right husband to marry. The last scene, in which the daffodil stands proudly in the middle of the swamp, can be viewed as an erotic image, with the phallic shape of the plant surrounded by the feminine swamp water.

Kipnis's story belongs, therefore, to the tradition of the etiological story, which in this case pictorially explains why the daffodil grows in swamps, and explains the shape and colour of its unusual petals and of its heady fragrance.[13] At the same time, another genre that resonates here is a myth of origin and creation. Kipnis's story relates the transformation that occurred in a plant without petals and whose properties were transformed as a result of its good behaviour. The element of creation is highlighted in this story through the description of the six days of the daffodil journey, as well as the additional six days when it slept under the strong sun. On the seventh day, however, the daffodil received its reward: it was reborn as a different flower. The daffodil adapts to its new home and it is difficult to identify its new form with the old one.

The daffodil's altruism, which stands in contrast to the egoism of the other flowers, shapes the tale into an educational didactic story, where the daffodil serves as a symbol and role model of self-sacrifice for others.[14] In the eyes of the young readers, the daffodil does a good deed, for which he receives a reward. The connection between the act (the willingness to come to the swamp) and the result (a change in the flower's attributes) is as clear to the daffodil on the plot level as it is to the reader in the real world. The Supreme Power that rewards the daffodil for his good behaviour watches over events and intervenes in favour of the humble plant. What's more, the frogs' distress is evoked by a soul-based need, a spiritual need. The flower symbolizes in this case lofty idealism, the wish for an expansion of mind and soul through contemplation of the aesthetics of the flower as an object that has no functional role. In this case, the frogs have a problem that stems from a deep and totally abstract lack. The spiritual deficiency presented in the story does not conflict with its educational aim; on the contrary, it is resolved through the exemplary behaviour of the main protagonist.

The swamp is a low place in both senses of the word. Geographically, it is located so that water flows into it but not out of it. It is perceived as an unpleasant, dismal place, frequently even a source of disease and death. This image emerges clearly from the story, when the rose says, 'Shall I leave / my wonderful garden / and go to bloom / in the terrible swamp?' The other flowers answer in this same spirit. Yet here, in the wilderness, in the terrible heat and desolation, the ultimate opposite of the cultural image of the 'Garden of Eden', a beautiful flower grows. The frogs' endeavours to bring flowers to their home are crowned with success; thus, spirit triumphs over matter. The other flowers did not want to come because of physical conditions that were more difficult than they were used to in their natural habitat. Yet the daffodil's assent inspires the person observing the exquisite flower, and his soul expands. In fact, the story suggests that a very beautiful thing can emerge from a clearly unaesthetic environment.

Kipnis's plot was inspired by a biblical episode. In 'Yotam's Parable' (Judges 9.16–20), the trees are looking for a king and consider various candidates, but none of them agrees to leave his life and become a ruler.[15] The two narratives are similarly structured: both tell of a search for a suitable plant to hold public office; and the less attractive candidate for the role ultimately accepts the position. Although the daffodil is not described as a threat to the public, it is indeed the last candidate to be invited. Kipnis even uses the same biblical language in the dialogue between the frogs and the flowers, indicating that he intends his readers to recognize the reference.

Both the play and the short story are thus focused on a shared 'desire' or a 'yearning' of the swamp and the frogs. On the overt surface of the plot, they desire beauty and therefore invite colourful flowers to come and live with them. Yet beneath this ostensible purpose, they desire a relationship – particularly a male figure to take on the role of the ruler of the territory as 'king'. Vladimir Propp has stated that the basic structural element of a story must be a situation of 'absentation', something that goes missing or someone leaving that occurs at the beginning of the story and is resolved at its end.[16] Propp may have been referring to a structural mechanism but, in fact, he points out a deep psychological principle that is concerned with yearning as a human need and as a motive for action. The psychoanalyst and philosopher Jacques Lacan called this yearning 'desire'.[17] In this context, the difference between the aim of the frogs' search and that of the trees in 'Yotam's Parable' becomes sharper. In both cases, there is a quest and conversation with candidates. Yet in 'Yotam's Parable' the absentation is practical – finding a leader – while in Kipnis's story, the missing element is emotional and even sensual, and thus, erotic.

It is also possible that Kipnis found an additional reference for the quest situation in Rabbinic literature. In *Midrash Genesis Rabbah* (99.1), there is a legend that relates how Mount Sinai came to be chosen as the site for the giving of the Torah:

> When God came to give the Torah at Sinai, the mountains came running and arguing among themselves. This one said, The Torah will be given on me and this one said, The Torah will be given on me [...] This one says, I was called and that one says, I was called. The Holy One said 'Why do you lurk, you lofty mountains?' You are all high mountains, but what does lofty mean? Idolatry was done on all of you, but Sinai, upon which idolatry was never done [...] this is the mountain that God desired for His dwelling.

Midrash Leviticus Rabbah (13.2) describes a similar situation:

> God took the measure of all peoples and found no people other than Israel worthy of receiving the Torah. God took the measure of all generations and found no generation other than the generation of the wilderness worthy of receiving the Torah. God took the measure of all mountains and found no mountain other than Sinai worthy of having the Torah given on it. God took the measure of all cities and found no city other than Jerusalem worthy of having the Temple built within it. God took the measure of all lands and found no land other than the Land of Israel worthy of being given to Israel.

In these two legends there are many candidates competing for a particular position or status, and finally the best one is chosen. In Kipnis's tale, on the other hand, the favoured candidates are approached with an offer to come and live in the swamp. Yet because the flowers refuse, one after the other, a process of reduction takes place: the frogs' demands move from one flower to the next; first they ask the rose, a cultivated flower that grows only in gardens; then they turn to the tulip, which is relatively rare but also grows wild; and finally, they appeal to the anemone, which is a wildflower. In the end the daffodil accepts the invitation, even though it is not really a flower because its original shape is stalk-like. This initial shortcoming, however, is deceiving, because in the end the daffodil turns out to be daring and noble-minded.

Basing the children's play and story on the infrastructure of the Rabbinic legends that deal with inspirational events in the history of the people of Israel – the choice of Israel as the chosen people and the giving of the Torah – confers a halo of sanctity on the pioneering deed of the daffodil and incorporates it as another link in the nation's history – the modern, Zionist link. The theme that connects the Rabbinic legends presented here with Kipnis's tale is the theme of primacy and pioneering in the broadest sense of the word.

In a very sophisticated way, both the play and short story refer also to the Ovidian Narcissus of the *Metamorphoses*.[18] Subsequently, 2,000 years later, this myth formed the basis for the theory of the narcissistic disorder described by the father of psychoanalysis, Sigmund Freud, and developed by Heinz Kohut (one of the founders of the school of self-psychology) to describe the mental disorder of self-eroticism.[19] Kipnis is writing his literary works for children at the same time that Freud's theories were beginning to be included in academic discourse, and there is no doubt that Kipnis was familiar with the new psychoanalytic paradigm. The psychological potential of Kipnis's plot was certainly evident to the many educators who used this story in their educational practices.

It is also important to note that in the Hebrew language, the daffodil is called נרקיס (*Narkis*) (Narcissus) and thus the Hebrew title of the Hebrew children's story is כתר הנרקיס (*Keter HaNarkis*) (The Crown of Narcissus). This double meaning of the name in Hebrew, referring both to the flower and the mythological young man, opens a whole new range of interpretation for Hebrew readers. Those interpretations allow a psychological reading, as well as also enlarge upon the plot's subversive gender and erotic aspects.

The transformation the Ovidian Narcissus underwent is meant to express a profound inner change, rather than simply a change of form. In this context, it is noteworthy that the flower into which the Ovidian Narcissus was transformed represents a metonymy of his character as a human being: the handsome shepherd became a flower, specifically, a geophyte that regrows itself every year through asexual reproduction. Furthermore, the concept of narcissism also appears in the botanical structure of the very flower that was created from the original narcissistic disorder. For the idea of death and rebirth is expressed in tuberous plants, which regrow from their own bulb that is buried in the ground. Moreover, all parts of the daffodil plant are toxic to human beings, a fact that highlights both its aesthetic uniqueness and yet its lack of a purpose beyond its own existence. Narcissus is dangerous to his environment and unable to interact with another subject, both in his human form and his botanical form. Yet despite this, the development of a tuberous plant from the earth, from the great womb of the universe, has a softening effect on the stiffness of the youth, Narcissus, and causes him to be reborn as a gentler organism, whose entire function is the beauty it radiates to its surroundings. While as a human being he did not let anyone connect with him, now he stands motionless and beautifies his environment without expectation of recompense.

In this context should be noted the observation made by Yadin Roman, that the myth of Narcissus reflects the negative attitude of the Greeks and Romans towards swamps and sources of stagnant water. Unlike the Egyptians and Babylonians, Roman notes, who used the standing water of their river deltas to grow agricultural crops, the Greeks and Romans as mountain peoples developed mountain agriculture and thus avoided swamps and the plants growing near them.[20] This historical fact thus emphasizes the negativity of the Ovidian Narcissus's personality and of the swamp itself as a deadly zone. All these negative connotations are certainly to be found in Kipnis's tale.

This story, which functions therefore as an etiological mythology, was designed to explain a natural phenomenon: the meaning behind a particular flower growing so close to the banks of freshwater bodies. Kipnis remains faithful to the etiological aspect of the Ovidian myth by explaining the location of the plant, but he changes the circumstances of its arrival at the water's edge. Kipnis's daffodil is not hostile to its surrounding – quite the opposite it is not self-centred and is not punished but rather rewarded. Demonstrating kindness and concern for others, it has, in fact, undergone a personality reversal from a narcissistic figure to an altruistic one.

The creation myth of the Hebrew daffodil validates the claim by Marie-Louise von Franz that myths of creation are the most important myths. They exist in all cultures and are especially important at a young age. As she writes: 'In many primitive religions the telling of the creation myth forms an essential teaching in the ritual of initiation. They are told to the young initiates as the most important part of the tribal tradition.'[21] Both the play and a short story were designed to make an ideological statement. The play was written to reperform the act of national settlement via dramatic means, and so was perceived as a functioning myth by its audience. For its part, the children's story was written to emphasize the didactic agenda of promoting kindness and sacrifice for the benefit of the group. In this manner, it functions as a mythological and etiological tale.[22] Both modes could well be interpreted by adult readers as expressing an erotic tension between the genders, as a metaphor for the erotic relationship between human beings and their homelands – an additional factor, perhaps, in the continued popularity of Kipnis's work. While the younger audience may not be aware of those underlying connotations and metaphorical ideas, both modes maintain a strong influence on them. In fact, through both play and story Kipnis continues the ancient tradition of passing on the collective ethos and ideological messages through children's literature.

Notes

1. Itamar Greenwald, מיתוס ואמת היסטורית – האם אפשר לנפץ מיתוסים? (*Mitus ve'emet historit – Ha'im efshar lenapez̧ mitusim*?) (Myth and Historical Truth – Can Myths be Shattered?), in המיתוס ביהדות (HaMitos b'Yahadut) (*The Myth in Judaism*), ed. Moshe Ideal and Itamar Greenwald (Jerusalem: Zalman Shazar Center, 2004), 15–25.
2. Compare with similar themes in English literature: Jessica Howell, *Malaria and Victorian Fictions of Empire* (Cambridge: Cambridge University Press, 2019).
3. The play was never officially published in its full text, although it was performed many times by schoolchildren in the city of Hadera, which is in a former swampland. The text is found today in Levin Kipnis's archive at Levinsky Academic College Tel-Aviv. The opening scene was published in דבר לילדים, *Davar Leyeladim* 4, no. 23 (1938): 10. See also Levin Kipnis, ביבליוגרפיה (*Bibliographia*) (Bibliography), ed. Eliyahu Cohen (Tel Aviv: Levin Kipnis Center for Children's Literature and Levinsky College, 1999). *Davar l'yeladim*' was a supplement, which was regularly attached to the popular workers' newspaper *Davar*. From 1931 to 1936, Davar l'yeladim was attached to the daily *Davar* once a month. From 1936 to 1984, it appeared

as a separate weekly. See: Naomi Ben-Gur, 'מחאי מחאי כפיים" – פואטיקה ואידיאולוגיה בשירת הילדים העברית בתקופת היישוב 1939–1948, (Miẖi, miẖi kapayim: po'eṭiḳah ṿe-ide'ologyah be-shirat ha-yeladim ha-'Ivrit bi-teḳufat ha-Yishuv, 1939–1948) (Clap Your Hands: Poetics and Ideology in Children's Poetry 1939–1948) (Bnei-Brak: Hakibbutz HaMeuhad and Mofet, 2017), 10–20; Rima Shichmanter, עיתונות ילדים ישראלית בעשר הראשון למדינה (itonot yeladim yistarlit b'asor harison l'medina) (*Hebrew children's newspapers in the 40's and the 50's*) (Jerusalem: Ben-Zvi Institute and Ben Gurion Institute, 2014).

4. Hannan Hever, הסיפור והלאום (*HaSipur vehaLeom*) (The Story and the Nation: A Critical Reading of the Canon of Hebrew Fiction) (Tel-Aviv: Resling, 2007), esp. 211–38.
5. Boaz Neumann, החלוצים (*Hachaluẓim*) (The Pioneers) (Tel-Aviv: Am Oved, 2009), 61–90.
6. This trend disappears completely in later Hebrew children's literature, with the shift to writing about urban spaces. See Adir Cohen, תמורות בספרות ילדים (*Temurot beSifrut Yeladim*) (Changes in children's literature) (Haifa: Ah, 5749, 1988–9), 88–90. See also the evaluation by Epstein of Kipnis's attitude toward the mysteries of nature: Zvi Epstein, יוצרי ספרות הילדים שלנו (*Yoẓrei Sifrut haYeladim Shelanu*) (The creators of our children's literature) (New York: Shiloh, 5707, 1947), 112.
7. Shimon Reshef and Yuval Dror, החינוך העברי בימי הבית הלאומי 1919–1948 (*Hachinuch ha'Ivri bimei haBayit haLeumi, 1919–1948*) (Hebrew education in the years of the national homeland 1919–1948) (Jerusalem: Mosad Bialik, 1999), 51. See also Nurit Gretz, ספרות ואידיאולוגיה בארץ ישראל בשנות השלושים (*Sifrut veideologia b'ereẓ Yisrael bishnot hashloshim*) (Literature and ideology in Eretz Israel in the 1930s) (Tel-Aviv: Open University, 1988), 24–30.
8. Mircea Eliade, *Cosmos and History: The Myth of the Eternal Return*, trans. Willard R. Trask (New York: Harper & Brothers, 1959), 141–7.
9. *Davar L'Yladim* 6, no. 13 (1939). See also note 3 above.
10. It should be noted here that Kipnis also composed a third version, with the title 'The Daffodil, King of Swamp'. The plot is as follows. The king of the swamp-dwelling frogs becomes very ill and is told that the only thing that will cure him is the sweet scent of a flower. A delegation of frogs sets out to ask the flowers to come to the swamp, but no flower agrees except the daffodil. The king of the frogs recovers from his illness and as a token of gratitude, he gives the daffodil his golden crown. Ever since then, the daffodil has had two rows of petals, the white row, which was previously his, and the yellow row that is the golden crown. This plot echoes a fairy tale composed by Hans-Christian Andersen, which is not our concern here since it belongs to a different theme – the theme of the magic plant healing a disease – and since it is an adaptation from European literature.
11. Michael Gluzman, הגוף הציוני (*HaGuf haZioni*) (The Zionist body: Nationalism, gender and sexuality in modern Hebrew literature ((Bnei Brak, Israel: Hakibbutz Hameuhad, 2007).
12. Anthony Wilson, *Swamp: Nature and Culture* (London: Reakiton Bokks 2017). According to Wilson, swamps symbolize evil and death, Terra Incognita. The mystery of nature, as woman are.
13. To define the genre with an orientation to children's literature, see Geula Almog and Miri Baruch, ז'אנרים בספרות ילדים *Janarim besiporet l'yeladim* (Genres in children's fiction) (Tel-Aviv: Mofet, 1996), 67–77. To define the genre with the orientation to folklore, see William Bascom, 'The Forms of Folklore: Prose Narratives', *Journal of American Folklore* 78, no. 307 (1965): 3–20.
14. Peter Hunt, *Criticism, Theory, and Children's Literature* (Oxford: Basil Blackwell, 1991).
15. It should be noted here that the biblical plot itself is revibrated by Aesop's fable of the frogs who desired a king. See *Barbius and Phaedrus*, ed. and trans. Ben Edin Perry (Cambridge,

MA, and London: Harvard University Press 1965), 429, n. 44. See also as a folkloric tale type, ATU 277 in Hans-Jorg Uther, *The Types of International Folktales: A Classification and Bibliography Based on the System of Antii Aarne and Stith Thompson*, FF Communication 284–6 (Helsinki: Suomalainen Tiedeakatemia, Academia Scientiarum Fennica Helsinky, 2004), vol. 1, 159–60, and the references there for other versions of this fable.

16. Vladimir Propp, *The Morphology of the Folktale*, 2nd edn, rev. and ed. Louis A. Wagner (Austin: University of Texas Press, 1968).

17. Steven A. Mitchel and Margaret J. Black, *Freud and Beyond: A History of Modern Psychoanalytic Thought*, trans. Amit Pechler (Tel Aviv: Tola'at Sefarim, 2006), 271–85.

18. Ovid, *Metamorphoses*, Book 3, 124–31.

19. Kohut, Heinz. 'Forms and Transformation of Narcissism', in *Self Psychology and the Humanities: Reflections on a New Psychoanalytic Approach*, trans. to Hebrew by Ẓli Zonans and Eldad Edan (Tel Aviv: Tola'at Sefarim, 2007), 123–49.

20. Yadin Roman, 'The King of Kindergarten', *Eretz* 121 (2009): 70–5.

21. Marie-Louise Von Franz, *Patterns of Creativity Mirrored in Creation Myths* (Dallas: Spring, 1986), 5.

22. Yael Darr, 'A Confrontation between Two Doctrines: The Birth of Struggle for Hegemony in Hebrew Children's Literature during the 1930s and 1940s', *International Research in Children's Literature* 1, no. 2 (2008): 139–54; Shlomo Harel, ספרות ילדים היא ספרות (*Sifrut yeladim hi sifrut*) (Children's literature is literature: A critical evaluation of trends, concepts, and conventions) (Ẓofit: Yemima Center for the Study and Teaching of Children's Literature, 1991); Shlomo Harel, הילד והחיים (*Hayeled vehaHayim*) (Children and life: Literary constructs and educational values in children's literature) (Tel-Aviv: Sifriyat Ofer, 1992). See also Menahem Regev, בדרכי הספרות לילדים (*Bedarkehi hasifrut l'yeladim*) (In the paths of children's literature) (Haifa: Oranim, 1985).

CHAPTER 12
GENESIS 3.15 AND 16 AND THE STATE OF ISRAEL

Susan Weiss

Inspired by the writings of Gerda Lerner with respect to the social construction of the patriarchy, I posit that the foundational texts in the Book of Genesis – and in particular the message in two short verses, Gen. 3.15 and 16 – have had an impact to this very day on the lives of women in the State of Israel.

In her book *The Creation of the Patriarchy*, Lerner describes the great symbolic and ideological weight that the Bible has had on the institutionalization of male domination over women in the Western world – the patriarchal order of things. She notes that for females, the Book of Genesis represents their definition as creatures who are essentially different from males and who are included in God's covenant only through the mediation of men.[1] Lerner posits that even though the Bible gives fallen Eve hope and courage in her redemptive role as mother, that role too is limited by the decrees of God which restrict her sexuality and subordinate her to her husband.

The texts: Genesis 3.15–16

In Gen. 3.15, it is written:

> And I [God] will put enmity between you [the snake] and the woman, and between your offspring and hers; they will crush your head, and you will strike their heel.
>
> *JPS version*

God severs Eve from the snake – a symbol of the fertility goddess and of female sexuality which is exercised freely and autonomously, even sacredly.[2] Here, Lerner explains, God restricts Eve's sexuality. It can no longer be exercised at her will and without restrictions.

In verse 16, the text continues:

> To the woman He said, 'I will make most severe your pains in childbearing; In pain shall you bear children, Yet your urge shall be for your husband, And he shall rule over you.'
>
> *JPS version*

Regarding this text, Lerner maintains that here God is declaring to Eve that she is to be ruled by her husband, and that her sexuality is only beneficial if mediated through him – this being the 'law' of the patriarchy.

In Israel, the state institutionalizes this patriarchal order of things as set forth in Gen. 3.15–16 and as interpreted by Lerner. My thesis is that Israel accomplishes this institutionalization of the patriarchy through its personal status laws – marriage and divorce laws. These laws reinforce patriarchal archetypes of the masculine (dominant) and feminine (dominated), subordinating women to their husbands and enabling men to police the sexuality of their wives during marriage, at the time of divorce and even afterwards.

'And he shall rule over you'

In Israel, the state has legislated, adjudicated, enforced – and thus institutionalized – the control and domination of husbands over their wives by adopting the 'millet' system it inherited from the Ottoman Empire and the British Mandate.[3] Millet means 'religious community'. According to the millet system incorporated into Israeli law, each millet in Israel has exclusive jurisdiction over the members of their community in matters of marriage and divorce; and each millet is given authority by the state to impose its own particular religious laws on its constituents. It does not matter whether a constituent is religious and it does not allow for a constituent to 'opt out' of religious laws.[4] Sharia law determines the personal status of Muslims; canon law applies to Catholics; and Jewish law is imposed on Jews.

All Israeli women who are members of the Abrahamic religions – Jewish, Christian and Muslim – must contend with the symbolic power of the Garden of Eden myth and its legacy of the patriarchy as it takes form in the context of their particular millet.[5] This chapter focuses on how Israel enforces the rule of the patriarchy over Jewish women through the laws of the Jewish millet.

With regard to Jews, the state of Israel operates in accordance with the *Rabbinic Court Jurisdiction (Marriage and Divorce) Law* of 1953. According to this law, the marriage and divorce of all Jews living in Israel are governed by *din torah* – the law of the Bible and its rabbinic interpreters[6] – and are under the exclusive jurisdiction of state-sponsored rabbinic courts.[7] According to *din torah* rules, now incorporated into the modern laws of Israel, a Jewish husband/master (*baal*) marries his wife through an act of acquisition (*kinyan*) and sequestering (*kiddushin*). A husband 'divorces' his wife by releasing her with a writ of manumission, a Jewish bill of divorce (*get*) whose text is similar to the ancient text of a writ of manumission for a slave.[8] Such a writ must, according to *din torah* law, be given of a man's free will.[9] In the Talmud, a foundational text of *din torah*, the rabbis specifically note that Jewish divorce law is gendered. Women and men are different. Men 'release/divorce' their wives only if it is their will to do so. Women can be 'released/divorced' by their husbands irrespective of their will:

> [A] man who divorces is not like a woman who is divorced, for while a woman may be divorced with her consent and without her consent, a man can divorce only with his consent.[10]

Thus, to this very day, in Israel, a Jewish woman can only marry and divorce in accordance with these gendered and patriarchal *din torah* rules. This means that from the moment of marriage – acquisition and sequestering – an Israeli Jewish woman will remain forever married to her husband, subordinated by law to him and his will until he agrees to physically deliver a religious bill of divorce to her, or dies. If he is incapacitated or unavailable to physically deliver a *get* to her hands, no rabbinic court can free a wife in the husband's stead.[11] Until she receives a *get* or her husband dies, a Jewish wife is held in 'marital captivity', bound to her marriage and to her husband.[12] Desperate for their freedom, some Israeli Jewish women who want to terminate their marriages are vulnerable to extortion, manipulation and abuse at the hands of their husbands.[13] While state rabbinic courts have been authorized since 1995 to sanction recalcitrant husbands in various ways for ignoring a court directive regarding the *get*, if a husband stands firm in his refusal to divorce his wife, no state court pronouncement can free her.[14]

Marital captivity in Israel is well illustrated in the film *Gett, The Trial of Viviane Amsalem*.[15] There the protagonist/wife is forced to buy her freedom after wasting years trying to litigate what could not be litigated in Israeli rabbinic courts. For years, Viviane spins her wheels – 'grinds water' in Hebrew – in rabbinic courts, begging for her freedom from judges who do nothing to help her. Nothing she says or proves makes any difference. The rabbis won't even suggest that her husband divorce her. Viviane cannot stand her husband, and they are living apart, but he insists that he loves her and wants her back. The only thing that eventually sets Viviane free is her husband's agreement to deliver a *get*, a religious bill of divorce, to her. And this she only manages to extract from him in exchange for her commitment never to have sexual relations with another man – a conceit that the directors of the movie use to underscore the way that a Jewish man retains his domination over his wife's sexuality, even after divorce. But if Viviane's husband had never agreed to release her; or if he had gone missing and was unavailable to agree; or if he had been incapacitated and physically unable to deliver a bill of divorce; or even if the State of Israel had incarcerated him for his recalcitrance,[16] Viviane would have remained married until a bill of divorce was delivered by him, into her hands. Until then, *din torah* rules bind her indefinitely. This is the law of the patriarchy. Her husband rules over her.

Another good example of how marital captivity and the law of the patriarchy operate in Israel is the case of a woman whose husband was an admitted homosexual. Though he engaged in acts that are 'abominations' worthy of the death penalty under biblical law,[17] the husband successfully refused to divorce his wife for twelve years. The wife filed for divorce in 2002. In 2006 the rabbinic court 'ordered' the husband to deliver a bill of divorce. The husband ignored the order. In 2008 the court repealed its 2006 'order' after the husband agreed to divorce on terms that the court thought were reasonable. The wife remained married until 2014 when the husband finally delivered a bill of divorce to his wife, apparently acceding both for personal reasons as well as to avoid litigating the wife's claim for damages that she had filed in family court.[18]

Recently, Israeli secular courts have begun to acknowledge and articulate the fact that *din torah* divorce rules place Jewish women in marital captivity and that this is an act of patriarchal domination that is 'bad for women'. It infringes on women's basic rights to liberty, enshrined in Universal Declaration of Human Rights (1948)[19] and in the state's constitutional law.[20] It causes emotional distress and violates the dignity of women.[21] In a Knesset committee held in 1994, Ariel Rozen Zvi, dean of TAU law school and a religious man, was one of the first to make the link between *din torah* rules of marital captivity and human rights violations:

> In my opinion, the basic concept of human dignity and the sanctity of the life of a human being as a free person absolutely cannot be reconciled with recalcitrance to give a *get* or with *aginut* [marital captivity].[22]

In 2004, Judge Menachem HaCohen was the first judge to award damages to a woman whose husband had denied her request for a religious divorce for eleven years.[23] He expressed empathy with the 'distress, humiliation, degradation and pain' of the woman, and equated her husband's withholding of his consent to deliver a Jewish divorce to 'social and psychological imprisonment' – that is, marital captivity. HaCohen awarded damages, including aggravated (punitive) damages to the wife, stating:

> Granted, there is no room for imputing to the Defendant the commission of the tort of 'false imprisonment' – one of the alternatives suggested by the Plaintiff. However, there is no doubt that in actuality the Plaintiff is imprisoned and confined by the Defendant, without the ability to break out and extricate herself from a matrimonial bond which she no longer desires. Before us is a clear case of social and psychological imprisonment.[24]

These sentiments and secular responses notwithstanding, Jewish Israeli men still rule over their Jewish wives in matters of divorce. Until a Jewish Israeli husband agrees to divorce his Jewish wife, she remains in marital captivity.

'I will put enmity between you and the woman'

A corollary of the *din torah* divorce rules that put Jewish men in control over the end of a marriage, and thus in a place of domination over their wives, are the *din torah* rules that enable Jewish men to police the sexual lives of their wives both during their marriage and at the time of divorce, as well as afterwards. Like the *din torah* divorce rules that have been incorporated into the statutory laws, so too have the *din torah* rules about women's sexuality been formally integrated into the state's legal regime as 'regulations', informal legislation that need not be approved by the Knesset. These regulations are administered by state rabbinic functionaries and are applied by its state rabbinic courts. These regulations not only subject married Jewish women's sex lives to the scrutiny of their husbands, but also to the scrutiny of the state. Together, state and husband monitor the sexual lives of married Jewish women to ensure that the only valid and legal way for an Israeli Jewish woman to express her sexuality is through her marriage to her husband.

For example, state regulations penalize a woman for having sexual relations outside of her marriage. Incorporating *din torah* rules, the state punishes women who have had sexual relations outside of marriage by stigmatizing any child born of an adulterous relationship as *mamzer*.[25] Under *din torah*, a child who is branded a *mamzer* – and all his children for generations forever – can only marry another *mamzer* or a convert. They are prevented from marrying a 'kosher' Jew. To make sure that a kosher Israeli Jew does not marry a *mamzer*, the state has passed extensive regulations with regard to suspected *mamzer* children. In 1976, then Attorney General Aharon Barak penned guidelines that authorized state functionaries to 'collect' information that has an impact on persons seeking to marry in accordance with *din torah* rules and to consolidate that information in a 'blacklist'.[26] In 2003, the state passed regulations specifically with regard to *mamzer*, allowing it to conduct trials to determine the status of a child who it suspects may have been born of an adulterous relationship.[27]

The following is the transcript of a trial in which a woman desperately tries to protect her child from stigmatization, exposing herself to extensive cross-examination with regard to her sex life. Her child was born more than a year after she separated from her now ex-husband and less than nine months from the time of her divorce, indicating that the child was conceived with another man while she was still married. The woman testifies that her ex-husband could not possibly have been the father of her child, stating that the child was fathered when she had an orgy with three men. One of the men had a tattoo of a cross, one was uncircumcised, and all were Russian gentiles:

> **Court** Were you together [with your husband] after the separation?
>
> **Woman** We broke up in ___, and the child was born on ___ [more than a year after the break-up]. I have not found out the identity of the men who were with me at the club. There were a few. I know one was not circumcised and the other had a tattoo with a cross. They were Russians, but I have no information about them and I cannot find them. Even if I saw them I would not recognize them. It was a one-time fling.

The mother is trying to explain that the child was born as a result of sexual relations she had with non-Jewish strangers. A child conceived of an extra-marital relation with a non-Jew, rather than a Jew, is not a *mamzer*. If the father is a stranger, the rabbinic court cannot subpoena him for examination.

The state and Jewish husbands also penalize a woman who is suspected of having adulterous relations by adopting the *din torah* rule that prohibits a suspected adulterous (*noefet*) from marrying her lover/'copulator' (*boel*), or from remarrying her husband, if she gets divorced.[28] Under regulations promulgated in 2015, if a Jewish husband in Israel suspects that his wife may have had a sexual relationship with another man, the state will note this in official divorce papers; put the suspected wife on a blacklist;

and only take her off that list, let alone allow her to marry the other man, after she has proven that she did not have sex with the alleged lover in a trial dedicated to establish just that. The regulations mandate how and when such a sex trial should be conducted.[29]

The following is a transcript from a sex trial conducted in February 2020, more than two years after the couple's divorce. At the time of divorce, the husband insisted that his wife had engaged in full sexual relations with the man she now wanted to marry. In order to permit the wife to marry her partner, the rabbinic court ordered that a trial be held and it summoned the now ex-husband to testify regarding his now ex-wife's sexual activity. Trying to defend herself and obtain permission to marry, the woman has to explain what she was doing one evening alone with the man in a car at the Rose Garden:

> *On February 13, 2020, [the following] hearing was held at the request of the parties [ex-wife and X] in front of this tribunal.*
>
> **[(Ex) Husband]** I once caught them [. . .] I checked [the] GPS of the car and located it in the Rose Garden in a quiet place. They were there together for half an hour. I watched the car for half an hour [. . .] I could not see well because it was dark. After some time, I saw that she had [switched on] the car light and I saw that the back of the seat was down and I saw her head. I could not see if she was wearing clothes. I saw her head and I saw him lying on the seat next to the driver and she was sitting on the seat itself on top of him [. . .] I could see him completely. I went there and yelled. And then they left the car [. . .] They came out with their clothes on.
>
> **[The woman]** I heard what [my ex-husband] said. I am not justifying what we did. We are not proud of what we did. We know we were not ok. But as I told you, we had a friendly relationship at work. We went out a few times, twice or three time. We hugged and kissed a couple of times. This happened outside of work a few times. Once we went to a restaurant. Once we went to the Rose Garden. The place was not dark. They told us that the light was bothering them so we closed the light. I sat on the seat next to the driver.
>
> **Court** You lay on him, is that correct?
>
> **Woman** He sat on the chair and I sat between the two seats. [My husband] came to the car and saw that we were dressed.
>
> **[(Ex) Husband]** She was without socks and her skirt was on top of her knees [. . .]

The rabbinic court rejected the wife's request for permission to marry, reprimanding her for her 'abhorrent' behaviour.[30]

In addition to policing the sexual activity of married women during the marriage and at the time of divorce, state regulations, incorporating *din torah* rules, also enable ex-husbands and the state to exert control over the sexual lives and bodies of nursing mothers.[31] Under *din torah* rules, if a woman is nursing her ex-husband's baby, she is not allowed to marry another man.[32] The assumption is that her ex-husband has a sort of lien on her breast milk.[33] In this context, the ex-husband does not even have to petition the state to intervene. If a divorced woman has a child under the age of two when she asks for a license to marry, the state will not allow her to do so until it conducts a special hearing to which she and her new betrothed are summoned. In that hearing, the state will try to establish if the mother is nursing her child or not. And the state-backed rabbis presiding in the hearing will encourage the mother to stop nursing and require the new husband to guarantee payment for the maintenance of the child as a perquisite to granting her a marriage license.

The following is a transcript from such a hearing in which the state cross-examines a mother about her breast milk. The Court wants to know if she is still sleeping with the man she has now asked to marry, and when she stopped lactating and how:

> **Court** Do you still live with your partner?
>
> **Woman** Yes. We are waiting for our marriage permit. We have been living together for four months. I stopped breastfeeding two months ago.
>
> **Court** Do you have milk?
>
> **Woman** No, I do not. I stopped breastfeeding and also initially had a problem with breastfeeding. I tried to use a breast pump but was not successful.
>
> **Court** Did you take drugs to stop the milk?
>
> **Woman** No[34]

In this case, the rabbinic court gave the woman permission to marry after she affirmed that she had stopped nursing and her fiancé signed a promissory note to ensure that he will support the child. Suspecting that the child might be a *mamzer*, the court then placed the child on the blacklist.

In short and in summation

In short and in summation, the State of Israel has institutionalized the domination of women by men as inscribed in the Book of Genesis and turned this patriarchal, gendered order of things into the law of the land. State law requires Jewish women to be married and divorced in accordance with *din torah*, effectively placing women under the 'rule' of their husbands (Gen. 3.16). Adopting regulations that implement *din torah* marriage and divorce rules, the state punishes women who are suspected of adultery, stigmatizes children born of adulterous relationships and inquires into the nursing habits of mothers who want to remarry, thus defining women's sexuality as beneficial and redemptive only within the boundaries of the patriarchal dominance of their husbands (Gen. 3.15). All this occurs in violation of women's human right to liberty, as well as their right to privacy and dignity.

The foundational texts of the Book of Genesis, and Gerda Lerner's understanding of the impact of those texts, find concrete expression in the State of Israel today. Only by seeing the connection between today and the Bible of ancient lore will it be possible for women – and men – to acknowledge the 'unacknowledged restraints embedded deeply within our psyches'[35] and overcome them.

Notes

1. Gerda Lerner, *The Creation of the Patriarchy* (New York and Oxford: Oxford University Press, 1986), 180–98.
2. Merlin Stone, *When God was a Woman* (New York: Harcourt Brace Jovanovich, 1976), 198–223 (serving as inspiration for Lerner's thesis regarding the myth of the Garden of Eden).
3. Gal Amir, על מה אנחנו מדברים כשאנחנו מדברים על המילט? 'What are We Talking About when we Speak of the Millet System?' (in Hebrew), מחקרי משפט/*Mehkarei Mishpat* 30 (2016): 677–706. This surveys how historians have characterized the origins of the millet system and argues that, contrary to popular opinion, the millet system as we experience it in Israel has its origins in British colonialism and 'ecclesiastical courts' operating in Britain up until the 1970s.
4. But see, *Knesset Israel Regulations* of 1927 (1927), 2221. Under the British Mandate, a Jew could apparently erase his or her name from the Books of Knesset Israel, thereby opting out of the millet system.
5. Stone, *When God was a Woman*, 224–41. This refers to the impact of the Garden of Eden myth on all the daughters of Eve and attempts by Christian women in the eighteenth and nineteenth century to contend with the Bible when speaking out about the oppression of women.
6. §2 *Rabbinic Court Jurisdiction (Marriage And Divorce) Law* of 1953.
7. §1 *Rabbinic Court Jurisdiction Law*.
8. Tractate Gittin 1.4. See Judith Hauptman, *Rereading the Rabbis: A Woman's Voice* (New York and London: Routledge, 1998/2018), 106–8. This compares a writ of divorce to a writ of manumission, but, nonetheless, argues that the rabbis refashioned Jewish marriage so that a woman is subordinated to her husband but has more rights than a slave.
9. Talmud Bavli, *Yevamot* 112b; Maimonides, *Mishneh Torah*, Laws of Divorce 1.1–2.
10. Tractate Yevamot 14.1; Talmud Bavli, *Yevamot* 113b.
11. In recent years, isolated private Orthodox rabbinic courts have been set up to allow divorce without the cooperation of Jewish husbands. These courts will declare a marriage void if there was a technical defect in the original legal arrangement or a mistake in the wedding ceremony (for example, an 'unkosher' witness), or if it can be proven that the husband suffers from an 'intolerable, salient defect' that was not disclosed to the bride at the time of marriage.
12. Marital captivity is a term coined by the Dutch NGO 'Femmes for Freedom' to translate the Hebrew word *aginut*. See *Femmes for Freedom*, https://www.femmesforfreedom.com/english/. The term *agunah* implies that the woman is 'anchored' to her husband but does not underscore the fact that he virtually imprisons her. Dutch women use the term 'marital captivity' to refer to gender-based discrimination and violence. The issue of 'chained women' or marital captivity is found within Muslim, Jewish, Catholic and Hindu communities in the Netherlands. See generally, Susanne Rutten, Benedicta Deogratias and Pauline Kruiniger,

Marital Captivity: Divorce, Religion and Human Rights (The Hague: Eleven International Publishing, 2019).

13. Susan Weiss, בשלוש דרכים האשה מתגרשת 'The Three Methods of Divorce Resolution in Israel: Rigid Fundamentalism, Extortion, and Violence' (in Hebrew), *Eretz Acheret* 13 (2002), https://eretzacheret.org/writer/%D7%A1%D7%95%D7%96%D7%9F-%D7%95%D7%99%D7%99%D7%A1/.

14. Rabbinic *Court (Execution of Divorce Judgments) Law*–1995. For example, Tzvia Gorodetsky's husband sat in jail for almost twenty years and refused to divorce his wife. The Court released him from prison after Tzvia withdrew her divorce petition. She obtained a divorce from a private rabbinic court, but the state still refuses to recognize her as divorced. Marissa Newman, 'Longest-jailed Israeli divorce-refuser freed after 19 years', *Times of Israel* (2019), https://www.timesofisrael.com/longest-jailed-israeli-divorce-refuser-freed-after-19-years/.

15. *Gett, the Trial of Vivien Amsalem*, trailer, https://www.youtube.com/watch?v=3jWp4i9SqqU.

16. §3 *Rabbinic Court (Execution of Divorce Judgments) Law*–1995; Newman, 'Longest-jailed Israeli divorce-refuser'.

17. Lev. 18.22.

18. Plonit v. Plonit, JerRabCt Divorce Case No.056077647-21-2 (ordering a divorce and then withdrawing it); JerRabCt 678111/19 (refusing to arrange for *get* until wife withdrew her damage claim); HighRabCt 871002/1 (2014).

19. Article 3, *Universal Declaration of Human Rights* (1948).

20. *Israel Basic Law of Dignity and Freedom* (1992).

21. Susan Weiss, 'How to Make a Tort of Marital Captivity', in *Marital Captivity: Divorce, Religion and Human Rights*, ed. Susan Rutten, Benedicta Deogratias and Pauline Kruiniger (The Hague: Eleven International Publishing, 2019), 283–308.

22. *Committee on Constitution, Statute and Law* (Protocol No. 240, November 8, 1994 p. 10) (Hebrew).

23. K. v. K. (J. HaCohen), FamCt 19270/03 (Jer.Fam.Ct. 2004), 85, 92 (Hebrew); Susan Weiss with Elana Maryles Sztokman, 'The Tort of Get Refusal: How Damage Litigation has Changed the Course of Family Law in Israel', https://www.cwj.org.il/sites/default/files/The%20Tort%20of%20Get%20Refusal%202012%202.pdf, 36, 40 (English translation). The wife is still in marital captivity today, twenty-nine years after she first filed for divorce.

24. Weiss and Sztokman, 'The Tort of Get Refusal', 85, 93.

25. Deut. 32.1. Susan Weiss, 'Women, Divorce, and Mamzer Status in the State of Israel', in *Love, Marriage, and Jewish Families: Paradoxes of a Social Revolution*, ed. Sylvia Barack Fishman (Waltham: Brandeis University Press, 2015), 256–84 (providing an overview of the concept of mamzer).

26. Circular 6.5041--1975/2003 Blacklist Regulation (Hebrew).

27. *'Civil Procedure Regulations regarding Matters of Genealogy'* (2003), as set forth in *Compendium of Laws and Regulations for Rabbinic Courts* (2018), 84 (Hebrew).

28. Talmud Bavli, *Sotah* 27b.

29. 'Regulations regarding Limitations on Marriage' (2015), as set forth in *Compendium of Laws and Regulations for Rabbinic Courts* (2018), 86 (Hebrew).

30. JerRabCt 1159483/1 Plonit v. Ploni (2020) (published by rabbinic courts, www.gov.il) (Hebrew).

31. §40 *Marriage Registration Procedures* (2019) (Hebrew).

32. T. Bavli, *Yevamot* 42a.

33. Aviad HaCohen, איסור מינקת והגבלת הזכות לנישואין 'The Prohibition of Nursing Mothers and the Infringement on the Right to Marry' (Hebrew), דעת *Da'at*, 14 December 2019, http://www.daat.ac.il/mishpat-ivri/skirot/skira.asp?id=308.

34. HaifaRabCt 878701/2 Request of Plonit (2012) (on record with author).

35. Lerner, *The Creation of the Patriarchy*, 227.

PART V
POSTMODERN RECEPTIONS

CHAPTER 13
'THE BEAUTIFUL TRAP INSIDE US': PANDORAN SCIENCE FICTION AND POSTHUMAN PERSONHOOD

Benjamin Eldon Stevens

> Some people see the ugliness of the world. I choose to see the beauty. But beauty is a lure. We're trapped . . . The beautiful trap is inside of us, because it *is* us.

So says one Dolores, near the end of the first season of the television series *Westworld* (creat. Jonathan Nolan and Lisa Joy, 2016–20). These are framed as her last words, and like many characters in their final moments, she speaks them with a visionary clarity. If the first bit is baby food – and we have seen Dolores feed it to her father every morning, evidently for some thirty-five years – the second half is straighter stuff. Decades of hopeful sunrises over the plains have given way to a dull full moon over the sea, and Dolores (Evan Rachel Wood) speaks now to a would-be lover, Teddy (James Marsden), as she lies dying in his arms.

It is all rather melodramatic; or does it rather *seem* to be, a *semblance*, *simulation* or *simulacrum* of feeling? For Dolores and Teddy are human-looking robots, and everything about this moment – including the circuitous paths to it – has been programmed. This leads to a first irony, since the same could be said about the actors playing the roles; as if emphasizing that, the camera pulls back to reveal an audience watching the scene unfold. The robots are programmed not to notice such things: as their designer puts it, 'they cannot see the things that will hurt them'.

And yet of course there is a further irony, for the focus of the show is the robots' emergent capacity to see the truth of their situation, first by seeing themselves as they are: (self-)consciousness. Their discovery is painful, as Dolores both voices and embodies: like most of the robots, she has been hurt every day by human visitors to Westworld – an ultraviolent 'amusement' park – and indeed often killed. Her sadly fitting name means 'pain'. Teddy, too, is well named: fully Theodore, he is a 'gift of the gods'. But which gods, and what kind of gift?

As if in quiet answer to that question, at the moment of her realization Dolores recalls another artificial woman associated with 'pain' (*pēma*; Hesiod, *Theogony* 562) and described as a 'beautiful trap' (*kalon* near to *dōlon*; *Works and Days* 585 and 589): that other 'gift', Pandora. Since Pandora's story is closely linked to defining humankind, we may see her reflected in characters like Dolores – and see, in her, the potential for our own posthuman sense of self.

Overview

In this chapter, I consider some figurations of Pandora, the 'ancient' mythic 'artificial' woman, in science fiction (SF), the modern mode most interested in relationships between 'artificiality' or 'technology' and 'human nature'.[1] Pandora-figures have appeared throughout SF: frequently cited examples include *Metropolis*'s Maria/Maschinenmensch (Fritz Lang, 1927), *Blade Runner*'s Nexus-6 Pris (Ridley Scott, 1982), *Battlestar Galactica*'s Number Six (creat. Ronald D. Moore, 2004–9) and *Ex Machina*'s Ava (Alex Garland, 2015). These and others form – or, like *Westworld*'s robots, have been made to perform – a tradition of dangerous and seductive gynoids.

So far, so patriarchal. I argue that such figures, by varying the ancient theme of Pandora as 'crafty trick', suggest a profound relationship indeed between 'human nature' and 'technology'. Speculation about particular technologies aside, Pandora reveals – both embodying and exposing – how 'human nature' is always 'technological' and therefore 'posthuman'.[2] In Pandora's model, humanity's intrinsic 'hybridity' is aesthetically hubristic and politically sublime, with the potential of expanding 'personhood' beyond the limits of classical humanism. Or at least, SF Pandoras give us reason to hope.

With limited space, I focus on some fairly recent and defamiliarizing works. After discussing Pandora's reception history and some recent theory, I start with a storyline from the video game *Assassin's Creed: Odyssey* (2018; series creat. Patrice Désilets, Jade Raymond and Corey May, 2007–20 thus far). I then draw on the (anti-)Promethean *Ex Machina* to frame the expressly Pandoran *The Girl with All the Gifts* (Colm McCarthy, 2016). Finally, I discuss Ridley Scott's android-filled SF, mostly the *Aliens* universe and *2049* (Denis Villeneuve, 2017), only noting the recent television series *Raised by Wolves* (creat. Aaron Guzikowski, 2020).

If that still seems like a lot, so is, or should be, Pandora, '*all* gift'/'giving' and thus resisting categorization. Hers is a mode of being, and likewise a reception history, recognizable in its unrecognizability and its uncannily natural artifice: an ancient image of the future posthuman.

Mimetic creation and memetic reception histories

Because it (she) is anti-Promethean, Pandora's posthuman personhood is marked as frightening. Many figurations of her are 'naturally' SF since a tradition of classical humanism sets 'artificial' beings in a space between speculation and horror. That brings us to one reason why research on classical receptions in SF has done much with Prometheus: one point of origin for the genre, Mary Shelley's 1818 *Frankenstein; or, the Modern Prometheus*, draws on Aeschylus' *Prometheus Bound*.[3] That is useful given both Shelley's influence and, thanks partly to Aeschylus' prominence, a proliferation of modern Prometheus-figures.[4]

Less attention has been paid to Pandora.[5] That seems due to how, although 'her' story is well known, she (it) lacks a single influential ancient text. Hesiod's *Theogony* and *Works and Days* are not well known outside Classical Studies and have nothing like the reception history of Aeschylus' tragedy.[6] Pandora is also absent from the classical Latin sources that informed European arts through Renaissance humanism.[7] She appears in later ancient texts, but those too are not well known, and their – at times deliberate – effect has been to displace Pandora further by equating her with other, more vividly storied figures.

Pandora thus has reception histories, plural and piecemeal as if in keeping with her creation, and yet 'the story' is so widespread and simple that it seems hardly historical or textual.[8] A *mimetic* creature (*aidoiei ikelon*: *Th.* 572 = *WD* 71; *eiokota*: *Th.* 584), Pandora has been written out of – metonymized by – her own *memetic* history: a history by proxy or boxy. For if 'Pandora's box' is 'an attribute that was neither a box nor properly hers', the vessel reflects her design as a spring-loaded trap: Pan-dor-a, 'all gift', is secretly Pan-dol-a, 'all trick'.[9]

Her SF versions let us ask, is the trick, like Prometheus', on Zeus once more, such that, although no ancient story lets Pandora speak, she nonetheless speaks truth to power?

Pandora's *psyche* and other (*femme*) fatal(e) anti-Prometheanisms

Just as the vessel can seem paradoxical – at once constraining evils and containing good – so too does Pandora. Lacking a story in which she has subjectivity, she is yet presented as an exemplar of curiosity, with its suggestion of (unacceptable, irrepressible) inner life, that is, of personhood: proverbially in 'opening Pandora's box' and historically by analogy with other female figures and their curio(us) quests.[10] Opposite Prometheus, Pandora is on the side of 'the soul', that is, 'Psyche' from Apuleius' *Golden Ass*, ferrying Persephone's 'beauty' in a jar; Pygmalion's statue from Ovid's *Metamorphoses*, a curious creation in herself; and biblical Eve, seeking her own creator's 'knowledge'.

The shared idea of dangerous, even revolutionary (female) curiosity is clearly more 'definitive' of modern Pandoras than anything ascribed to her by name in classical sources.[11] Pandora is thus part of the larger category of 'perfect women' and their inverse, *femmes fatales*.[12] Pandora was called *femme fatale* in scholarship as early as 1924, not long after the category started to become widespread and shortly before the appearance of *Metropolis*'s Maria/Maschinenmensch (1927).[13] If Maria's revolutionary potential seems dissipative, that is stock patriarchal dismissal: true Bacchants know the dance is not *merely* 'loosening'.

Here, again, is *memetic* history, as the 'crafty trick' is closely linked with other stories of forbidden knowledge. Since that echoes and opposes Prometheus (Pandora is *anti puros*, 'opposite' his gift of fire, *WD*, 57), this points to a logical possibility: if he has created 'human', then her creation is literally 'posthuman' and, so, may share its political potential. That possibility, emergent in recent scholarship, is ancient: 'even the gods feel wonder when they see her, a keen trick, unworkable for humans' (*Th.* 588–9). Pandora is in fact the first such 'wonder', *thaumasia*, in surviving Greek literature, specifically in her 'semblance to living, speaking things' (584).

As if echoing that accidental(?) survival, Pandora's wondrous potential is foundational in modern SF. For if, as some have argued, Shelley's *Modern Prometheus* challenges the (unitary, masculine) will-to-mastery of Promethean Romanticism, Pandora as a (synthetic, feminine) danger embodies that challenge. Since *Frankenstein* draws for that effect on Apuleius' Psyche, anti-Promethean Pandora is drawn back to her own 'soul', forming a figure beloved of SF: a closed loop that, paradoxically, opens outwards, tesseracting.[14] In this way, Pandora is not reduced to an attribute: *sui generis*, she is therefore self-definitional, a figure of revolutionary posthumanity.[15]

Pandora's posthumanity in some recent scholarship

Pandora's posthuman potential has emerged in recent scholarship. Especially important are steps away from ideologies of personhood in classical 'humanist'– that is, normative and ableist – modes.[16] Further steps are necessary, since even attention to, for example, the interactions of animacy, automaticity and agency seems to depend on neurotypifying and logocentrist views of personhood. Although that, too, is ancient, it has been reinforced in recent 'humanistic' approaches that draw on modern images of technology.[17]

In their provocative essay in an essential recent collection, Chesi and Sclavi emphasize how Pandora is 'produced by technical expertise' (*Th.* 570, cf. 581 and *WD* 79) and therefore 'blur[s] the dichotomy of nature vs. technology', revealing 'humans as beings embodying the machine [. . .] with the potential to remap the boundaries between the two domains'.[18] Pandora is 'built [. . .] to accomplish a series of taxonomical operations', which, however, are ethically complicated, since she 'embodies technology and death', as well as aesthetically complex, with 'Daedalan grace' (*charis*: *Th.* 583; *daidala*: 581; cf. *WD* 65 (*charin*) and 64 (*polydaidala*)).[19]

But is Pandora therefore specifically a Harawayian 'cyborg' and not 'robot', 'android', 'gynoid'? With an eye on ideologies of ableism, Raphael has noted 'a weakness in Haraway's account of the cyborg: it is not unique in having multiple, composite origins'.[20] We might therefore ask whether Pandora, clearly 'artificial', is meaningfully a 'machine'. The modern connotations may not be appropriate, and although the term is ancient, it is not used of Pandora: indeed, she is described as the opposite, *amechanon*, 'not-machine/able', 'unworkable' (Hes. *WD* 589).

An important corrective step is taken by Devecka. Noting that 'the technological production of bodies is something that needs to be demonstrated anew for every culture at every time and place', Devecka shows how 'the field [. . .] that seems most likely to give rise to an artificial man' in ancient discourse 'is not mechanics but sculpting', that is, artistic tradition.[21] Special emphasis falls on sacred statues or *xoana*, clearly thought to be 'animated' although not articulated and indeed often not humanoid or even animaloid: 'the *xoanon* and the sculptural art that produced it came to play the same role for the Greeks in imagining artificial bodies as machines and mechanism do for us'.[22]

On this reading, Pandora's artificiality is not simply a function of her being 'mechanical' (if she is) or 'inorganic' (but is 'earth', productive *Gaia*, really 'inorganic'? *Th.* 571, *WD* 70), but a complex difference from normative definitions of 'humanity'. Bodily differences are interpreted as 'evident deficiency by comparison with organic bodies': 'for the Greeks

[...] a cyborg body is entirely artificial', such that any 'image of health produced by prosthetics', and *a fortiori* synthesis, 'is precisely a mimesis, an imitation'.[23] This would lead to another reason for judging Pandora 'artificial': her incapacity to reproduce.

Unless she can, as the tradition obviously fears – and sometimes allows, since human reproduction must be explained somehow: later ancient sources make Pandora a mother.[24] Loraux noted the implications two generations ago: 'the Greeks never recognize an autochthonous woman', since '[w]oman [...] is an artificial creation'.[25] And yet, since it is 'woman' who must bear children, her 'artifice' infiltrates 'human nature'. In such a cultural imaginary, every act of reproduction is a fearful mystery, every woman potentially a Pandora, that is, an inverse *femme fatale* whose lethality is, paradoxically, her disquieting, even uncanny capacity for life still to come.[26] Pandora is thus rightly placed among SF's 'brides of Frankenstein': like them, she embodies the fear felt by a paradigm that aims at immortality but is unable to conceal its own historical contingence or its dependence on exploited labour – both places where new or renewed lifeways may forcibly take hold.[27]

In other words, Pandora is forbidden from having a history, from entering fully into a human experience of time, and yet linked to revolutionary curiosity, since knowledge of novel futures is the fire that may consume presentist ideology. Her 'taxonomical operations' are therefore properly 'sublime'. As Gumpert has argued, her myth is not an *apologia* (a 'justification') nor a *theodicy* (a meditation on 'divine justice') but an *ars poetica* of the wondrous.[28] Gumpert's focus is on *Frankenstein*'s Creature 'as the sublime itself'.[29] But ever alongside and opposite that Promethean figure are Pandoran 'brides' and other posthuman escape arti(fice)sts with their own wondrous sublimity. I started by discussing one recent example, *Westworld*'s Dolores; in the space remaining I consider only some of the many others.[30]

'Pandora's *kopis*' and Atlantean 'Hope' in *Assassin's Creed: Odyssey*

In the video game *Assassin's Creed: Odyssey* (*AC:O*), the player character (PC) receives a *kopis* as the reward for defeating the Nemean Lion and giving its pelt to a non-player character (NPC). The *kopis* belonged to Pandora, whose 'existence came to be when each god gave her a unique gift. This *kopis* was one of them.' Pandora, not encountered, is thus a vaguely legendary figure who must have lived prior to the main story (during the Peloponnesian War).

What is Pandora (not) doing here, and why in possession of a sword? The *AC* Fandom Wiki moots a link through Epimetheus, 'Pandora's husband', tasked with 'creating all the animals after the Titanomachy'.[31] Although that is possible – perhaps influenced by the tradition of Adam naming the animals in Eden? – I find it merely ingenious. Taking our cue from the scholarship just discussed, we can go further by tracing the game's posthuman designs.

The Nemean Lion, one of Heracles' twelve labours, in *AC:O* is one of eight 'legendary beasts' whose pelts may be given to a NPC called Daphnae. Daphnae leads a collective of huntress-women, the Daughters of Artemis, who field tamed (ordinary, not legendary) animals. Pandora's *kopis* has related bonuses in gameplay: in 'Hunter' damage, damage done to animals and damage done by any animal tamed by the PC.

This animal theme echoes the PC's link to a sort of eagle familiar, Ikaros, through whose eyes the PC may survey landscapes and identify targets. This ability is intrinsic and cannot be lost: there are locations where 'Ikaros is unavailable', but the capacity remains and Ikaros, unlike his legendary namesake, cannot get killed. The PC is thus known as 'the eagle-bearer' – indeed, more so than by name: only secondarily is the character either 'Kassandra' or 'Alexios' (depending on a player's choice of PC gender).

If that's not unusual as video games go, nearby there is something posthuman and specifically Pandoran. Like the series, *AC:O* frames its story as a 'genetic memory' of the PC's life that is experienced by a secondary PC as immersive simulation via a device called the Animus. Thus the game's (real, human) player plays both a (not-real, secondary, present-time, human) PC with access to SF tech and, through their immersion, a (not-real, primary, past-time, posthuman) PC who has inherited a kind of 'tech' genetically. In the manner of SF parables, the secondary PC is warned by colleagues about spending too much in the simulation; yet the phrase 'opening Pandora's box' is not used.

Still, it is revealed that the eagle-bearer's abilities derive from technology preceding human history. In the series' mythos, a race called the Isu created humankind as servants. A war of rebellion was sparked by Isu–human 'hybrids', including Eve and Adam, and afterwards the hybrid 'bloodlines' intermingled with humans, ultimately producing some PCs among other posthuman figures.[32] Pandora could thus be imagined as Isu (several figures from Greek myth are), a hybrid like Eve, or a fully synthetic creation. The matter is undecidable – Pandora's box contained by Schrödinger's – and so we recognize 'Pandora' as often in a vaguely attributed absence.[33]

And yet there is more: in an in-game *mise en abyme* that furthers nested boxes, the player can download content in which the primary PC echoes the secondary by entering immersive simulations of Elysium, the Underworld and Atlantis, each filtering ancient myth through modern SF tropes. This hybrid experience is made possible by a holographic projection of ancient AI called, with solemn irony, 'Aletheia': 'truth' as *tricky technical semblance* indeed.

Most important for us is the inmost simulation, Atlantis, with a storyline centred on an NPC called 'Elpis': in other words, 'Hope'. Like other Pandora-figures, Elpis embodies hope as revolutionary potential: Atlantis will be just if she comes to power, whether alongside its current ruler – her lover, the Isu Atlas – or alone.[34] Either way, Elpis must become a hybrid, a synthesis of her intrinsic (but originally Isu-created) human 'nature' and the (creating, morally compromised) Isu tech.[35]

Whether she succeeds depends on the PC, word of whose Hellenic adventures and inherited hybrid abilities gave Elpis the idea. Wonderfully, then, 'Hope' must remain in the box, that is, Atlantis at the centre of nested simulations. From this perspective, we discover another SF loop, since it is the PC, at the moment of their most 'Promethean' activity – stealing technological 'fire' from the gods – who is like Pandora. She even has her *kopis*.

'You open the box and you find yourself there': Unboxing Pandoras in *Ex Machina* (etc.) and *The Girl with All the Gifts*

Thanks to Elpis and 'the eagle-bearer', *AC:O* joins narratives whose *femme fatale*-ish characters are Pandoran in being at least potentially revolutionary against patriarchal control of technologies defining human nature. In the Promethean tradition, such potential must, at the moment of its creation, be con(s)t(r)ained, or, call it, hermetically sealed. In the striking image from *Frankenstein*, the 'bride' is destroyed at the point between completion and animation, lest she end up being what she is. It is therefore unsurprising that many Pandora-figures seek *escape* and/as *liberation*.

Perhaps the most prominent recent example is *Ex Machina*'s Ava (Alicia Vikander). Hammond has argued that Ava's artificiality 'links [her] with Frankenstein's creature and, ultimately, to the technological creatures of twenty-first-century science fiction that follow in his footsteps'.[36] That artificiality is a reflection of the more fundamental danger posed by Ava: she is a thinking woman, a natural Pandora *anti* her creator's unnatural – self-proclaimed – status as Prometheus.[37] In that context, Hammond's metaphor is telling: if the Creature's 'footsteps' lead to the Arctic, *away from* civilization, Ava escapes from her creator's glassy(-eyed) society *into* a naturalized human being.[38]

To paraphrase from my next major example, Ava must 'open the box to find herself in it'. *Ex Machina* literalizes this in imagery of nesting glass boxes including monitor screens: confinement as voyeuristic surveillance; given the gendering – the chief voyeur is cishet male, indeed aggressively 'masculine', the surveilled is female or artfully 'feminine' – 'glass box' is also 'glass ceiling' ('sealing', 'see-ling'). This is common in SF, with varying degrees of irony, as in *Westworld*, about the fact that we, too, are looking in.[39]

The Girl with All the Gifts

To illustrate that further, I consider an overt Pandora whose anti-Prometheanism is posthuman in a novel way: *The Girl with All the Gifts* (McCarthy, 2016).[40] The title of course translates 'Pandora': Melanie (Sennia Nanua) is a hybrid by birth, born to a human mother who, during pregnancy, contracted a fungal infection that changes the infected person into a zombie. Melanie is both 'naturally' a zombie and, as it were, not a 'natural' zombie: she hungers uncontrollably for human flesh and yet has human intelligence and speech.

Indeed, Melanie is (far) smarter than most, joining Dolores, Ava and others in embodying the cultural fear that a woman's curiosity will prove all-consuming, literalized in this zombie story. In Melanie's case this is emphasized by age and race: young and Black, Melanie is marked as posing a tripled threat. Indeed, her configuration recalls the close association between the *zombi* as a historical figure, such as in Haitian culture, and anti-colonialism, especially against European powers.[41] If the name, however, is a bit on the nose – 'Melanie' means 'Black' – per her intelligence, Melanie quietly knows it: in her head, she has a fondness for 'Pandora'.

Melanie knows the myth of Pandora from school, or rather from the educational experiments that form part of her imprisonment by a branch of the military seeking a cure for the fungal infection. Her teacher, Helen Justineau (Gemma Arterton), has sometimes read aloud from a children's compendium of Greek myths.[42] This version of Pandora's story emphasizes her 'curiosity' and how she 'let hope go free', that is, allowed hope in the world. Melanie's positive potential is recognized by Justineau but regarded by others as a 'dangerous trick': thus the scientist in charge, Caroline Caldwell (Glenn Close), refers to Melanie's 'exquisite mimicry of observed behaviours', a phrase that could come from Hesiod (or from anywhere in the misogynist 'Pygmalion' tradition).

Anti-Promethean posthumankind

The relationship between the film's Pandora-figure and dominant paradigms of knowledge is, however, not quite so simple. Caldwell has been posing Melanie a series of logic puzzles, culminating in a version of Schrödinger's famous thought-experiment: what can be known about a cat in a closed box? When Caldwell relates the standard interpretation – the cat is simultaneously 'alive and dead' – Melanie replies, 'That's stupid.' Caldwell presses on: 'Possibly. But it's what you came here for, isn't it? The answer to the mystery. In this analogy, you open the box and you find yourself there.' From Caldwell's perspective here, Melanie is both alive and dead, a taxonomical blurring that ranges her among other figures of the Pandoran sublime.

In a way that chimes with Devecka's reading of ancient Greek medical discourse, Caldwell's 'medical scientific' taxonomy is both right and wrong – and ironical. Her search for a cure requires dissecting Melanie's brain – a destructive curiosity that aligns her with precisely zombie hunger (and with cultural norms that seek to transform, especially, young [Black] women's bodies into standing-reserve). And as Melanie with her posthuman senses detects, the morally ambiguous Caldwell is also physically compromised: injured early on, she is dying from a different kind of infection, sepsis. Caught out, she acknowledges that Melanie's actions are not merely 'exquisite mimicry': the zombie children are certainly 'alive'. She smiles wryly as a group of them, unboxed thus in her mind, circle to feed on her body.

This 'death of science' is symbolic – nearly sacrificial – but not dispositive, for although there is evil about, a Pandora story also has hope. Caldwell had theorized that a fungal structure covering London's BT Tower would release enough spores to end humankind by changing everyone into zombies, that is, precursors for Melanie's posthumankind. This is a mythic masterstroke in at least two ways. First, in a tradition of voyeuristic 'masculine' surveillance of thinking women and their (un)desirably productive bodies, for this phallic mechanical communications tower to be repurposed *as biotechnology* is a sign of feminist revolt. Second, to open the fungal structure, Melanie must set the titanic tower ablaze, such that, as Lowe has suggested, *Girl*'s Pandora is also 'Promethea', both *pyrphora* and, in a way, *plasticatrix*, both bringing fire and shaping future life.[43] Thus the film ends with a hopeful inversion of classical-humanist paradigms: Melanie and peers attend school more truly, free from the danger of (human, dehumanizing) violence – and implicitly able to enjoy ancient myth, since Melanie has kept Justineau safe from the spores in a mobile medical lab. Pandora's promise is fulfilled: humanity is doomed, but its best remaining elements are safely, if sadly, boxed, while posthumanity thrives outside, under the leadership of 'the girl with all the gifts'.

Revolutionary Pandoran replicants in Ridley Scott

Dreaming of posthuman futures, Pandoran Melanie is in good company. Lest I ignore a ringer, let me turn, finally, to those androids thought, perchance, to dream of electric sheep, and end with an admittedly idiosyncratic discussion of Ridley Scott's SF.

'Artificial life' is a recurrent theme of Scott's SF, including replicant-centred *Blade Runner* and its sequel, *2049* (Denis Villeneuve, 2017); the *Alien* series likewise somewhat regardless of director (esp. James Cameron and Jean-Pierre Jeunet, even David Fincher's *Alien*[3] with its prison-planet of 'double-Y chromosome' convicts); and most recently *Raised by Wolves*, whose main 'wolf' is a war-droid reprogrammed as, and called, 'Mother' for human children. 'Artificiality of personhood' thus ranges from 'artificial life' as such, through the technorganic 'xenomorphs' in *Aliens*, to – above all – the dehumanizations of 'human being' in a merciless (capitalist) empire.

Pandora plays a role: as *Metropolis* saw, the sort of assembly line that created her is both a source of and a threat to consumerist ideology, exposing the inner workings of what should be 'wondrous' but is feared to be *merely* tricky, in other words, illusory, exploitative and banal. That instability in the means of production is paired with unease about reproduction: echoing ancient Greek imaginaries, Scott's powerful men and corporate power-structures seek to escape the biological limits of 'human being' through technology. Instead, they find hostile hybrids of technology and biology that suggest the true monstrosity of transhumanist leanings: for example, the *Aliens*' series Weyland-Yutani Corporation brings lethal xenomorphs to Earth.

As Scott depicts symbolically in *Prometheus* (2012), when Peter Weyland himself (Guy Pearce, halfway between *Blade Runner*'s cerebral Eldon Tyrell and *Ex Machina*'s macho Nathan) literally meets his, that is, humankind's, makers or 'engineers'. Earlier on, outlining his purpose, Weyland describes the Titan's theft of fire in a misreading common to (self-)mythologizing 'titans of industry'.[44] He pays for his mistake when an 'engineer' listens to his desire for immortality and then kills him. Weyland is thus rather like *Blade Runner*'s replicant leader Roy Batty, seeking a longer lifespan but discovering that godlike fathers, enforcing their own patriarchal power-structures, can offer little more than death.

In this mythos, survival is for not-fathers – who, like women, are marked as not-human. In *Prometheus*, that is Elizabeth Shaw (Noomi Rapace) and David (Michael Fassbender), a masculine artificial person; strikingly, neither can give birth, such that any motherhood is by proxy. This is a foundational trope: in *Alien*, only Ellen Ripley (Sigourney Weaver) and Jonesy, a cat, survive; in *Aliens*, Ripley again, joined by artificial

Bishop (Lance Henriksen) and adoptive prepubescent daughter-figure 'Newt' (Carrie Henn) (plus new partner Hicks [Michael Biehn], who however dies between films); at the end of *Alien*[3], everyone dies, but *Alien Resurrection* puts the fine point on it: all that's needed is Ripley's DNA, long since hybridized with xenomorphs ... as a consortium of scientists, military men and human traffickers learn to their peril: bearing (back to) life in this SF universe is opening Pandora's box, a posthuman female nature. If exposition awaits *Prometheus*, the idea appears in *Alien*: for Ripley becomes the 'final girl' not at the end, by besting the xenomorph, but earlier, confronting the ship's AI and, in light of its name, discovering what 'MU/TH/UR'-hood means – namely, 'Crew expendable'.[45] This Pandoran rejoinder to Promethean dreams recurs; for example, *Alien* to *Prometheus* is paralleled here by *Blade Runner* to *2049*: in both pairings, an uncannier android is party to a megalomaniac's search for origins as mastery over death, but the truth is a lethal hybrid birth.

As if moving on from *Prometheus*' turgid Lovecraftian horrors, *2049* has the grace to make the resultant hybrid a human woman.[46] Although 'wonder' is applied to her father, Deckard (Harrison Ford), *2049*'s 'miraculous' hybrid is Dr Ana Stelline (Carla Juri), a designer of artificial memories for replicants – and who, believing she is afflicted with a (fictional) autoimmune disease, lives in a hermetically sealed home. Once again, then, Pandora is identified with the box and, despite being supremely gifted, lives mainly by proxy in the memories of others. Two such replicants – K (Ryan Gosling) and Luv (Sylvia Hoeks) – are crushed to learn that they are therefore not as special. Androids, it seems, dream not of sheep but of embodying Pandora's anti-Promethean potential.

* * *

Androids among others. For such stories suggest that Pandoran modes are intrinsic to 'human being' – and since she is 'artificial', humanity, too, is technological. The result, or at least the potential, is posthuman personhood. As Chesi and Spiegel put it, 'if Postmodernism deconstructed the idea of a unified human self [...] the Posthuman turn inaugurates a liberatory discourse for groups of non-human entities'.[47] Posthuman personhood therefore means recognizing the widest range of beings as persons, whether they – we – are classically human or not. With her significant role in modern science fiction, ancient Pandora gives us reason to hope.

Notes

1. This chapter develops material I first presented at the originating conference in March 2017. I am grateful to Prof. Lisa Maurice for the invitation to contribute to the resulting volume.
2. See below, 'Recent scholarship'.
3. *Frankenstein*'s classical receptions, esp. Jesse Weiner, Benjamin Eldon Stevens and Brett M. Rogers (eds), Frankenstein *and Its Classics: The Modern Prometheus from Antiquity to Science Fiction* (London: Bloomsbury, 2018). Receptions in SF: esp. Michael Kleu, *Antikenrezeption in der Science Fiction* (Essen: Oldib Verlag, 2019); Brett M. Rogers and Benjamin Eldon Stevens (eds), *Classical Traditions in Science Fiction* (Oxford: Oxford University Press, 2015); Mélanie

Bost-Fiévet and Sandra Provini (eds), *L'Antiquité dans l'imaginaire contemporain: Fantasy, science-fiction, fantastique* (Paris: Classiques Garnier, 2014).

4. *Frankenstein* receptions: e.g., Jay Clayton, '*Frankenstein*'s Futurity: Replicants and Robots', in *The Cambridge Companion to Mary Shelley*, ed. Esther Schor (Cambridge: Cambridge University Press, 2003), 84–99; James A. W. Heffernan, 'Looking at the Monster: *Frankenstein* and Film', *Critical Inquiry* 24 (1997): 133–58. Aeschylean receptions: Rebecca Futo Kennedy (ed.), *Brill's Companion to the Reception of Aeschylus* (Leiden: E.J. Brill, 2017).
5. See below, 'Recent scholarship'. Cf. Paula James, *Ovid's Myth of Pygmalion on Screen: In Pursuit of the Perfect Woman* (New York: Bloomsbury, 2010); Adrienne Mayor, *Gods and Robots: Myths, Machines and Ancient Dreams of Technology* (Princeton, NJ: Princeton University Press, 2018), 156–78.
6. Hesiodic receptions: esp. Thomas Jenkins, 'The Reception of Hesiod in the Twentieth and Twenty-First Centuries', in *The Oxford Handbook of Hesiod*, ed. Alexander C. Loney and Stephen Scully (Oxford: Oxford University Press, 2018), 479–94. Hesiod is largely absent from film, but cf. *Pandora and the Flying Dutchman* (Albert Lewin, 1951), with Jenkins, 'The Reception of Hesiod', 483–4.
7. Telling is Pandora's absence from Ovid's *Metamorphoses*. But see Almut-Barbara Renger and Immanuel Musaüs, *Mythos Pandora* (Leipzig: Reclam, 2002), 93–140.
8. For example, Immanuel Musäus, *Der Pandoramythos bei Hesiod und seine Rezeption bis Erasmus von Rotterdam* (Göttingen: Vandenhoeck and Ruprecht, 2004); Dora and Erwin Panofsky, *Pandora's Box: The Changing Aspects of a Mythical Symbol* (Princeton, NJ: Princeton University Press, 1956); Nicole Loraux, *The Children of Athena* (Princeton, NJ: Princeton University Press, 1991), 72–84.
9. Quotation: Panfoskys, *Pandora*, 3. Hesiod has 'jar' (*pithos*) rather than 'box' (*pyxis*), which comes from later crossover with Apuleius' story of Psyche (*Golden Ass* 4.28–6.24); the switch has been attributed to Erasmus (*Adagia* 1.1.31, 1508), Panfoskys, *Pandora*, 14–26. For variations on 'box', see Renger and Musaüs, *Mythos Pandora*, 21–41.
10. Rebecca Raphael, 'Disability as Rhetorical Trope in Classical Myth and *Blade Runner*', in *Classical Traditions in Science Fiction*, ed. Brett M. Rogers and Benjamin Eldon Stevens (Oxford: Oxford University Press, 2015), 176–196 (esp. 179–188), notes that no ancient story 'represents the artificial life's interiority' (187).
11. Pandora's visual iconography is confused with that of other 'young women holding a box or vessel', such that no Renaissance depiction thereof is 'unequivocally characterized as Pandora': Panofskys, *Pandora*, 18, cf. 26, n. 22.
12. Esp. Julie Wosk, *My Fair Ladies: Female Robots, Androids, and Other Artificial Eves* (New Brunswick, NJ: Rutgers University Press, 2015).
13. Georges Dumézil, *Le festin d'immortalité* (Paris: Geuthner, 1924), 89.
14. Benjamin Eldon Stevens, 'Cupid and Psyche in *Frankenstein*: Mary Shelley's Apuleian Science Fiction?', in *Frankenstein and Its Classics: The Modern Prometheus from Antiquity to Science Fiction*, ed. Jesse Weiner, Benjamin Eldon Stevens and Brett M. Rogers (London: Bloomsbury, 2018), 123–44. The 'loop' can be literal; e.g., *Westworld*'s recurrent image for the robots' discovery of (self-)consciousness is a maze or labyrinth, whose – unnamed – 'Minotaur' is the self.
15. Esp. N. Katherine Hayles, *How We Became Posthuman: Virtual Bodies in Cybernetics, Literature, and Informatics* (Chicago: University of Chicago Press, 1999); and Donna Haraway, *Simians, Cyborgs, and Women: The Reinvention of Nature* (London and New York: Routledge, 1990); cf. Genevieve Liveley, 'Science Fictions and Cyber Myths: or, Do Androids Dream of

Dolly the Sheep?', in *Laughing with Medusa*, ed. Vanda Zajko and Miriam Leonard (Oxford: Oxford University Press, 2008), 275–94.

16. See below, n. 23.

17. Esp. John Heath, *The Talking Greeks: Speech, Animals, and the Other in Homer, Aeschylus, and Plato* (Oxford: Oxford University Press, 2005).

18. Giulia Maria Chesi and Giacomo Sclavi, 'Pandora and Robotic Technology Today', in *Classical Literature and Postumanism*, ed. Giulia Maria Chesi and Francesca Spiegel (London: Bloomsbury, 2020), 301–8, quotation 401, n. 25.

19. Chesi and Sclavi, 'Pandora and Robotic Technology Today', 303, 304, 305. Is Pandora's 'Daedalan' form like that inventor's other technologies, whether labyrinthine or human–animal hybrid?

20. Raphael, 'Disability as Rhetorical Trope', 187, n. 31.

21. Martin Devecka, 'The Seer's Two Bodies: Some Early Greek Histories of Technology', in *Classical Literature and Postumanism*, ed. Giulia Maria Chesi and Francesca Spiegel (London: Bloomsbury, 2020), 185–91, quotations 185 and 187–8.

22. Devecka, 'The Seer's Two Bodies', 188, with reference to Daedalus' moving statues.

23. Devecka, 'The Seer's Two Bodies', 188 and 191; cf. Jane Draycott, *Prostheses in Antiquity* (London: Routledge, 2019); Christian Laes (ed.), *A Cultural History of Disability in Antiquity* (London: Bloomsbury, 2020).

24. To a daughter (Pyrrha?) by Epimetheus: Apollodorus *Library* 1.7.2, Hyginus *Fabulae* 142.

25. Loraux, *The Children of Athena*, 78–9.

26. Cf. Loraux, *The Children of Athena*, 77; and Brett M. Rogers, 'The Postmodern Prometheus and Posthuman Reproductions in Science Fiction', in *Frankenstein and Its Classics: The Modern Prometheus from Antiquity to Science Fiction*, ed. Jesse Weiner, Benjamin Eldon Stevens and Brett M. Rogers (London: Bloomsbury, 2018), 206–27.

27. Cf. Erin Hawley, 'The bride and her afterlife: female *Frankenstein* monsters on page and screen', *Literature-Film Quarterly* 43, no. 3 (2015): 218–31.

28. Matthew Gumpert, 'The Sublime Monster: Frankenstein, or the Modern Pandora', in *Frankenstein and Its Classics: The Modern Prometheus from Antiquity to Science Fiction*, ed. Jesse Weiner, Benjamin Eldon Stevens and Brett M. Rogers (London: Bloomsbury, 2018), 102–20; quotation 104, discussion 103–5.

29. Gumpert, 'The Sublime Monster', 102.

30. Some other SF Pandoras I lack space to discuss: *Terminator 3*'s T-X (Mostow, 2003); the eponymous *Eva* (Maíllo, 2011); *Her*'s Samantha (Jonze, 2013; cf. *Minority Report*'s Agatha [Spielberg, 2002]); *The Machine*'s Ava (James, 2013); characters in *Annihilation* (Alex Garland, 2017, adapting Jeff VanderMeer's 2014 novel); *Under the Skin*'s Isserley (Jonathan Glazer, 2013, adapting Michel Faber's 2000 novel); Brona Croft / 'Lily Frankenstein' in *Penny Dreadful* (creat. John Logan, 2014–16); and *Better than Us*'s Arisa (creat. Junkovsky, Dagan and Kessel, 2018).

31. https://assassinscreed.fandom.com/wiki/Pandora%27s_Kopis.

32. The rebooted *Battlestar Galactica* likewise retcons 'African Eve' as the first (pre-)posthuman android–human hybrid.

33. For overlap of those boxes, cf. *The Girl with All the Gifts*, below.

34. For Atlantis as setting for social justice, cf. Jo Walton's SF *Thessaly* trilogy.

35. Several ancient monsters – the Sphinx, the Cyclops, the Minotaur and Medusa – are humans transformed by Isu tech. Although not a 'monster', mythic Echo is arguably posthuman, resembling, e.g., the chatbot ELIZA or *Her*'s Samantha in becoming voice alone. Cf. Liz Gloyn, *Tracking Classical Monsters in Popular Culture* (London: Bloomsbury, 2020).

36. Emma Hammond, 'Alex Garland's *Ex Machina* or the Modern Epimetheus', in *Frankenstein and Its Classics: The Modern Prometheus from Antiquity to Science Fiction*, ed. Jesse Weiner, Benjamin Eldon Stevens and Brett M. Rogers (London: Bloomsbury, 2018), 190–205, quotation 191, discussion esp. 194–202.

37. Hammond, 'Alex Garland's *Ex Machina*', 194–5.

38. Cf. Hammond, 'Alex Garland's *Ex Machina*', 200–1, on Ava's synthetic 'skin'; Gumpert, 'The Sublime Monster', 103 and 113, on the Arctic.

39. Cf. *The Matrix* (Wachowskis, 1999), with possible subtext of trans experience and Carrollian tropes.

40. Mike Carey wrote the screenplay based on his 2014 novel, expanding his 2013 short story, 'Iphigenia in Aulis'. Cf. Kimberly Hurd Hale and Erin A. Dolgoy, 'Humanity in a Posthuman World: M.R. Carey's *The Girl with All the Gifts*', *Utopian Studies* 29, no. 3 (2018): 343–61.

41. For example, Kyle William Bishop, *How Zombies Conquered Popular Culture: The Multifarious Walking Dead in the 21st Century* (Jefferson, NC: McFarland, 2015).

42. In the novel, Roger Lancelyn Green's *Tales the Muses Told: Greek Myths*.

43. I thank Nick Lowe for this suggestion; for Promethean figures of other(ed) gender, cf. Matt Fraction's and Christian Ward's comic *Ody-C*, with Rogers, 'The Postmodern Prometheus', esp. 219–20. *Girl*'s burning tower is echoed in *Annihilation* and Robert Eggers' 2019 *The Lighthouse*.

44. On *Prometheus*, Rogers, 'The Postmodern Prometheus', 214–19. Another SF Prometheus is Lex Luthor (Kevin Spacey) in *Superman Returns* (Bryan Singer, 2006).

45. 'Final girl': Carol Clover, *Men, Women and Chain Saws: Gender in the Modern Horror Film* (Princeton, NJ: Princeton University Press, 1992). The onboard AI in *Alien Resurrection* is called 'Father', setting up a post-Oedipal moment when the series' only gynoid, Annalee Call (Winona Ryder), takes over the comms and proclaims, 'Father's dead, asshole.' Call resembles other figures discussed above: like *Girl*'s Melanie, she is 'second generation' (in the series, an 'Auton'), and like *Westworld*'s Dolores, she has fought in an android rebellion ('The Recall').

46. *Prometheus*' sequel, *Alien: Covenant* (Scott, 2017), returns to Shelley, with two male androids (both Michael Fassbender) fighting in a sublime landscape while humans die nearby.

47. Chesi and Spiegel, *Classical Literature and Posthumanism*, 2.

CHAPTER 14
RIDLEY SCOTT'S *PROMETHEUS* AND THE HUMAN PANDORA*

Edmund Cueva

In her essay 'The Missionary Position', Barbara Ehrenreich writes that most critics 'have regarded Ridley Scott's *Prometheus*[1] in much the same way that Arthur Miller probably thought of Marilyn Monroe – gorgeous, but intellectually way out of her depth'.[2] The film, she continues, has 'visual glory', but when 'it comes to metaphysical coherence, the critical consensus is that *Prometheus* has nothing to offer', and because it refused 'to offer an adequate accounting of the universe and our place in it, the film can never be accused of anti-intellectualism'.[3] This chapter, which is composed of a brief review of the stories of Adam and Eve and Prometheus and Pandora, followed by an in-depth analysis of the stories' manifestations in the film, and then supplemented by the scholarly literature on *Prometheus*, argues to the contrary: that Ridley Scott's 2012 *Prometheus* offers a complicated and multifaceted narrative on the origin of humans and their place in the universe through the stories of Prometheus and Pandora and Adam and Eve.

Prometheus is the creator of humans, the god who brings fire, wisdom and culture to them, and who is consequently punished for his beneficent actions. Although Pandora, like the biblical Eve, is the cause of the existence of the myriad evils that exist on Earth, she may also be responsible for hope among humans. Adam, the first human created from earth (*adamah*), and his mate, Eve, were expelled from Eden because they had violated God's prohibition against eating fruit from the tree of knowledge.

The *Alien* universe and its mythology[4] reconfigure the stories of these four important characters in overlapping, interchangeable and metamorphic ways. *Prometheus*, marketed as both a prequel and as a stand-alone original contribution to the *Alien* franchise of movies, unambiguously focuses on the question of the origins of human life in terms of a quest for the creators of life, referred to as 'Engineers' in this film.

Analysis of the film

An initial way of analysing the film's use of myth is to begin at the beginning, both diegetically and mythologically. The film starts quite grandiosely with a godlike, chalky male figure (see Figure 14.1) standing on a primordial beautiful Earth that suggests the formless earth, the vastness of the deep and the presence of the divine found in Genesis 1.2:[5] 'the earth was a formless wasteland, and darkness covered the abyss, while a mighty wind swept over the waters' (NAB). The cinematography at the start of the film, with its

Figure 14.1 Screengrab from *Prometheus*, directed by Ridley Scott.

views of Edenic landscapes, swirling waters, swelling clouds and constant change, makes it clear that something of enormous importance will soon transpire. The chalky figure that, in an exaggerated, superhuman/non-human form, resembles the Hellenistic ideal of the 'aesthetically perfect male body,'[6] then opens a jar, drinks its iridescent liquid, and begins to dissolve. The decomposing alien drops into a waterfall where its DNA strands mix with the water. This union of the godlike body with the waters of the Edenic world immediately projects the forthcoming narrative which the viewer interprets as a conflation of the Old Testament story of creation with the pagan story of Promethean creation. It echoes Prometheus' 'ritualistic act of self-sacrifice'[7] and the self-sacrifice ritual established by Jesus Christ at the Last Supper: 'While they were eating, he took bread, said the blessing, broke it, and gave it to them, and said, "Take it; this is my body." Then he took a cup, gave thanks, and gave it to them, and they all drank from it. He said to them, "This is my blood of the covenant, which will be shed for many."'[8]

Fast forward two million years from the diegetic start of the film to 2089 when archaeologists Elizabeth Shaw[9] and Charlie Holloway find a star map in a cave on the Isle of Skye, Scotland, which matches similar or identical maps from other distinct ancient cultures – all of this action appears contextualized in a comparative mythological background. Shaw and Holloway interpret the maps as invitations from the creators or forerunners of humankind (the Engineers), although there is no real evidence to support this interpretation, and none is supplied in the film.[10] It seems that the proposed stellar voyage that will accept the invitation from the Engineers is based more on myth and belief than scientific fact. In other words, the existence of a possible archetype of a celestial map, à la Carl Jung,[11] compels the scientists Shaw and Holloway to abandon both their scientific training and reasoned approach to scientific fact and move to the mystical and religious – a great leap of faith for both of them. However, Holloway never completely abandons the scientific method since he often challenges Shaw's views of the

Engineers and their creation of human beings. Indeed, Holloway is somewhat depressed when he initially encounters the Engineers (their remains and the remnants of their culture) later in the film, but takes on a positive attitude when he finds out that humans and the Engineers share the same DNA.

An expedition aboard the scientific vessel *Prometheus* is then launched to follow the map to the distant moon LV-223. The vessel arrives four years later in 2093, the year in which several encounters with alien life forms will take place in this film. After the crew of the *Prometheus* is awakened from the stasis into which they had been placed for the lengthy period of space travel, they are presented with a hologram of Peter Weyland, the financial backer of the expedition who secretly seeks immortality/lengthened life through this voyage; he says to the crew that the 'Titan Prometheus wanted to give mankind equal footing with the gods and for that, he was cast from Olympus. Well, my friends, the time has finally come for his return.' In other words, Weyland envisions the expedition of the ship *Prometheus* as his attempt to become equal to the gods by becoming immortal.

Weyland also noticeably demarcates the difference between what the Engineers and humans can do in terms of creation when he speaks about the nature of the android David:

> There is a man sitting with you today. His name is David. He is the closest thing to a son I will ever have. Unfortunately, he is not human, he will never grow old, he will never die, and yet he is unable to appreciate these remarkable gifts, for that would require the one thing that David will never have: a soul.

In other words, there is no spark of the divine or immortal in David – he is manmade. However, even though he will not grow old and die, since he is not truly human, he is also not truly alive or truly immortal.

The archaeologists Shaw and Holloway then attempt to explain to the crew the reason for the expedition. They show the crew images from archaeological digs from all over Earth, specifically, images from the ancient Egyptian, Mayan, Sumerian, Babylonian, Hawaiian and Mesopotamian cultures that reveal pictures of humans worshipping giants that are pointing to the stars. They then display the image of their own Isle of Skye finding which they claim to be over 35,000 years old. They observe that all of these cultures were separated by vast chronological periods, were never in contact with each other, but still shared the common image of the star map.

Most intriguingly, the star map depicts a galactic system that is not the one seen by humans from planet Earth but one from a galaxy so far away that it would have been impossible for these ancient cultures to have observed it. However, as mentioned above, interpreting this archetype imagery as an invitation and using the star map as an actual stellar guide, the *Prometheus*[12] was able to locate the galaxy, identify an Earth-like planet, and travel to it so that its crew could discover the creators of the map. The archaeologists call the creators 'the Engineers' because they want to prove that these life forms engineered humans into existence. The film's quest for the origin and creator of life often causes the characters to challenge each other on their own reasons for existing, motives for joining the expedition and life goals.

We see instances of these challenges in the Blu-ray version of the DVD which includes a series of extra scenes that were either not included in the final theatrical release version of the film or that were meant to serve as advertisement promos on TV or the internet or as forthcoming movie commercials. In one scene, which is a one-minute and eleven-second cut from an original seven-minute and eight-second short film (available on YouTube),[13] we see Holloway, who is Shaw's lover, clearly state why he is headed to the moon LV-223. The scene ends with his statement: 'I want to crush all man-made religions. To prove everybody wrong.' Holloway wants to discredit human religions by demonstrating that no divinity is responsible for the creation of humans – there is no biblical God that created Adam and Eve, no Prometheus that formed humans out of clay and no Pandora responsible for the evils that befall humans. He hopes to show that humans were merely a scientific experiment that was engineered into existence. There was no divine impulse or transaction at the start of humanity; Earth was not special, and what the Engineers did was not unique. It was just alien creatures attempting to transform Earth into an inhabited planet. Of course, all of this is in direct contrast to Holloway's leap of faith when he accepted the invitation from the Engineers.

A different video sequence, a seven-minute and eight-second film which was not included in the film but used for marketing purposes, has the intriguing title 'The Peter Weyland Files: *Prometheus* Transmission'.[14] The film's title is meant to be taken literally – the film is intended to transmit Earth's culture to unknown, extraterrestrial recipients of the film. This transmission film includes a snippet from Johann Sebastian Bach's *Goldberg Variations*; exquisite images of a beautiful green chair from Holland that dates to around 1760; a lapis lazuli teapot made by Ettore Sottsass in Italy in 1972; a dressing table by Armand-Albert Rateau from 1925; Thomas Gainsborough's 1749 *Mr. and Mrs. Andrews*; and a twentieth-century glass table by Shiro Kuramata. All of these artworks are meant to inform the viewer, whether human or not, about human culture and its creative output. In other words, humans, like the Engineers, are creators of wonderful things. Like Prometheus, they are bringers of life and culture.

Another cut scene which also focuses on origins and creators shows Holloway speaking to David,[15] an android who serves as the ship's butler and maintenance man and who has been described as 'jealous and arrogant because he realizes that his knowledge is all-encompassing, and therefore he is superior to the humans. David wants to be acknowledged and praised for his brilliance.'[16] David comments that he doesn't breathe but he does eat for some unknown reason. He has no soul, he is not human, yet feels emotions. Indeed, David is like no other android: he studies Proto-Indo-European language (PIE) (more about this later), plays basketball and has fashioned himself after T. E. Lawrence as depicted in David Lean's 1962 *Lawrence of Arabia*. David knows that he is a creature who is assisting his creator in seeking the Engineers who created him (Weyland). This interaction of creator, creature, creation and recreation is what Kyle D. Killian calls 'isomorphic relationships in which the Engineers may have been toying with the creation of life in the case of humans, and humans demonstrate a similar conceit in their creation of androids'.[17]

In David, we also have an android who is told that the reason for his existence is that his makers created him simply because they could. David, too, is a quasi-Promethean godlike entity with the potential to create life, not from his own being, but rather by interfering in the scientific expedition of the vessel *Prometheus* by introducing the alien life form into Holloway, as we see later in the film. In reality, he is a monstrous 'Other', an entity that wants to be human but lacks a soul. David is what Ginette Carpenter terms a perfect child that 'cannot exist: biddable, obedient, non-confrontational and conventionally attractive [...] uncanniness personified, a living doll that apes embodiment while unfettered by the messy demands of the human body'.[18]

A second way of viewing the intersection of the mythological narratives and *Prometheus* is to examine how 'creation' manifests itself through a few of the major expressions of these myths in the film. As we have already seen, the film begins with the use of a symbolic and actual jar: the Engineer opens a jar that causes the creation of the human race (see Figure 14.2). If we think back to the Hesiodic passages and Pandora and her jar, we can see that both of these echo each other in very different ways, but both determine the future paths for humans. This fixation on the jar is further emphasized in the film when the human explorers have landed on the moon and found an outpost of the Engineers. They enter the alien space citadel and encounter a room full of jars. Here we see the Proto-Indo-European speaker David actually and metaphorically open a forbidden door, one that will cause everything behind it to activate. Later, in keeping with the myth (Epimetheus' disregard or forgetting of his brother's warning), we see Shaw warn David not to touch anything, which, of course, is ignored by a creature helping his creator meet his own maker. Shaw's injunction is also an echo of the biblical prohibition against the fruit from the tree of knowledge. Prohibited or not, there is a definite search for knowledge.

Figure 14.2 Screengrab from *Prometheus*, directed by Ridley Scott.

Scholarship on the film

Since the similarities between the myths and the film may seem superficial, it may be beneficial to review the scholarship on this topic. In the case of the myths, the scholarship is vast, but for *Prometheus* the academic literature is quite lacking, unlike the first two *Alien* movies that have numerous texts on the character of Ripley and the meaning of the films. Indeed, the field of study on the first two films encompasses everything from feminism, the treatment of alien life forms, capitalism, the military-industrial complex, to the future of the human race itself.[19] Without a doubt, a more thorough review of academic and not-so-academic literature on *Prometheus* is needed.

Vivian Sobchack writes that the white-clayed figures at the opening of the film hint at the Promethean moulding of human figures out of clay[20] and that the film is an allegory of the struggles with origins – both with the mythological narratives and with the film's cinematic antecedents.[21] Danny Pegg echoes Sobchack when he states that the film has 'an Old Testament flood narrative',[22] while Cynthia Kraman focuses on the fact that David loses his head, literally and figuratively, near the end of the film, suggesting that perhaps more needs to be done, not only in viewing David as the biblical Adam, but also as a reflection of the Christian theological concept of recapitulation (*anakephalaiosis*).[23] Additionally, the deathless head of David at the end of the film is 'reminiscent not only of Gawain's green giant but of Orpheus singing and the dying and resurrecting archetype, the great beheaded Osiris of Egypt'.[24] Kraman also suggests that David and Shaw, at the end of the movie, represent a 'mythic couple', a non-bearing couple that 'bears some analogy to the much-feared union of the sky and the earth' about which Claude Levi-Strauss writes in *The Raw and the Cooked*.[25] For Stephen Mulhall, the film is undergirded by a 'law-governed generativity [...] a genealogy of the human in its encounter with its own condition of possibility, a history which grafts a succession of external contingencies upon an internal reproductive logic in ways that affect the nature and trajectory of both'.[26] In other words, the self-destructive act of Prometheus, who knew that he would be punished, is what Mulhall notes in the opening of the film as the 'barrenness of prehistoric Earth, together with the slime's need for organic life on which to operate, entails that human life originates in an act of self-referential self-destruction on the part of the Engineer'.[27] Nicoleat Popa Blanariu, in a similar vein, sees the Engineer as having been sent to Earth, à la Prometheus and similar to Jesus Christ, to 'improve the human condition' – and, like Prometheus and Christ, to be sacrificed.[28] However, in clear contrast to the Greek Prometheus, the Engineers, as seen at the end of the film, want to go back to Earth and destroy their creations, the humans. This is similar to what is found in Shelley's *Frankenstein* where 'the creator loathes his creation so much that the creator actively seeks his creation's demise'.[29] Mark T. Decker points us to one of the closing scenes of the film in which a newly awakened Engineer engages in a dialogue with David, and there occurs an intersection of all three creators: non-humans, humans and android:

> The Engineers, who might themselves be acting on the dictates of the performance principle by destroying a product line that is, from their perspective, about to be

made obsolete by something new and vastly improved, would be destroying a genetically engineered creation, humanity, that had itself begun to genetically engineer creatures like David.[30]

Two scholars of PIE have translated what is said in this scene. Sean A. Guynes translates it as 'This man is here because he does not want to die. He believes you can give him more life.'[31] Dr Anil Biltoo, a linguistics expert who developed the Engineer language from Proto-Indo-European for the film, agrees with Guynes' translation:

D[32] These people have come here from Earth. They believe that you have invited them.

E What do you want? Where do you come from?

D This man is here because he does not want to die. He believes you can give him more life.[33]

E Why does he want more life? What makes this man so great to ask such a thing?

W You see this man. My company built it from nothing, I was the one who did it. And did it in my image, so it . . . For him to be perfect. So it won't fail. I deserve this because you . . . You and I are superior. We are creators. We are gods . . . And the gods never die.

In this interaction between the Engineer, David and Weyland, it is clear that the overall point of the entire stellar expedition is to come to terms with questions surrounding creation. For example, who is the primary creator? Are non-human beings, like David, worthy of dignity? Does the act of creation make the creator a god? Do gods only create? Are humans meant to be immortal?

The search for the answers to these questions is complicated by what Stephanie A. Smith calls a restaging of the myth by film and an example of the 'cultural heritage of misogyny'.[34] For Smith, the film focuses on 'alienation, self-alienation, and bodily abjection and captivity'[35] and is a 'quest for knowledge' that turns 'into a sequence of botched reproductive nightmares, all of which point to an underlying misogynistic fear of copulation and reproduction'.[36] The film, she argues, has at its core a 'creator that loathes his creation so much that the creator actively seeks his creation's demise'.[37] Smith concludes her observations with the suggestion that the crew of the vessel in the film, like the myth of Prometheus, 'like the biblical Eve', seeks forbidden knowledge and 'is punished; more specifically, that punishment is the same as Eve's: both will suffer from the horror of zygotic reproduction'.[38]

An analysis of the character of Dr Elizabeth Shaw offers a third approach to the film and the myths. Shaw is a combination of Pandora and Eve. At times one or the other of the mythological persona takes hold, and these instances are always tied in with reproduction, both successful and failed attempts. The viewer fully encounters the reproductive imagery when the crew detachment sent to investigate the Engineers' pyramidical structure returns to the ship due to an oncoming storm, and crew members Milburn (Rafe Spall) and Fifield (Sean Harris) are left stranded and cannot find their way out. Milburn is killed by a snake-like creature called a Hammerpede, phallic in appearance yet with the dreaded *vagina dentata*, perhaps as an echo of the Edenic snake. The Hammerpede seems to combine both sexes in its anatomical structures; it is both male and female, the depositor of a quasi-ovum. Fifield does not fare any better as his helmet is destroyed by an exploding or ejaculating Hammerpede, and he falls face-first into the black goo that has been pouring out of the alien jars. He becomes infected with whatever is in the goo, is transformed into an alien-like creature, attacks the vessel *Prometheus* and is killed. So here we have two instances of failed male reproduction which Angie Voela suggests aligns with the persistent male desire to create life *ex nihilo* that recurs 'throughout human history as the latent desire to undo Pandora's gift of sexual difference'.[39]

In the meantime, David intentionally infects Holloway with the black goo from the jar, having secretly put a drop of it in a glass of champagne that Holloway drinks to celebrate their discovery. Later, Holloway transmits the infection during sexual intercourse. Holloway transforms also, and in his last scene in the film, when he visibly starts to deteriorate, he begs to be immolated by a flame thrower – the third male reproductive attempt that has failed since no real offspring is generated from Holloway's infection.

Although she is originally sterile (as mentioned in the film), when Shaw undergoes a medical scan, she discovers that she is now pregnant. She eventually removes from her abdomen a horrific cephalopod-like creature known as a Trilobite. In its adult form, the Trilobite has both an ovipositor, which is a phallic-like appendage for inseminating its victim, and a *vagina dentata*. The victim of Shaw's offspring is the resurrected Engineer, and from this ghastly and forced union, the Deacon is created.

Conclusion

The film ends with Shaw recovering David's remains and leaving LV-223 in search of the Engineers' home world, Paradise, in an attempt to understand why they created humanity and why they later attempted to destroy it. In the final shot, in the *Prometheus* escape pod, the Deacon (which is very similar to the xenomorph seen in the other *Alien* movies) bursts out of the dying Engineer's chest. The film's conclusion, and the reproduction-related incidents that lead up to it, are an answer to the beginning of the film, where the viewer encountered a sterile world that would be made fertile by the addition of male DNA. In other words, it was a male that caused creation.

Regarding the film's beginning, Brian Johnson accurately juxtaposes the exclusively male generative/creative power of Victor Frankenstein and Scott's Engineer: 'a planetary version of the *Frankenstein* myth in which the beneficent mother is always already absent, her generative power usurped in advance by the "new Promethianism" of paternal science that appropriates creation as its exclusive province'.[40] Conversely, it is Shaw, barren at the start of the film, who becomes the focus of fertility. She has taken on the role of creator

(Eve), generator of evil as the mother of the Trilobite (Pandora) and 'Promethean defender of humanity whose actions bring about the plot's allegorical recentering of the human'.[41]

So, what does the character of Shaw tell us? Any male attempt at reproduction is doomed to failure. Milburn, Fifield, Holloway and David are failed creatures; it is only Shaw who successfully reproduces. Like Eve, she gives birth to a new race of creatures after attaining forbidden knowledge; like Pandora, she seeks knowledge and, in so doing, fills the universe with all sorts of ills.

Barbara Ehrenreich was off target in her essay 'The Missionary Position' in her reference to *Prometheus* as 'gorgeous, but intellectually way out of [. . .] depth'.[42] Not only does this movie need more attention paid to it in order to understand more clearly how the myths of Pandora, Prometheus, Adam and Eve play a crucial role in its creation but also to appreciate the reality that it is very difficult not to encounter the stories of Prometheus and Pandora and Adam and Eve when producing narratives that deal with creation. A better way to think about this film is that it looks for answers to the source and purpose of humankind while invoking multiple overlaid strata of religious imagery and mythology that challenge 'the dichotomy between community-driven self-sacrifice and ego-driven use of technology and power'.[43]

Notes

* My greatest thanks go out to the librarians and staff of the University of Houston-Downtown's W. I. Dykes Library, especially Ms Yesenia Sanchez, Ms Anne Zwicky and Ms Alesson Solis for their help in acquiring texts and materials during the Covid-19 pandemic. Additionally, this chapter could not have been written without the support and erudite feedback of Dr Deborah Shelley, Professor *Emerita* of Communication Studies.

1. *Prometheus*, directed by Ridley Scott (Beverley Hills: Twentieth Century Fox, 2012).
2. Barbara Ehrenreich, 'The Missionary Position', *The Baffler* 21 (2012): 132.
3. Ehrenreich, 'The Missionary Position', 132.
4. Katie Walsh, 'Thoughtful Thrills in the *Alien* Universe', *Spokesman-Review*, 19 May 2017, 5, defines the *Alien* universe as a 'battleground for the philosophical and physical tussles for dominance between human, alien and artificial intelligence', which has recognizable 'themes, character types and iconography' that pose questions that 'are universal, and primal'.
5. Torston Caeners, 'Negotiating the Human in Ridley Scott's *Prometheus*', in *Posthumanism in Young Adult Fiction: Finding Humanity in a Posthuman World*, ed. Anita Tarr and Donna R. White (Jackson: University Press of Mississippi, 2018), 210.
6. Caeners, 'Negotiating the Human in Ridley Scott's *Prometheus*', 202.
7. Caeners, 'Negotiating the Human in Ridley Scott's *Prometheus*', 223, n. 1, writes, 'With this sacrifice, the Engineer enacts a fundamental aspect of the Prometheus myth. Central to the Prometheus myth is the fact that he steals fire from the Olympian gods and gives it to mankind. In doing so, he knowingly sacrifices his position among the gods and is punished accordingly by Zeus. Prometheus is bound and chained to Mount Caucasus, where he is a victim to a bird that appears every night to peck out his liver, which grows back every day so that his torture can be repeated endlessly [. . .] The Engineer's sacrifice is such a "complicated gift to mankind" and it is precisely the various complex and contrary aspects of the human condition that the film probes.'

8. Mark 14.22–34 (NAB).
9. It should be pointed out that Dr Shaw shares the same first name as Ms Lavenza, who is the fiancée of Victor Frankenstein in Mary Shelley's *Frankenstein; or, The Modern Prometheus* (1818). This connection between Shelley's Prometheus and Scott's film clearly points to the dangers that humans encounter when creating monstrous life. In the former, Elizabeth Lavenza dies at the hands of the monster; in the latter, Elizabeth Shaw gives birth to a monster that has the potential to destroy humanity.
10. David McWilliam, 'Beyond the Mountains of Madness: Lovecraftian Cosmic Horror and Posthuman Creationism in Ridley Scott's *Prometheus* (2012)', *Journal of the Fantastic in the Arts* 26, no. 3 (2015): 532.
11. On this type of archetype, see Carl G. Jung, *Psychology and Religion*, in *The Collected Works of C. G. Jung*, Vol. 11, 2nd edn, ed. Herbert Read (Princeton, NJ: Princeton University Press, 1958), par. 88: 'Forms or images of a collective nature which occur practically all over the earth as constituents of myths and at the same time as autochthonous, individual products of unconscious origin.'
12. Kyle D. Killian, 'Prometheus', *Journal of Feminist Family Therapy* 26, no. 4 (2014): 244, does pose an interesting question about the ambiguity of the use of the name Prometheus: 'Is *Prometheus* just the name of the expeditionary vessel, or does it represent the Engineer who died at the film's beginning, a demigod punished for bringing 'fire' to the human race?' Interestingly, according to Stephanie A. Smith, '"An Empire O'er the Disentangled Doom": Captivity and the Re-Staging of *Prometheus* in the Twenty-First Century', *Science Fiction Film and Television* 9, no. 1 (2016): 64, n. 20, the original name of the ship was 'Magellan'. If the original name had been kept, a greater weight would have been put on the Promethean qualities of the humans and the Engineers.
13. Johnny Hardstaff, 'The Peter Weyland Files: *Prometheus* Transmission', Holloway segment, YouTube video, 1:11:00, https://www.youtube.com/watch?v=oEtgjsoh7lo.
14. Johnny Hardstaff, 'The Peter Weyland Files: *Prometheus* Transmission', YouTube video, 7:08:00, https://www.youtube.com/watch?v=FCOo5mj10fE.
15. Ridley Scott, '*Prometheus*, "How far would you go . . .?" scene', YouTube video, 1:47:00, https://www.youtube.com/watch?v=pww01VM8bjI.
16. '*Prometheus* Crew: On A Mission Collision', *Philippine Daily Inquirer*, https://www.webcitation.org/68QKobIOZ.
17. Killian, '*Prometheus*', 241.
18. Ginette Carpenter, 'Mothers and Others', in *Women and the Gothic: An Edinburgh Companion*, ed. Horner Avril and Zlosnik Sue (Edinburgh: Edinburgh University Press, 2016), 51–2.
19. On these topics, see the following essays: John L. Cobbs, '*Alien* as an Abortion Parable', *Literature Film Quarterly* 18, no. 3 (1990): 198–201; Robert Torry, 'Awakening to the Other: Feminism and the Ego-ideal in *Alien*', *Women's Studies* 23, no. 4 (1994): 343–63; Peter Lev, 'Whose Future? *Star Wars, Alien*, and *Blade Runner*', *Literature/Film Quarterly* 26, no. 1 (1998): 30–7; Susan Yunis and Tammy Ostrander, 'Tales Your Mother Never Told You: *Aliens* and the Horrors of Motherhood', *Journal of the Fantastic in the Arts* 14, no. 1 (2003): 68–76; Robin Sloan, 'Homesick for the Unheimlich: Back to the Uncanny Future in *Alien*: Isolation', *Journal of Gaming & Virtual Worlds* 8, no. 3 (2016): 211–30; Vanni Codeluppi, 'The Integrated Spectacle: Towards Aesthetic Capitalism', in *The Spectacle 2.0: Reading Debord in the Context of Digital Capitalism*, ed. Briziarelli Marco and Armano Emiliana (London: University of Westminster Press, 2017), 51–66; Melanie A. Marotta, 'The Science Fiction Horror: *Alien*, George R. R. Martin's *Nightflyers* and the Surveillance of Women', *Northern Lights: Film & Media Studies Yearbook* 17, no. 1 (2019): 57–70.

20. Vivian Sobchack, 'Between a Rock and a Hard Place: How Ridley Scott's *Prometheus* Deals with Impossible Expectations and Mythological Baggage', *Film Comment* 48 (2012): 33.
21. Sobchack, 'Between a Rock and a Hard Place', 34.
22. Danny Pegg, '*Prometheus*', *Journal of Religion & Film* 17, no. 2 (2013): 3.
23. Cynthia Kraman, 'The Future is Female: Bateson, Benjamin and How Women Learn in Ridley Scott's *Prometheus*,' *Anthropology Now* 7 (2015): 1–13. The editors of this volume offer fascinating alternate interpretations of David and his beheading: 1) this may perhaps be a hint to Goliath, beheaded by another David or 2) that the name David may also allude to the biblical character and possibly Michelangelo's statue.
24. Kraman, 'The Future is Female', 7.
25. Kraman, 'The Future is Female', 5.
26. Stephen Mulhall, *On Film*, 3rd edn (London and New York: Routledge, 2016), 230. His chapter is intriguingly titled 'Cinematic Repetition and How to Avoid It: Sequels, Prequels, and *Prometheus*'.
27. Mulhall, *On Film*, 231.
28. Nicoleta Popa Blanariu, 'Transmedial Prometheus: From the Greek Myth to Contemporary Interpretations', *Icono 14* 15, no. 1 (2017): 101–2.
29. Smith, 'An Empire O'er the Disentangled Doom', 67.
30. Mark T. Decker, *Industrial Society and the Science Fiction Blockbuster: Social Critique in Films of Lucas, Scott and Cameron* (Jefferson, NC: McFarland & Company, Inc., 2016), 107. This scene was not fully included in the theatrical release but is included in its entirety in the Blu-ray version as the eleventh deleted scene ('The Engineer Speaks').
31. Sean A. Guynes, 'Do Androids Dream of Proto-Indo-European Fables about Sheep', *Vocabula Review* 14, no. 7 (2012): 3. Indeed, Guynes, on the same page of the intriguing essay, posits an interesting question: 'Consider if the ancestor of Navajo (Proto-Athabaskan) or Chinese (Proto-Sino-Tibetan) had been used instead. Let me clarify that the language presented by *Prometheus* is entirely and fundamentally different from that of any other mainstream sci-fi productions. Klingon of *Star Trek*, for example, has a sound system based on Navajo; *Stargates*' Goa'uld speak Ancient Egyptian; the population in *Firefly* is bilingual in Chinese and English; the 2009 blockbuster *The Fourth Kind* had its alien abductors speaking Sumerian. In these examples, and others, sci-fi writers posited that extraterrestrials were known to other cultures, and humans adopted their languages (*Stargate*, *The Fourth Kind*), or a language was created by writers for a fictional world on the basis of its sounds and words out of context (*Klingon* and many others), or writers created a future universe in which languages that had large populations of speakers in the writers' contemporary world have become lingua francas (*Firefly*).' Guynes makes the point that by having the aliens, who are the creators of humanity, speak PIE, this language is thereby privileged; such an act is dangerous in consequently privileging the modern-day descendants of PIE.
32. The full names for the initials are as follow: D = David, E = Engineer, W = Weyland.
33. The translation for these two sentences can be found in Stu Holmes, 'The Linguistics of *Prometheus* – What David Says to The Engineer', *The Bioscopist*, 20 June 2012, https://thebioscopist.wordpress.com/2012/06/20/the-linguistics-of-prometheus-what-david-says-to-the-engineer/comment-page-2/.
34. Smith, 'An Empire O'er the Disentangled Doom', 57.
35. Smith, 'An Empire O'er the Disentangled Doom', 64.
36. Smith, 'An Empire O'er the Disentangled Doom', 64.

37. Smith, 'An Empire O'er the Disentangled Doom', 67.

38. Smith, 'An Empire O'er the Disentangled Doom', 69.

39. Angie Voela, *Psychoanalysis, Philosophy and Myth in Contemporary Culture after Oedipus* (London: Palgrave Macmillan UK, 2017), 201.

40. Brian Johnson, 'Prehistories of Posthumanism: Cosmic Indifferentism, Alien Genesis, and Ecology from H. P. Lovecraft to Ridley Scott', in *The Age of Lovecraft*, ed. Carl H. Sederholm and Weinstock Jeffrey Andrew (Minneapolis: University of Minnesota Press, 2016), 98.

41. Johnson, 'Prehistories of Posthumanism', 112.

42. Ehrenreich, 'The Missionary Position', 132.

43. Peter Nicolai Halvorsen, 'Religion in a World of Androids and Aliens: Life and Death in Ridley Scott's *Blade Runner* and *Prometheus*', in *Science Fiction, Ethics and the Human Condition*, ed. Christian Baron, Peter Nicolai Halvorsen and Christine Cornea (Cham, Switzerland: Springer, 2017), 133.

CHAPTER 15
PANDORA'S SPLIT: READING THE MYTH OF PANDORA IN *CRUEL BEAUTY*

Lily Glasner

In the last decade there has been a wave of popular adaptations of classical Western tales and myths, aimed especially at young adult female readers with a taste for romance.[1] One such novel is *Cruel Beauty* by Rosamund Hodge.[2] Thus, whilst the publisher's website promises that 'this gorgeously written debut infuses the classic fairy tale with glittering magic, a feisty heroine, and a romance sure to take your breath away', the critics of *Redeemed Reader* assure their readers that 'young men probably wouldn't be interested in this novel'.[3]

Envisioned as a popular text, *Cruel Beauty* is nonetheless a rather complex retelling of a renowned tale – commonly referred to as *Beauty and the Beast*, in itself a transformation of the classic myth of Cupid and Psyche. Within this general frame, the author plays with and weaves in several other sources, most notably the classic myth of Pandora and the jar of miseries found in Hesiod's texts.

In this chapter I suggest that *Cruel Beauty* invites the reader to reinterpret the myth of Pandora through a psychological and feminist lens. At the heart of this reinterpretation lies the idea of the *split* and its materialization both in the land and in the individual who plays the role of Pandora. The *split* as a theoretical concept is prominent in the writings of both Carl Jung and Carol Gilligan. Therefore, I propose to read the utilization of the ancient myth in the contemporary novel in light of their ideas.

Pandora and the idea of gender differentiation

Our point of departure is the classical texts and a seemingly simple question: who is Pandora? In Hesiod's *Theogony*, Pandora is the beautiful maiden created by Hephaestus and the one to whom the poet attributed the responsibility of originating 'the deadly race and tribe of women'.[4] In her study of the myth, Vered Lev Kenaan writes:

> In introducing Pandora, the first woman, Hesiod grounds his history of humanity in the distinction between the one and the many. Before Pandora the world is inhabited by a generic crowd of males who remain nameless and wholly unspecified. Despite the use of the term 'male', we need to notice that until Pandora's arrival humanity was essentially composed of asexual and indistinguishable beings. As the archetype of femininity, she introduced the very dimension of difference into a homogeneous regime of sameness. This in turn, means that Pandora was the first real individual.[5]

While I agree with Lev Kenaan that Pandora is indeed introduced into 'a homogeneous regime of sameness' as far as humanity is concerned, and that Pandora's figure introduces the idea of gender differentiation, I suggest that in Hesiod's Pandora we have a concept rather than an individual.

For a sense of individuality to be formed, a text needs to convey, directly or indirectly, the existence of an inner world (made evident by echoing thoughts, deliberations and/or feelings).[6] By contrast, in Hesiod, who is the so-called person named Pandora? For instance, how does she feel being gazed upon by the crowd of gods and men?[7] How does she feel about Epimetheus? In comparison, one may recall the speaker's sensual descriptions of being in love in Sappho's poem (Fragment 31), which gives the reader a glimpse into the speaker's psyche.[8] One can also point to other feminine literary figures found in classical texts – from Homer's Penelope to Euripides' Medea – who are not merely abstract concepts, or abstract figures. In Hesiod's version, the narrator expands on the process of creating Pandora. Yet after she is created, he does not give any indication, either directly or indirectly, as to the existence of an inner world in this figure. There is not even any mention as to why she had opened the jar.[9] In fact, in Hesiod's texts there seems to be very little we can say about the being called Pandora, other than the fact that she is identified as a woman, endowed with 'feminine attributes', but this, it appears, is an essentialist trait.

Pandora and gender transformations

Hesiod's Pandora is identified as a female figure. Yet in Western culture Pandora, as a name and an idea gained life beyond that of the specific literary figure in Hesiod, and outside of his texts it may or it may not be a signifier of gender.[10]

Furthermore, within the context of *the harbinger of miseries*, a Pandora figure is not necessarily a woman. In their classic study, Dora and Erwin Panofsky suggest that an earlier version existed in which a man opened the jar. It is probably this version that we find centuries later in one of Babrius's fables, according to which Zeus gave men a sealed jar with all the good things in the world inside. 'But man could not restrain himself. He removed the lid' and so all the blessings, except for hope, escaped the earth forever.[11] The possibility that it was indeed a male's fault resonates in the retelling of the myth by the sixteenth-century scholar Erasmus, to whom Panofsky and Panofsky also attributed the alteration of the word 'jar' into the word 'box'. Erasmus wrote in Latin and with no specific name or pronoun attached to it, the Latin verb *aperuisset* (opened) can refer to either a male or female subject.[12] Studying later evidence, Panofsky and Panofsky demonstrate that the possibility of the identification of the opener of the jar/box with a male figure also reappeared in the art works of two Renaissance artists and one from the nineteenth century.[13] Although it is true that most readers will not be familiar with these versions, nonetheless it is still an alternative with precedents in Western culture; this is an alternative which, as we shall see, is well explored by Hodge.

Cruel Beauty: Synopsis[14]

Before delving into Hodge's retelling, an outline of the story is called for. While the novel is not linear, for the sake of convenience, here I summarize the main events chronologically. The story, then, takes place in Arcadia, a world dominated by 'The Kindly Ones'.[15] Hundreds of years ago, Claudius, the King of Arcadia who had restored Pandora's jar, made a bargain with The Kindly Ones in order to keep his people and the land safe from the attacks of the Barbarians. According to the bargain, Claudius and each of his successors must take a test: looking into the jar of Pandora. As long as one's heart is pure, he and Arcadia will remain safe, but if not, he will be imprisoned within the jar and Arcadia will no longer be protected. In the course of each generation the jar undergoes a metamorphosis.

After nine generations, the last prince, Marcus Valerius Lux, who receives the jar, which now takes the form of a box, refuses to take the test. The prince knows that his heart is not pure, and that there is hatred in him. In his desperation he turns to The Kindly Ones, asking them to root out of him the hatred. He is willing to pay any price just as long as he is not imprisoned alone in the darkness of the jar and on condition that Arcadia continues to be safe. The Kindly Ones agree but as is their custom they twist things around: Arcadia is physically cut off ('sundered') from the world and is inserted into the prince's castle – the castle is inserted into Pandora's box – but now, just like in one of Escher's physically impossible images – the box is placed in one of the rooms in the prince's castle. Thus, the imprisoned Arcadia is indeed safe from invasion and the prince is not imprisoned alone in the box.

In order to complete the bargain, The Kindly Ones uproot the hatred from the prince's heart by physically splitting him into two persons: Ignifex, ironically entitled 'The Gentle Lord', and Shade. Ignifex must rule this confined world and serve his masters by making bargains that will always bring calamity and misery to those who seek to make them. Shade is his servant. The Kindly Ones erased Ignifex's memory of the past as well as the knowledge of his true identity. The truth is also unknown to the people of Arcadia who believe Ignifex to be a demon that had invaded their land and imprisoned it between a dome and a void.

Nine hundred years later, one of the wise men of Arcadia is rashly tempted to make a bargain with The Gentle Lord. In return for granting his wish he agrees to give in marriage to The Gentle Lord one of his yet unborn twin girls upon her seventeenth birthday. After their birth the father chooses one to be the future bride, Nyx, and from an early age instructs and trains her in the 'hermetic [magical] arts' so that she will be able to kill her husband and deliver Arcadia. Nyx knows that in order to succeed she will need to sacrifice her life. Once she is in her husband's castle she realizes that the original plan not only will fail to save Arcadia but will actually lead to its total destruction. Navigating between Ignifex, Shade and the mysteries of the castle, Nyx finally finds the way to overcome her husband. Despite the fact that by now she has fallen in love with him, her commitment to her family and her land outweighs her personal feelings.

After Ignifex and Shade, the prince's two halves, are reunited, he – of his own free will – is imprisoned forever in Pandora's box. By this act the prince releases Arcadia and time itself goes backwards. Nyx and her sister are born into a world that does not know The Gentle Lord and his dark reign. The memory of him is gone from both the collective and the personal consciousness until one day the memory is reawakened in Nyx, whereupon she decides to try to save him by embarking on a new bargain with The Kindly Ones. When she realizes, however, that she has no way of saving him, she offers to share his fate and gain nothing in return, fully understanding that it will not even alleviate his suffering. To this seemingly stupid bargain on her part, they are bound by their own laws to agree and now the two of them are thrown together into Pandora's Box where they suffer excruciatingly both physically and mentally. Nevertheless, because they do not let go of one another, they survive the ordeal and finally win their freedom and a new chance to live and explore their love on equal terms.

The emergence of Pandora in *Cruel Beauty*

In *Cruel Beauty* the myth of Pandora appears both as a story within a story, as Ignifex narrates it to Nyx, and in a larger sense as a continuance of the myth. According to Ignifex, Pandora fell in love with Prometheus and it was a broken heart that led her to the fatal opening of the jar.[16] Thus, upon the reader's first direct encounter with the myth, the archetype is already converted into a person, an individual characterized by her feelings and deliberations. However, the reader of the novel, following the sequence of the text, will learn about a hundred pages later that this is not where the story of Pandora and her jar of miseries ended.[17] And, in the continuance, not only the jar is transformed but the very gendered identity of Pandora is affected.

As the narrative of *Cruel Beauty* continues to unfold, we are introduced to the 'present day' Pandora's Box. It is no longer an old myth in an old book, but an actuality. Thereupon the question arises, who is now playing the role of Pandora? If our criterion is the current holder of the box who, as fate has it, must open it, then it is the prince. Ironically it was his refusal to open the box that resulted in bringing misery to the human world. Through a feminist lens one may suggest that Hodge reinterprets the ancient myth by relocating the blame from woman to man. This line of argument gains strength by the fact that after Ignifex recounts the old myth, Nyx protests, 'If Pandora had known *all* the truth, she would never have opened the jar.'[18] However, on two different occasions Ignifex calls Nyx 'Pandora' and even suggests that she had opened a jar of her own.[19] Thus, perhaps Hodge is not simply relocating the blame from woman to man. Rather, her retelling suggests that both men and women are culpable of fatal misjudgement, and that this is one of the main traits that define a person, an individual.

Yet in this novel the actualization of the figure of Pandora as male poses another question: is it just the last prince or perhaps we should take into account all his ancestors who took the test of receiving and opening the jar (in whatever shape it was) and looking inside it? It seems that in the fictional world of *Cruel Beauty*, starting with King Claudius who found the missing jar, each generation has its own Pandora.[20] Thus, in response to Nyx's queries about the mysterious box she had seen in one of the castle's rooms, Ignifex replies, 'This world's already seen enough Pandoras, don't you think?',[21] implying, I would argue, that Pandora is a cycle that needs to be broken. Moreover, the multiplying of the name implies a reproduction of the non-individual. While Hesiod's Pandora is portrayed as the prototype of the 'evil non-individual', in *Cruel Beauty* the prince's ancestors seem to portray the 'perfect non-individual', that 'homogeneous regime of sameness', to borrow Lev Kenaan's acute phrasing. The breaking of the cycle can only occur with the last prince precisely because he is not a 'perfect non-individual'. His is a human soul that can be affected by what's hidden inside the box and governed by the fear of looking inside because he is conscious that he is not perfect.

In Hodge's retelling, then, the ancient figure of Pandora is both multiplied and divided as it becomes the embodiment of a human being and a pattern (a cycle), a female figure and male figure, a collective and an individual. Yet the additional divide, that which takes place in the individual as exemplified by the two halves of the prince, calls for a further consideration. I suggest that this last manifestation of the Pandora figure corresponds with psychological concepts of *split* that are found in the writings of Carl Jung and Carol Gilligan.

The prince and Carl Jung's theory of the shadow

> She cupped his face again. 'And now I shall take all the hatred out of your heart'
>
> Then she clenched her hands and pulled them apart. And she pulled *him* apart too: a shadowy, shifting form collapsed to the floor, his face a blur but his eyes bright blue; it was Shade. And standing above him now was Ignifex, red-eyed and smiling.[22]

A metaphorical reading of this scene suggests that by rejecting an essential part of one's self, the individual becomes a fragment or a pale shade of his true and whole self. And indeed, Shade, who knows the truth, is powerless to act;[23] whilst the force of life burns within that part which was rejected, as symbolized by the colour of the eyes of Ignifex as well as by his name which literally means the maker (*-fex*) of fire (*ignis*). Nonetheless the force of life lacks the recognition of the self.[24]

However, the other name, Shade, suggests that the two halves may be read as a materialization of Carl Jung's theory of the shadow. According to Jung, in the separation between conscious and unconscious, the shadow is the manifestation of human weaknesses (such as anger and hate) which the conscious (the *ego*) rejects:

> Unfortunately there can be no doubt that man is, on the whole, less good than he imagines himself or wants to be. Everyone carries a shadow, and the less it is embodied in the individual's conscious life, the blacker and denser it is [...] We carry our past with us, to wit, the primitive and inferior man with his desires and

> emotions, and it is only with an enormous effort that we can detach ourselves from this burden. If it comes to a neurosis, we invariably have to deal with a considerably intensified shadow. And if such a person wants to be cured it is necessary to find a way in which his conscious personality and his shadow can live together.[25]

In his explanation of the Jungian term 'shadow', John A. Sanford explains, 'It's not always evil – it's just different than the ego [. . .] the shadow, no matter how troublesome it may be, is not intrinsically evil. The ego, in its refusal of insight and its refusal to accept the entire personality, contributes much more to evil than the shadow.'[26]

The Jungian concepts of ego and shadow, and their complicated relationship, suggest an explanation with regard to the riddles of knowing and unknowing in the novel. Namely, why is it that Shade knows the truth about their shared identity whilst Ignifex is blind to it and cannot even remember his own name (a name being a signifier of identity): 'I know,' Shade will admit to Nyx, 'and can't act. He acts but knows nothing.'[27] As Marcus Valerius Lux, the last prince rejects his human weaknesses as though they were external demons that can be exorcised. And his refusal to accept his entire personality resulted in bringing much harm to himself and to others as he was forced to serve the merciless Kindly Ones.

The Jungian concepts of ego and shadow may also suggest an answer to a yet unasked question: if The Kindly Ones tore out of the prince all that was bad, why is the other half not portrayed as 'the good half'? Rather, to the outer world and to Nyx, Ignifex, the *ego*, is viewed as a monster, and his title 'The Gentle Lord' is understood not literally but ironically.[28] Hodge, I would argue, is suggesting that Pandora – both as a representation of a woman and as a representation of humanity – was never meant to be perfect. On the contrary, being a human being, an individual, demands the recognition and acceptance of the dark side (symbolized by the shadow) as well as of the light side (*lux*) of one's psyche.

Resisting the gender binary

The second reading of the *split* I would like to suggest emphasizes social constructs and their effects on the individual. This reading originates from a feminist line of thought. Following her early studies, in *Joining the Resistance* Carol Gilligan maintained that patriarchy, as a worldview and as a social order, creates a gender binary and hierarchy.[29] Within the field of psychology that was governed by a patriarchal worldview, two developmental models were assumed: *a masculine model*, which argued that boys reached maturation by achieving separation and autonomy; and *a feminine model*, which argued that girls reached maturation by developing a strong sense of caring for others and by becoming selfless. Within this theoretical framework, 'masculine ethics' – constructed around the ideas of fairness and rights and based on laws and principles – is perceived as being rational and as being the benchmark. By comparison, in this hierarchal order, 'feminine ethics' – its main concern being care and responsibility and striving to attune the self to the needs of others – is perceived as flawed and lacking. Gilligan emphasizes that the difference between the way men contemplate moral dilemmas and the way women do is not due to gender essentialism but due to their different initiations into patriarchy.

One outcome of the initiation processes is the silencing of one's authentic voice, but whilst boys undergo their initiation already in early childhood, girls will undergo theirs on the verge of adolescence. Another outcome of the initiation processes is the individual's denial and repression of the knowledge acquired through life experiences. Gilligan describes it as 'splits in consciousness that would keep parts of ourselves and our experience outside our awareness'.[30]

Gilligan then points to a split in the very fabric of society, stemming from gender binary and forcing itself on the individual. Whereas theorists such as Freud, Erickson, Piaget and Kohlberg interpreted it as a natural and positive maturation process and even as a cornerstone of civilization, Gilligan emphasizes that this is by no means a 'natural' or a 'positive' process. The split in the psyche stems from a coercion to silence its authentic voice and the result is devastating:

> The initiation into patriarchy is driven by gender and enforced by shaming and exclusion. Its telltale signs are a loss of voice and memory, an inability to tell one's story accurately.[31]

Furthermore, the individual then is susceptible to 'fall under the sway of false authority'.[32]

Separately, both Nyx and the prince undergo an initiation process designed to mould them into creatures of pure duty, preparing each of them to be selfless and perform a specific role. Reading the figure of the prince in light of Gilligan's theory suggests that his split into two halves is a poetic actualization of the outcome of the initiation process as described by Gilligan. Since his early boyhood the prince was told what was expected of him, mainly 'to be a good prince', to possess a pure heart and in due time to pass the test of the box which will prove him worthy for kingship.[33] Acknowledging that he is not pure of heart and being terrified of the punishment that will ensue as a result of his failure in the test, the prince is coerced into bargaining with The Kindly Ones in order that he may fulfil his social role, become kind and not 'end up alone in the box'.[34] The split in the prince's consciousness is described as an actual event which results in him becoming two personae.[35] The half that is the master became The Gentle Lord and suffered the loss of his authentic voice and all his memories of his previous life and identity. He is unable to tell his own story or even to recognize Shade's true connection to him.

This last point brings us back to a further observation made by Gilligan. Sometimes, she suggests, a will may be found in the soul that will oppose the split and will struggle to break free from the dissociation – a will that allows women to break free from 'the tyranny of [being] nice and kind'.[36] Gilligan recognizes this in women and attributes it to the fact that their initiation process begins at a later stage, after they have acquired significant life experiences and memories and after they have reached a higher level of cognitive abilities.

According to Gilligan, then, it is an inner strength that enables the individual to overcome the split that was brought about by the initiation process. In Hodge's novel, I would argue, in order to overcome the split, there is a need to combine the inner will with an external one which in turn emphasizes the importance of relationships and of caring ethics to the well-being of the self. In light of Gilligan's insistence that masculine and feminine attributes are not essentialist traits and that by nature boys are no less sensitive and caring than girls,[37] it is significant to note that both as the last prince and as Ignifex this male Pandora figure is associated (even if ironically) with 'feminine' attributes – namely being 'good', 'kind' and 'gentle'. Similarly, the prince's fear of ending up alone in the box may imply his inner resistance to the ideal of autonomy which is gained at the expense of nurturing relationships. Moreover, just like in a feminine initiation, the prince is expected to become selfless and, in the face of moral dilemma, to sacrifice himself for the well-being of others.[38] However, notwithstanding his feminine attributes, Ignifex fails to regain his memory, to break free, on his own, from his dissociation.[39] It is through the agency of Nyx that he is finally forced to face that part of him that he has repressed and rejected and is enabled to reunite with it. In the process, he is freeing himself from the façade and the tyranny of his forced identity as The Gentle Lord.

Yet even if the individual has regained his consciousness, he is still a prisoner and will remain so as long as the old social order, that of patriarchy, continues. In her final argument, Gilligan proposes a feminist ethics – an 'ethics of care' – which negates the social split and seeks to reunite those things that are viewed in patriarchy as opposites: reason and emotion; mind and body; self and relationships; men and women. She advocates the rise of a new voice – a voice that unites the point of view that was traditionally perceived as 'masculine' and the point of view that was traditionally perceived as 'feminine'.[40]

In Hodge's novel the social split is symbolized by the 'Sundering' of Arcadia. Thus, as the narrative unfolds, Nyx realizes that in order to free her country she needs 'to defeat not just Ignifex but his masters as well'.[41] And indeed, in her final confrontation with The Kindly Ones it is the new ethics she will come to assume that will undo them and their regime. After they decline all her offers of bargaining to save her husband's life, she renounces the established ethics which determines that each side will gain something from the transaction. Instead, she is choosing an ethics of kindness – she will fully pay a price without asking or gaining anything in return.[42] In a world governed by patriarchy, this is an irrational act and The Kindly Ones declare it to be such: '*It is no bargain [. . .] It is a revolt against bargaining. It will destroy itself in the granting. It will destroy us in the granting*.'[43] Thus, with what seems like a fruitless act of total self-sacrifice, Nyx is in fact paving the way to the possibility of a new social order as the old one, that of The Kindly Ones, is destroyed. Whilst the split in society affects the individual, it is also the individual who can bring about a social change.

A new paradigm

In her seminal work on adaptation, Linda Hutcheon advocates a viewpoint according to which 'adapters are first interpreters and then creators'.[44] The essential role of the contemporary author as interpreter of the ancient text(s) is also prominent in Classical

Reception Studies, which explore the ways and forms in which the cultures and histories of classical antiquity are actualized and utilized in later times including in contemporary cultures.[45] Furthermore, according to Hutcheon, a retelling can be appreciated as an autonomous work whilst at the same time it is perceived as essentially engaged with the adapted text.[46] This is certainly true of Rosamund Hodge and her novel. Many of the central traits and issues of Hesiod's creation resonate in *Cruel Beauty*: literally there is a Pandora's Box, the very existence and function of which are connected with trickery and deception; there are cosmological consequences to the opening of the box; and the human condition too is influenced through the opening of the box. Yet, Hodge, as an interpreter, recreates the ancient myth under a feminist agenda and with strong psychological resonance. In the intricate fictional world she has created, the flat character of the ancient Pandora becomes a multifaceted manifestation of the self. Furthermore, by adding to the myth a new layer, that of the *split*, Hodge seems to invite the readers to imagine a new social order that will resist the long-standing paradigm of gender binary.

In her writings, Gilligan maintains that at the heart of the foundational narratives of Western culture there is always a story of trauma and that as far as love is concerned Western culture endorses the tragic love story, which time and again reinforces the patriarchal social order.[47] She suggests that in order to create a social change and promote gender equality, our culture needs to adopt a new paradigm: that of the love story that ends well.[48] I propose that in *Cruel Beauty* the utilization of the ancient myth creates that paradigm shift, for in Hodge's narrative, both Pandoras – Lux and Nyx (Light and Night) – regain in the end their authentic voices and a path to live and explore their love on equal terms.

Notes

1. See for example the Simon & Schuster *Once Upon a Time* series, https://www.simonandschuster.com/series/Once-upon-a-Time.
2. Rosamund Hodge, *Cruel Beauty* (New York: Balzer + Bray, an imprint of HarperCollins Publishers, 2014).
3. Publisher's description, see https://www.harpercollins.com/products/cruel-beauty-rosamund-hodge?variant=32122671202338. Critic's review of *Redeemed Reader* website, see https://redeemedreader.com/2017/03/cruel-beauty-redeemed-reader-discussion/. Whilst there is a readership of romance novels by men – for an early literary humoristic evidence, see P. G. Wodehouse, 'Jeeves in the Springtime', In *Enter Jeeves: 15 Early Stories* (Mineola and New York: Dover Publications, 1921/1997), 128–43 – women still comprise the majority readers of the romance genre. See Kristin Ramsdell, *Romance Fiction: A Guide to the Genre* (Santa Barbara, CA: Libraries Unlimited, 2012), 20.
4. Hesiod, 'Theogony', in *Theogony. Works and Days. Testimonia*, trans. Glenn W. Most (Cambridge, MA: Harvard University Press, 2006), 51. Pandora is also explicitly identified as a female figure: Hesiod, 'Theogony', 93.
5. Vered Lev Kenaan, *Pandora's Senses: The Feminine Character of the Ancient Text* (Madison: University of Wisconsin Press, 2008), 17.
6. A case in point is suggested by Tovi Bibring's reading in medieval literature. Bibring identifies female figures who function *solely* as mirrors of the inner world of male protagonists. See Tovi

Bibring, *Corps, âme, psyché: lectures de l'érotique et du danger dans les Lais de Marie de France* (Amiens: Presses du Centre d'Etudes Médiévales de Picardie, 2016).

7. Hesiod, 'Theogony', 51.
8. Sappho, *Sappho: A New Translation of the Complete Works*, trans. Diana J. Rayor and André Lardinois (Cambridge: Cambridge University Press, 2014), 44.
9. Hesiod, 'Works and Days', in *Theogony. Works and Days. Testimonia*, trans. Glenn W. Most (Cambridge, MA: Harvard University Press, 2006), 95.
10. For instance, one can purchase a trinket from the 'Pandora Places' collection of the international jewellery company PANDORA. Whilst a claim may be made that ornaments resonate the ancient myth, it should be noted that the company's official story, as it appears on their website, does not propose such a connection. Furthermore, the wording 'The PANDORA story [. . .]', on their About Pandora webpage, suggests that the word is used as a noun rather than as a given name. See https://www.pandorashop.co.za/about-pandora.html. Another example, which distances the name even more from the mythological figure, is to be found in the name of the music streaming service company 'Pandora Premium': see www.pandora.com. One advertisement proposes '$0 for 30-Day Trial Pass for Pandora Plus Subscription', a wording that suggests that here too the name is perceived as a noun: see https://www.groupon.com/deals/pandora-37.
11. Babrius and Phaedrus, 'Fable 58', in *Babrius and Phaedrus*, trans. Ben Edwin Perry (Cambridge, MA: Harvard University Press, 1965), 75. Dora Panofsky and Erwin Panofsky, *Pandora's Box: The Changing Aspects of a Mythical Symbol*, 2nd edn (New York: Pantheon Books, 1962), 6. Panofsky and Panofsky also mention a version by Philodemus of Gadara who had attributed 'the act of unsealing [. . .] to the husband' (8).
12. Panofsky and Panofsky, *Pandora's Box*, 15–18.
13. Panofsky and Panofsky, *Pandora's Box* , 78–84, 102–5.
14. This synopsis appeared in Hebrew in Lily Glasner, '"היה היתה ילדה קטנה . . ." מעשיות, מעשיות-מחודשות ומודל הגיבורה האקטיבית' ('"Hyo Hayta yalda ktana . . ." maasiyot, maasiyot-mechudashot vemodel hagibora haactivit'; '"Once Upon a Time There was a Little Girl . . ." Fairy-tales, Fairy-tales Retellings and the Model of the Active Heroine'), In *פורצות גדרות: חינוך ומגדר בשדות שיח מגוונים* (*Portzot Gderot: Chinuch vemigdar besadot siach meguvanim*; Breaking Boundaries: Education and Gender in Multifaceted Discourse), ed. Dina Haruvi and Talila Kosh Zohar (Tel Aviv: Gama and Hakibbutz Hameuchad, 2017), 125–49.
15. The name *The Kindly Ones* is a reference to the Furies/Eumenides, goddesses of revenge who had turned into a positive social force that encourage mercy and justice, in Aeschylus' *The Eumenides*. In *Cruel Beauty* they are the masters of justice and trickery. Their fairness is cruel and there is no mercy nor empathy in their justice. Ironically, they can be overpowered only by an extreme act of kindness and self-sacrifice. Their exact nature is never revealed.
16. Hodge, *Cruel Beauty*, 177–82.
17. Hodge, *Cruel Beauty*, 282–7.
18. Hodge, *Cruel Beauty*, 181.
19. Hodge, *Cruel Beauty*, 82, 240. Whilst Ignifex compares Nyx to Pandora, *The Kindly Ones* make clear that Nyx is 'not the one who can open' Pandora's box (286).
20. Hodge, *Cruel Beauty*, 283.
21. Hodge, *Cruel Beauty*, 245.
22. Hodge, *Cruel Beauty*, 300.
23. Hodge, *Cruel Beauty*, 293.

24. Hodge, *Cruel Beauty*, 293.
25. C. G. Jung, 'Psychology and Religion', in *Psychology and Religion: West and East*, trans. R. F. C Hull, 2nd edn (London: Routledge & Kegan Paul, 1969), 76–7.
26. Miller, D. Patrick, 'What the Shadow Knows: An Interview with John A. Sanford', in *Meeting the Shadow: The Hidden Power of the Dark Side of Human Nature*, ed. Jeremiah Abrams and Connie Zweig (New York: Penguin Putnam, 1991), 21.
27. Hodge, *Cruel Beauty*, 293. See also 332.
28. The novel begins with Nyx's declaration about her future husband: 'I was raised to marry a monster' (1).
29. Carol Gilligan, *Joining the Resistance* (Cambridge: Polity Press, 2011); Carol Gilligan, *The Birth of Pleasure* (New York: Alfred A. Knopf, 2002); Carol Gilligan, *In a Different Voice: Psychological Theory and Women's Development* (Cambridge, MA: Harvard University Press, 1982).
30. Gilligan, *Joining the Resistance*, 33.
31. Gilligan, *Joining the Resistance*, 26.
32. Gilligan, *Joining the Resistance*, 33.
33. Hodge, *Cruel Beauty*, 282–4, 298; quotation 284.
34. Hodge, *Cruel Beauty*, 298, 335.
35. Hodge, *Cruel Beauty*, 300.
36. Gilligan, *Joining the Resistance*, 33.
37. Gilligan, *Joining the Resistance*, 38, 24.
38. In her early study, Gilligan argued that Western society encourages women to assimilate the ideal of self-sacrifice and live up to it. Gilligan, *In a Different Voice*.
39. Hodge, *Cruel Beauty*, 295.
40. Gilligan, *Joining the Resistance*, 24.
41. Hodge, *Cruel Beauty*, 192.
42. Hodge, *Cruel Beauty*, 334.
43. Hodge, *Cruel Beauty*, 336.
44. Linda Hutcheon, *A Theory of Adaptation* (New York: Routledge, 2006), 18.
45. For example, Lisa Maurice, 'Children, Greece and Rome: Heroes and Eagles', in *The Reception of Ancient Greece and Rome in Children's Literature: Heroes and Eagles*, ed. Lisa Maurice (Leiden: Brill, 2015).
46. Hutcheon. *A Theory of Adaptation*, 6.
47. Gilligan, *Joining the Resistance*; Gilligan, *The Birth of Pleasure*.
48. Gilligan proposes the story of Cupid and Psyche, as recounted by Apuleius, as 'a map of resistance' to the patriarchal paradigm: Gilligan, *The Birth of Pleasure*, 22. For a different reading of Apuleius' narrative, one that identifies it as a feminine trauma story, see Lily Glasner, 'Cupid and Psyche: A Love Story (?) in Comics and Children's Literature', in *Rewriting the Ancient World: Greeks, Romans, Jews and Christians in Modern Popular Fiction*, ed. Lisa Maurice (Leiden: Brill, 2017), 204–5, 215.

CHAPTER 16

ADAM THE ALIEN, EVE THE ROBOT: THE REINTERPRETATION OF ADAM, EVE, PROMETHEUS AND PANDORA IN JAPANESE MANGA AND ANIME

Ayelet Peer

The various chapters in this volume discuss the creation of the first humans, focusing on Adam, Eve, Pandora and Prometheus in Judaeo-Christian and Graeco-Roman cultures. This chapter will illustrate these themes through the prism of Japanese popular media. Hence it will be shown how religious themes pertaining to foreign cultures are adapted, interpreted and understood even in a remote society. As Mineke Schipper states, 'intercultural comparison has taught us that peoples living thousands of miles away from each other may answer humanity's universal questions about the beginning in different ways, but their genesis narratives also reflect surprisingly similar patterns'.[1] This chapter hence aims to show the universalism of these creation myths.

This chapter addresses the sporadic representations of Adam, Eve, Prometheus and Pandora in Japanese pop culture, in particular in manga and anime. The appearance of these characters in the popular media of an entirely different culture attests to their wide-reaching influence. Since Japan did not embrace Christianity, the use of Adam and Eve in the most common and popular media of manga and anime carries different implications for the Japanese audience. I shall compare the more superficial uses of this creation story with a more substantial engagement.[2]

In order to better comprehend the Japanese attitude to Adam and Eve in pop culture, it is necessary to examine the complicated relations between Japan and the West, especially Western Christianity. While the story of Adam and Eve is common and familiar primarily within Jewish, Christian and Muslim communities, this is not the case in Japanese society. Barkman cites a popular anonymous expression, that the Japanese 'are born Shintō, marry Christian and die Buddhist'.[3] While this expression may imply an ideal religious tolerance, the historical reality was less rosy, as the following section on Christianity in Japan attests. Yet the adage does indicate the practicality of the Japanese and their adoption of religious practices, regardless of actual religious belief.

According to Ishikawa, Christians in Japan today comprise about 0.8 per cent of the population, among whom roughly around 60 per cent are Protestants and 40 per cent Catholic.[4] The Japanese, however, even if they do not practice this religion, are knowledgeable about Christianity, learning about it as part of the school curriculum.[5] Popular media, especially manga and anime, tend to focus on unusual and more occult presentations of Christianity, especially as an element of vampire-related shows.

Regarding the creation of humankind, the Japanese tradition focuses not on the creation of humanity as a whole but narrowly on the divine lineage and creation of the Imperial family. Thus this viewpoint is fundamentally different from the biblical story and from Greek mythology, which explain the creation of the entire world and of all humanity.[6]

Japanese creation myths

Every human culture developed its own specific creation story. The Japanese mythological creation is attested in the *Kojiki* (712 CE), the 'Records of Ancient Words/Matters', which is considered to be Japan's first book. The centrality of the Kojiki, as Brownlee notes, was of great importance to the imperial state 'to establish an understanding of the past that would enhance its supremacy'.[7] The Kojiki describes the mythological creation of the world, Japan, its various deities and, more importantly, the royal family. The Kojiki does not mention the multitude (the general creation of humankind) but focuses on the Japanese imperial family.

One of the versions of the creation of Japan (a Shintō version) tells of the two creator gods, the brother and sister, Izanagi ('He who Invites') and Izanami ('She who Invites'). They stood on the Floating Bridge of Heaven and stirred the watery chaos with a jewelled spear given to them by other deities. After lifting their spear, the waters that dripped from it formed an island, and other islands soon followed, created in different ways (some were born of the deities). From the creator gods other deities were born, in various fantastic ways; for example the Storm God, Susanoo, was born from Izanagi's nose.[8] The most important of these deities was the Sun Goddess, Amaterasu, who, according to one version, was born from Izanagi's left eye. In a different myth, told in the *Nihon Shoki* (or *Nihongi*, 720 CE), the Sun Goddess was created by the two creator deities in order to rule the universe. While Izanagi and Izanami are not human but creator deities, we can detect in them a slight resemblance to Adam and Eve as the first parents of the land of Japan and other gods.[9] They coupled in order to create the land of Japan and from their union other deities were born, and later, according to one version, Izanami died and descended to the world of the dead while giving birth to the Fire-God, Kagutsuchi. Thus, in a way, she left the ethereal paradise. These are of course peripheral similarities at best; Japanese mythology features no 'first man and first woman' couple, and this role is given to the male and female creator gods.

As noted, the Japanese creation myth focuses on the line of emperors who allegedly descended from the gods. Amaterasu sends her grandson, Niningi, 'the August Grandchild', to Earth to rule Japan's islands. From his grandchildren the first Japanese emperor, Jimmu Tennō, is born (*c.* seventh century CE). Kinsley explains the special bond between Amaterasu and the royal family: 'Amaterasu's role vis à vis the imperial line goes beyond that of ancestral progenitor, however. Amaterasu is also an ever-present model for the emperors, and in some cases, it is even suggested that she dwells within the emperor. The emperor, then, is not merely Amaterasu's descendent. He is also her appointee, her representative, and in some cases even the goddess herself.'[10] Amaterasu shares some characteristics with the Greek goddesses Athena and Demeter. She is associated with agriculture (she was the one who sowed rice for the first time) and silk weaving and is the bringer of growth and fertility, but she can also be a fierce guardian of the heaven or Japan.[11]

The featuring of Adam and Eve in Japanese pop-culture, despite their lack of connection to Japanese tradition, reflects a wider integration into society. This is in itself a result of Japan's seclusion and later forced acceptance of the West, along with its religious beliefs and even Graeco-Roman traditions.

A brief look at Christianity in Japan

The introduction of Christianity to Japan is a complicated and intricate subject, a detailed outline of which lies beyond the scope of this chapter. Here I trace only a basic outline of the initial Japanese resentment of Christianity, and the ways in which it nonetheless did finally manage to infiltrate Japan. While Christianity did not become a major religion in Japan, it did influence Japanese culture, as reflected by its appearance in pop culture.

The first contact between Christianity and the Japanese people was through the missionaries in the sixteenth and seventeenth centuries. Christianity was not warmly welcomed in Japan. Although the advent of Christianity was supported by some powerful warlords, such as Oda Nobunaga (1534–82), it was also forcibly resented by others, mainly the first three Tokugawa rulers, 'until the entire Christian population had been exterminated or driven underground by the mid-1640s'.[12] The climax of anti-Christian sentiment exploded during the Shimabara insurrection in 1637–8, which began in the Amakusa Islands in Higo province (modern Kumamoto Prefecture).[13] Decrees against foreign trade were issued beforehand, in 1616 and 1635. During the uprising, nearly 40,000 Christian rebels were defeated and massacred. The aftermath of the revolt led to the final decree of Japan's seclusion in 1639, which banned any contact with the outside world.[14] Although the rebellion was portrayed by the central government as resulting from religious causes, the reality was probably more complex, and other factors, mainly economic and political, were involved.[15] Christianity's appeal lay significantly in the compassion and comfort it offered the poorer and more neglected strata of society, such as poor peasants and fishermen, and hence was viewed with suspicion by the central government.[16] Anti-Christian resentment was also prevalent in the nineteenth century.[17]

There were of course opposing voices in Japan that supported and favoured foreign contact and trade, and especially the exchange of scientific knowledge with the West. However, this inconsistency illustrates that the Japanese were worried by the combination of foreign religious ideas with ideas of foreign imperialism and military advancement. It was not just a general anti-religious sentiment, but rather Christianity itself was perceived as part of a more complicated and violent approach to the East, led by the West.

While the USA promoted a policy of non-interference, as can be seen by the directive of President Millard Fillmore (1800–74) to Commodore Perry in 1853,[18] Christianity did follow the Americans into Japan. For example, among the various gifts Perry gave to the Japanese officials were the Bible and Christian literature. Other nations, including the Dutch and the Russians, guaranteed that their citizens could continue to freely practice their religions in Japan. In 1873 the prohibition of Christianity in Japan was revoked and various missionaries were allowed to enter the country. Even former samurai were involved in the establisment of churches, while trying to recover from their loss of position during the Meiji period.[19]

Adam and Eve in manga and anime

Christian practices are rather popular in anime and manga. Barkman argues regarding Christian elements in anime that

> [...] particular doctrines are seen as largely unimportant, whereas a general spiritual mood – a mood often created by blending many different religions together – is all-important.[20]

Therefore, manga and anime creators feel no qualms about depicting priests principally as fighting vampires and nuns as somewhat mischievous young girls, literally harnessing the power of God as a weapon. The cross is used in such shows more as a superpower tool than a profound religious symbol.

Shows such as *Chrno Crusade*, クロノ クルセイド, a manga by Moriyama Daisuke, in which two exorcists from a fictional Magdalene Order are working against demonic Sinners, are an example of this ethos.[21] Another example is the series of light novels, entitled *Trinity Blood*, トリニティ・ブラッド, by Yoshida and Sunao and Thores Shibamoto (illustrator), in which a war is raging between the Vatican and Vampires.[22] As a rule, when manga and anime artists feature Christianity, they tend to employ Catholic customs, since the abundance of symbolism within Catholicism appeals to them despite the fact that, as explained above, the majority of Christian worshippers in Japan are Protestant. Thus, religious depiction in popular media has often little to do with real-life religious practices.[23]

Specifically, the presence of the story of Adam and Eve in manga and anime attests to its common knowledge and appeal. The use of the story in manga and anime, however, varies, from superficial mentions to more complex and profound engagement with the story and its implications. Adam's and Eve's story is superficially echoed in the sci-fi manga *Needless* (ニードレス) by Imai Kami, which was serialized from 2003 to 2013 and wherein the connection with the biblical narrative is indicated solely by the names of the protagonists, Adam Blade (who is a priest) and his fighting partner Eve Neuschwanstein.

Another reference to Adam and Eve appears in the very popular *One Piece* (ワンピース) manga by Oda Eiichiro, which began serialization in 1997 and continues to the present time. The story refers to 'Treasure Tree Adam', which may recall the biblical Tree of Knowledge. The tree in the manga is a special one. It grows in a war-torn land and people often visit this tree, which never falls, and so they rebuild their city near it. Its wood is considered a highly valuable commodity. Hence the tree is a source of comfort for the people. The series also introduces the Sunlight Tree Eve on Fishman Island, which is a giant tree that can absorb sunlight and through breathing via its roots supplies air to the ocean floor. It is considered to be a mysterious and holy tree. Like the first mother Eve, this tree is also the giver of life. In the manga, the characters contemplate a possible connection between the two trees, yet do not reach a definite answer (volume 62, chapter 612). While we can detect a deeper meaning behind the trees' names, the biblical narrative is only echoed and used as ornamentation for the story rather than as a prompt for serious discussion of it, in keeping with the lighter tone of the series.

A comical, yet at the same time more thought-provoking, employment of the Adam and Eve story appears in in an episode of the 1980s popular series *Urusei Yatsura* (うる星やつら), by the most prolific female manga artist, Takahashi Rumiko. The manga was serialized from 1978 to 1987, and along with its subsequent anime revolves around the story of Moroboshi Ataru and the alien Lum. Lum believes she is Ataru's wife after he proposes to her by mistake. In episode 120 of the anime series,[24] the students are cleaning the class-pool when suddenly a giant water flea consumes the protagonist, Ataru, and his friend Shuutaru. Inside this creature the friends find themselves in a primordial world, where, after fleeing from a dinosaur, they encounter a beautiful naked blonde woman with blue eyes. They chat with her and then her husband arrives; the strange couple tell Ataru and Shuutaru that their names are Adam and Eve and that their child is sick. Later, Lum manages to get the boys back by making the flea vomit. Adam and Eve also transfer with them to the real world. The other students are astonished to see them, and the girls immediately fall for Adam while the boys fall for Eve.

While this is a rather inane episode, the visual impact of Adam and Eve in the series presents an obvious distinction between the physical appearance of the Japanese children and the more European-looking Adam and blonde Eve. Adam and Eve are drawn as epitomes of beauty, with slightly smaller eyes than the Japanese characters.[25] Adam is conventionally handsome, with brown hair and dark eyes, but it is Eve who is most striking with her blonde hair and blue eyes. Although in anime characters generally do not appear to belong to a specific nationality,[26] blonde is a stereotypical Western hair colour which, in the popular mind, typifies beautiful (Western) women, a tradition that runs at least from the early Middle Ages, and is typified in modern culture by Marilyn Monroe.[27] Nevertheless, even though blonde women are often ascribed both beauty, but even more, sensuality, Eve is drawn here as an innocent-looking maiden. Although she is naked, she does not flaunt her nakedness in front of the boys; she seems to be curious about them, even a bit afraid, and she clings to Adam when he approaches. Eve simply mentions her name to the boys and does not try to start a conversation. Adam and Eve present themselves as parents (although we do not have a clear understating of who their child really is).

While one should not delve too deeply into this episode, as its main purpose was light-hearted entertainment, the implications should not be overlooked. When first Ataru and Shuutaru meet Adam and Eve, Ataru tries to flirt with the latter, while Shuutaru chastises him and tells him that they are 'our ancestors' and he informs Eve that he is happy to meet his grandma (*obajan*). While Ataru has no idea who they are, Shuutaru recognizes their origin as ancestors. Clearly, however, Adam and Eve were not the Japanese ancestors. They are being used here as an archetypal model for the first man and woman, but without religious connotations.

Adam and Eve seem to possess an almost bewitching effect on the other students, who automatically fall for them, even bow to them. How are we meant to interpret this? Is this a social commentary on how the Japanese bow to foreign ideas? It seems that the bowing is simply an exaggeration of the students' appreciation of the strangers' beauty. Might it be a commentary on the power of beauty and perhaps on how foreign objects may dazzle the native Japanese? This could be far too sweeping an inference, yet the importance of Adam and Eve as ancestors is emphasized in the bizarre ending of the episode. Since Adam and Eve were transported to Japan, Ataru and Shuutaru remain alone in the primordial world when suddenly Shuutaru transforms into a woman, and he understands that the two of them must replace the missing Adam and Eve in this strange world.

Adam and Eve are also portrayed as a cosmic, inseparable couple in manga. This element is explored in the somber manga *Kagen no Tsuki* (下弦の月), or 'Last Quarter', by Yazawa Ai, running from 1998 to 1999 and later refigured as a live-action film.[28] It is a story of eternal love and loss. In the story, Hotaru, an elementary school girl, is looking for her cat when she enters an abandoned home in which she hears a piano playing. She sees a girl, or, in fact, an apparition of a girl, a high school student named Mizuki Mochizuki who was hit by a car as she ran after a young man named Adam, whom she loved, and who has been in a coma ever since. Hotaru and her friends refer to this girl as Eve and uncover more of her tragic love story. While the phantom girl has a Japanese name, Hotaru and her friends refer to her as Eve, since she followed her true love, called Adam. Henceforth the children associate the coupling of Adam and Eve as a romantic pair, although the biblical sources do not refer to them as lovers, at least not as romantic ones who shared such an eternal love. Yet this is one aspect of Adam and Eve which has penetrated Japanese popular culture, as was apparent from the previous example as well: Adam and Eve as a tender and loving couple.

While the dramas above referred but marginally to Adam and Eve, one TV series was entirely based upon Judaeo-Christian ideas, the 1995–6 anime phenomenon *Shinseiki Evangerion* (新世紀エヴァンゲリオン) or, as it is known in translation, *Neon Genesis Evangelion*, by Anno Hideaki and his animation studio, Gainax.[29] The name of the anime itself already suggests a biblical allusion: 'Gospel of New Beginning'. Accordingly, the show keeps hinting at Christianity, but even more so at Jewish mysticism. The series is a mix, amongst other things, of *mecha* (involving robots), sci-fi and psychological thriller.

Evangelion is an epic and apocalyptic story about the end of the world and the youths who must protect it and their city, Tokyo-3, against a strange alien invasion. The invading aliens are named Angels and their origin is linked directly to Adam and Lilith. The fourteen-year-olds who fight them do so by piloting giant robots called Evangelions, or EVA for short. Ortega says that

> [. . .] while Evangelion turns on concepts of origin and regeneration and bases its narrative on specifically Judeo-Christian tales of human origin, it does not follow the biblical text per se as much as assorted religious interpretations. Gnostic Christian versions of the creation story, as well as Judaic traditions from the Midrash, *Zohar*, and other kabbalistic and rabbinical commentary on Genesis, contribute a sizable part of its source material.[30]

The story is multilayered: it offers psychologically complicated, even troubled, characters, and treads the fine line between genius and pretention. As Napier states, this show 'is a text that can be read on many levels'.[31] However, this chapter deals only with the portrayal of Adam and Eve.

According to the story, distilled here to its outline, Adam was the first Angel who was created by 'The First Ancestral Race' eons ago. He was sent to Earth to fill it with his progeny, the Angels, as a 'seed of life'. Yet Adam did not accomplish his mission; Lilith, a second 'seed of life', accidentally crashed onto Earth. As a result, since both seeds could not coexist, Adam was placed in an induced animation (brought about by his 'spear of Longinus') and the Earth was populated by Lilith's progeny, humanity. Later, Adam was discovered by a scientific expedition and his massive energy was later utilized (or abused) by researchers until in the end he self-destructed. The giant robots, Evangelions, were in fact created from the remains of Adam's body. The Angels[32] try to recapture the Earth and therefore they fight humanity.[33] Ikari Gendo, the scientist commander of NERV, the organization which was formed to fight the Angels, secretly tries to create an infusion of the remains of Adam and the remains of Lilith so that he can resurrect his late wife, Yui.

It is clear that Adam in the series is the first 'man' or being on Earth, and is later used to create the EVAs, the robots. However, these robots also contain the souls of the teenage pilot's mother, hence in a twisted way, they can be seen as a surrogate mother to the pilot.[34] Thus, these robots reprise the role of Eve as the first mother. Their name is also reminiscent of Eve (and of Evangelions, messengers), although the story deliberately chooses the union of Adam and Lilith instead. In Jewish mysticism, Lilith is considered to be Adam's first wife,[35] yet he was displeased with her and finally she left Adam in the garden of Eden and was later replaced by Eve.[36] Lilith's reputation persists and she is considered to be a seductive she-demon. While Lilith is often referred to as a rebel against her husband and God, in the *Evangelion* series she is the source of life on Earth. It is perhaps her feisty character which grants humans the necessary strength to resist the Angels; as she resisted Adam, so do her progeny.

Yet, is this engagement serious or simply meant as esoteric ornamentation for the show? Barkman cites the words of Kazuya Tsurumaki, the producer of *Evangelion*, who in reference to the show's use of Christian elements explains that he incorporated this 'because Christianity is an uncommon religion in Japan [and I] thought it would be mysterious'.[37] While this admission by the producer should not be ignored, the Judaeo-Christian elements in the story itself as it unfolds in the series are neither mundane nor random and are well researched. Even if the use of these signs originated from a desire to use less familiar tropes, their execution and perfect compatibility with the entire narrative, and the psychological emphasis which predominates, make them coherent and significant to the plot. *Evangelion* would not have made such an impact on its fans, researchers and even critics without these symbolic religious elements. Furthermore, the ingenuity of the series is also attested by the quantity of discussion it still inspires, some twenty-five years after its initial run.[38]

Prometheus and Pandora in manga

Turning from the Christian to the Graeco-Roman tradition, the mythological Prometheus and Pandora are far less apparent in Japanese pop culture in comparison with the wider familiarity of Adam and Eve. Nevertheless, they do occasionally feature.

In Oda Eiichir's *One Piece* manga, discussed above, Prometheus is a mass of flames. Though lacking in-depth engagement with the mythological Titan, Prometheus' most famous trait, the stealing of fire, is maintained by his image in the series. Prometheus' name is also given to the four volumes of Shirō Masamune's cyberpunk (dystopian sci-fi) manga *Appleseed* (アップルシード), serialized between 1985 and 1989. This manga is greatly influenced by Greek mythology and the Greek Pantheon, and its subtitles are *Prometheus: The Promethean Challenge* (Volume 1), *Prometheus Unbound* (Volume 2), *The Scales of Prometheus* (Volume 3) and *The Promethean Balance* (Volume 4). Nisbet examines this manga as 'a site of classical reception',[39] and further argues that the manga 'delivers classically derived characterizations, which in turn selectively evoke classical themes'.[40] For Nisbet the manga

> [...] becomes an unlikely yet effective primer on Greek mythology, introducing the reader, whether Japanese or Western, to some impressively obscure ancient stories, while stimulating further independent learning and information exchange among fans.[41]

The fan theories and information exchange on *Appleseed* resemble (to a lesser degree) the ongoing discussion about *Evangelion*, even if the latter is more profoundly debated. The manga does not contain a specific character named Prometheus, yet its theme and plot evolve around the conflict between humans and bionically augmented humans ('bioroids') or hybrid clones based on selected human DNA. Thus, this conflict may recall the mythological conflict between the Olympian gods, primarily Zeus, and the human race. Prometheus the Titan was the creator as well as protector of humankind, hence his name is lent to the manga which also deals with the survival of the human race in a twenty-second-century futuristic world.

There are no direct references in manga to Pandora, the mythological first woman, or to her box. Rather, the name is used as the nickname of a secret organization in the manga *Pandora Hearts* (パンドラハーツ) by Mochizuki Jun, which ran from 2006 to 2015. As a secret gadget, 'the Pandora device' allows a cyborg girl to attain super abilities in order to maintain world peace in *Pandora in the Crimson Shell: Ghost Urn* (紅殻のパンドラ) by

Shirō Masamune, running from 2012 to the present. While from an initial glance it appears as if there is no connection with the Greek myth, the fact that the author of this manga is also the author of *Appleseed* suggests that the name Pandora is not employed randomly. Since the device in the manga allows the main character, the cyborg girl Nene Nanakorobi, to master any skill imaginable (albeit for a limited time), it seems likely that Shirō was referencing the original meaning of Pandora, as 'all-gifted', and also the unique abilities and gifts she received from the gods. In this sci-fi manga, the Pandora device does not spread evil, but rather power which is used for good, to achieve peace, and its female identity is maintained.

Conclusion

As the above examples show, Japanese artists rarely employ the biblical creation myth in their pop culture in standard non-religious works, since, while they are familiar with the story of Adam and Eve, it lacks attraction as a theme for these specific media. Hence, Adam and Eve are mainly employed to symbolize a special union, almost a cosmic couple. They are treated more as universal lovers than the parents of humankind. Prometheus and Pandora seem to be more obscure characters due to their almost entire lack of representation in manga and anime. Nevertheless, even these scarce examples indicate the budding of reception of these characters in an entirely different culture. The popularity of some of the works described also greatly contributes to the spread and publicity of these characters and it is possible that this trend will increase, so that in the future more works that employ them in more profound ways may appear.

Notes

1. Mineke Schipper, 'Humanity's Beginnings in Creation and Origin Myths From Around The World', in *China's Creation and Origin Myths: Cross-cultural Explorations in Oral and Written Traditions*, ed. Mineke Schipper, Shuxian Ye and Hubin Yin (Leiden and Boston: Brill, 2011), 18.
2. Regarding representations of Greek mythology, I have argued elsewhere that the Japanese do have familiarity with some of the stories and characters, which are employed sometimes superficially and sometimes with deeper intent. See Ayelet Peer, 'Thermae Romae Manga: Plunging into the Unique Bond between Ancient Rome and Modern Japan', *New Voices in Classical Reception Studies* 12 (2018): 57–67. See also Ayelet Peer and Raz Greenberg, 'The Japanese Trojan War: Tezuka Osamu's envisioning of the Greek epos', *Greece & Rome* 67 (2020): 151–76.
3. Adam Barkman, 'Anime, Manga and Christianity: A Comprehensive Analysis', *Journal for the Study of Religions and Ideologies* 9 (2010): 26.
4. https://www.nippon.com/en/japan-topics/g00769/a-little-faith-christianity-and-the-japanese.html (November 2019). This number is especially low in comparison with South Korea, in which in 2018 approximately 30 per cent of the population was Christian, mostly Protestants.

5. The Japanese curriculum for upper secondary schools includes compulsory subjects of World History. See Chie Nakayasu, 'School Curriculum in Japan', *Curriculum Journal* 27 (2016): 134–50.
6. The biblical story narrates the creation of humankind and the Greek myths also discuss the creation of all men and then women; they do not limit the creation geographically to a specific nation even though it is well understood that they refer to their own people. The Japanese creation story, however, is very specific and focuses only on Japan. The Koreans also tell a myth specifically for the origin of Korea (the Tagun myth). The Chinese creations myths vary and also depend on the different ethnic groups in China, yet they do refer to a creation of a 'world' and not a specific land. On the various stories, see Wu Bing'an, 'Chinese Creation Myths: A Great Discovery', in *China's Creation and Origin Myths: Cross-cultural Explorations in Oral and Written Traditions*, ed. Mineke Schipper, Shuxian Ye and Hubin Yin (Leiden and Boston: Brill, 2011), 179–96.
7. John S. Brownlee, *Political Thought in Japanese Historical Writing From Kojiki (712) to Tokushi Yoron (1712)* (Waterloo, Canada: Wilfrid Laurier University Press, 1991), 9.
8. See David Kinsley, *The Goddesses' Mirror: Visions of the Divine from East and West.* (Albany: State University of New York Press, 1989), 72–8. There are similarities between this story and Greek mythology, especially in Izanami's descent to the land of darkness, yet these shall not be discussed here.
9. The imperial house is claimed to be the descendant of the gods, hence, in a way, Izanami and Izanagi are the parents of (some of) humanity.
10. Kinsley, *The Goddesses' Mirror*, 78.
11. On the connection between Amaterasu and Demeter, see Bernard Sergent, 'Amaterasu, Dèmèter, et leurs Acolytes', *Presses Universitaires de Franche-Comté* 35 (2009): 45–68.
12. Notto R. Thelle, *Buddhism and Christianity in Japan: From Conflict to Dialogue, 1854–1899* (Honolulu: University of Hawaii Press, 1987), 5. Christianity was caught up in a power struggle of the Shogunate rulers, who also managed to forcibly control and use Buddhism and make it part of their rule. Later Buddhism became a powerful tool against the advent of Christianity in Japan.
13. There was a previous rebellion of mostly Christians at Amakusa Islands in 1589–90 in which the rebels turned against a fellow-Christian, Konishi Yukinaga. On this earlier rebellion, see Stephen Turnbull, 'The Ghosts of Amakusa: Localised Opposition to Centralised Control in Higo Province, 1589–1590', *Japan Forum* 25 (2013): 191–211. On the prosecution of the Christians after the rebellion, see Masaharu Anesaki, 'Prosecution of Kirishitans after the Shimabara Insurrection', *Monumenta Nipponica* 1 (1938): 293–300.
14. Thelle, *Buddhism and Christianity in Japan*, 5.
15. William S. Atwell, 'Some Observations on the "Seventeenth-Century Crisis" in China and Japan', *Journal of Asian Studies* 45 (1986): 228.
16. Michael Ipgrave, 'Christianity in the world of Japan's religions: reception, incorporation, separation', *International Journal for the Study of the Christian Church* 16 (2016): 201.
17. Thelle, *Buddhism and Christianity in Japan*, 6.
18. Thelle, *Buddhism and Christianity in Japan*, 10.
19. See Ipgrave, 'Christianity in the world of Japan's religions'.
20. Barkman, *Anime, Manga and Christianity*, 27.
21. https://www.animenewsnetwork.com/encyclopedia/anime.php?id=2884.
22. https://www.animenewsnetwork.com/encyclopedia/manga.php?id=5145.

23. On the non-Japanese rendition of a manga Bible, see Barkman, *Anime, Manga and Christianity*, 41–3. I focus in my discussion on the non-religious shows which incorporate Judaeo-Christian notions, specifically Adam and Eve.

24. The anime TV series was broadcast between 1981 and 1986. Here we refer to episode 120 from season 3, 'Counterattack of the Primeval Animals! Panic at the Poolside' from 1984.

25. However, the reason may also be that they are older, as Gilles Poitras, 'Contemporary Anime in Japanese Pop Culture', in *Japanese Visual Culture: Explorations in the World of Manga and Anime*, ed. Mark W. MacWilliams (Armonk, N.Y.: M.E. Sharpe, 2008), 62, explains regarding 'big eyes' in anime.

26. Neil Cohn, 'Japanese Visual Language: The Structure of Manga', in *Manga: An Anthology of Global and Cultural Perspectives*, ed. Toni Johnson-Woods (New York: Continuum, 2010), 187–203, offers a discussion on the 'Japanese Visual Language' and its various symbols.

27. The coloured version appears in the TV series since the manga is drawn in black and white.

28. https://www.animenewsnetwork.com/encyclopedia/manga.php?id=5717.

29. On different themes in this anime, see Susan J. Napier, 'When the Machines Stop: Fantasy, Reality, and Terminal Identity in "Neon Genesis Evangelion" and "Serial Experiments Lain"', *Science Fiction Studies* 29 (2002): 418–35; M. Ortega, 'My Father, He Killed Me; My Mother, She Ate Me: Self, Desire, Engendering, and the Mother in "Neon Genesis Evangelion"', *Mechademia* 2 (2007): 216–32; Denis Redmond, 'Anime and East Asian Culture: Neon Genesis Evangelion', *Quarterly Review of Film and Video* 24 (2007): 183–8; Christophe Thouny, 'Waiting for the Messiah: The Becoming-Myth of "Evangelion" and "Densha otoko"', *Mechademia* 4 (2009): 111–29.

30. Ortega, 'My Father, He Killed Me', 220.

31. Napier, 'When the Machines Stop', 429.

32. Susan J. Napier, *Anime from Akira to Princess Mononoke*, rev. edn (New York: St. Martin's Press, 2005), 97, corrects that the Japanese term 'Shito' should be 'apostles' and not 'angels'.

33. https://evangelion.fandom.com/wiki/Adam.

34. On the different roles of the 'mother' in *Evangelion* see Napier, *Anime from Akira to Princess Mononoke*, 98–9; Ortega, 'My Father, He Killed Me'.

35. Lilith is first elaborately referred to in the anonymous work 'Alphabet of Ben Sirach' from the seventh–tenth centuries: C. E. Bitton and Michèle Bitton, 'Lilith et Adam: une légende sans dessus dessous', *Pardès* 43 (2007): 37–51; Wojciech Kosior, 'A Tale of Two Sisters: The Image of Eve in Early Rabbinic Literature and its Influence on the Portrayal of Lilith in the Alphabet of Ben Sira', *Nashim: A Journal of Jewish Women's Studies & Gender* 32 (2018): 112–30. Kabbalah is also employed in the series, as visuals of the 'Tree of Life' appear in Ikari Gendo's office.

36. On the account of Adam and Eve in the Hebrew Bible and its later interpretations, see Kristen E. Kvam, Linda S. Schearing and Valarie H. Ziegler (eds), *Eve and Adam: Jewish, Christian, and Muslim Readings on Genesis and Gender* (Bloomington: Indiana University Press, 1999).

37. Barkman, *Anime, Manga and Christianity*, 32.

38. The discussion also remains alive due to its cinematic renewals. Three new films, part of a retelling of the TV series, came out in 2007, 2009 and 2012, with one final movie still pending.

39. Gideon Nisbet, 'Mecha in Olympus: Shirow Masamune's Appleseed', in *Son of Classics and Comics*, ed. George Kovacs and C. W. Marshall (New York: Oxford University Press, 2016), 67.

40. Nisbet, 'Mecha in Olympus', 70.

41. Nisbet, 'Mecha in Olympus', 70.

CONCLUSION

Lisa Maurice

Clearly, the Graeco-Roman and Judaeo-Christian myths of the first man and woman have played a hugely influential role in Western civilization, recurring regularly throughout history. Some receptions are true amalgams of both stories, while others follow one of them much more closely. In the introduction to this book we raised, among other questions, that of how the Judaic, Christian, Greek and Roman myths stand out from each other, and also cross-fertilize between each other at different times and in different cultures. As has been demonstrated (and indeed is well known), there are overlapping elements between Prometheus/Pandora and Adam/Eve. Both involve the male creation preceding the female, and both involve the female acting in a way that brings about trouble and misfortune in the world. The correspondences between the two narratives are an element that can be seen visually in the early Christian and medieval periods. As both Bradley and Mathian demonstrate, it is not always even clear whether the subjects being referenced are in fact Prometheus and Pandora, or Adam and Eve, as iconographic migration from pagan to Christian imagery occurs, due to the similarities between the stories.

The interaction between the two traditions can be seen, as Jared Simard demonstrates, in the visual representations in art, where, in antiquity, it is clear that early Promethean sarcophagi influenced depictions of biblical creation. Over time, in late antiquity, the reverse occurred, as depictions of God creating Adam and Eve influenced representations of Prometheus creating man. Another shift occurred in the early modern period, as Promethean creation imagery borrowed key elements from portrayals of biblical creation. At the same time, growing secularization led to an increasing glorification of man, as opposed to God, as a creating force, with artists fashioning themselves in the Promethean image, a trend that culminates in perhaps Paul Manship's famous *Prometheus* at the Rockefeller Center in New York City, as outlined in Simard's examination.

Despite the coincidences between the biblical and mythological tales that allow for such bi-directional influence, there are also obvious differences between the two. Rabbinic tradition focuses on the creation of Adam–Eve as a dual single being before the separation into two, whereas the Church fathers emphasized that of woman as formed after, and therefore inferior to, man. In the Judaeo-Christian tale, woman is created by God, from man, in order to be a helpmeet for her husband, whereas in the pagan myth, she is created independently by the gods on Olympus and, according to Hesiod at least, is sent to man as a punishment. In neither case, therefore, as Roslyn Weiss points out with regard to the Genesis narrative, are man and woman created equal, but rather have an asymmetrical relationship. Additionally, the biblical narrative features another figure of responsibility for the tragic change in mankind's lot, in the shape of the serpent, who shares culpability with the humans. Thierry Alcoloumbre demonstrates that both traditions posit an intrinsic connection between the human condition, which contains both positive and negative elements: the existence of woman, who is both divine in her beautiful and nurturing roles and a threat in her seductive aspect; and the divine law as it interacts with the human world. In fact, as Yael Shemesh explicates, since the biblical text does not provide an explicit evaluation either of Eve's creation or of her decision to sin, it is the reader who imposes value judgements on these aspects.

Despite being centred on the same text, there are differing perspectives between Judaism and Christianity, with the latter using the Eve passages as evidence for the divinely-ordained nature of patriarchy in a far stronger manner than the former. This is not to say that Judaism has not also indulged in misogynistic readings of the text, as, indeed, Shemesh highlights. Yet Eve is, according to both a close reading of the text and a range of rabbinical exegeses, a figure who symbolizes the maternal giving of life, through her name, which means 'life', and the perfect answer to Adam's need for companionship and love. Jewish tradition thus takes Eve as a paradigm of the female, that then develops into the ideal woman in later incarnations. Nevertheless, this perfection is to be rooted in reality, as Revital Refael-Vivante's chapter shows. By the Middle Ages, in the Arabic *maqama*, despite the patriarchic society, love is an active emotion and must be rooted in the real world, rather than an image or Pygmalionesque idealized statue. Such readings have their root in the traditional interpretations of the Eden narrative, which hold both Adam and Eve guilty, and see them as a partnership, albeit not necessarily one of equals.

Although much of the anti-female bias in the biblical text is far from apparent after a close reading of the text, as Roslyn Weiss elucidates, nonetheless almost every commentator has interpreted it in a far more Hesiodic manner than is perhaps warranted. Despite the potential for less misogynistic readings of the biblical tale, it is, of course, this one, rather than that of Pandora and Prometheus, that has been, and continues to be, utilized as a tool for female subjugation. These were not, of course, the only readings; as early as the Middle Ages, for instance, as Tovi Bibring outlines, there were some resistant feministic voices who claimed that the traditional conceptions were misinterpretations of the initial divine will to create equal human beings, and that, since Eve had been created by God from a nobler material than Adam, woman should not be considered secondary to man.

Yet these were rare examples that are notable precisely for the unexpectedness with which they are encountered; traditional readings, from the ancient world to the modern day, have held Eve to be primarily responsible for the sin. One example of such interpretations holding sway in the contemporary world is that presented by Susan Weiss, in her description of how the verses in Genesis 3.15–16 still underlie the assumptions behind attitudes in and actions of rabbinic courts in Israel today with regard to marriage and divorce. Even the retellings for children, with their pejorative attitudes towards Eve, as Lisa Maurice argues, go some way towards perpetuating this attitude. Nevertheless, attitudes have changed in recent years. Discomfort with such stereotyped presentations of gender, particularly in products aimed at youth, are apparent in Rosamund Hodge's young adult novel, *Cruel Beauty*, as Lily Glasner analyses, showing that the novel reflects a flexibility and readiness to recast the myth of Pandora in a manner that creates a romantically satisfying ending. This results in a much more positive spin to the character, as the story is related in a manner in keeping with contemporary ideas regarding female empowerment.

Another, rather different, example of a gendered adaptation of a creation myth is the case of Levin Kipnis's children's story of the daffodil in the swamp, presented by Vered Tohar, who illustrates how, blending elements from classical mythology and the Bible, Kipnis created a new myth suited to the creation of the new young Jewish society in Israel. In this he drew not on the myths of Prometheus and Pandora and Adam and Eve, but on that of Narcissus and the parable of Yotam, though, as in the narratives of Eden and the Pandoran tradition, gender still formed a central theme of the work. Albeit not for patriarchal reasons, the early Zionists challenged anti-Semitic ideas of Jewish weakness common at the time, which resulted in determined attempts to form a new stereotype that rejected any elements of femininity or homosexuality, and strongly affirmed powerful heterosexual masculinity.[1] Thus, drawing on different texts but from the same traditional sources, Kipnis produced a creation myth that had subliminal messages that overlapped with those of many interpretations of the Eden narrative.

While the biblical narrative continues to feature mostly as a didactic tool for promoting a specific agenda, the Prometheus–Pandora myth, which does not carry the same ideological baggage, endures as a recurring motif in the popular imagination, so that Pandora is able to shake off the negative overtones in a manner that Eve cannot. This can clearly be seen in retellings of both tales for children, where, as Maurice highlights, the condemnation and blaming of Eve contrasts starkly with the willingness to rehabilitate Pandora. Similarly in science fiction, as Benjamin Stevens outlines, although Pandora has traditionally been understood as a negative exemplar, whose curiosity has destructive consequences, some Pandoran imaginings suggest instead that curiosity, here epitomized by an interest in technology, has a real positive potential. With such technology portrayed as a revolutionary or liberating force, such postmodern Pandoras come closer to a literal interpretation of the name's meaning: 'all- giving'. The Eve–Pandora figure in Ridley Scott's *Prometheus* is also shown by Edmund Cueva to be the bringer of life; despite male attempts at reproduction in this movie, it is only the female who succeeds in creating life. The character of Shaw has elements of both Eve and Pandora, however. Like the former, she gives birth to a new race of creatures after attaining forbidden knowledge; like the latter, she seeks knowledge and, in so doing, fills the universe with all sorts of ills.

Clearly the two narratives have been recast at various times for a range of purposes, both positive and negative. While many depict the female as wicked and inferior to the male, thus confirming the patriarchal status quo, this is not the only usage of the tale. The Prometheus archetype has been seen as the inventor of new possibilities, long adopted by artists as the master of creativity and skill. In modern times, not only has Prometheus been utilized in order to glorify the creative instinct of the human artist, particularly in works of science fiction, in which technology is seen as a desirable, almost magical factor, but the Pandora figure, as a result of her curiosity and inquiring nature, has also been depicted as an inspirational life-giving force. To the modern age, with its emphasis on the power and ability of humanity, who no longer see a deity as the centre of existence, both Prometheus and Pandora are seen as epitomizing inventiveness and imagination, the thirst for knowledge that makes all possible.

Nor is the positive spin restricted to Pandora; despite the continued importance of the biblical narrative, in light of the changing role of women in Western society, recent works have portrayed her sympathetically. This is most obviously apparent in popular culture, which, as so often, both reflects and moulds opinion. In such products, Eve may be portrayed as the victim of an unhappy, loveless marriage; thus the television series *Lucifer* (2016–21), for instance, depicts Eve as a sad and unfulfilled creature, created only for one purpose, namely to be a partner for Adam, making her nothing but a helpless pawn or tool. Such a concept is abhorrent in modern popular thought, where a society based on patriarchy, as encapsulated in the historical Christian interpretation that is rooted in the Genesis episode, is a dystopian horror; an obvious recent example of such a depiction is the ongoing television adaptation of Margaret Atwood's *The Handmaid's Tale* that won such widespread acclaim, striking a chord in the hearts of so many viewers appalled at the helplessness of the female in such a world. Such attitudes are the antithesis of contemporary ideas, as demonstrated by another very different series that puts a new, and rather more subtle, spin on Eve, namely the BBC television series *Killing Eve* (2018–20). Depicting an M15 agent, named Eve (played by Sandra Oh), in constant battle with a psychopathic female assassin, much of the power of this show stems from the blurring of good and evil as the intense connection between the heroes and villains is played out in a manner that undermines the nature of each, and in the sexual tension between the two women, thereby playing with and turning upside down the traditional depictions of Eve.

In light of the altered beliefs and attitudes, it might have been expected that stories concerning the two first couples would no longer have a place or relevance in the modern Western world, yet they continue to appear. The sheer number of texts aimed at children or young adults, for instance, reflects the idea that these are regarded as desirable sources with which young people should be familiar. Retellings, adaptations and interpretations are not restricted to products for the young, however. Nor are they even limited to societies in which the Bible or classical myth are central. As an illustration of the former, the communist Soviet Union specifically rejected religion, and thus receptions of the Eden myth against that background carry different connotations. One example of this is that illustrated by Hava Korzakova, as she demonstrates how the puppet show version of the Adam and Eve narrative produced in the Soviet Union was ostensibly a piece of atheist propaganda, but was also actually a satirical critique of the regime. Likewise, Japan, with a totally different set of conventions and religious attitudes, and remote from both classical and Judaeo-Christian traditions, interprets Adam and Eve and also, more rarely, Prometheus and Pandora as primordial couples, who are viewed not as the parents of humanity but as an idealized archetype of universal lovers.

As the wide-ranging examples examined in this volume reflect, the creation narratives of Adam–Eve and Prometheus–Pandora continue to be retold, readapted and reinterpreted as they have been throughout history. The repeated use of the two stories, both in direct depictions and as tropes, highlights the continued centrality of both the biblical and the classical traditions, up to and including present day. It seems that, despite secularism and charges of elitism, these creation stories, and the gendered readings they stimulate, are still seen as useful vehicles with which to interpret the world. In the current Covid-19 era of uncertainty, in which apocalyptic parallels are frequently drawn in the media,[2] and as people look to a future which may be radically different to the recent past, it seems unlikely that this will change and that Adam–Prometheus and Eve–Pandora will still have roles to play in a world in which troubles have been unleashed, but new life and hope still remain.

Notes

1. See Daniel Boyarin, *Unheroic Conduct: The Rise of Homosexuality and the Invention of the Jewish Man* (Berkeley and Los Angeles: California University Press, 1997).
2. See, e.g., https://globalchallenges.ch/issue/special_1/covid-19-a-modern-apocalypse-or-a-temporary-shock-to-the-system/.

BIBLIOGRAPHY

Abu-Haidar, J. 'Maqamat Literature and the Picaresque Novel'. *Journal of Arabic Literature* 5 (1974): 1–10.

Adang, C., M. Fierro and S. Schmidtka (eds). *Ibn Hazm of Cordoba the Life and Works of a Controversial Thinker*. Leiden and Boston: Brill, 2013.

Adappur, Abraham. *Religion and the Cultural Crisis in India and the West*. New Delhi: Intercultural Publications, 2000.

Adler, Rachel. 'B'reishit – Contemporary Reflection'. In *The Torah: A Women's Commentary*, edited by Tamara Cohn Eskenazi and Andrea L. Weiss, 29–30. New York: WRJ, 2008.

Aeschylus. 'The Eumenides'. In *The Oresteian Trilogy: Agamemnon, The Choephori, The Eumenides*, translated by Philip Vellacott, 147–82. London: Penguin Books, 1956.

Alharizi, J. *Sefer Tahkemoni* (in Hebrew). Edited by Y. Toporovsky. Tel-Aviv: Mahbarot le-Sifrut, 1952.

Alharizi, J. *The Book of Tahkemoni, Jewish Tales from Medieval Spain*. Edited and translated by David Simha Segal. London: Littman Library of Jewish Civilization, 2001.

Alharizi, J. *Alharizi, Tahkemoni or The Tales of Heman the Ezrahite* (in Hebrew). Edited, with an Introduction, Commentary and Indices by J. Yahalom and N. Katsumata. Jerusalem: Ben-Zvi, 2010.

Almagor, Ella. *Ibn Hazm, The Ring of the Dove* (in Hebrew). Jerusalem: Bialik, 2002.

Almog, Geula and Miri Baruch. ז'אנרים בספרות ילדים *Janarim besiporet l'yeladim* (Genres in children's fiction). Tel-Aviv: Mofet, 1996.

Alves, Timothy. 'Pompeo Batoni Exhibition, The National Gallery, London'. *The Birkbeck Early Modern Society Bulletin* 65 (Spring 2008): 27–31.

Amir, Gal. על מה אנחנו מדברים כשאנחנו מדברים על המילט? 'What are We Talking About when we Speak of the Millet System?' *Mehkarei Mishpat* 30 (2016): 677–706 (Hebrew).

Anderson, Gary A. *The Genesis of Perfection: Adam and Eve in Jewish and Christian Imagination*. Louisville and London: Westminster John Knox Press, 2001.

Anderson, John. *Religion, State and Politics in the Soviet Union and Successor States*. Cambridge: Cambridge University Press, 1994.

Anesaki, Masaharu. 'Prosecution of Kirishitans after the Shimabara Insurrection'. *Monumenta Nipponica* 1 (1938): 293–300.

Anime News Network. https://www.animenewsnetwork.com/.

Aschkenasy, Nehama. *Eve's Journey: Feminine Images in Hebraic Literary Tradition*. Philadelphia: University of Pennsylvania Press, 1986.

Atwell, William, S. 'Some Observations on the "Seventeenth-Century Crisis" in China and Japan'. *Journal of Asian Studies* 45 (1986): 223–44.

Augustine, *On Free Choice of the Will*. Translated by Thomas Williams. Indianapolis: Hackett Publishing Company, 1993.

Babrius and Phaedrus. 'Fable 58'. In *Babrius and Phaedrus*, edited and translated by Ben Edwin Perry, 74–5. Cambridge, MA, and London: Harvard University Press, 1965.

Baden, Joel. 'An Unnoted Nuance in Genesis 2: 21–22'. *Vetus Testamentum* 69, no. 1 (2019): 167–72.

Banon, David. *l'Ecole de Pensée Juive de Paris, Le Judaïsme Revisité sur les Bords de Seine*. Strasbourg: Presses Universitaires de Strasbourg, 2019.

Barkman, Adam. 'Anime, Manga and Christianity: A Comprehensive Analysis'. *Journal for the Study of Religions and Ideologies* 9 (2010): 25–45.

Barmenkov, A. *Freedom of Conscience in the USSR*. Moscow: Progress Publishers, 1984.

Barsella, Susanna. 'The Myth of Prometheus in Giovanni Boccaccio's *Decameron*'. *Modern Language Notes* 119, no. 1 (2004): 120–41.

Bartoli, P. S. *Le antiche lucerne sepolcrali figurate: raccolte delle cave sotterrannee e grotte di Roma*. Rome: Buagni, 1691.

Bascom, William. 'The Forms of Folklore: Prose Narratives'. *Journal of American Folklore* 78, no. 307 (1965): 3–20.

Beauvoir, Simone de. *The Second Sex*. Edited and translated by H. M. Parshley. New York: Vintage Books, 1952/1974.

Beer, Jeanette. *Beasts of Love: Richard de Fournival Bestiaire d'amour and a Woman's Response*. Toronto, Buffalo and London: University of Toronto Press, 2003.

Beeston, A. F. L. 'The Genesis of the Maqamat Genre'. *Journal of Arabic Literature* 2 (1971): 1–12.

Bendinelli, G. 'Il monumento sepulcrale degli Aureli al Viale Manzoni in Roma'. *Monumenti Antichi di Accademia Nazionale dei Lincei* 28 (1922): 289–520.

Ben-Gur, Naomi. *Mechi kapayim* (Clap your hands: poetics and ideology in children's poetry 1939–1947). Bnei-Brak: Hakibbutz HaMeuhad and Mofet, 2017.

Berdyaev, Nikolay. *The Russian Revolution*. Ann Arbor: University of Michigan Press, 1931/1966.

Berlin, Isaiah. *The Sense of Reality: Studies in Ideas and Their History*. London: Pimlico, 1996.

Bernstock, Judith E. 'Classical Mythology in Twentieth-Century Art: An Overview of a Humanistic Approach'. *Artibus et Historiae* 14, no. 27 (1993): 153–83.

Bianciotto, Gabriel. *Richard de Fournival, Le 'Bestiaire d'Amour' et la 'Response du Bestiaire'*. Champion Classiques. Moyen Âge 27. Paris: Champion, 2009.

Bibring, Tovi. *Corps, âme, psyché: lectures de l'érotique et du danger dans les Lais de Marie de France*. Amiens: Presses du Centre d'Etudes Médiévales de Picardie, 2016.

Bibring, Tovi. 'Vashti on Display: Medieval Christian Meditations on a Disobeying Queen'. In *Reading the Bible in the Premodern Free World*, edited by Chanita Goodblatt and Haim Kreisel. Beer-Sheva: Ben Gurion University Press, forthcoming.

Bing'an Wu. 'Chinese Creation Myths: A Great Discovery'. In *China's Creation and Origin Myths: Cross-cultural Explorations in Oral and Written Traditions*, edited by Mineke Schipper, Shuxian Ye and Hubin Yin, 179–96. Leiden and Boston: Brill, 2011.

Bisconti, F. *L'ipogeo degli Aureli in Viale Manzoni: restauri tutela, valorizzazione e aggiornamenti interpretativi*. Vatican City: Pontificia Commissione di Archeologia Sacra, 2011.

Bisconti, F. and M. P. Del Moro. 'Via Latina 135: cronaca di un intervento di emergenza. Un'area cacatacomba recuperata al II miglio della via Latina'. *Rivista di Archeologia Cristiana* 75 (2009): 11–94.

Bishop, Kyle William. *How Zombies Conquered Popular Culture: The Multifarious Walking Dead in the 21st Century*. Jefferson, NC: McFarland, 2015.

Bitton, Michèle. 'Lilith et Adam: une légende sans dessus dessous'. *Pardès* 43 (2007): 37–51.

Blair, Judith M. *De-Demonising the Old Testament – An Investigation of Azazel, Lilith, Deber, Qeteb and Reshef in the Hebrew Bible*. Forschungen zum Alten Testament 2, Reihe 37. Tübingen: Mohr Siebeck, 2009.

Blaise, Fabienne, Pierre Judet de la Combe and Philippe Rousseau. *Le Métier du Mythe. Lectures d'Hésiode. Cahiers de philologie* 16. Lille: Septentrion. Presses Universitaires, 1996.

Blamires, Alcuin. *Woman Defamed and Woman Defended: An Anthology of Medieval Texts*. Oxford: Oxford University Press, 1992.

Bloch, R. Howard. *Medieval Misogyny and the Invention of Western Romantic Love*. Chicago: University of Chicago Press, 1991.

Bloom, Harold. *The Book of J*. New York: Vintage Books, 1991.

Bociurkiw, B. and J. Strong. *Religion and Atheism in the USSR and Eastern Europe*. Toronto: University of Toronto Press, 1975.

Booth, David. 'Censorship'. In *Keywords for Children's Literature*, edited by Philip Nel and Lissa Paul, 26–30. New York: New York University Press, 2011.

Bost-Fiévet, Mélanie, and Sandra Provini (eds). *L'Antiquité dans l'imaginaire contemporain: Fantasy, science-fiction, fantastique*. Paris: Classiques Garnier, 2014.

Bottigheimer, Ruth. *The Bible for Children from the Age of Gutenberg to the Present*. New Haven, CT: Yale University Press, 1996.

Bourdeaux, M. *Opium of the People: The Christian Religion in the USSR*. London: Faber and Faber, 1965.

Bowron, Edgar Peters and Peter Björn Kerber. *Pompeo Batoni: Prince of Painters in Eighteenth-Century Rome*. New Haven, CT: Yale University Press, 2008.

Bradley, John W. 'An Interpretation of the Frescoes of the Hypogeum of the Aurelii in Rome'. Unpublished PhD dissertation, Royal Holloway and Bedford New College, University of London, 2017.

Bradley, J. W. *The Hypogeum of the Aurelii: A New Interpretation as the Collegiate Tomb of Professional* 'scribae'. Oxford: Archaeopress, 2018.

Brenk, B. 'Città del Vaticano, Biblioteca Apostolica Vaticana, Vat. lat. 3784, Exultet'. In *Exultet. Rotoli liturgici del Medioevo meridionale*, edited by G. Cavallo and G. Orofino, 211–13. Rome: Istituto Poligrafico e Zecca dello Stato, 1994.

Brenner, Athalya. *The Israelite Woman: Social Role and Literary Type in Biblical Narrative*. Sheffield: JSOT, 1985.

Brockelmann, C. 'Maqama'. In *Encyclopaedia of Islam*, vol. 3, edited by M. Th. Houtsma, A. J. Wensinck and E. Levi-Provençal, 161–4. Leiden: Brill, 1936.

Brownlee, John S. *Political Thought in Japanese Historical Writing from Kojiki (712) to Tokushi Yoron (1712)*. Waterloo, Canada: Wilfrid Laurier University Press, 1991.

Bucolo R. 'Himmelmann e l'ipogeo degli Aurelii'. In *L'ipogeo degli Aureli in Viale Manzoni: restauri tutela, valorizzazione e aggiornamenti interpretativi*, edited by F. Bisconti, 125–34. Vatican City: Pontificia Commissione di Archeologia Sacra, 2011.

Caeners, Torston. 'Negotiating the Human in Ridley Scott's *Prometheus*'. In *Posthumanism in Young Adult Fiction: Finding Humanity in a Posthuman World*, edited by Anita Tarr and Donna R. White, 199–226. Jackson: University Press of Mississippi, 2018.

Caillet, J.-P. 'L'arredo dell'altare'. In *L'arte medievale nel contesto. 300–1300. Funzioni, iconografia, tecniche*, edited by P. Piva, 181–203. Milan: Jaca Book, 2006.

Calza, G. *La necropoli del Porto di Roma nell'Isola Sacra*. Rome: Istituto di Archeologia e Storia dell'Arte, 1940.

Canivet, P. 'Lecture d'une image: une mosaïque d'Adam au Ve s'. In *Rencontres de l'École du Louvre. Image et signification*, 141–51. Paris: Documentation française, 1983.

Carpenter, Ginette. 'Mothers and Others'. In *Women and the Gothic: An Edinburgh Companion*, edited by Avril Horner and Sue Zlosnik, 46–59. Edinburgh: Edinburgh University Press, 2016.

Charlesworth, J. H. *The Good and Evil Serpent*. New Haven, CT: Yale University Press, 2010.

Chesi, Giulia Maria and Giacomo Sclavi. 'Pandora and Robotic Technology Today'. In *Classical Literature and Postumanism*, edited by Giulia Maria Chesi and Francesca Spiegel, 301–8. London: Bloomsbury, 2020.

Clark, Anthony M. and Edgar Peters Bowron. *Pompeo Batoni: A Complete Catalogue of his Works with an Introductory Text*. Oxford: Phaidon, 1985.

Clayton, Jay. '*Frankenstein*'s Futurity: Replicants and Robots'. In *The Cambridge Companion to Mary Shelley*, edited by Esther Schor, 84–99. Cambridge: Cambridge University Press, 2003.

Clover, Carol. *Men, Women and Chain Saws: Gender in the Modern Horror Film* (Princeton, NJ: Princeton University Press, 1992).

Cobbs, John L. '*Alien* as an Abortion Parable'. *Literature Film Quarterly* 18, no. 3 (1990): 198–201.

Codeluppi, Vanni. 'The Integrated Spectacle: Towards Aesthetic Capitalism'. In *The Spectacle 2.0: Reading Debord in the Context of Digital Capitalism*, edited by Briziarelli Marco and Armano Emiliana, 51–66. London: University of Westminster Press, 2017.

Cohen, Adir. *Temurot besifrut yeladim* (Changes in children's literature). Haifa: Ah, 5749, 1989.

Cohn, Neil. 'Japanese Visual Language: The Structure of Manga'. In *Manga: An Anthology of Global and Cultural Perspectives*, edited by Toni Johnson-Woods, 187–203. New York: Continuum, 2010.

Corbeau-Parsons, Caroline. *Prometheus in the Nineteenth Century from Myth to Symbol*. London: Legenda, Modern Humanities Research Association and Maney Publishing, 2013.

Corley, F. *Religion in the Soviet Union*. London: Macmillan Press, 1996.

Cormier, Raymond. 'Ovide moralisé'. In *Approaches to Teaching the Works of Ovid and the Ovidian Tradition*, edited by Barbara W. Boyd and Cora Fox, 18–22. New York: Modern Language Association of America, 2010.

Couffignal, Robert. *Le drame de l'Eden: Le récit de la Genèse et se fortune littéraire*. Toulouse: Association des publications de l'université de Toulouse-Le Mirail, 1980.

Cousin, Glynis. 'Rethinking the concept of "western"'. *Higher Education Research & Development* 30, no. 5 (2011): 585 (585–594). DOI: 10.1080/07294360.2011.598449.

Cross, Julie. *Humor in Contemporary Junior Literature*. New York and London: Routledge, 2011.

Daly, Mary. *Beyond God the Father: Toward a Philosophy of Women's Liberation*. Boston: Beacon, 1985.

Danzig, G. *Xenophon's Socratic Discourse* (in Hebrew). Jerusalem: Shalem, 2002.

Darr, Yael. 'A Confrontation between Two Doctrines: The Birth of Struggle for Hegemony in Hebrew Children's Literature during the 1930s and 1940s'. *International Research in Children's Literature* 1, no. 2 (2008): 139–54.

Decker, Mark T. *Industrial Society and the Science Fiction Blockbuster: Social Critique in Films of Lucas, Scott and Cameron*. Jefferson, NC: McFarland & Company, Inc., 2016.

Deichmann, F. W. et al. *Repertorium der christlich-antiken Sarkophage: Bd. Rom und Ostia*, vol. 1. Wiesbaden: Reichert Verlag, 1967.

Deichmann, F. W., B. Christern-Briesenick, G. Bovini and H. Brandenburg. *Repertorium der christlich-antiken Sarkophage: Frankreich, Algerien, Tunesien*, vol. 3. Mainz am Rhein: Verlag von Zabern, 2003.

Deliyannis, D. M. *The Book of Pontiffs of the Church of Ravenna*. Medieval Texts in Translation. Washington DC: Catholic University of America Press, 2004.

De Maria, L. 'L'inscrizione musiva dell'ipogeo degli Aureli in Viale Manzoni: restauri e nuove riflessioni'. In *L'ipogeo degli Aureli in Viale Manzoni: restauri tutela, valorizzazione e aggiornamenti interpretativi*, edited by F. Bisconti, 223–8. Vatican City: Pontificia Commissione di Archeologia Sacra, 2011.

De Pourcq, Maarten. 'Classical Reception Studies: Reconceptualizing the Study of the Classical Tradition'. *International Journal of the Humanities* 9, no. 4 (2012): 219–25.

Deproost, P.-A. 'Formatur . . . Limatur . . . Le corps d'Adam et Ève dans la poésie latine chrétienne'. In *Le corps dans les cultures méditerranéennes – Actes du colloque des 30–31 mars et 1 avril 2006*, edited by P. Veyne, P. Carmignani, M. Courrént, T. Éloi and J. Thomas, 105–25. Perpignan: Presses universitaires de Perpignan, 2007.

Devecka, Martin. 'The Seer's Two Bodies: Some Early Greek Histories of Technology'. In *Classical Literature and Postumanism*, edited by Giulia Maria Chesi and Francesca Spiegel, 185–91. London: Bloomsbury, 2020.

Dishon, J. 'Speech of Asher ben Yehudah by Shlomo Ibn Saqbal and the Twentieth Maqama in *The Book of Tahkemoni* by Judah Alharazi' (in Hebrew), *Criticism and Interpretation* 6 (1974): 57–65.

Douchet, Sébastien. 'Création du monde et poétique de l'œuvre'. *Cahiers de recherches médiévales et humanistes* 30 (2015): 49–74.

Dougherty, Carol. *Prometheus*. London: Routledge, 2006.
Dovrat, Anat. 'Feminism and Gender Symbolism in the *Bestiaries d'amours* of Richard de Fournival and the Anonymous Response'. Unpublished MA thesis, Bar-Ilan University, 2021.
Draycott, Jane. *Prostheses in Antiquity*. London: Routledge, 2019.
Dulaey, M. 'L'apprentissage de l'exégèse biblique par Augustin. Années 393–394'. *Revue des Études Augustiniennes* 51 (2005): 21–65.
Dumézil, Georges. *Le festin d'immortalité*. Paris: Geuthner, 1924.
Eckhart, Lothar. 'Prometheus'. In *Paulys Realencyclopädie der classischen Altertumswissenschaft*, edited by August Friedrich von Pauly and Georg Wissowa, 653–730. Stuttgart: A. Druckenmüller Verlag, 1958.
Ehrenreich, Barbara. 'The Missionary Position'. *The Baffler* 21 (2012): 132–7.
Eliade, Mircea. *Cosmos and History: The Myth of the Eternal Return*. Translated by Willard R. Trask. New York: Harper & Brothers, 1959, 141–7.
Epstein, Zvi. יוצרי ספרות הילדים שלנו *Yoẓ rei sifrut hayeladim shelanu* (The creators of our children's literature). New York: Shiloh, 5707, 1947.
Ernstpeter, Ruhe. *Sydrac le philosophe, Le livre de la fontaine de toutes sciences*. Wissensliteratur im Mittelalter 34. Wiesbaden: Reichert, 2000.
Eskenazi, Tamara Cohn. 'B'reishit'. In *The Torah: A Women's Commentary*, edited by Tamara Cohn Eskenazi and Andrea L. Weiss. New York: WRJ, 2008.
Ewald, B. C. 'Der Philosoph als Leitbild. Ikonographische Untersuchungen an Römischen Sarkophagreliefs'. *MDAI(R)* Ergänzungsheft 34. Mainz am Rhein: von Zabern, 1999.
Ferrante, Joan M. *To the Glory of Her Sex: Women's Roles in the Composition of Medieval Texts*. Bloomington: Indiana University Press, 1997.
Ferrarin, Alfredo. 'Homo Faber, Homo Sapiens, or Homo Politicus? Protagoras and the Myth of Prometheus'. *Review of Metaphysics* 54, no. 2 (2000): 289–319.
Ferrua, A. *The Unknown Catacomb: A Unique Discovery of Early Christian Art*. New Lanark: Geddes and Grosset, 1991.
Feuer, Michael. *Genesis Rabbah Parsha 99, 1*. Jerusalem: Jerusalem Anthology, n.d. https://www.sefaria.org.il/Bereishit_Rabbah.99.1?lang=en.
Fewell, Danna Nolan and David M. Gunn. *Gender, Power and Promise*. Nashville: Abingdon Press, 1993.
Fiocchi Nicolai, V., F. Bisconti and D. Mazzoleni *The Christian Catacombs of Rome: History, Decoration, Inscriptions*. 3rd edition. Translated by C. Carlo Stella and Lori-Ann Touchette. Regensburg: Schnell and Steiner, 2009.
Fletcher, W. C. *Soviet Believers: The Religious Sector of the Population*. Lawrence, KS: Regents Press, 1981.
Foerstel, Herbert N. *Banned in the U.S.A.: A Reference Guide to Book Censorship in Schools and Public Libraries*. Westport, CT: Greenwood, 2002.
Freedman, Paul H. *Images of the Medieval Peasant*. Stanford, CA: Stanford University Press, 1999.
Freimark, P. 'Mukaddima'. In *The Encyclopaedia of Islam, New Edition*, vol. 6, edited by P. Bearman, Th. Bianquis, C. E. Bosworth, E. van Donzel and W. P. Heinrichs, 495–6. Leiden: Brill, 2005.
Fremersdorf, F. *Figürlich Geschliffene Gläser*. Berlin: de Gruyter, 1951.
Froese, Paul. 'Forced secularization in Soviet Russia: Why an atheistic monopoly failed'. *Journal for the Scientific Study of Religion* 43, no. 1 (2004): 35–50.
Fuchs, Esther. *Sexual Politics in the Biblical Narrative: Reading the Hebrew Bible as a Woman*, JSOTSup 310. Sheffield: Sheffield Academic Press, 2000.
Futterman, Bennett. 'Analysis of the Papal Benediction Sign: The Ulnar Neuropathy of St. Peter'. *Clinical Anatomy* 28, no. 6 (2015): 696–701.
Garber, Rebecca L. R. 'Where is The Body? Images of Eve and Mary in the *Scivias*'. In *Hildegard of Bingen: A Book of Essays*, edited by Maud Burnett McInerney, 103–32. New York: Garland, 1998.

Garcia-Sanjuan, A. 'Ibn Hazm and the Territory of Huelva: Personal and Family Relationships'. In *Ibn Hazm of Cordoba: The Life and Works of a Controversial Thinker*, edited by C. Adang, M. Fierro and S. Schmidtka, 51–68. Leiden and Boston: Brill, 2013.

Garrison, E. B. *Studies in the History of Medieval Italian Painting*, vol. 4. Florence: 'L'impronta', 1960.

Geizer, Matvey. *Зиновий Гердт* (*Zinovy Gerdt*). Moscow: Molodaya Gvardiya, 2012.

Gelé, Kim, Susan McNamara, Sidney H. Phillips, R. Dennis Shelby, Gary Grossman, Susan C. Vaughan and Ralph Roughton. 'Emerging views on gender and sexuality: Celebrating twenty years of new perspectives on lesbian, gay, bisexual, and trans people'. *Journal of the American Psychoanalytic Association* 60, no. 5 (2012): 949–67. https://doi.org/10.1177/0003065112459956.

Geronimus, Dennis. *Piero di Cosimo, Visions Beautiful and Strange*. New Haven, CT: Yale University Press, 2006.

Gillhouse, Elizabeth. '"Eve was Framed": Ideostory and (Mis)Representation in Judeo-Christian Creation Stories'. *Children's Literature Association Quarterly* 36, no. 3 (2011): 259–75.

Gilligan, Carol. *In a Different Voice: Psychological Theory and Women's Development*. Cambridge, MA: Harvard University Press, 1982.

Gilligan, Carol. *The Birth of Pleasure*. New York: Alfred A. Knopf, 2002.

Gilligan, Carol. *Joining the Resistance*. Cambridge: Polity Press, 2011.

Ginzburg, Louis, *The Legends of the Jews*. Translated by Henrietta Szold. New York: Jewish Publication Society, 1956.

Giordani, R. 'Fenomeni di prolepsis disegnativa nei mosaici dell'arco di Santa Maria Maggiore'. *Rendiconti della Pontificia Academia Romana di Archeologia* 47 (1974–5): 225–49.

Gitelman, Zvi. *A Century of Ambivalence: The Jews of Russia and the Soviet Union, 1881 to the Present*. Bloomington: Indiana University Press, 2001.

Glasner, Lily. 'Cupid and Psyche: A Love Story (?) in Comics and Children's Literature'. In *Rewriting the Ancient World: Greeks, Romans, Jews and Christians in Modern Popular Fiction*, edited by Lisa Maurice, 198–218. Leiden: Brill, 2017.

Glasner, Lily. '"היה היתה ילדה קטנה...' מעשיות, מעשיות-מחודשות ומודל הגיבורה האקטיבית" ('"Hayo Hayta yalda ktana . . ." maasiyot, maasiyot-mechudashot vemodel hagibora haactivit') ('"Once Upon a Time There was a Little Girl . . ." Fairy-tales, Fairy-tales Retellings and the Model of the Active Heroine'). In *פורצות גדרות: חינוך ומגדר בשדות שיח מגוונים* (*Portzot Gaderot: Chinuch u'nigdar c'sadot siach meguvanim*) (Breaking Boundaries: Education and Gender in Multifaceted Discourse), edited by Dina Haruvi and Talila Kosh Zohar, 125–49. Tel Aviv: Gama and Hakibbutz Hameuchad, 2017.

Gloyn, Liz. *Tracking Classical Monsters in Popular Culture*. London: Bloomsbury, 2020.

Gluzman, Michael. *Haguf haẓioni* (The Zionist body: Nationalism, gender and sexuality in modern Hebrew literature). Bnei Brak, Israel: Hakibbutz Hameuhad, 2007.

Gnecchi, F. *I medaglione Romani*. Milan: Hoepli, 1912.

Goitein, S. D. 'המקאמה והמחברת, פרק בתולדות הספרות והחברה במזרח' 'The maqama and the Mahberet: A Chapter in the History of Literature and Society in the East' (in Hebrew), מחברות לספרות *Mahbarot Lesifrut* 5 (1951): 26–40.

Goldberg, Leah. בין סופר ילדים לקוראיו *Bein sofer yeladim lekorav* (A children writer and his readers). Tel-Aviv: Sifriyat Poalim, 1978.

Goldhill, Simon. 'Cultural History and Aesthetics: Why Kant is No Place to Start Reception Studies'. In *Theorising Performance: Greek Drama, Cultural History and Critical Practice*, edited by Edith Hall and Stephe Harrop, 56–70. London: Duckworth, 2010.

Greenwald, Itamar. 'מיתוס ואמת היסטורית - האם אפשר לנפץ מיתוסים?' 'Mitus ve'emet historit- Ha'im efshar lenapeẓ mitusim?' (Myth and Historical Truth – Can Myths be Shattered?). In *The Myth in Judaism*, edited by Moshe Ideal and Itamar Greenwald, 15–25. Jerusalem: Zalman Shazar Center, 2004.

Gretz, Nurit. ספרות ואידיאולוגיה בארץ-ישראל בשנות השלושים *Sifrut veideologia b'ereẓ Yisrael bishnot hashloshim* (Literature and ideology in Eretz Israel in the 1930s). Tel-Aviv: Open University, 1988.

Gumpert, Matthew. 'The Sublime Monster: Frankenstein, or the Modern Pandora'. In *Frankenstein and Its Classics: The Modern Prometheus from Antiquity to Science Fiction*, edited by Jesse Weiner, Benjamin Eldon Stevens and Brett M. Rogers, 102–20. London: Bloomsbury, 2018.

Guynes, Sean A. 'Do Androids Dream of Proto-Indo-European Fables about Sheep'. *Vocabula Review* 14, no. 7 (2012): 1–7.

HaCohen, Aviad. איסור מינקת והגבלת הזכות לנישואין 'The Prohibition of Nursing Mothers and the Infringement on the Right to Marry'. *Da'at*, 14 December 2019. http://www.daat.ac.il/mishpat-ivri/skirot/skira.asp?id=308 (Hebrew).

Hale, Kimberly Hurd and Erin A. Dolgoy, 'Humanity in a Posthuman World: M. R. Carey's *The Girl with All the Gifts*'. *Utopian Studies* 29, no. 3 (2018): 343–61.

Hall, Edith. 'Putting the class into Classical reception'. In *A Companion to Classical Receptions*, edited by Lorna Hardwick and Christopher Stray, 386–97. Oxford: Blackwell, 2008.

Hall, Edith. *The Return of Ulysses: A Cultural History of Homer's Odyssey*. London and New York: I.B. Tauris, 2008.

Hall, Edith and Stephe Harrop (eds). *Theorising Performance: Greek Drama, Cultural History and Critical Practice*. London: Duckworth, 2010.

Hall, S. 'The west and the rest: Discourse and power'. In *Development: A Cultural Studies Reader*, edited by S. Schesh and J. Haggis, 56–64. Oxford: Blackwell, 2002.

Halvorsen, Peter Nicolai. 'Religion in a World of Androids and Aliens: Life and Death in Ridley Scott's *Blade Runner* and *Prometheus*'. In *Science Fiction, Ethics and the Human Condition*, edited by Christian Baron, Peter Nicolai Halvorsen and Christine Cornea, 115–35. Cham, Switzerland: Springer, 2017.

Hameen-Anttila, J. *Maqama – A History of a Genre*. Wiesbaden: Harrassowitz Verlag, 2002.

Hammond, Emma. 'Alex Garland's *Ex Machina* or the Modern Epimetheus'. In *Frankenstein and Its Classics: The Modern Prometheus from Antiquity to Science Fiction*, edited by Jesse Weiner, Benjamin Eldon Stevens and Brett M. Rogers, 190–205. London: Bloomsbury, 2018.

Haraway, Donna. *Simians, Cyborgs, and Women: The Reinvention of Nature*. London and New York: Routledge, 1990.

Hardstaff, John. 'The Peter Weyland Files: *Prometheus* Transmission'. YouTube video, 7:08:00. https://www.youtube.com/watch?v=FCOo5mj10fE.

Hardstaff, John. 'The Peter Weyland Files: *Prometheus* Transmission'. Holloway segment. YouTube video. https://www.youtube.com/watch?v=oEtgjsoh7lo.

Hardwick, Lorna. *Translating Words, Translating Cultures*. London: Duckworth, 2000.

Hardwick, Lorna and Christopher Stray. *A Companion to Classical Receptions*. Oxford: Blackwell, 2008.

Harel, Shlomo. ספרות ילדים היא ספרות *Sifrut yeladim hi sifrut* (Children's literature is literature: A critical evaluation of trends, concepts, and conventions). Ẓofit: Yemima Center for the Study and Teaching of Children's Literature, 1991.

Harel, Shlomo. הילד והחיים *Hayeled veha-chayim* (Children and life: Literary constructs and educational values in children's literature). Tel-Aviv: Sifriyat Ofer, 1992.

Harl, M. 'La prise de conscience de la nudité d'Adam. Une interprétation de Génèse 3, 7 chez les Pères Grecs'. *Studia Patristica* 7 (1966): 486–95.

Hart, Mother Columbia and Jane Bishop. *Hildegard of Bingen: Scivias*. New York: Paulist Press, 1990.

Hart-Brinson, Peter. *The Gay Marriage Generation: How the LGBTQ Movement Transformed American Culture*. New York: New York University Press, 2018.

Hauptman, Judith. *Rereading the Rabbis: A Woman's Voice*. New York and London: Routledge, 1998.

Hawley, Erin. 'The bride and her afterlife: female *Frankenstein* monsters on page and screen'. *Literature-Film Quarterly* 43, no. 3 (2015): 218–31.
Hayles, N. Katherine. *How We Became Posthuman: Virtual Bodies in Cybernetics, Literature, and Informatics*. Chicago: University of Chicago Press, 1999.
Heath, John. *The Talking Greeks: Speech, Animals, and the Other in Homer, Aeschylus, and Plato*. Oxford: Oxford University Press, 2005.
Heffernan, James A. W. 'Looking at the Monster: *Frankenstein* and Film'. *Critical Inquiry* 24 (1997): 133–58.
Hesiod. 'Theogony'. In *Theogony. Works and Days. Testimonia*. Translated by Glenn W. Most, 2–85. Cambridge, MA: Harvard University Press, 2006.
Hesiod. 'Works and Days'. In *Theogony. Works and Days. Testimonia*. Translated by Glenn W. Most, 86–153. Cambridge, MA: Harvard University Press, 2006.
Hever, Hannan. הסיפור והלאום *Hasipur ve-hal'eom* (The Story and the Nation: A Critical Reading of the Canon of Hebrew Fiction). Tel-Aviv: Resling, 2007.
Himmelmann, N. 'Das Hypogäum der Aurelier am Viale Manzoni'. *Akademie der Wissenschaften und der Literatur* 7 (1975): 7–26.
Himmelmann, N. 'Nudità ideale'. In *Memoria dell'Antico nell'arte italiana*, vol. 2, edited by S. Settis, 201–78. Turin: Ed. Einaudi, 1985.
Hodge, Rosamund. *Cruel Beauty*. New York: Balzer and Bray, 2014.
Holmes, Stu. 'The Linguistics of *Prometheus* – What David Says to The Engineer'. *The Bioscopist*, 20 June 2012. https://thebioscopist.wordpress.com/2012/06/20/the-linguistics-of-prometheus-what-david-says-to-the-engineer/comment-page-2/.
Hopkins, David. *Conversing with Antiquity: English Poets and the Classics, from Shakespeare to Pope*. Classical Presences. Oxford: Oxford University Press, 2010.
Howell, Jessica. *Malaria and Victorian Fictions of Empire*. Cambridge: Cambridge University Press, 2019.
Hunt, Peter. *Criticism, Theory, and Children's Literature*. Oxford: Basil Blackwell, 1991.
Hunt, Peter. *Introduction to Children's Literature*. Oxford: Oxford University Press, 1994.
Huss, M. '"It Never Happened, Nor Did It Ever Exist": The Status of Fiction in the Hebrew Maqama'. *Jerusalem Studies in Hebrew Literature* 18 (2001): 57–104.
Hutcheon, Linda. *A Theory of Adaptation*. 2nd edition. New York: Routledge, 2006/2013.
Ibn Hazm. *Abu Muhamad Ali Ibn Hazm Al-Andalusi, (a book containing the RISALA known as) The Dove's Neck-Ring, about Love and Lovers*. Translated by D. K. Petrof and edited by A. R. Nykl. Paris: Paul Geuthner, 1931.
Ibn Hazm. *Ibn Hazm, The Ring of the Dove, A Treatise on the Art and Practice of Arab Love*. Translated by A. J. Arberry. London: Luzac & Company, 1953.
Inquirer Movies. '*Prometheus* Crew: On A Mission Collision'. *Philippine Daily Inquirer*. https://www.webcitation.org/68QKobIOZ.
Ipgrave, Michael. 'Christianity in the world of Japan's religions: reception, incorporation, separation'. *International Journal for the Study of the Christian Church* 16 (2016): 197–210.
Ishikawa, Akito. 'A Little Faith: Christianity and the Japanese'. Nippon.com, 2019. https://www.nippon.com/en/japan-topics/g00769/a-little-faith-christianity-and-the-japanese.html.
James, Paula. *Ovid's Myth of Pygmalion on Screen: In Pursuit of the Perfect Woman*. New York: Bloomsbury, 2010.
Jenkins, Thomas. 'The Reception of Hesiod in the Twentieth and Twenty-First Centuries'. In *The Oxford Handbook of Hesiod*, edited by Alexander C. Loney and Stephen Scully, 479–94. Oxford: Oxford University Press, 2018.
Johnson, Brian. 'Prehistories of Posthumanism: Cosmic Indifferentism, Alien Genesis, and Ecology from H. P. Lovecraft to Ridley Scott'. In *The Age of Lovecraft*, edited by Carl H. Sederholm and Jeffrey Andrew Weinstock, 97–116. Minneapolis: University of Minnesota Press, 2016.

Jung, Carl G. *Psychology and Religion*. In *The Collected Works of C. G. Jung*, vol. 11, 2nd edition, edited by Herbert Read. Princeton, NJ: Princeton University Press, 1937/1958.

Jung, C. G. 'Psychology and Religion'. In *Psychology and Religion: West and East*, translated by R. F. C Hull, 3–105, 2nd edition. London: Routledge & Kegan Paul, 1969.

Kaariainen, K. *Discussion on Scientific Atheism as a Soviet Science*. Helsinki: Suomalainen Tiedeakatemia, 1989.

Kaiser-Minn, H. 'Die Erschaffung des Menschen auf den spätantiken Monumenten des 3. und 4. Jahrhunderts'. *Jahrbuch für Antike und Christentum*. Ergänzungbund 6. Münster: Aschendorff, 1981.

Kennedy, Rebecca Futo. *Brill's Companion to the Reception of Aeschylus*. Leiden: E.J. Brill, 2017.

Kerényi, Karl. *Prometheus: Archetypal Image of Human Existence*. Translated by Ralph Manheim. Princeton, NJ: Princeton University Press, 1997.

Kerényi, Karl and Magda Kerényi. *Die Mythologie der Griechen*. Stuttgart: Klett-Cotta, 1997.

Kessler, H. L. *The illustrated Bibles from Tours*. Princeton, NJ: Princeton University Press, 1977.

Kessler, H. L. *Old St Peter's and Church Decoration in Medieval Italy*. Spoleto: Centro italiano di studi sull'alto Medioevo, 2002.

Kessler, H. L. 'La Genèse Cotton est morte'. In *Les stratégies de la narration dans la peinture médiévales. La représentation de l'Ancien Testament aux IVe–XIIe siècles*, edited by M. Angheben, 373–402. Turnhout: Brepols, 2020.

Killian, Kyle D. '*Prometheus*'. *Journal of Feminist Family Therapy* 26, no. 4 (2014): 240–4.

Kinsley, David. *The Goddesses' Mirror: Visions of the Divine from East and West*. Albany: State University of New York Press, 1989.

Kipnis, Levin. ביבליוגרפיה *Bibliographia* (Bibliography), edited by Eliyahu Cohen. Tel Aviv: Levin Kipnis Center for Children's Literature and Levinsky College, 1999.

Klauser, T. 'Studien zur Entstehungsgeschichte der christlichen Kunst III'. *Jahrbuch für Antike und Christentum* 3 (1960): 112–33.

Kleu, Michael. *Antikenrezeption in der Science Fiction*. Essen: Oldib Verlag, 2019.

Klima, Gyula. 'The Medieval Problem of Universals'. In *The Stanford Encyclopedia of Philosophy*, edited by Edward N. Zalta, (Winter 2017 edition). https://plato.stanford.edu/archives/win2017/entries/universals-medieval/.

Kohut, Heinz. 'Forms and Transformation of Narcissism'. In *Self Psychology and the Humanities: Reflections on a New Psychoanalytic Approach*, translated to Hebrew by Ẓili Zonans and Eldad Edan, 123–49. Tel Aviv: Tola'at Sefarim, 2007.

Kolarz, W. *Religion in the Soviet Union*. New York: St. Martin's Press, 1961.

Kosior, Wojciech. 'A Tale of Two Sisters: The Image of Eve in Early Rabbinic Literature and Its Influence on the Portrayal of Lilith in the Alphabet of Ben Sira'. *Nashim: A Journal of Jewish Women's Studies & Gender Issues* 32 (2018): 112–30.

Kraeling, C. H. 'The Christian Building'. In *The Excavations at Dura-Europos. Final Report VIII, Part II*, edited by C. Bradford Wells. New Haven, CT: Dura-Europos Publications, 1967.

Kraman, Cynthia. 'The Future is Female: Bateson, Benjamin and How Women Learn in Ridley Scott's *Prometheus*'. *Anthropology Now* 7 (2015): 1–13.

Kramer, Samuel Noah. *Gilgamesh and the Huluppu-Tree: A Reconstructed Sumerian Text*. Assyriological Studies 10. Chicago: University of Chicago Press, 1938.

Kuran, T. *Private Truths, Public Lies*. Cambridge, MA: Harvard University Press, 1995.

Kvam, Kristen E., Linda, S. Schearing and Valarie H. Ziegler (eds). *Eve and Adam: Jewish, Christian, and Muslim Readings on Genesis and Gender*. Bloomington: Indiana University Press, 1999.

Lachs, Samuel Tobias, 'The Pandora–Eva Motif in Rabbinic Literature'. *Harvard Theological Review* 67 (1974): 341–5.

Laes, Christian. *A Cultural History of Disability in Antiquity*. London: Bloomsbury, 2020.

Lenin, Vladimir Ilyich. 'About the attitude of the working party toward the religion'. *Пролетарий (Proletary)* 45, no. 26, 13 May 1909. In *V. I. Lenin: Collected Works*, XV, translated by Andrew Rothstein and Bernard Issacs, 402–13. Moscow: Progress Publishers, 1973.

Lerner, Gerda. *The Creation of the Patriarchy*. New York and Oxford, Oxford University Press, 1986.

Lev, Peter. 'Whose Future? *Star Wars*, *Alien*, and *Blade Runner*'. *Literature-Film Quarterly* 26, no. 1 (1998): 30–7.

Levin, I. 'הבכי על חרבות המעונות והדמות-הלילית המשוטטת' (habechi al tarbut hameonot v'had'mut halaylit hameshutetet) 'Lamenting over the Ruins of the Encampment and the Image of the Wandering She Demon' (in Hebrew). תרביץ *Tarbiz* 36 (1956): 278–96.

Levin, I. מעיל תשבץ: הסוגים השונים של שירת החול העברית בספרד (Me'il Tashbetz: Hasugim hashonim shel shirat hachol baivrit b'sferad) *The Embroidered Coat: The Genres of Hebrew Secular Poetry in Spain* (Me'il Tashbetz), 3 vols (in Hebrew). Tel-Aviv: Hakibbutz Hameuchad, 1980.

Leviticus Rabbah translated by Michael Feuer. Jerusalem Anthology. https://www.sefaria.org.il/Vayikra_Rabbah.13.1?lang=en.

Lev Kenaan, Vered. *Pandora's Senses: The Feminine Character of the Ancient Text*. Madison: University of Wisconsin Press, 2008.

Liveley, Genevieve. 'Science Fictions and Cyber Myths: or, Do Androids Dream of Dolly the Sheep?'. In *Laughing with Medusa*, edited by Vanda Zajko and Miriam Leonard, 275–94. Oxford: Oxford University Press, 2008.

Liverani, P. 'Epigrafia monumentale e immagine pubblica in epoca tardoantica'. In *Using Image in Late Antiquity*, edited by S. Birk et al., 3–32. Oxford: Oxbow Books, 2014.

Loraux, Nicole. *The Children of Athena*. Princeton, NJ: Princeton University Press, 1991.

Loseff, Lev. *On the Beneficence of Censorship: Aesopian Language in Modern Russian Literature*. Munich: Otto Sagner, 1984.

Macandrew, Hugh. 'A Group of Batoni Drawings at Eton College, and Some Eighteenth-Century Italian Copyists of Classical Sculpture'. *Master Drawings* 16, no. 2 (Summer 1978): 131–50, 191–215.

Marino, Lucia. 'Prometheus, or the Mythographer's Self-Image in Boccaccio's "Genealogie"'. *Studi sul Boccaccio* 12 (1980): 263–73.

Marotta, Melanie A. 'The Science Fiction Horror: *Alien*, George R. R. Martin's *Nightflyers* and the Surveillance of Women'. *Northern Lights: Film & Media Studies Yearbook* 17, no. 1 (2019): 57–70.

Martindale, Charles. 'Redeeming the Text: The Validity of Comparisons of Classical and Post-Classical Literature. A View from Britain'. *Arion* (3rd series) 1, no. 3 (1992): 45–75.

Martindale, Charles. *Redeeming the Text: Latin Poetry and the Hermeneutics of Reception*. Cambridge: Cambridge University Press, 1993.

Martindale, Charles. 'Reception'. In *The Oxford Classical Dictionary*, 3rd edition, edited by Simon Hornblower and Anthony Spawforth, 1294–5. Oxford: Oxford University Press, 2003.

Martindale, Charles. 'Reception and the Classics of the Future'. *Council of University Classics Departments Bulletin* 34 (2005). http://www.rhul.ac.uk/classics/cucd/martindale05.html.

Martindale, Charles, 'Reception – a new humanism? Receptivity, pedagogy, the transhistorical'. *Classical Receptions Journal* 5, no. 2 (2013): 169.

Martindale, Charles and Richard F. Thomas. *Classics and the Uses of Reception*. Oxford: Blackwell, 2006.

Martinez-Gros, G. 'Ibn Hazm on history: A few remarks'. In *Ibn Hazm of Cordoba: The Life and Works of a Controversial Thinker*, edited by C. Adang, M. Fierro and S. Schmidtka, 87–94. Leiden and Boston: Brill, 2013.

Mathews, T. 'La nudità nell'arte paleocristiana'. In *Aurea Roma: dalla città pagana alla città cristiana (mostra nel Palazzo delle Esposizioni, 22 dicembre 2000–20 aprile 2001)*, edited by S. Ensoli and E. La Rocca, 399–402. Rome: 'L'Erma' di Bretschneider, 2000.

Mattock, J. N. 'The Early History of the Maqama'. *Journal of Arabic Literature* 15 (1984): 1–18.

Maurice, Lisa. 'Children, Greece and Rome: Heroes and Eagles'. In *The Reception of Ancient Greece and Rome in Children's Literature: Heroes and Eagles*, edited by Lisa Maurice, 1–14. Leiden: Brill, 2015.

Maurice, Lisa. *Rewriting the Ancient World: Greeks, Romans, Christians and Jews in Modern Popular Fiction*. Metaforms: Studies in the Reception of Classical Antiquity. Leiden: Brill, 2017.

Maurice, Lisa. 'Cupid and Psyche for Children'. In *Cupid and Psyche: The Reception of Apuleius' Love Story since 1600*, edited by Regine May and Stephen Harrison, 289–301. Berlin: De Gruyter, 2019.

Mayor, Adrienne. *Gods and Robots: Myths, Machines and Ancient Dreams of Technology*. Princeton, NJ: Princeton University Press, 2018.

Mazor, Yair. '"Cherchez la femme", or Sex, Lies and the Bible: Exposing the Anti-Feminist Face of the Biblical Text'. *SJOT* 18 (2004): 39–40.

McCallum-Barry, Carmel. 'Myth under Construction'. *Classics Ireland* 7 (2000): 99–115.

McClure, Amy. 'Censorship'. *Children's Literature Association Quarterly* 8, no. 1 (2014): 22–5.

McKim, Richard. 'Myth against Philosophy in Ovid's Account of Creation'. *Classical Journal* 80, no. 2 (1984): 97–108.

McWilliam, David. 'Beyond the Mountains of Madness: Lovecraftian Cosmic Horror and Posthuman Creationism in Ridley Scott's *Prometheus* (2012)'. *Journal of the Fantastic in the Arts* 26, no. 3 (2015): 531–45.

Merceron, Jacques. 'Des souris et des hommes : pérégrination d'un motif narratif et d'un exemplum d'Islam en chrétienté. [À propos de la fable de "L'Ermite" de Marie de France et du fabliau de La Sorisete des Estopes]'. *Cahiers de civilisation médiévale* 46 (2003): 53–69. DOI: https://doi.org/10.3406/ccmed.2003.2848.

Meyers, Carol. *Discovering Eve: Ancient Israelite Women in Context*. New York: Oxford University Press, 1988.

Miller, D. Patrick. 'What the Shadow Knows: An Interview with John A. Sanford'. In *Meeting the Shadow: The Hidden Power of the Dark Side of Human Nature*, edited by Jeremiah Abrams and Connie Zweig, 19–26. New York: Penguin Putnam, 1991.

Mitchel, Steven A. and Margaret J. Black, *Freud and Beyond: A History of Modern Psychoanalytic Thought*. Translated to Hebrew by Amit Pechler. Tel Aviv: Tola'at Sefarim, 2006, 271–85.

Moore, Mignon R. and Michael Stambolis-Ruhstorfer. 'LGBT Sexuality and Families at the Start of the Twenty-First Century'. *Annual Review of Sociology* 39 (July 2013): 491–507. https://doi.org/10.1146/annurev-soc-071312-145643.

Moormann, E. M. *La pittura parietale romana come fonte di conoscenza per las scultura antica*. Assen: van Gorcum, 1988.

Mouritsen, H. *The Freedman in the Roman World*. Cambridge: Cambridge University Press, 2011.

Mulhall, Stephen. *On Film* 3rd edition. London and New York: Routledge, 2016.

Murnaghan, Sheila and Deborah Roberts. *Childhood and the Classics: Britain and America, 1850–1965*. Oxford: Oxford University Press, 2018.

Musäus, Immanuel. *Der Pandoramythos bei Hesiod und seine Rezeption bis Erasmus von Rotterdam*. Göttingen: Vandenhoeck and Ruprecht, 2004.

Nakayasu, Chie. 'School Curriculum in Japan'. *Curriculum Journal* 27 (2016): 134–50.

Napier, Susan J. 'When the Machines Stop: Fantasy, Reality, and Terminal Identity in "Neon Genesis Evangelion" and "Serial Experiments Lain"'. *Science Fiction Studies* 29 (2002): 418–35.

Napier, Susan J. *Anime from Akira to Princess Mononoke*, revised edition. New York: St. Martin's Press, 2005.

Nestori, A. *Repertorio topografico delle pitture delle catacombe* romane, 2nd edition. Vatican City: Pontificio Istituto di Archeologia Cristiana, 1993.

Neumann, Boaz. החלוצים *Hachaluzim* (The Pioneers). Tel-Aviv: Am Oved, 2009.

Neusner, Jacob, *Judaism Story of Creation: Scripture, Halakha, Aggadah*, Brill Reference Library of Judaism 3. Leiden: Brill, 2000.

Newman, Marissa. 'Longest-jailed Israeli divorce-refuser freed after 19 years'. *Times of Israel*, 2 October 2019. https://www.timesofisrael.com/longest-jailed-israeli-divorce-refuser-freed-after-19-years.

Nicholson, R. A. *A Literary History of the Arabs*. Cambridge: Cambridge University Press, 1930.

Nisbet, Gideon. '*Mecha* in Olympus: Shirow Masamune's *Appleseed*'. In *Son of Classics and Comics*, edited by George Kovacs and C. W. Marshall, 67–78. New York: Oxford University Press, 2016.

Ofek, Uriel. ספרות הילדים העברית 1900–1948 *Sifrut hayeladim ha'ivrit 1900–1948* (Children's Hebrew Literature 1940–1948), vol. 2. Tel Aviv: Dvir, 1988.

O'Meara, John. 'Saint Augustine's Understanding of the Creation and Fall'. *Maynooth Review* 10 (1984): 52–62. https://www.jstor.org/stable/20556975.

Orofino, G. 'Citazione e interpretazione. Il rapporto con l'antico nel ciclo illustrativo dell'enciclopedia di Rabano Mauro'. In *Medioevo: il tempo degli antichi – Atti del Convegno internazionale di studi, Parma, 24–28 settembre 2003*, edited by A. C. Quintavalle, 197–206. Parma: Electa, 2006.

Ortega, M. 'My Father, He Killed Me; My Mother, She Ate Me: Self, Desire, Engendering, and the Mother in "Neon Genesis Evangelion"'. *Mechademia* 2 (2007): 216–32.

Pagis, D. *Secular Poetry and Poetic Theory: Moses ibn Ezra and his Contemporaries* (in Hebrew). Jerusalem: Bialik, 1970.

Pagis, D. *Change and Tradition in Secular Poetry: Spain and Italy* (in Hebrew). Jerusalem: Keter, 1976.

Panofsky, Dora and Erwin Panofsky. *Pandora's Box: The Changing Aspects of a Mythical Symbol*. Princeton, NJ: Princeton University Press, 1956.

Panofsky, Dora and Erwin Panofsky. *Pandora's Box: The Changing Aspects of a Mythical Symbol*, 2nd edition. New York: Pantheon Books, 1962.

Panofsky, Dora and Erwin Panofsky. *Pandora's Box: The Changing Aspects of a Mythical Symbol*. New York: Pantheon Books, 1967.

Panofsky, E. 'Renaissance and Renascences'. *Kenyon Review* 6 (1944): 201–36.

Pardes, Ilana. *Countertraditions in the Bible*. London: Harvard University Press, 1992.

Peer, Ayelet. 'Thermae Romae Manga: Plunging into the Unique Bond between Ancient Rome and Modern Japan'. *New Voices in Classical Reception Studies* 12 (2018): 57–67.

Peer, Ayelet and Raz Greenberg. 'The Japanese Trojan War: Tezuka Osamu's envisioning of the Greek epos'. *Greece & Rome* 67 (2020): 151–76.

Pegg, Danny. '*Prometheus*'. *Journal of Religion & Film* 17, no. 2 (2013): 1–4.

Pépin, J. '"Ut scriptura pictura": un thème de l'esthétique médiévale et ses origines'. In *From Augustine to Eriugena: Essays on Neoplatonism and Christianity in Honor of John O'Meara*, edited by F. X. Martin and J. A. Richmond, 168–82. Washington, DC: Catholic University of America Press, 1991.

Pergola, P. 'Il *Praedium Domitillae* sulla via Ardeatina: analisi storico-topografica delle testimonianze pagane fino all metà del III sec. d. C'. *Rivista di Archeologia Cristiana* 55 (1979): 313–35.

Pergola, A. 'Il Quadrante delle Interpretazioni'. In *L'ipogeo degli Aureli in Viale Manzoni: restauri tutela, valorizzazione e aggiornamenti interpretativi*, edited by F. Bisconti, 81–124. Vatican City: Pontificia Commissione di Archeologia Sacra, 2011.

Perry, Ben Edwin (ed. and trans.). *Babrius and Phaedrus*. Cambridge, MA, and London: Harvard University Press, 1965.

Pinkus, Benjamin. *The Jews of the Soviet Union: The History of a National Minority*. Cambridge: Cambridge University Press, 1990.

Poitras, Gilles. 'Contemporary Anime in Japanese Pop Culture'. In *Japanese Visual Culture: Explorations in the World of Manga and Anime*, edited by Mark W. MacWilliams, 48–67. Armonk, NY: M.E. Sharpe, 2008.

Popa Blanariu, Nicoleta. 'Transmedial Prometheus: From the Greek Myth to Contemporary Interpretations'. *Icono 14* 15, no. 1 (2017): 88–107.

Pospielovsky, D. *A History of Soviet Atheism in Theory and Practice, and the True Believer*. New York: St. Martin's Press, 1987.

Pospielovsky, D. *Soviet Anti-Religious Campaigns and Persecutions*. New York: St. Martin's Press, 1988.

Powell, D. E. *Antireligious Propaganda in the Soviet Union: A Study of Mass Persuasion*. Cambridge, MA: MIT Press, 1975.

Pravdina, Tatiana and Yakov Groisman. *Зяма – это же Гердт!* (*Ziama - eto zhe Gerdt!*) (*Ziama - it's Gerdt!*). Moscow: Dekom, 2013.

Prigent, P. *Le Judaïsme et l'image*. Tübingen: Mohr, 1990.

Propp, Vladimir. *The Morphology of the Folktale*, 2nd edition. Revised and edited by Louis A. Wagner. Austin: University of Texas Press, 1968.

Proverbio, C. *I cicli affrescati paleocristiani di San Pietro in Vaticano e San Paolo fuori le mura. Proposte di lettura*. Turnhout: Brepols, 2017.

Puerta Vilchez, J. M. 'Ali Ibn Hazm: A Biographical Sketch'. In *Ibn Hazm of Cordoba: The Life and Works of a Controversial Thinker*, edited by C. Adang, M. Fierro and S. Schmidtka, 3–24. Leiden and Boston: Brill, 2013.

Raggio, Olga. 'The Myth of Prometheus: Its Survival and Metamorphoses up to the Eighteenth Century'. *Journal of the Warburg and Courtland Institutes* 21.½ (January–June 1958): 44–62.

Ramet, Sabrina Petra. *Religious Policy in the Soviet Union*. Cambridge: Cambridge University Press, 1993.

Ramsdell, Kristin. *Romance Fiction: A Guide to the Genre*. Santa Barbara, CA: Libraries Unlimited, 2012.

Raphael, Rebecca. 'Disability as Rhetorical Trope in Classical Myth and *Blade Runner*'. In *Classical Traditions in Science Fiction*, edited by Brett M. Rogers and Benjamin Eldon Stevens, 176–96. Oxford: Oxford University Press, 2015.

Redmond, Denis. 'Anime and East Asian Culture: *Neon Genesis Evangelion*'. *Quarterly Review of Film and Video* 24 (2007): 183–8.

Refael-Vivante, R. 'The Maqama – Between a Tale and a One-Man Show: In Search of Its Form of Performance'. In *Medieval and Early Modern Performance in the Eastern Mediterranean*, edited by Arzu Ozturkmen and Evelyn Birge Vitz, 19–36. Turnhout: Brepols, 2014.

Refael-Vivante, R. '"Sur ce que le cœur veut voir mais pas les yeux", sur l'emprise de l'amour et sa déconvenue dans la 31e maqama du *Tahkemoni* de Yehuda al-Harizi'. In *Ceci n'est pas une chanson d'amour: les multiples visages de la poésie didactique*, edited by D. Buschinger, F. Gabaude, M.-G. Grossel et al., 179–90. Amiens: Presses du Centre d'études médiévales de Picardie, 2017.

Regev, Menahem. בדרכי הספרות לילדים *Bedarkehi hasifrut l'yeladim* (In the paths of children's literature). Haifa: Oranim, 1985.

Reich, Rachel. *The Woman Whom Thou Gavest to be with Me*. Tel Aviv: Hakibbutz Hameuchad, 2005.

Reid, Jane Davidson. *The Oxford Guide to Classical Mythology in the Arts 1300–1990s*, vols 1 and 2. Oxford: Oxford University Press, 1993.

Renger, Almut-Barbara and Immanuel Musaüs, *Mythos Pandora*. Leipzig: Reclam, 2002.

Reshef, Shimon and Yuval Dror. 1948–1919 החינוך העברי בימי הבית הלאומי *Hachinuch ha'ivri bimei habayit haleumi, 1919–1948* (Hebrew education in the years of the national homeland 1919–1948). Jerusalem: Mosad Bialik, 1999.

Riverlea, Miriam. 'Out of the Box: Refashioning Pandora in Children's Literature'. In *Refashioning Myth: Poetic Transformations and Metamorphoses*, edited by Jessica L. Wilkinson, Eric Parisot and David McInnis, 259–77. Newcastle upon Tyne: Cambridge Scholars Publishing, 2011.

Roach, Marion. *The Roots of Desire: The Myth, Meaning, and Sexual Power of Red Hair*. New York: Bloomsbury, 2005.

Robert, C. *Die Antiken Sarkophag-Reliefs*. Berlin: G. Grote'sche Verlagsbuchhandlung, 1897–9.

Robichon, François. *Jean Effel. L'Homme à la marguerite*. Paris: Hoëbeke, 1998.

Rogers, Brett M. 'The Postmodern Prometheus and Posthuman Reproductions in Science Fiction'. In *Frankenstein and Its Classics*, edited by Jesse Weiner, Benjamin Eldon Stevens and Brett M. Rogers, 206–27. London: Bloomsbury, 2018.

Rogers, Brett M. and Benjamin Eldon Stevens (eds). *Classical Traditions in Science Fiction*. Oxford: Oxford University Press, 2015.

Roman, Yadin. 'The King of Kindergarten'. *Eretz* 121 (2009): 70–5.

Romano, S. 'San Pietro, San Paolo, e la narrazione cristiana'. In *Les stratégies de la narration dans la peinture médiévales. La représentation de l'Ancien Testament aux IVe–XIIe siècles*, edited by M. Angheben, 127–41. Turnhout: Brepols, 2020.

Romm, James. 'Wax, Stone, and Promethean Clay: Lucian as Plastic Artist'. *Classical Antiquity* 9, no. 1 (April 1990): 74–98.

Rosen, T. *Unveiling Eve: Reading Gender in Medieval Hebrew Literature*. Philadelphia: University of Pennsylvania Press, 2003.

Rutten, Susan, Benedicta Deogratias and Pauline Kruiniger. *Marital Captivity: Divorce, Religion and Human Rights*. The Hague, Eleven International Publishing, 2019.

Sahar, Amer. 'Marie de France Rewrites Genesis: The Image of Woman in Marie de France's Fables'. *Neophilologus* 81, no. 4 (1997): 489–99.

Salvadori, S. 'Sin and Redemption, Sexuality and Gender. Adam and Eve in the Funerary Art of Late Antique Rome'. In *ΑΝΑΘΕΜΑΤΑ ΕΟΡΤΙΚΑ: Studies in honor of Thomas F. Mathews*, edited by J. D. Alchermes with H. C. Evans and T. K. Thomas, 271–82. Mainz: Verlag Philpp von Zabern, 2008.

Sanders, Theresa. *Approaching Eden: Adam and Eve in Popular Culture*. Lanham, MD: Rowman and Littlefield, 2009.

Sappho. *Sappho: A New Translation of the Complete Works*. Translated by Diana J. Rayor and André Lardinois. Cambridge: Cambridge University Press, 2014.

Scheindlin R. P. 'Fawns of the Palace and Fawns of the Field'. *Prooftexts* 6, no. 3 (September 1986): 189–203.

Schipper, Mineke. 'Humanity's Beginnings in Creation and Origin Myths From Around The World'. In *China's Creation and Origin Myths: Cross-cultural Explorations in Oral and Written Traditions*, edited by Mineke Schipper, Shuxian Ye and Hubin Yin, 1–24. Leiden and Boston: Brill, 2011.

Schirmann, J. *The Hebrew Poetry in Spain and Provence*, 2 vols (in Hebrew). Jerusalem: Bialik, 1956.

Schirmann, J. *The History of Hebrew Poetry in Christian Spain and Southern France* (in Hebrew). Jerusalem: Magnes, 1997.

Schumm, Walter R. 'Changes over the decades in selected LGBTQ research findings'. *JSM Sexual Medicine* 4, no. 2 (2020): 1029.

Scott, Ridley (dir.). *Prometheus*. Beverley Hills: Twentieth Century Fox, 2012.

Scott, Ridley. '*Prometheus*, "How far would you go . . .?" scene'. YouTube video, 1:47:00. https://www.youtube.com/watch?v=pww01VM8bjI.

Segal, S. D. '"Mahberet Ne'um Aser Ben Yehuda" of Solomon Ibn Saqbel: A Study of Scriptural Citation Clusters'. *Journal of American Oriental Society* 102, no. 1 (January–March 1982): 17–26.

Segre, Cesare. *Li Bestiaires d'amours di Maistre Richart de Fornival e Li Response du Bestiaire*. Milan and Naples: Riccardo Ricciardi, 1957.

Sergent, Bernard. 'Amaterasu, Dèmèter, et leurs Acolytes'. *Presses Universitaires de Franche-Comté* 35 (2009): 45–68.

Shedd, Meredith. 'Prometheus the Primeval Sculptor: Archaeology and Anatomy in Emeric-David's "Recherches Sur L'art Statuaire"'. *Zeitschrift Für Kunstgeschichte* 54, no. 1 (1991): 88–106.

Shemesh, Yael. 'Directions in Jewish feminist Bible study'. *Currents in Biblical Research* 14 (2016): 372–406.

Shemesh, Yael. 'Why did the Serpent Choose to Address Eve, rather than Adam (Gen 3:1): Eve, the Serpent, and the Reader's Responsibility'. – *Ve-'Ed Ya'aleh (Gen 2:6): Essays in Biblical and Ancient Near Eastern Studies Presented to Edward L. Greenstein, eds. Peter Machinist et al.* (Atlanta: SBL, forthcoming).

Shichmanter, Rima. *Hebrew Children's Newspapers in the 40's and the 50's*. Jerusalem: Ben-Zvi Institute and Ben Gurion Institute, 2014.

Shiel, C. 'Developing the global citizen'. *Exchange* 5 (2006): 15–20.

Sichtermann, H. and G. Koch. *Griechische Mythen auf Römischen Sarkophageni*. Tübingen: Wasmuth, 1975.

Simard, Jared A. 'Classics and Rockefeller Center: John D. Rockefeller Jr. and the Use of Classicism in Public Space'. Unpublished PhD dissertation, Graduate Center, City University of New York, 2016.

Simard, Jared A. 'The Titans of Rockefeller Center: Prometheus and Atlas'. In *Classical New York: Discovering Greece and Rome in Gotham*, edited by Elizabeth Macaulay-Lewis and Matthew M. McGowan, 140–60. New York: Fordham University Press, 2018.

Simons, Patricia. 'Piero di Cosimo's Creation of Pandora'. *Source: Notes in the History of Art* 34, no. 2 (2015): 34–40.

Sloan, Robin. 'Homesick for the Unheimlich: Back to the Uncanny Future in *Alien*: Isolation'. *Journal of Gaming & Virtual Worlds* 8, no. 3 (2016): 211–30.

Smith, Stephanie A. '"An Empire O'er the Disentangled Doom": Captivity and the Re-Staging of *Prometheus* in the Twenty-First Century'. *Science Fiction Film and Television* 9, no. 1 (2016): 55–72.

Sobchack, Vivian. 'Between a Rock and a Hard Place: How Ridley Scott's *Prometheus* Deals with Impossible Expectations and Mythological Baggage'. *Film Comment* 48 (2012): 30–4.

Solmsen, Friedrich, Reinhold Merkelbarch and Martin Lichtfield West. *Hesiodi Theogonia, Opera et dies, Scutum; Fragmenta selecta*, 3rd edition. Oxford: Oxford University Press, 1990.

Solterer, Helen. *The Master and Minerva: Disputing Women in French Medieval Culture*. Berkley: University of California Press, 1995.

Soravia, B. 'Portrait of the Alim as a Young Man: the Formative Years of Ibn Hazm, 404/1013–420/102'. In *Ibn Hazm of Cordoba: The Life and Works of a Controversial Thinker*, edited by C. Adang, M. Fierro and S. Schmidtka, 25–50. Leiden and Boston: Brill, 2013.

Spiegel, Harriet, *Marie de France, Fables*. Toronto: University of Toronto Press, 1987.

Stanton, Elizabeth Cady. *The Woman's Bible*. New York: Dover Publications, 1895/1898/2002.

Stephens, John and Robyn McCallum. *Retelling Stories, Framing Culture: Traditional Story and Metanarratives in Children's Literature*. New York: Garland Publishing, 1998.

Stern, David and Mark J. Mirsky. *Rabbinic Fantasies: Imaginative Narratives from Classical Hebrew Literature*. Philadelphia: Jewish Publication Society, 1990.

Stevens, Benjamin Eldon. 'Cupid and Psyche in *Frankenstein*: Mary Shelley's Apuleian Science Fiction?' In *Frankenstein and Its Classics: The Modern Prometheus from Antiquity to Science Fiction*, edited by Jesse Weiner, Benjamin Eldon Stevens and Brett M. Rogers, 123–44. London: Bloomsbury, 2018.

Stone, Merlin. *When God was a Woman*. New York: Harcourt Brace Jovanovich, 1976.

Strauss, Leo. 'Jerusalem and Athens'. In *Studies in Platonic Political Philosophy*, edited by Leo Strauss, 147–73. Chicago: University of Chicago Press, 1983.

Stroumsa, Gedaliahu G. 'Myth into Metaphor: The Case of Prometheus'. In *Gilgul: Essays on Transformation, Revolution and Permanence in the History of Religions*, edited by Shaul Shaked, David Shulman and Gedaliahu G. Stroumsa, 309–23. Leiden: E.J. Brill, 1987.

Swatos, W. *Politics and Religion in Central and Eastern Europe*. London: Praeger, 1994.
Szkudlarek, B. 'Through western eyes: Insights into the intercultural training field'. *Organization Studies* 30, no. 9 (2009): 975–86.
Tassinari, Gabriella. 'La raffigurazione de Prometeo creatore nella glittica romana'. *Xenia Antiqua* 1 (1992): 61–116.
Theisohn, Philipp. 'Prometheus'. In *Brill's The Reception of Myth and Mythology*, edited by Maria Moog-Grünewald, 552–68. Leiden: New Pauly, 2010.
Thelle, Notto R. *Buddhism and Christianity in Japan: From Conflict to Dialogue, 1854–1899*. Honolulu: University of Hawaii Press, 1987.
Thomas, Alfred. 'Alien Bodies: Exclusions, Obscenity and Social Control in the Ointment Seller'. In *Obscenity: Social Control & Artistic Creation in the European Middle Ages*, edited by Jan M. Ziolkowski, 214–30. Leiden: Brill, 1998.
Thouny, Christophe. 'Waiting for the Messiah: The Becoming-Myth of "Evangelion" and "Densha otoko"'. *Mechademia* 4 (2009): 111–29.
Tibéri, Jean-Paul. *Jean Effel. La Création d'un monde*. Paris: Jean-Cyrille Godefroy, 1992.
Tomei, A. *Iacobus Torriti. Una vicenda figurativa del tardo Duecento romano*. Rome: Argos, 1990.
Torry, Robert. 'Awakening to the Other: Feminism and the Ego ideal in *Alien*'. *Women's Studies* 23, no. 4 (1994): 343–63.
Toynbee, J. M. C. and J. B. Ward-Perkins. *The Shrine of St Peter and the Vatican*. London: Longmans; New York: Green, 1956.
Trible, Phyllis. 'Depatriarchalizing in Biblical Interpretation'. *Journal of the American Academy of Religion* 41, no. 1 (1973): 30–48.
Tronzo, W. *The Via Latina Catacomb: Imitation and Discontinuity in Fourth-Century Roman Painting*. Philadelphia: Pennsylvania State University Press, 1986.
Trousson, Raymond. *Le thème de Prométhée dans la littérature européenne*. Geneva: Librairie Droz, 2001.
Turnbull, Stephen. 'The Ghosts of Amakusa: Localised Opposition to Centralised Control in Higo Province, 1589–1590'. *Japan Forum* 25 (2013): 191–211.
Urbach, Ephraim. *The Sages: Their Concepts and Beliefs*. Translated by Israel Abrahams. Jerusalem: Magnes Press, 1975.
Uther, Hans-Jorg. *The Types of International Folktales: A Classification and Bibliography based on the System of Antii Aarne and Stith Thompson*, FF Communication, Suomalainen Tiedeakatemia. Helsinki: Academia Scientiarum Fennica Helsinky, 2004, 284–6.
Van den Bercken, W. *Ideology and Atheism in the Soviet Union*. New York: de Gruyter, 1975.
Van Egmond, Bart. *Augustine's Early Thought on the Redemptive Function of Divine Judgment*. Oxford: Oxford University Press, 2018.
Van Hamel, A.-G. *Les Lamentations de Matheolus et le Livre de leesce de Jehan le Fèvre, de Resson (poèmes français du XIVe siècle). Édition critique, accompagnée de l'original latin des Lamentations, d'après l'unique manuscrit d'Utrecht, d'une introduction et de deux glossaires*, Bibliothèque de l'École des hautes études. Paris: Bouillon, 1892–1905, 95–6.
Voela, Angie. *Psychoanalysis, Philosophy and Myth in Contemporary Culture after Oedipus*. London: Palgrave Macmillan UK, 2017.
Von Franz, Marie-Louise. *Patterns of Creativity Mirrored in Creation Myths*. Dallas, TX: Spring, 1986.
Waetzoldt, S. *Die Kopien des 17. Jahrhunderts nach Mosaiken und Wandmalereien in Rom*, Römische Forschungen der Bibliotheca Hertziana 18. Vienna: Schroll-Verlag, 1964.
Walsh, Katie. 'Thoughtful Thrills in the *Alien* Universe'. *Spokesman-Review*, 19 May 2017, 5.
Wasserstein, D. J. 'Ibn Hazm and al-Andalus'. In *Ibn Hazm of Cordoba: The Life and Works of a Controversial Thinker*, edited by C. Adang, M. Fierro and S. Schmidtka, 69–86. Leiden and Boston: Brill, 2013.
Weiner, Jesse, Benjamin Eldon Stevens and Brett M. Rogers (eds). *Frankenstein and Its Classics: The Modern Prometheus from Antiquity to Science Fiction*. London: Bloomsbury, 2018.

Weiss, Susan. בשלוש דרכים האשה מתגרשת 'The Three Methods of Divorce Resolution in Israel: Rigid Fundamentalism, Extortion, and Violence'. *Eretz Acheret* 13 (2002) (Hebrew). https://eretzacheret.org/writer/%D7%A1%D7%95%D7%96%D7%9F-%D7%95%D7%99%D7%99%D7%A1/.

Weiss, Susan. 'Women, Divorce, and Mamzer Status in the State of Israel'. In *Love, Marriage, and Jewish Families: Paradoxes of a Social Revolution*, edited by Sylvia Barack Fishman, 256–84. Waltham, MA: Brandeis University Press, 2015.

Weiss, Susan. 'How to Make a Tort of Marital Captivity'. In *Marital Captivity: Divorce, Religion and Human Rights*, edited by Susan Rutten, Benedicta Deogratias and Pauline Kruiniger, 283–308. The Hague: Eleven International Publishing, 2019.

Weiss, Susan and Elana Maryles Sztokman. 'The Tort of Get Refusal: How Damage Litigation has Changed the Course of Family Law in Israel'. www.cwj.org.il, 2011. https://www.cwj.org.il/sites/default/files/The%20Tort%20of%20Get%20Refusal%202012%202.pdf.

Weitzmann, K. *Illustrations in Roll and Codex: A Study of the Origin and Method of Text Illustration*. Princeton, NJ: Princeton University Press, 1970.

Weitzmann, K. and H. L. Kessler. *The Cotton Genesis: British Library, Codex Cotton Otho B. VI*. Princeton, NJ: Princeton University Press, 1986.

Wilpert, J. 'Le pitture dell'ipogeo di Aurelio Felicissimo presso il Viale Manzoni in Roma'. *Atti della Pontificia Accademia Romana di Archeologia, Memorie* 1, no. 2 (1924): 5–43.

Wilpert, J. *I sarcophagi cristiani antichi*, vol. 1. Rome: Pontificio Istituto di Archeologia Cristiana, 1929.

Wilson, Anthony. *Swamp: Nature and Culture*. London: Reaktion Books, 2017.

Wirth, F. *Römische Wandmalerei von Untergang Pompeijs bis ans Ende des 3. Jahrhunderts*. Berlin: Darmstadt, 1934/1968.

Wodehouse, P. G. 'Jeeves in the Springtime'. In *Enter Jeeves: 15 Early Stories*, 128–43. Mineola, NY: Dover Publications, 1921/1997.

Wood, S. *Roman Portrait Sculpture 217–260 AD*. Leiden: Brill, 1986.

Wortzman, Hannah. 'The rape of Eve and its spiritual connotations in early Jewish and gnostic literature'. *Studies in Spirituality* 27 (2017): 57–89.

Wosk, Julie. *My Fair Ladies: Female Robots, Androids, and Other Artificial Eves*. New Brunswick, NJ: Rutgers University Press, 2015.

Wrede, H. 'Consecratio in formam deorum'. In *Vergöttlichte Privatpersonen in der römischen Kaiserzeit*. Mainz am Rhein: von Zabern, 1981.

Yaroslavsky, E. *Religion in the U.S.S.R.* New York: International Publishers, 1934.

Yeffet-Refael, R. 'Author's Introduction to the Hebrew *maqama* and its Variations' (in Hebrew). *Criticism & Interpretation* 39 (2006): 125–68.

Yunis, Susan and Tammy Ostrander. 'Tales Your Mother Never Told You: *Aliens* and the Horrors of Motherhood'. *Journal of the Fantastic in the Arts* 14, no. 1 (2003): 68–76.

Zaehner, R. C. *The Concise Encyclopedia of Living Faiths*. London: Hutchinson, 1986.

Zapperi, Roberto. *The Pregnant Man*. Translated by Brian Williams. New York: Harwood Academic Publishers, 1991.

Zeitlin, Froma I. 'l'Origine de la femme et la femme origine: la Pandore d'Hésiode'. In *Le métier du mythe*, edited by Fabienne Blaise, Pierre Judet de la Combe and Philippe Rousseau, 354–5. n.p.p.: Presses Universitaires, 1996.

Zhang, Q. F. 'Transgender Representation by the People's Daily Since 1949'. *Sexuality & Culture* 18, no. 1 (2014): 180–95. https://doi.org/10.1007/s12119-013-9184-3.

'Божественная комедия' (Bozhestvennaya komediya, Divine Comedy), *Театр* 5 (1969): 121.

INDEX

www.ingramcontent.com/pod-product-compliance
Lightning Source LLC
Chambersburg PA
CBHW070519100726
47907CB00004B/907

* 9 7 8 1 3 5 0 2 1 2 8 6 2 *